TRANSNATIONAL CORPORATIONS

VERSUS THE STATE

TRANSNATIONAL CORPORATIONS VERSUS THE STATE

The Political Economy of the Mexican Auto Industry

BY

DOUGLAS C. BENNETT AND
KENNETH E. SHARPE

PRINCETON, NEW JERSEY
PRINCETON UNIVERSITY PRESS

CONTENTS

TABLES

ACKNOWLEDGMENTS

The field work for this project was conducted between 1975 and 1981. Between us, we spent over three years in Mexico collecting data, conducting interviews, and immersing ourselves in the context of the political economy of Mexico.

Both government and industry officials made available reliable data on the performance of the industry: production, sales, trade, and the like. None of the three episodes of bargaining between the Mexican government and the transnational automobile corporations around which this book is organized, however, ever found more than the briefest mention in the Mexican news media. To learn about the formulation and implementation of policy toward the automobile industry, we have had to rely on extensive interviews, often extending over several sessions, with those most closely involved.

Many of the people involved in automobile industry policy since 1960 are still active in government or industry. To insure candor, we promised our interviewees that, in our publications, we would not attribute to them anything they said to us. Consequently, there are no specific citations to the interviews, even though these constitute the principal source of information for the book. However, we have used nothing from the interviews that was not confirmed by a second interview or by a reliable published source. If the interviews gave conflicting evidence, we have stated this in the text. In appendix B, we provide a list of those we interviewed. We are very grateful for the time and care these people took in trying to reconstruct complex events, some of which had happened a decade or two before. Without their extraordinary cooperation, this book would not have been possible.

While we were conducting the field work, we received valuable advice and encouragement from quite a number of people, including José Luis Reyna, Rosario Green, and Miguel Wionczek (all at the Colegio de Mexico), and from Nora Hamilton, Susan Kaufman Purcell, Kevin Middlebrook, John Purcell, and Rose Spaulding. We also had high-spirited and skillful research assistance from Ines Cifuentes, Sarah Holmes, Peggy McKernan, Bonnie Sharpe, and Richard Valelly.

For several years, we had the good fortune to be members of the Working Group on Transnational Corporations in Latin America, sponsored by the Social Science Research Council. It allowed us to present our work in progress and to hear about the research of others

ix

well in advance of publication. This group engendered a second one that met a few times to discuss the political economy of the Latin American automobile industry. We would like to thank Reid Andrews, Peter Evans, Michael Fleet, Gary Gereffi, Lou Goodman, Rhys Jenkins, Richard Kronish, David Martin, Ken Mericle, David Moore, Ted Moran, Moises Naim, Richard Newfarmer, Al Stepan, Phil Shepherd, Peter West, and Van Whiting for all that they taught us during these sessions.

Bruce Bagley, Clark Reynolds, Arthur Schmidt, and Laurence Whitehead read one or more chapters and provided useful advice and criticism. Gary Gereffi, Kevin Middlebrook, and Robert Feldmesser each read the entire manuscript; we are especially grateful to them. Sandy Thatcher at the Princeton University Press has been both a supportive and a patient editor.

For secretarial assistance, we are most appreciative of the efforts of Eleanor Greitzer and the diligent staff of the Swarthmore College typing pool, and of Kathy Fairchild at Temple University. None of this research could have been conducted without the generous financial support given to one or both of us at various times by the Social Science Research Council, the Carnegie Endowment for International Peace, the Doherty Foundation, the Tinker Foundation, and the Woodrow Wilson International Center for Scholars. We are also indebted to Swarthmore College, Temple University, and Dartmouth College for their support and assistance.

The two of us started together early in graduate school, while working on a study of graduate education for the American Political Science Association. We quickly came to understand that writing together is not easy, at least if it is going to be more than a simple division of responsibility for chapters or a set of compromises that reduce quality to the lowest common denominator. At times in this project, we have benefited from the incisive criticism of Moss Blachman, another colleague and friend from the APSA study. We owe a special debt of gratitude to him.

We have frequently been asked about our previous collaborations: Who wrote which part? The truth is that, by the time we finish a piece, neither of us can tell. We are each so thoroughly involved, from the initial brainstorming of ideas and the collection of data through the writing and rewriting of drafts, that each of us has difficulty locating even individual sentences we can call our own. Egos are regularly on the line is this process, hidden behind a turn of phrase or embedded in a particular way of organizing an argument. No doubt there are more efficient ways to write. Writing together as we do depends on (and strengthens, most days) the mutual intellectual respect and the deep personal friendship that allow us to weather the heated debate that ultimately produces material we both—at the end—agree is better than the drafts we started with.

ABBREVIATIONS

AMIA	Asociación Mexicana de la Industria Automotriz
AMPPA	Asociación Mexicana de Productores de Partes Automotrices
ANFPA	Asociación Nacional de Fabricantes de Productos Automotrices
APTA	Automotive Products Trade Agreement
CANACINTRA	Cámara Nacional de Industrias de Transformación
CEDI	certificado de devolución de impuestos
CKD	completely knocked down
CNC	Confederación Nacional de Campesinos
CNOP	Confederación Nacional de Organizaciones Populares
CTM	Confederación de Trabajadores Mexicanos
DINA	Diesel Nacional
DINA-MAN	Diesel Nacional—Maquiladora Automotriz Nacional
FANASA	Fábrica Nacional de Automóviles, S.A.
ICA	Ingenieros Civiles Asociados
INA	[Consejo de la] Industria Nacional de Autopartes
LAFTA	Latin American Free Trade Association
LICIT	Labor-Industry Coalition for International Trade
MORESA	Motores y Refacciones, S.A.
NAFIN	Nacional Financiera
PEMEX	Petróleos Mexicanos
PRI	Partido Revolucionario Institucional
SAE	Society of Automotive Engineers
SEPAFIN	Secretaria de Patrimonio y Fomento Industrial
SIC	Secretaria de Industria y Comercio
SOMEX	Sociedad Mexicana de Crédito Industrial
TREMEC	Transmisiones y Equipos Mecánicos
VAM	Vehículos Automotores Mexicanos
VISA	Valores Industriales, S.A.

TRANSNATIONAL CORPORATIONS

VERSUS THE STATE

·1·

INTRODUCTION

In 1960, the automobile industry in Mexico consisted of a dozen small firms that assembled vehicles from imported kits. By 1970, there was substantial automobile manufacture in Mexico: 60 percent of each vehicle sold in Mexico was produced there. By 1980, Mexico had become a significant exporter of automotive parts, particularly to the United States. Cars "made in the U.S." had a fair chance of containing Mexican-built engines, springs, windshields, or transmissions, and automotive exports had become a point of friction between the U.S. and Mexican governments. Moreover, during these years, the automobile industry was the engine for a new surge of industrial growth in the Mexican economy. This book explores this transformation at three levels:

First, it aims to provide a historical account of the growth of automobile manufacturing in Mexico, a significant element in the industrialization of the country and an important chapter in the history of the internationalization of the automobile industry.

Second, it aims to understand bargaining and dependency relations between transnational corporations (TNCs) and the state in developing countries. The coming of automobile manufacture to Mexico has been accompanied by a steadily increasing domination by transnational firms—Ford, General Motors, Chrysler, Volkswagen, Nissan, Renault, and American Motors. Nevertheless, the development of automobile manufacture would not have occurred without the continuous exertions of the Mexican state. The twenty-year history of the automobile industry in Mexico thus provides an unusually rich case for examining bargaining between states and TNCs in the overall context of the dependency of a developing country.

Third, most generally and for us most importantly, it seeks to exemplify a historical-structural method, demonstrating the ability of this approach to address the fundamental issues of social-science inquiry. The approach, simply stated, follows Marx's maxim: "Men make their own history, but they do not make it just as they please; they do not make it under circumstances chosen by themselves, but under circumstances directly found, given and transmitted from the past."[1]

---

[1] Karl Marx, "The Eighteenth Brumaire of Louis Bonaparte," in Robert C. Tucker, ed., *The Marx-Engels Reader* (New York: W. W. Norton, 1972), p. 437.

However much this may seem like common sense, it is decidedly not the established position in the social sciences, particularly in the United States. All too often, theorists a priori assume either that there are certain historical laws or social structures that determine and thus explain human action, or that individuals or groups exercising their free will can voluntaristically re-create themselves or society. Our intention is to use a historical-structural method that is neither deterministic nor voluntaristic. We will explore what possibilities for human action are open or closed at a particular time within given social structures; we will try to explain the interests of actors and their power to create change within these historical limits; and we will look at how actions taken over time (i.e., human history) change or maintain social structures, which themselves open possibilities for, as well as limit, future action.

The structures with which we are most concerned are those of capitalism as a world system. These are the structures that define dependency in less-developed countries (LDCs). Proceeding from our historical-structural approach, we see these as constricting but not determining the chances for development. There are possibilities for action—in this case, by the state—to make development happen. But whether this development can be rapid and whether its fruits can be equitably shared are among the questions for our analysis.

BARGAINING AND DEPENDENCY

Three episodes of bargaining between the Mexican state and the transnational automobile firms were particularly important in moving the automobile industry in Mexico from simple assembly to domestic manufacture to exports. These three bargaining conflicts and the changes they brought about are the substance of our narrative. The central actors were the Mexican government and the transnational automobile firms, but Mexican entrepreneurs and the home-country governments of the TNCs played important supporting roles. Though vital to the development of the industry, labor in Mexico was never involved in shaping industrial policy toward the automobile sector. Bargaining among the key actors moved the industry forward from assembly to domestic manufacture to exports, but this bargaining took place within structures that were both national and international. The political economy of Mexico has been continually shaped by its dependent relationships with the world capitalist system, and the Mexican automobile industry by its dependent relationships with the world auto industry.

4

These complex structures delimited the alternatives and shaped the interests of the actors and their power to choose among them.

Our analysis proceeds, though not uncritically, within the broad perspective of dependency theory. The theory of modernization of the 1950s and 1960s sought to explain underdevelopment by viewing some countries as simply starting later and proceeding more slowly than others along the path to development because of an adherence to traditional values and institutions.[2] In this perspective, all countries follow essentially the same route to "modernity." By contrast, the dependency perspective argues that the earlier development of some countries significantly alters the terms and chances of development of others. "Underdevelopment" in Latin America, Africa, and Asia (the "periphery") is not an inherent condition but rather a consequence of the earlier "development" of Europe and North America (the "center") and of the integration of the peripheral countries into a capitalist world economy on terms which are generally disadvantageous to them. In this perspective, Mexico is not simply "behind," nor can it simply follow in the footsteps of the United States. Rather, relationships with the industrialized countries hinder the development of those following after them. The complex and often subtle ways that such relationships impede development have been the primary concern of the *dependencia* perspective.

Central to this perspective is capitalism viewed as a world system. The intellectual origins of the *dependencia* framework were rooted in the concern of Latin American scholars for the domestic consequences of imperialism. The world capitalist system, the dependency approach argues, is "characterized by a functional division of labor" between the center and the periphery.

> Countries of the center are industrially advanced and viewed as capable of developing dynamically in accordance with their internal needs; they are the main beneficiaries of global links. The periphery has a less autonomous type of development, conditioned

---

[2] For explications of the modernization approach, see Gabriel A. Almond and James S. Coleman, eds., *The Politics of Developing Areas* (Princeton: Princeton University Press, 1960); Walt W. Rostow, *The Stages of Economic Growth: A Non-Communist Manifesto* (Cambridge: Cambridge University Press, 1960); and Cyril E. Black, *The Dynamics of Modernization* (New York: Harper and Row, 1966). Important critiques of the modernization theory include Reinhard Bendix, "Tradition and Modernity Reconsidered," *Comparative Studies in Society and History* 9 (1967):292-346; Joseph R. Gusfield, "Tradition and Modernity: Misplaced Polarities in the Study of Social Change," *American Journal of Sociology* 72 (1967):351-362; and Robert A. Packenham, *Liberal America in the Third World* (Princeton: Princeton University Press, 1973).

by the requirements of the center's expansion. Dependency analysis attempts to understand, and evaluate, the developmental implications of peripheral capitalism.[3]

Simply stated, dependency is a situation "in which the rate and direction of accumulation are externally conditioned."[4] Dependency is not inconsistent with development: there may be significant economic growth, as there has been in Mexico over the past half-century. It is rather that actors and processes outside the country undergoing development are principally responsible for setting the opportunities for and the limits to development. Nor does external conditioning mean that the benefits of development accrue only to those outside the country. The dependency perspective is concerned with the internal analogies of external structures and processes. Relationships of dependency serve to benefit a domestic elite that draws wealth and power from its privileged position within the linkages that tie a developing country to the world capitalist system.

This external conditioning is largely defined by a complex web of international relationships between center and periphery, involving trade, finance, and investment, which have varied in their relative

---

[3] Gary Gereffi, *The Pharmaceutical Industry and Dependency in the Third World* (Princeton: Princeton University Press, 1983), pp. 7-8.

[4] Peter Evans, *Dependent Development: The Alliance of Multinational, State, and Local Capital in Brazil* (Princeton: Princeton University Press, 1979), p. 27. Compare the more elaborate definition of Theotonio dos Santos: "By dependence we mean a situation in which the economy of certain countries is conditioned by the development and expansion of another economy to which the former is subjected. The relation of interdependence between two or more economies, and between these and world trade, assumes the form of dependence when some countries (the dominant ones) can expand and be self-sustaining while other countries (the dependent ones) can do this only as a reflection of that expansion, which can have either a positive or a negative effect on their immediate development." Theotonio dos Santos, "The Structure of Dependence," *American Economic Review* 60 (1970):236. Other important treatments of *dependencia* are: Celso Furtado, *Economic Development of Latin America: A Survey from Colonial Times to the Cuban Revolution* (London: Cambridge University Press, 1970); Helio Jaguaribe, *Economic and Political Development: A Theoretical Approach and a Brazilian Case Study* (Cambridge: Harvard University Press, 1968); Frank Bonilla and Robert Girlin, eds., *Structures of Dependency* (Stanford: Stanford University Press, 1973); Suzanne Bodenheimer, "Dependency and Imperialism: The Roots of Latin American Underdevelopment," in K. T. Fann and Donald C. Hodges, eds., *Readings in U.S. Imperialism* (Boston: Porter Sargent, 1971), pp. 155-181; André Gunder Frank, *Capitalism and Underdevelopment in Latin America: Historical Studies of Chile and Brazil* (New York: Monthly Review Press, 1967); James T. Petras, *Latin America: From Dependence to Revolution* (New York: John Wiley, 1973); Osvaldo Sunkel, "Big Business and 'Dependencia'," *Foreign Affairs* 50 (1972):517-531; and Fernando Henrique Cardoso and Enzo Faletto, *Dependency and Development in Latin America* (Berkeley and Los Angeles: University of California Press, 1979).

importance but which have tended to reinforce one another. Since World War II, investments by transnational corporations have been particularly critical in shaping situations of dependency. Whereas direct foreign investment was once confined primarily to mining and agriculture, and to activities closely connected with these, such as railroads, direct foreign investment in manufacturing has been dominant in recent decades. These investments were triggered in part by import substitution policies of LDCs that were seeking to induce domestic manufacturing and thus to lessen trade dependency (the export of primary products to pay for imports of manufactured goods), but they stemmed as well from the postwar international expansion of transnational corporations based in the U.S., Europe, and Japan.

While the modernization approach has tended to see TNCs as beneficent agents of change bringing capital, technology, and management skills to LDCs, the dependency approach has inclined toward a more critical view, arguing that investments by TNCs have posed a threat to domestic capital accumulation and that manufacturing industries in LDCs have been shaped more in response to world market conditions and the global strategies of TNCs than in response to the needs of the populations of developing countries. One important concern of the dependency approach with transnational corporations has to do with their consequences for distribution. TNCs, it is argued, not only impede national accumulation, but they also foster an inequitable international distribution of income by shifting capital from developing to developed countries (through profit repatriation, payments for technology, and sales of parts and equipment). Further, it is argued that TNCs reinforce an inequitable distribution of income *within* developing countries. Important as this concern is, it is not the one on which we will primarily focus. Our main interest, rather, lies in the possible distortions of an LDC's economy, society, and politics that can follow from the activities of TNCs. Transnational corporations, it has been argued, are unwilling to invest in activities that would promote growth and industrialization. They utilize inappropriate (capital-intensive) technology and introduce inappropriate products into LDCs. Further, they prevent the development of an indigenous economic base, squeezing out local entrepreneurs or pre-empting their entry into the most dynamic sectors of the economy; and they distort local market structures, visiting upon LDCs the oligopolistic structures and practices of globally organized industries. Finally, it is claimed, TNCs co-opt local elites or form alliances with domestic entrepreneurs to block government efforts at regulation, and they use their influence with home-country governments to keep host-country governments in line.

7

INTRODUCTION

These hypothesized distortions will be foremost in our attention as we examine the consequences of TNC activities during two decades of development of the automobile industry in Mexico. The nature of these consequences has depended not only on the actions of the transnational automobile corporations, however, but also on the actions of the Mexican state. There has been a decided tendency in *dependencia* analyses to depict the state as passive and powerless in the face of the TNCs, not as an actor able or inclined to oppose them in any significant respect. In this work, we proceed from a different assumption: that in certain circumstances, the state in developing countries can and will attempt to alter the behavior of TNCs and the consequences of that behavior. It may even seek to alter some of the structural aspects of dependency in which TNCs have a substantial stake. Exploring this assumption requires attention to *bargaining* between the state and TNCs.

This study seeks to advance the understanding of dependency and development processes in a number of different ways:

(1) It focuses on a *single industry* over two decades of growth and change. Dependency studies that take entire countries as their focus of analysis tend to sketch the mechanisms of dependency only in very broad strokes. Studies of single industries can provide a much clearer understanding of the predicaments faced by specific actors and what they can and cannot do in them. On the other hand, studies of single industries within the dependency perspective have largely been restricted to the extractive industries. We focus on a manufacturing industry because this has been the most dynamic sector of foreign investment in recent decades and because the lack of industrialization was a defining feature of dependency before World War II that many third-world governments have sought to overcome. Furthermore, the particular industry examined, automobile manufacture, is one that has gone through significant changes in its global organization, thus allowing us to follow the consequences of changes in international structure for actors in Mexico.

(2) It pays particular attention to *public policy* toward the industry. Many dependency studies concentrate so much on the structural constraints that define situations of dependency, or presume the state to be so passive, that they fail to make a serious inquiry into public policy. The automobile industry in Mexico has been an object of government policy for the past quarter-century. We want to analyze not only the constraints imposed by situations of dependency but also the alternatives for action within these constraints and the consequences of choices made. At least in the Mexican case, this requires an examination of the making and implementing of public policy.

8

(3) For related reasons, this study pays particular attention to *bargaining* between the Mexican state and the transnational automobile firms. The Mexican state has by no means been able to establish by fiat whatever policy it chooses. Instead, it has had to negotiate with the transnational automobile firms. Although there have been a number of excellent studies of bargaining between third-world governments and transnational firms, these have not been fully integrated into the dependency perspective.

(4) It is a case study of the limits of possibility for a state seeking to *overcome dependency* while abiding by the norms of global capitalism. The Mexican government has not attempted to remove Mexico from the world capitalist system. Rather, it has pursued policies aimed at providing both growth and increased autonomy for Mexico *within* that system, and nowhere has this been more evident than in the automobile industry. Our study therefore is a kind of test case for the dependency perspective.

(5) It employs a *historical-structural approach* that gives equal emphasis to structures and actions, to limits and possibilities. A historical-structural approach is already embodied in the best examples of the dependency perspective; what we seek now to contribute is a deliberate and consistent application of this approach to both of our principal actors, the Mexican state and the transnational automobile corporations.

The Historical-Structural Approach

Taken together, dependency and bargaining manifest the central methodological perspective of this book—the historical-structural approach. The dominant approaches in American social science have tended toward either determination or voluntarism and have thus led to fundamental distortions of the human condition and subtle betrayals of the proper aims of social analysis. In contrast, the historical-structural approach holds that human beings are social products, but that society itself is a product of human actions. In the words of Cardoso and Faletto, this approach "emphasizes not just the structural conditioning of social life, but also the historical transformation of structures by conflict, social movements and class struggles."[5]

The dependency perspective places particular emphasis on structures—particularly the structures of the world capitalist system—that "condition" development. These structures, to quote Cardoso and Fa-

[5] Cardoso and Faletto, *Dependency and Development in Latin America*, p. x.

letto again, "impose limits on social processes and reiterate established forms of behavior."[6] In the hands of some dependency analysts, this structural conditioning tends toward a certain determinism; possibilities for significant choice within these structures and for action to transform structures are denied. We are interested, however, in the possibilities for change within and against existing structures. Structures condition but do not fully determine; they impose limits but also shape possibilities. The task for social analysis is to explore, concretely, the structural limits and the possibilities for action in particular historical situations. Our emphases on state policy and on bargaining are intended to make explicit these concerns with alternative possibilities and with the transformation of structures.

Structures shape the interests and power of the actors within them. Insofar as structures bequeath overwhelming power to some actors or mold a fundamental convergence of interests among actors, structures will tend to persist. Efforts to alter them will be ineffectual. However, structures tend to "generate contradictions and social tensions"[7]—i.e., conflicts of interest—and these set the stage for change. One major task of this study is to explain the interests of the Mexican state and the transnational automobile firms, to reach some understanding of how and why their interests converged at some points and diverged into conflict at others.

The historical-structural approach to the actors in a set of events proceeds from three leading ideas: (1) Each actor has interests and power of its own—the wherewithal to make its own history. (2) The possibilities for action are limited by the structures in which actors are enmeshed, and each actor's interests and power are shaped by its position within these structures. (3) These structures are historical products of past human actions and, in certain circumstances, are susceptible to marginal change or transformation by the concerted efforts of the actors.

For an elaboration of a historical-structural approach applied to transnational corporations, we turn to industrial-organization theory. First formulated in the United States and most widely employed in the study of the U.S. economy, industrial-organization theory has been used almost exclusively in the analysis of industries within the geographically constrained national market of a developed country. Because our concerns are with a developing country and with transnational corporations, which operate simultaneously in several different

[6] Ibid., p. xi.
[7] Ibid.

10

INTRODUCTION

national markets, several revisions of industrial-organization theory
will be necessary to fit it to our purposes.

The structure most important (though hardly the only one) in shaping the interests and power of the transnational automobile firms in
the Mexican setting is the structure of the industry in which they
compete, both globally and in Mexico. Two aspects of this structure
will be salient in our analysis: (a) the structure of the market, principally
the number of firms in the industry, and (b) the structure of ownership,
principally the extent of domination by transnational firms. These
aspects of the Mexican automobile industry structure were in part the
result of struggle between the state and the TNCs. Once created, they
have been crucial in shaping the behavior of the firms and the performance of the industry in Mexico.

Unlike the case for the transnational firms, there is no single structure which is of pre-eminent importance in shaping the interests and
power of the state or in delimiting its possibilities for action. The
relevant structures are many: they are domestic and international, and
they are political, economic, social, military, and cultural. Moreover,
despite the renaissance of attention to "the state," there is no single
theory of the state to which we can turn for an elaboration of the
historical-structural approach; we have had to fashion our own, drawing on a number of perspectives.

Consistent with the historical-structural approach, we depict the state
as an actor with interests and power of its own—a conception that is
denied, explicitly or implicitly, by a number of current perspectives.
This hardly means the state can act "just as it pleases," nor is it an
insistence on the autonomy of the state. While state action may be
shaped and constrained, for example, by its relationship to the domestic class structure or to the structure of international finance, the
state is nevertheless an actor, capable of formulating its own policies
and of exerting power in an effort to carry them through.

Our approach to the state understands its interests as being "embedded orientations" that have been acquired and institutionalized in the
course of its history as the state has responded to problems and opportunities facing it. The power of the state is set both by internal
characteristics (unity, technical capability) and by its relationship to the
structures around it, particularly the domestic class structure. In the
Mexican situation, it is particularly important to see the active role of
the state in shaping this relationship to domestic classes; it has not
merely been an object that was captured or shaped in the conflict
among them.

The historical-structural approach—this concern with structure and

11

action, with dependency and bargaining—informs the organization of this book. Chapters 2 through 4 introduce the major actors and the structures within which they are enmeshed, and it sets forth in greater detail the theoretical perspectives that guide our analysis. Chapter 2 provides an overview of the political economy of Mexico, focusing on the changing character of dependency within the world capitalist system, and lays out our theoretical approach to the Mexican state as an actor. Chapter 3 does the same for the world automobile industry, showing Mexico's place within that structure in 1960 and setting forth our theoretical approach to the transnational automobile corporations. Chapter 4 elaborates our framework for the analysis of bargaining between the state and transnational corporations.

Drawing on this foundation, chapters 5 through 10 analyze dependency and bargaining in the automobile industry in Mexico between 1960 and 1980, concentrating on three major episodes. For each, we will (a) examine the structures that determined the limits and possibilities for action and shaped the interests and power of the actors, (b) examine the conflict itself and show how its resolution led to change or continuity in the structure of the automobile industry in Mexico, and (c) show how this new structure set the stage for the next conflict, imposing new limitations but opening other possibilities for action. Chapters 5 and 6 are concerned with the 1962 bargaining: the effort of the Mexican state to create a manufacturing industry in Mexico by means of an import-substitution policy, the resulting enactment and implementation of a governmental decree, and the structure of ownership and of the market that resulted. Within these new structures, there arose a series of problems for the state and for some of the firms, particularly the Mexican-owned ones. Chapters 7 and 8 deal with a second major conflict in 1968-1969, growing out of these problems. The bargaining that took place in this connection led to a decision to move away from import substitution and toward export promotion as the basic thrust of policy. The chapters examine the difficulties this change engendered and the way in which the problems were rendered more serious by a crisis in the political economy of Mexico in the mid-1970s, as well as a series of changes in the structure of the world automobile industry which had important implications for Mexico and the transnational corporations. Chapter 9 considers a third bargaining episode, in 1977, the result of which was a new decree strengthening export requirements, and chapter 10 treats a variety of problems that resulted from this Decree.

Chapter 11 draws a number of conclusions about the historical-structural approach, the consequences of TNCs for developing countries, and the possibilities for altering these consequences by state action. In a postscript, we provide a brief discussion of a new automotive policy, promulgated in September 1983, while Mexico was in the midst of an economic crisis.

·2·

THE STATE AND DEPENDENCY
IN MEXICO

Shortly after taking office in December 1958, the López Mateos administration singled out the automobile industry to be a centerpiece of its efforts to stimulate further industrial growth in Mexico. The Great Depression and World War II had deprived Mexico of manufactured imports, and this artificial protection had propelled the country into a surge of industrialization along an import-substitution path. Following the war, the policy instruments of tariffs and quotas were instituted to continue the protection of the domestic market, but by the mid-1950s this surge of industrialization was showing signs of exhaustion. Domestic manufacture of virtually all consumer nondurable goods had already commenced. If industrial growth were to continue, the López Mateos administration reasoned, import substitution would have to move on to consumer durable goods or producer goods. The automobile industry seemed like a perfect candidate, particularly because of its many connections with other industries—steel, glass, paint, plastics, metalworking, and electrical components.

Understanding the terms of success of this effort—which would occupy the attentions of not just the López Mateos administration but of its successors as well—requires an understanding of the broad context of dependency in which the country found itself during these years. It also requires an understanding of the Mexican state as an actor: how its interests and power were shaped within this situation of dependency, and why it sought in part to challenge and in part to accommodate itself to the conditions in which it found itself.

Because of the Mexican Revolution, the devastation it wreaked upon the domestic class structure, and the extreme separation it engendered between political and economic elites, the Mexican state does not easily fit standard generalizations about the state in capitalist society. The state came to serve the interests of capital, but until recently the domestic bourgeoisie has lacked the power to make the state an instrument of its will. The state has regularly acted to protect national against transnational capital, and it has played a vigorous role as an entrepreneur. Despite the mobilization of the lower classes and the state's partial reliance upon their support, the state has turned a deaf ear to the claims of workers and peasants without (so far) risking a new upheaval.

14

In short, the state has acted to transform some aspects of dependency but not others. How do we account for this?

Independence in 1821 had brought political sovereignty to Mexico but no significant change in the country's relationships with the world capitalist system nor in the internal consequences of these relationships. Mexico's economy remained dependent, its functioning externally conditioned and controlled. Growth depended on trade relationships first with Europe and later with the United States. Exports of mining and agricultural products continued to pay for imports of luxury and manufactured goods for the agricultural, commercial, and mining elites.

After several decades of stagnation and political instability, the ascent to power of Porfirio Díaz in 1877 strengthened the power of the Mexican state and initiated several decades of economic growth. Mexico's dependency did not, however, lessen significantly. By the end of the nineteenth century, foreign control of Mexico's banking system and substantial foreign investment in a variety of sectors had been added to trade as external relationships that shaped the Mexican economy.[1]

In this situation, the possibilities for sustained economic growth were limited and political power was being used to sustain a system of highly unequal classes. The Mexican Revolution challenged foreign control of the economy and the internal social and political order associated with it. In the first two parts of this chapter, we will explore persistence and change in the dependency of postrevolutionary Mexico. In each of the periods covered, we will focus on trade, finance, and investment as three aspects of Mexico's dependent relationship with the international political economy, and we will explore the consequences of such relationships both for growth and for distribution. The third part of the chapter will draw on the discussion in chapter 1 to develop a theoretical framework for analyzing the Mexican state as an actor within the continuing structures of dependency. This will provide a basis for examining the industrial policy of the Mexican state in its effort to shape industrialization in the automotive sector between 1960 and 1980. In focusing on the state as an actor, we seek to avoid an economic determinism that would define the state as a mere instrument of dominant class interests in maintaining dependent relationships, but neither do we want to lose sight of the severe limits that constrict state action and dampen its effects.[2]

---

[1] For a fuller discussion of the character of dependency in the postindependence period in Mexico and elsewhere in Latin America, see Barbara H. Stein and Stanley J. Stein, *The Colonial Heritage of Latin America* (New York: Oxford University Press, 1970).

[2] Classic works employing a dependency approach include Theotonio dos Santos, "The Structure of Dependence," *American Economic Review* 60 (1970):231-236, and André Gun-

The Postrevolutionary Consolidation, 1917-1940

The Porfiriato and the Mexican Revolution

The Mexican Revolution that began in 1910 shattered the harsh political order that had been constructed under Porfirio Díaz, and it also demolished an economic system that had discouraged national accumulation and fostered suffering among the vast majority of Mexico's population.

Many of the problems of Mexico during the *Porfiriato* were rooted in the continuing character of its dependent position within the world capitalist system. Mexico's economy was based on the export of primary products—industrial minerals (copper, lead, zinc), petroleum, and agricultural goods—and the importation of manufactured products. With the exception of the iron and steel operations begun in Monterrey in 1903, industrialization was limited to very simple consumer non-durables—textiles, processed foods (especially sugar), beer, glass, and tobacco products—produced for a national market that was severely constricted in size by the highly skewed distribution of income and the marginal existence of most of the population.

Economic growth was tied not to the internal market but to the world demand for Mexico's primary product exports. When this demand slackened, as it did in the first decade of the twentieth century, it generated a series of economic and social problems. The number of employment opportunities declined, the percentage of the labor force employed in manufacturing fell, there was pressure on the agricultural sector to absorb an increasing number of workers, and the small but growing middle class found its position threatened. Mexico fit Peter Evans's paradigmatic depiction of the predicament of dependent countries "whose histories of involvement with the international market have led them to specialize in the export of a few primary products."

der Frank, *Capitalism and Underdevelopment in Latin America: Historical Studies of Chile and Brazil* (New York: Monthly Review Press, 1979). Some notable works that use the dependency approach but do begin to focus on state action to alter aspects of dependent development are Cardoso and Faletto, *Dependency and Development* (see especially pp. 199-216); Theodore H. Moran, *Multinational Coporations and the Politics of Dependence: Copper in Chile* (Princeton: Princeton University Press, 1974); Franklin Tugwell, *The Politics of Oil in Venezuela* (Stanford: Stanford University Press, 1975); Gary Gereffi, "Drug Firms and Dependency in Mexico: The Case of the Steroid Hormone Industry," *International Organization* 32 (1978):237-286; Gary Gereffi and Peter Evans, "Transnational Corporations, Dependent Development, and State Policy in the Semiperiphery: A Comparison of Brazil and Mexico," *Latin American Research Review* 16 (1981):31-64.

While the income from these few products is absolutely central to the process of accumulation in the dependent country, for the center each product represents only a tiny fraction of total imports, and can usually be obtained from several different sources. The development of the dependent country, however, requires the continued acceptance of its products in the center. Therefore, economic fluctuations in the center may have severe negative consequences for the periphery, whereas an economic crisis in the periphery offers no real threat to accumulation in the center.[3]

Mexico's small internal market and export-led growth based on primary products thus made it particularly vulnerable to world market conditions, and these problems were exacerbated by foreign ownership in the major export sectors. British and U.S. firms owned the petroleum industry (then the largest in the world outside the United States). U.S. companies owned millions of acres of rich agricultural lands—75 percent of the irrigable land in the border state of Sinaloa, for example. The mining and smelting industries were predominantly foreign, U.S. firms accounting for 60 percent of the total. U.S. and British interests owned most of the railroads. The banks that financed these export activities were largely foreign owned as well—predominantly French, though with some British and U.S. participation. The utilities were British-owned. French capital dominated the cotton textile industry and was found as well in the paper, flour-milling, brewing and distilling, and steel industries.[4] Such foreign ownership of leading sectors not only foreclosed opportunities for Mexican entrepreneurs but also posed serious obstacles to national capital accumulation: profits accrued to European and U.S. investors, so that much of the comparative advantage Mexico might have gained from its exports was lost.

The Mexican state and important economic groups with which it was linked helped sustain rather than challenge this structure of dependency. The Díaz regime actively encouraged foreign investment by granting lucrative concessions, tax exemptions, and subsidies. It insisted that "it was necessary to make an extreme effort, even to making sacrifices, rather than lose the opportunity of gaining by the investment of foreign capital in Mexico, the impetus that would bring

---

[3] Evans, *Dependent Development*, p. 26.

[4] See Eric Wolf, *Peasant Wars of the Twentieth Century* (New York: Harper and Row, 1973); Mira Wilkins, *The Emergence of Multinational Enterprise* (Cambridge: Harvard University Press, 1970), pp. 115ff.; and Harry K. Wright, *Foreign Enterprise in Mexico: Laws and Policies* (Chapel Hill: University of North Carolina Press, 1971), pp. 54-56.

prosperity.["5] Many of the *científicos* (highly placed, technically trained state officials, in function if not in intent the forerunner of today's *técnicos*) were enriched by the help they gave foreign corporations in negotiating concessions. Some actually became shareholders or directors, or gained title to land. This favoritism to foreign interests generated opposition among Mexican capitalists in mining, light industry, and commercial agriculture (especially in the North). The nationalist, antiforeign sentiment among these groups was important in sparking the revolution and in shaping its settlement.

Not only did the Mexican state fail to encourage or protect national capitalists or to increase national capital accumulation; it also fostered an internal social structure whose maldistribution of the benefits from trade stunted the growth of an internal market. The members of the small but increasingly educated and politically important middle class were eager to find jobs for themselves and their children, but upward mobility was limited both by a backward agricultural sector dominated by large landowners, or *hacendados*, and by the declining growth in activities associated with the foreign-dominated export sector. After the turn of the century, the state bureaucracy, the major source of employment, could no longer expand fast enough to absorb new middle-class job-seekers, and access to top positions was blocked by the aging and corrupt political elite around Díaz.[6]

Meanwhile, wages were kept low, and the Díaz regime offered foreign investors what one contemporary observer called "an absolute freedom from strikes and labor trouble."[7] The police were employed to repress, often violently, any attempts at labor organization. Peasants suffered at the hands of those who misused the 1856 Ley Lerdo, a liberal measure aimed at parceling out to individuals the communal *ejido* that Spanish legislation had granted each Indian village. With the protection and often the encouragement of the Díaz regime, these lands were appropriated through fraud and force by *hacendados*, "surveying" companies, and state officials. The export economy encouraged increasing commercialization of agriculture and encroachments on Indian land and water rights.[8] It was out of this rural Mexico that

[5] An official of the Díaz regime, as quoted in Wilkins, *Emergence of Multinational Enterprise*, p. 115.

[6] Roger Hansen, *The Politics of Mexican Development* (Baltimore: The Johns Hopkins University Press, 1971), chap. 6.

[7] Quoted in Wilkins, *Emergence of Multinational Enterprise*, p. 119.

[8] For an excellent discussion of the effects of expanding capitalist commercial agriculture in the sugar zones of Morelos, see John Womack, Jr., *Zapata and the Mexican Revolution* (New York: Vintage, 1969), chap. 2. Other insightful discussions of the diverse forms of

Indian and mestizo peasants, seeking return of traditional lands or defending their precarious positions, rose to join labor and middle-class groups in toppling Díaz, precipitating seven years of revolutionary turmoil.

Creating a New Political Order

Those who finally prevailed and undertook the task of reconstituting the Mexican state were neither the agrarian radicals, who saw the revolution as a social movement for massive land reform, nor those drawn from the more advanced factions of the labor and intellectual groups, who nurtured socialist and anarcho-syndicalist ideas. Instead, they were predominantly of the middle class, many from the north, from Sonora particularly; some, like Carranza and Obregón, were from landowning families (though not the largest of these), and a few, like Calles, were small businessmen.[9] Not surprisingly, they created a state apparatus that would nurture a capitalist economy, but the precise character of the new political order—the power of the state and the central party and the orientations of the state toward growth, distribution, and foreign control—took shape only gradually in the two decades following the revolution.

The creation of a new political order was the first problem facing postrevolutionary Mexico. Armed peasants struggled to reclaim land; attempted coups by military leaders led to armed rebellions in 1920, 1923, 1927, and 1929; armed regional strongmen resisted federal power. A crucial element in reestablishing a stable, institutionalized political order was the creation in the 1920s of a central party by Plutarco Elías Calles, who was president from 1924 to 1928. By building an independent party bureaucracy with its own funds and by centralizing the process of nominating candidates for office, Calles was able to undermine the independence of regional strongmen and undercut the strength and autonomy of the peasant and labor organizations. His control over Mexican politics continued until 1934, when Lázaro Cárdenas, his personal choice, was elected and then challenged his domination. During his administration, which ended in 1940, Cárdenas

---

agricultural production and the varying character of rural revolt are to be found in Nathan L. Whetten, *Rural Mexico* (Chicago: University of Chicago Press, 1948); Eyler N. Simpson, *The Ejido: Mexico's Way Out* (Chapel Hill: University of North Carolina Press, 1937); and Friedrich Katz, "Labor Conditions and Haciendas in Porfirian Mexico: Some Trends and Tendencies," *Hispanic American Historical Review* 54 (1974):1-47.

[9] See Arnoldo Cordova, *La ideología de la revolución mexicana: La formación del nuevo régimen* (Mexico City: Ediciones Era, 1973).

strengthened the party further, incorporating the more radical elements of militant labor and peasant organizations.[10] The three sectors of today's Revolutionary Institutional Party (Partido Revolucionario Institucional, or PRI) are the results of Cárdenas' 1938 reorganization: labor, as represented by the Mexican Confederation of Labor (CTM); peasants, as represented by the National Peasant Confederation (CNC); and various middle-class groups (at first, mostly government bureaucrats, but later teachers, private farmers, and professionals as well), as represented by the National Confederation of Popular Organizations (CNOP). A fourth sector organized by Cárdenas was the military, but this was later dismantled.

If a strong official party was important in establishing political order, a strong state apparatus was essential for economic recovery. What Alvaro Obregón (1920-1923) and especially Calles created had at its center a strong president, in practice largely unrestricted by the checks and balances of a legislature or court system. The crucial economic instruments of presidential power were the Ministry of Finance (*Hacienda*); other public financial institutions closely allied with it, such as the Bank of Mexico (the central bank) and Nacional Financiera (the major state development bank); and, under Calles, the Ministry of Public Works. The orientations of the state were shaped by the class origins and personal convictions of the postrevolutionary political elite, their experiences in office, and their confrontation with domestic and international problems.[11]

Given the middle-class origins and economic positions of the "Revolutionary Family" or "Revolutionary Coalition," the pro-capitalist orientations of the state they founded are understandable.[12] Indeed many of them—and not just the more conservative-minded ones—used their political positions to become millionaires.[13] In contrast to the political elite under Díaz, however, they were strongly nationalist and infused this orientation into the central ministries of the state. The resentment of these northerners to *entreguismo* (giving away to foreigners what is

[10] See Howard F. Cline, *Mexico: Revolution to Evolution, 1940-1960* (London: Oxford University Press, 1962).

[11] For further details, see Douglas Bennett and Kenneth Sharpe, "The State As Banker and As Entrepreneur: The Last Resort Character of the Mexican State's Economic Interventions, 1917–1976," *Comparative Politics* 10 (1980):165-189.

[12] The first phrase is from Frank Brandenburg, *The Making of Modern Mexico* (Englewood Cliffs, N.J.: Prentice-Hall, 1964), pp. 1-18; the second is from Hansen, *Mexican Development*, p. 129.

[13] Calles's personal fortune was estimated at no less than twenty million pesos. He acquired enough real estate to make his heirs "political *hacendados*." Hansen, *Mexican Development*, pp. 158-159.

rightfully Mexican) stemmed from their everyday experience with foreign capital, whose dominance under Díaz was strongest in the north, and it wove a strongly nationalist thread through their thinking. This outlook took on concrete form in article 27 of the 1917 constitution, which, as Wright has put it, "established the nation's direct ownership of all subsurface mineral deposits, abolished private property rights in petroleum deposits, and reincorporated petroleum into the legal system that governed other mining."[14] Foreigners could not own land along any of Mexico's borders, and elsewhere they could not unless they renounced the protection of their home-country governments.

If the proximity to the United States had allowed a foreign domination which rankled, it also put before the eyes of these Sonorans the image of a modern, rapidly developing country. After political consolidation, their greatest concern was with economic growth, and the model to be copied was the capitalist system to the north with its dramatic successes in industrialization and in large-scale commercial agriculture. It is important to remember that no noncapitalist model existed to be copied—Russia's path was still uncertain—but it is more important that the Sonoran constitutionalists had no inclinations to socialism and that no other social-class forces pushed strongly in that direction. Still, the decision to reintegrate Mexico into the world capitalist economy left open a choice of routes. Although the United States was to be the model for development, it was more in the sense of showing the shape and extent of what could be achieved than in the sense of showing a precise method to be followed. Among the alternatives available were a minimalist, laissez-faire state that would leave the speed and direction of growth to the private sector, and the Porfirian model of growth through active encouragement of foreign capital. The latter had just been rejected, however, and the former presumed the existence of the sort of national bourgeoisie that had led development in the United States but was still nascent in Mexico: a "yeoman" agricultural class to promote agricultural modernization, and an entrepreneurial class to lead industrialization. Mexico's peculiar conditions and its later start would require, they recognized, a forceful role for the state. The orientation chosen would place primary reliance on the private sector, and the private sector would be given inducements and assistance, particularly to encourage it in certain directions marked out by the state as critical for development, but the state would stand ready to take on those tasks that the private sector was unable or unwilling to do.

[14] Wright, *Foreign Enterprise*, p. 63.

21

The postrevolutionary victors knew that reconstruction demanded a redefinition of the Porfirian structure of finance, trade, and investment if nationalist and capitalist growth were to be achieved by this route. It also meant that they would have to restrain efforts on behalf of the revolutionary goal of social justice.

Growth and Capital Accumulation

Finance. Crucial to economic reconstruction was a set of state institutions created to exert strong national control over the financial and monetary system, previously under foreign domination and left in a shambles by the revolution. The Bank of Mexico, organized in 1925 by Finance Minister Alberto Pani, restored Mexican currency and directed the re-establishment of a private banking system. Later it developed a scheme of reserve requirements, which were used to channel private bank loans into high-priority sectors. A network of state investment banks was created to do what the private sector could not or would not: the Agrarian Credit Bank, the Ejidal Bank, the Worker's and Industrial Development Bank, the Foreign Commerce Bank, the Small Merchant's Bank, and, most importantly, Nacional Financiera (NAFIN).

Slowly, responding to the ministrations of the state, a private banking system controlled almost entirely by Mexican capital began to grow. Around the private-sector banks, a fledgling national bourgeoisie began to appear. In the absence of an effective stock or bond market for raising capital, and with permissive bank regulations, banks became the core institutions of powerful economic groups—a dozen or so major ones (e.g., Banamex, Bancomer, the Monterrey-based Garza-Sada group) and many smaller ones, each having at its center a bank or bank complex whose deposits came to be utilized for investments in affiliated manufacturing, mining, and commercial enterprises.[15]

National control over the banking system was decisive in directing Mexico's industrial and agricultural growth, but it did not end the country's fundamentally dependent relationship as a debtor in international financial markets. Mexico's extraordinarily weak financial position after the revolution gave international bankers and the U.S. government power which they used to influence Mexico's economic policies. Mexico was ultimately forced to accept the terms of the bank-

[15] See Salvadore Cordero and Rafael Santín, "Los grupos industriales: Una nueva organización Económica en Mexico," *Cuadernos del CES*, no. 23 (Mexico City: Colegio de Mexico, 1977).

ers for the amount of principal and interest to be paid on the foreign debt incurred by the Díaz and Huerta governments overthrown by the revolution, and it had to agree (among other things) to return the nationalized railways to private management, to maintain existing taxes on the railroads for the debt service payments, and to allocate revenue from the oil production taxes to payment on the foreign debt.[16]

Trade and Investment. In the two decades following the Mexican Revolution, economic growth continued to be based chiefly on exports of primary products. Petroleum became particularly important as mining and agricultural exports declined. Most manufactured products were imported, including machinery for the petroleum industry, automobiles and components, and threads, yarn, and other intermediate goods for the textile industry.[17]

However, when the depression reduced Mexico's capacity to import, some growth in the domestic manufacture of formerly imported goods was stimulated. The policies of the Cárdenas government encouraged the use of excess industrial capacity and new investments in manufacturing. Import and export duties were raised, the Mexican peso was devalued, and state banks made loan capital available to private enterprises for industrial projects. A public works program and deficit spending in the late 1930s also helped to promote industrial investment. Manufacturing output increased 42 percent between 1935 and 1940, leading to an increase from about 14 percent of gross domestic product (GDP) to about 17 percent.[18] But because of the small national market and the instability of the economic climate in the wake of Cárdenas's agrarian and petroleum policies, there was not the same surge of industrialization in response to the depression as occurred in Argentina, Chile, and Brazil. Import substitution did not begin in earnest until 1940.

Even though Mexican administrations between 1917 and 1940 deeply resented foreign ownership, and despite the strong constitutional provisions regarding subsoil rights, direct foreign ownership of national assets increased during that period, particularly in traditional export activities. One U.S. analyst estimated that in 1926, 98 percent of the mining industry was foreign owned; cotton, 86 percent; sugar

[16] Robert F. Smith, *The United States and Revolutionary Nationalism in Mexico, 1916-1932* (Chicago: University of Chicago Press, 1972), pp. 242-243.

[17] Clark Reynolds, *The Mexican Economy: Twentieth-Century Structure and Growth* (New Haven: Yale University Press, 1970), pp. 200-202.

[18] Reynolds, *Mexican Economy*, pp. 167, 208; Timothy King, *Mexico: Industry and Trade Policies since 1940* (Oxford: Oxford University Press, 1970), p. 12.

refining, 95 percent; the production of chicle, rubber, and guayule, and of bananas and other fruits, almost 100 percent; and foreign ownership of henequen and coffee production was increasing.[19]

A 1937 Mexican government report on the oil companies captured the spirit of the general nationalist case against foreign investment:

> The principal oil companies operating in Mexico have never been fully integrated into the country and their interests have always been alien, and at times even opposed, to the national interests. The principal oil companies operating in Mexico have left the Republic only wages and taxes, without in reality having cooperated in the social progress of Mexico.[20]

The oil companies were accused of having "earned enormous profits in the exploitation of the subsoil" influencing "national as well as international political events," paying lower real wages than those earned by workers in the mines or on the national railways, charging higher prices in Mexico than they charged for the oil they exported, and making higher profits in Mexico than in the United States.[21]

The struggle of the Mexican state to wrest control from foreign firms encountered the strong resistance not only of these firms but of the U.S. government.[22] Nevertheless, some headway was made. By the end of the Cárdenas period, and largely through his efforts, a Federal Electricity Commission (CFE) had been set up to regulate rates and the concessions of the mostly foreign-owned firms, the holdings of foreign owners of railroad bonds had been expropriated and the railroads returned to state management, and, in a spectacular showdown, the foreign-owned oil companies had also been expropriated. Mexico became a pariah in the international world of oil, escaping more serious sanctions from the British and U.S. governments largely because of strategic calculations in anticipation of imminent world war.

The Social and Political Goals of the Revolution

The postrevolutionary economic order increased national control over the economy and created the conditions for rapid economic growth, but the revolutionary goals of social justice were mostly either post-

---

[19] Smith, *U.S. and Revolutionary Nationalism*, p. 145.

[20] Quoted in Wilkins, *Emergence of Multinational Enterprise*, p. 226.

[21] Ibid.

[22] For discussions of these conflicts, see Smith, *U.S. and Revolutionary Nationalism*; Wright, *Foreign Enterprise*; Marvin Bernstein, *The Mexican Mining Industry, 1890-1950* (New York: SUNY Press, 1964); and Lorenzo Meyer, *Mexico and the United States in the Oil Controversy, 1917-1942* (Austin: University of Texas Press, 1977)

poned or sacrificed altogether. By choosing the institutions and practices of capitalism and by accepting the conditions necessary for reintegration into the world economic system, the leaders of the new Mexican state also accepted, consciously or otherwise, severe limits on the degree of redistribution and political democracy that could be attained.

The modern capitalist economy sought by persons such as Finance Minister Pani demanded first and foremost financial reconstruction and stabilization, so that Mexico's international trade could be normalized and its debt renegotiated to allow the resumption of foreign borrowing. In accepting the resulting policies of austerity, Calles gave second priority to agrarian and social reform measures; only limited revenues were directed toward public works and infrastructure investments.[23] The eagerness of some in the new political elite for their own enrichment placed a further brake on the use of state power to pursue redistribution. Thus, the growth strategy chosen, the requisites of international financial good behavior, and institutionalized corruption converged to limit land reform severely during the 1920s and early 1930s.[24]

Although Cárdenas never fundamentally challenged the capitalist nature of the political economy, his initiatives in the control of foreign capital were joined to efforts to use state power on behalf of peasants and workers in their conflicts with property owners. Under Cárdenas, the peasant and labor sectors of the ruling party had their interests genuinely represented to a greater extent than would ever subsequently be the case. Indeed, Cárdenas's reorganization of the PRI along corporatist lines would be used by his successors to co-opt and control these lower classes. Cárdenas encouraged labor-union organization, and his administration often sided with workers in conflicts with employers. His strong support for the peasants was manifested in the

---

[23] William P. Glade and Charles W. Anderson, Jr., *The Political Economy of Mexico* (Madison: University of Wisconsin Press, 1963), p. 117. Dwight Morrow, formerly of J. P. Morgan and Company and, after 1927, U.S. ambassador to Mexico, was influential in the government's decision to halt agrarian reform, convincing officials that the costs to the federal treasury were unacceptable. Nora Hamilton, *The Limits of State Autonomy: Post-Revolutionary Mexico* (Princeton: Princeton University Press, 1982), chap. 4.

[24] Hansen, *Mexican Development*, pp. 33-34. Hamilton, drawing from a number of sources, concludes that "in 1930, 70 percent of the non-ejidal rural population who owned land held less than one percent of the privately owned land, in holdings of less than five hectares, while 2.2 percent of the landowners held over 33 percent of the privately owned land in holdings of 500 hecateres or more. An estimated 2.3 to 3 million peasants . . . were without land, while the ejiditarios, comprising 15 percent of the agrarian population, often had small holdings of less than one hectare." Hamilton, *Limits of State Autonomy*, p. 100.

redistribution of 17.9 million hectares (more than 9 percent of Mexico's surface area), three times the total redistributed by the previous post-revolutionary administrations.[25] To avoid new domination by moneylenders and middlemen, Cárdenas established the Ejidal Bank in 1935 to make available to the new smallholding *ejiditarios* the credit denied them by commercial banks and the existing state Agrarian Credit Bank.[26] To help the peasants defend themselves against attacks by the landlords' "white guards," Cárdenas also armed 60,000 peasants organized into militias.[27]

State-sponsored reform waned during the last years of Cárdenas's administration, as he encountered limits inherent in Mexico's dependent situation within the world capitalist system. The private sector mobilized its diverse sources of power to resist: antigovernment propaganda, company unions, and simple refusal to invest.[28] At the same time, there was a tightening of fiscal constraints on the state. The renewal of the depression in the United States in 1937, the oil company boycott, and U.S. trade reprisals all reduced the import and export taxes on which the state relied.[29] The Ejidal Bank and the Agrarian Credit Bank were forced to cut their credit to peasants. The amount of land redistributed declined from about 5.8 million hectares in 1937 to 2.7 million in 1940.[30] There was also a marked weakening of Cárdenas's support for labor mobilization. Strike activity declined and more emphasis was placed on "class conciliation" and "national unity"—which for labor meant a postponement of its struggle for redistribution.[31]

ECONOMIC DEVELOPMENT FROM 1940 TO 1960

The Import-Substitution Strategy

When Manuel Avila Camacho came to office in 1940, he inherited an economy still characterized by a classic pattern of growth dependent on exports from agriculture and extractive industries. There had been

[25] Hansen, *Mexican Development*, p. 33.

[26] Glade and Anderson, *Political Economy of Mexico*, pp. 122-123.

[27] Gerrit Huizer, *The Revolutionary Potential of Peasants in Latin America* (Lexington, Mass.: D. C. Heath, 1972), p. 79.

[28] Nora Hamilton, "Mexico: The Limits of State Autonomy," *Latin American Perspectives*, 2 (1975):100-101.

[29] Merrill Rippy, *Oil and the Mexican Revolution* (Luden, Netherlands: E. J. Brill, 1972), p. 259.

[30] Centro de Investigaciones Agrarias, *Estructura agraria y desarrollo agrícola en México: Tenencia y uso de la tierra* (Mexico City: Fondo de Cultura Económica, 1977), p. 50.

[31] Hamilton, *Limits of State Autonomy*, chap. 7.

two significant changes in Mexico's relationship with the world capitalist system, however. Domestic ownership of banking and other financial institutions enhanced the government's ability to channel investments into areas that it deemed crucial, and foreign control of the economy had been reduced as increased domestic ownership and control of agricultural land, extractive industries, electric-power generation, and railroads laid the foundation for increased capital accumulation. The enhanced national control over the economy would allow Avila Camacho and his successors to shape the import-substitution industrialization that began with World War II and lasted for three decades.

Import substitution was not initially a deliberate policy. Mexico slipped into it when war-imposed restrictions on exports to Mexico created a sizeable market for Mexican manufacturers in Mexico and in the United States. When the end of World War II destroyed this "natural" protection, the regime of Miguel Alemán Valdés (1946-1952) instituted tariffs and import licenses to protect the nation's fledgling manufacturing sector. Import substitution then became a conscious policy, the foundation of Mexico's postwar "miracle" of economic growth. Between 1940 and 1970, industrialization for internal markets, not for exports, was the prime generator of the growth in gross national product (GNP) of 6 to 7 percent a year. Capital stock in manufacturing doubled in the 1940s and doubled again in the 1950s. Imports of manufactured consumer goods dropped from 28 percent of total commodity imports in 1940 to 14 percent in 1963.[32]

State action shaped the direction and rate of growth with more than import protection. Pursuing a policy of "stabilized development" (*desarrollo estabilizador*), it systematically created conditions of high profitability to encourage private-sector investment. State investment banks provided long-term, low-interest loans for industrial development, and the Bank of Mexico used its system of reserve requirements to encourage private banks to do the same. Taxes were kept low, and tax exemptions and fiscal subsidies were granted through a Law of New and Necessary Industries. Corporatist control of labor kept wages down, and, after 1954, orthodox fiscal and monetary policies kept inflation low. As Reynolds has pointed out, "the profit share of national

[32] Reynolds, *Mexican Economy*, pp. 184, 211. To sustain this industrialization, Mexico had to increase its imports of intermediate and capital goods, and such imports were still paid for largely by primary-product exports. The inefficiency of the new industries prevented much increase in manufactured exports; between 1940 and 1960, they rose only from 3 percent to 8 percent of total exports. The composition of exports did change dramatically, however. Between the same two years, minerals and fuels fell from 73 percent of commodity exports to 26 percent, while agricultural, forest, livestock, and fish products rose from 24 to 67 percent. Ibid., p. 206.

income increased rapidly during the 1940s and remained high during the following decade."[33]

In those sectors crucial to industrial growth in which the private sector was unwilling to invest (because of low or uncertain returns) or unable to do so (because of high capital costs), the state itself made the needed investments. Between 1940 and 1970, the public sector accounted for 30 percent of the country's aggregate investments.[34] Such investments were not only in the infrastructure (irrigation, transportation and communication, electric power), but also in basic industries such as steel, fertilizers, and petroleum. Moreover, acting as a last resort, the state became an entrepreneur of considerable importance in the Mexican economy, making investments in dozens of state enterprises in the manufacture of automobiles, auto parts, freight cars, paper, and cement, and in mining and sugar refining.[35]

In concert with the favorable world market conditions of the Pax Americana following World War II, the import-substitution policies of the Mexican state were successful in generating rapid and sustained economic growth. Gross domestic product increased in the decade of the 1950s at an average annual rate of 5.8 percent; the manufacturing sector alone grew at the rate of 7.3 percent. Beneath the surface of the economic miracle, however, were two serious problems: the lack of progress toward the revolutionary goal of social justice, and the difficulties in sustaining growth and national capital accumulation that were inherent in Mexico's dependent situation within the world capitalist system.

Inequality and Authoritarian Control

The policies so successful at promoting economic growth had several adverse effects on movement toward the revolution's goal of social justice. The light burden of the tax system that encouraged private-sector investment put heavy constraints on public spending. After 1954, the policy of *desarrollo estabilizador*, as part of the effort to hold down inflation, intensified these constraints by ruling out the use of unsupported central bank credits to finance increased spending. Social welfare expenditures were kept very low. Educational support (just 1.4 percent of GNP in the late 1950s) and, even more dramatically, social-security coverage lagged well behind their counterparts in Argentina,

---

[33] Ibid., p. 190.
[34] Hansen, *Mexican Development*, p. 211.
[35] See Bennett and Sharpe, "State As Banker."

Brazil, Chile, Peru, and Venezuela. In 1967, only 6.1 percent of the population, or 18.9 percent of the work force, was covered by social security.[36] State expenditures were targeted instead to investments in infrastructure and in bottleneck industries, so as to stimulate growth in agriculture and manufacturing. The benefits of these were primarily captured in profits by the private sector. Beyond what "trickled down," there was little benefit in state policy for the lower classes—and their circumstances were even worsened by a regressive tax structure.

Redistribution was also inhibited by state policies that prevented wages from rising and severely limited the ability of labor unions to strike. In agriculture, the pace of land reform declined dramatically. From 1940 to 1958, less land was redistributed than had been redistributed during the six years of the Cárdenas administration. Despite an increase under Adolfo López Mateos (1958-1964), there were still in the mid-1960s millions of hectares of cropland that strict enforcement of the laws would have made subject to expropriation. In 1960, despite the continued promise of land reform, 1.4 percent of all holdings contained more than 36 percent of Mexico's cropland, while half the landholders worked less than 12 percent of the cropland. To make matters worse, state investments in irrigation and the allocation of credit from state banks were centered on the large private holdings, not on the *ejidos* and small private holdings.[37]

State policies thus maintained, and in some respects increased, the degree of inequality in Mexico.[38] This inequality discouraged the creation of a broad national market in Mexico, though it did stimulate middle- and upper-middle-class demand for those consumer goods upon which the import-substitution strategy depended. At the end of the 1960s, Hansen concluded:

[36] Hansen, *Mexican Development*, pp. 85-86. For a very useful discussion of social security in Mexico, see Rose Spaulding, "State Power and Its Limits: Corporatism in Mexico," *Comparative Political Studies* 14 (1981):139-161.

[37] Roger Hansen, *Mexican Development*, pp. 33, 81-83.

[38] On the distribution of income in Mexico, see Ifigenia M. de Navarrete, "La distribución del ingreso y el desarrollo económico de México" (Mexico City: Instituto de Investigaciones Económicas, Escuela Nacional de Economía, 1960). This work has been updated and defended against a variety of criticisms in David Felix, "Income Distribution Trends in Mexico and the Kuznets Curves," in Sylvia Hewlitt and Richard Weinert, eds., *Brazil and Mexico: Patterns in Late Development* (Philadelphia: ISHI Press, 1982), pp. 265-316. Felix argues that the top 40 percent of families in the income pyramid increased their share of national income from 75 percent in the 1950s to about 80 percent in the 1960s. The biggest relative gainers were those in the 80th to 95th percentile interval (i.e., those just below the very top). The bottom 40 percent suffered a dramatic decline in their share, while the top 5 percent more or less held their own.

> While those on the lower half of the Mexican income scale have clearly lost ground in a relative sense, and possibly in absolute terms for the lowest 20-30 percent, shifts in the upper income brackets have benefited the emerging Mexican middle and upper-middle class . . . which provides an effective market for Mexican domestic manufactures . . . [The members of this class] are increasingly able to purchase those durable consumer goods now being manufactured in Mexico. Many of these products cannot yet meet international competitive standards, and must be sold in Mexico. By providing a growing domestic market for them, the redistribution of income away from both the top and bottom of the Mexican income scale toward the upper-middle sectors has undoubtedly supported the process of Mexican industrialization as it has developed since 1940.[39]

What this implied was greater production of luxury consumer goods, notwithstanding the unmet basic needs of the majority of the population. The selection, in the early 1960s, of automobiles as a major target sector for industrialization is one particularly significant example.[40]

The sacrifice of the goal of social justice in favor of the goal of growth can be explained by reference to certain political choices made within the limits of the capitalist structure of Mexico's economic institutions and class system and of the dependent relationship of Mexico's economy to the world capitalist system. But how could such political choices be made without stirring violent opposition from those who had fought during the revolution for social justice and who were now being made to shoulder the burden of the economic "miracle"?

A full explanation would have to trace out the complex rural and urban class structure and examine the history of peasant and labor organization. Here we will only stress the importance of political institutions—the state and the PRI—in limiting and repressing the claims of the lower classes for a more equitable share of the fruits of growth.[41]

[39] Hansen, *Mexican Development*, pp. 76-77.

[40] For a similar argument in the case of Brazil, see Evans, *Dependent Development*, p. 97.

[41] This view is most cogently elaborated in Hansen, *Mexican Development*, pp. 102-124, and we rely heavily on that line of analysis. Hansen also discusses alternative theories about the PRI and points to the role of culture in enforcing political stability; ibid., pp. 181-208. For other discussions of the state and the PRI in relation to the lower classes, see Susan Eckstein, *The Poverty of Revolution: The State and the Urban Poor in Mexico* (Princeton: Princeton University Press, 1977); David Ronfeldt, *Atencingo: The Politics of Agrarian Struggle in a Mexican Ejido* (Stanford: Stanford University Press, 1973); José Luis Reyna, "Redefining the Authoritarian Regime," in José Luis Reyna and Richard Weinert, eds.,

The PRI has been the central instrument of institutionalized control. Although its formal structure appears to give power and representation to its labor, peasant, and middle-class constituencies, it is the party leadership that actually controls Mexican politics, and it does so in two principal ways. First, it controls the nomination and election of virtually all municipal, state, and national officials. In consultation with other members of the political elite, the president nominates his successor as well as all state governors. Candidates for other elected offices are nominated by the political elite rather than through a bargaining process at the PRI's nominating convention. The PRI's nominees always win the presidency and all other offices, giving the party control of the governorships, state legislatures, and all but a fraction of Mexico's 2,300 mayoralties.[42] Secondly, through the PRI the political elite controls, from the top down, the various sectors of the party itself. There are few strong and independent unions in Mexico. Government recognition of a union has been largely conditioned on its membership in the PRI's labor sector (the CTM), and strikes by unrecognized unions are illegal. Unions outside the CTM have been tolerated to the extent that they do not create any economic or political disturbances. Government domination of the unions is gained either by imposing its own leadership on the unions or by co-opting existing leaders (awarding them legislative offices, for example). Union leaders, like the political elite that supports them, often use their official positions for private enrichment. In the agrarian sector, the imposition of leaders from above is even more prevalent, and the spoils of office are frequently used to ensure loyal support. The state's Ejidal Bank and the ministries concerned with agriculture are also important in maintaining control over the peasantry, often publicly voicing support for land redistribution claims while delaying and subverting them.

When co-optation, corruption, and subversion fail as control mech-

---

Authoritarianism in Mexico (Philadelphia: ISHI Press, 1977), pp. 155-171; Evelyn P. Stevens, Protest and Response in Mexico (Cambridge: MIT Press, 1974); Judith Hellman, Mexico in Crisis (New York: Holmes and Meier, 1978); and Pablo González Casanova, Democracy in Mexico (New York: Oxford University Press, 1970).

[42] The role of the PRI in Mexican politics is discussed in a number of studies, including Hansen, Mexican Development; Kenneth Johnson, Mexican Democracy: A Critical View (Boston: Allyn and Bacon, 1971); and Vincent Padgett, The Mexican Political System, 2nd ed. (Boston: Houghton Mifflin, 1976). A recent political reform has opened up representation in the legislature for opposition parties, but it is unclear what long-term consequences this may have for the political system. See Kevin Middlebrook, "Political Change and Political Reform in an Authoritarian Regime: The Case of Mexico," Working Papers, no. 91, Latin America Program, Woodrow Wilson International Center for Scholars, Washington, 1980.

anisms, state power is used for repression. The political controls of the PRI and the state apparatus are so well institutionalized that the tools of repression have been called on only infrequently. Nevertheless, the use of the army to crush strikes and force the resignation of labor leaders under Alemán, the jailing of railroad union leaders and their allies in 1958-1959 for demanding not only wage boosts but a more independent union, the actions taken against physicians in 1964, and the bloody repression of students in 1968 are all grim reminders of the political elite's willingness to use repression when other forms of control fail.

Dilemmas of Development

By the late 1950s, it had become clear to political leaders that growth would be difficult to sustain in the absence of new and vigorous state initiatives. The first (or "easy") stage of import substitution—the domestic manufacture of nondurable consumer goods—had neared completion by the end of the 1940s.[43] Between 1950 and 1958, the process of import substitution showed signs of stagnation. The share of imports in the total supply of nondurable consumer goods remained constant during those years, and there was a slowing in the rate of growth in GNP. Reinvigorating the growth process would require either expanding the size of the domestic market through income redistribution or extending the process of import substitution into consumer durables and producer goods. The first option would threaten the position of the middle and upper classes, and thus would be politically difficult, perhaps impossible, to carry through. The second demanded sophisticated technology and greater capital outlays. It also faced the opposition of certain domestic groups—importers of manufactured goods, for example—but its political costs would be considerably lower.

In the administration of Adolfo López Mateos (1958–1964), the Mexican state undertook important initiatives to reignite economic growth through an extension of import-substitution industrialization. One of these initiatives was an effort to compel the domestic manufacture of automobiles. Despite important changes in the character of Mexico's trade, financial, and investment relations, such action was vulnerable to currents in the international economic order.

[43] In 1950, nondurable consumer goods constituted only 17.6 percent of total imports. René Villarreal, "The Policy of Import-Substituting Industrialization, 1929-1975," in José Luis Reyna and Richard S. Weinert, eds., *Authoritarianism in Mexico* (Philadelphia: ISHI Press, 1977), p. 71.

Trade. The character of Mexico's international trade relations had altered as imports of consumer goods decreased. The import-substitution process was itself import-intensive, since imports of parts, machinery, and raw materials were needed to sustain the new and growing manufacturing industries; in 1960, they made up 85 percent of Mexico's commodity imports, an increase from 69 percent in 1940. Cash crops and manufactured goods were added to minerals and fuels to diversify Mexico's exports, but the country's trade position remained precarious in important ways. Primary products still constituted 92 percent of exports, and more than three-quarters of Mexico's trade was with one country, the United States. Any reduction of exports, in turn reducing the capacity to import, would have an even greater impact on production and employment in Mexico than had been true in the past.[44]

Finance. A private Mexican banking system had been re-established in national hands after the revolution, and it came to form the nucleus of the entrepreneurial elite of the new system. In 1965, the threat of foreign purchases of sizeable blocks of bank stocks spurred the administration of Gustavo Díaz Ordaz (1964-1970) to amend the banking laws to forbid ownership of bank and insurance company stock by foreign interests.[45] State banks filled gaps left by the private banking system. But despite this enhanced domestic control over the financial sector, the state came to rely increasingly on foreign loans to finance its projects.

There were three major ways to raise revenues to meet rising governmental expenditures: (a) tax the private sector, (2) borrow abroad, and (3) borrow at home by channeling private savings into public investment through financial intermediaries. There was some increase in income taxes after 1940, but basically the state maintained low taxes on personal and industrial earnings as part of its strategy to encourage private-sector investment. In the years following World War II, tax revenues were insufficient to finance increased government expenditures. The state resorted to unsupported credits from the central bank, resulting in severe inflation and to peso devaluation in 1948 and 1954. From the mid-1950s through the 1960s, however, it was possible for the state to pursue the policy of *desarrollo estabilizador* with the use of both domestic and foreign borrowing.

This mode of financing of public-sector expenditures, however, imposed serious constraints on state action. In order to be able to channel

[44] Reynolds, *Mexican Economy*, chap. 6.
[45] Wright, *Foreign Enterprise*, p. 91.

private savings into public investment, it was essential that the state maintain an economic climate that would encourage savings. In addition to low inflation, this demanded high real interest rates and a stable exchange rate to protect savers against the losses that would accompany devaluation.[46] It also disposed the state to shy away from exchange controls, which would discourage foreigners from bringing their savings into Mexico and which would, in view of the long common border with the United States, be extremely difficult to enforce. These policies enhanced the power of the private sector to oppose state action. Any widespread inclination on the part of the business community (itself quite concentrated in a few large groups) to pull its savings out of Mexico and place them in securities across the border would pose an immediate threat to growth, to the balance of payments, and to state fiscal resources. Countermeasures by the Mexican state could only make matters worse. Another problem was that the more the government relied on funds drawn out of the private sector, the scarcer and more costly became loanable funds in the private sector.[47] A contradiction had arisen between public and private investment.

The sensitivity and power of the private sector was made clear in its reaction to López Mateos's aggressive moves to control foreign investment and to his early support of Fidel Castro, who had taken power in Cuba in 1959. López Mateos was branded a socialist by some in the business community, and there was a flight of capital amounting to about $200 million in 1960-1961. In Vernon's words, there followed "an extraordinary effort on the part of the Mexican government to demonstrate its continued esteem for, and appreciation of, the critical role of business in Mexico's economic life."[48]

Foreign borrowing, the remaining source for financing state expenditures (and an important one for managing the conflict between public and private investment) also placed constraints on state action. Mexico's external public debt, already $816 million by 1960, quadrupled to $3,227 million by 1970.[49] Increasingly, the principal and interest payments on this debt ate into Mexico's earnings from the

[46] For a discussion of the reserve requirements and other mechanisms for channeling private savings into public investments, see Dwight Brothers and Leopoldo Solis, *Mexican Financial Development* (Austin: University of Texas Press, 1966), pp. 90-94.

[47] Brothers and Solis, *Mexican Financial Development*, p. 94.

[48] Raymond Vernon, *The Dilemma of Mexico's Development* (Cambridge: Harvard University Press, 1963), pp. 121-122. On this episode, see also Miguel Wionczek, *El nacionalismo mexicano y la inversión extranjera* (Mexico City: Siglo XXI, 1967), pp. 240-241.

[49] E.V.K. Fitzgerald, "The State and Capital Accumulation in Mexico," *Journal of Latin American Studies* 10 (1978):281.

export of goods and services. Although this level of foreign borrowing was, in the eyes of some economists, already perilously high in 1970, it was not until a few years later that the resultant international financial constraints on state action were felt (see chapter 8). The new character of Mexico's dependent relationship with international financial markets took shape in the 1950s and 1960s, however. Not only was Mexico increasingly vulnerable to changes in world financial markets (availability of loans, interest rates), but international banks, both public and private, also acquired potential influence over domestic policy by the terms they could set when this debt needed to be refinanced.

Foreign Investment. By the late 1950s, the Mexican manufacturing sector was producing a broad range of finished consumer goods, but many consumer durables and producer goods continued to be imported. This manufacturing sector tended to be inefficient: oligopolistic market structures displaced domestic competition in a number of industries, and the import barriers which encouraged industrialization shielded these industries from foreign competition. Unused capacity and high prices were the consequences. Not only did this situation stifle manufactured exports; it also hindered exports of primary products whose prices were affected by expensive industrial inputs.[50] And state policies aimed at furthering import substitution, improving efficiency, and promoting exports had to confront an increasingly important characteristic of the manufacturing sector: the domination of crucial industries by subsidiaries of transnational corporations.

By 1940, foreign investment had been severely restricted in many of those sectors where its presence had been most provoking before the revolution, such as agriculture, banking, petroleum, and railways. Two strategies had been predominantly employed. Either foreign firms had been excluded from the sector (reserving it for private Mexican ownership) or existing foreign-owned firms had been nationalized (public ownership). The successive administrations of Avila Camacho, Alemán, and Adolfo Ruiz Cortines (1952-1958) were ones of relative quiescence with regard to the control of foreign investment, but the next administration, that of López Mateos, was more aggressive. In 1960, the two remaining foreign-owned electric power companies were nationalized, and a year later new legislation for the mining sector barred firms with majority foreign ownership from new concessions and established a series of new subsidies available only to firms with majority Mexican ownership. In both these cases, state managers

[50] Villarreal, "Import-Substituting Industrialization," p. 75.

35

judged that the global interests of the foreign-owned firms so conflicted with the needs of Mexican development that only full or partial Mexican ownership, either public or private, could rectify the situation.[51]

Having been limited to or even eliminated from those sectors in which it had once been strongest, foreign investment began to make large inroads in the manufacturing sector, the most dynamic sector of the Mexican economy. Less than 7 perecent of foreign investment was in manufacturing in 1940, but more than 70 percent was by 1970. Of the 300 largest manufacturing enterprises, more than half were foreign-controlled in 1972. A sectoral breakdown shows the domination of transnational corporations to have been especially strong in areas demanding sophisticated technology and large amounts of capital, such as rubber, chemicals, fabricated metals, electrical and nonelectrical machinery, and transportation. Transnational corporations had come to dominate in just those sectors that, because of the amounts of capital and degree of technology utilized and their backward and forward linkages to the rest of the economy, were critical to continued industrial growth.[52]

This direct foreign investment in manufacturing was principally of U.S. origin. The U.S. share of total foreign investment rose from 69 percent in 1950 to a peak of 85 percent in 1962, at which time the volume of European (mostly West German) investment began to grow more rapidly. Nevertheless, in 1970 the United States still accounted for 79 percent of foreign investment in Mexico. In the years between 1950 and 1972, U.S. investment in Mexico grew at an annual rate of 11.2 percent, faster than the growth of the manufacturing sector as a whole.[53]

The quarter-century following World War II was a period of rapid international expansion by U.S.- and then by European- and Japanese-based manufacturing firms. Direct investment was their preferred

[51] For a fuller discussion, see Douglas Bennett, Morris Blachman, and Kenneth Sharpe, "Mexico and Multinational Corporations: An Explanation of State Action," in Joseph Grunwald, ed., *Latin America and World Economy: A Changing International Order* (Beverly Hills, Cal.: Sage, 1978), pp. 257-282.

[52] On transnational corporations in the Mexican economy, see Fernando Fajnzylber and Trinidad Martínez Tárrago, *Las empresas transnacionales: Expansión a nivel mundial y proyección en la industria mexicana* (Mexico City: Fondo de Cultura Económica, 1976); Richard Newfarmer and Willard Mueller, *Multinational Corporations in Brazil and Mexico: Structural Sources of Economic and Non-Economic Power*, report prepared for the Subcommittee on Multinational Corporations of the Senate Committee on Foreign Relations, 94th Cong., 1st sess., 1975; and Bernardo Sepulveda Amor, Olga Pellicer De Brody, and Lorenzo Meyer, *Las empresas transnacionales en México* (Mexico City: El Colegio de México, 1974).

[53] Newfarmer and Mueller, *Multinational Corporations in Brazil and Mexico*, p. 50.

mode of expansion.[54] The import-substitution policies of Mexico (and other countries) were in part responsible for this preference: faced with the possible loss of a market because of the erection of trade barriers, transnational corporations created local subsidiaries (or bought out existing firms) to enter into domestic manufacture. "Denationalization"—the transfer of ownership of local firms to foreign corporations—had become a major issue in Mexico by 1970. The older strategies for containing foreign investment—outright exclusion or nationalization—were deemed inappropriate for manufacturing (as well as for mining and a variety of other sectors), for they would shut out the capital, technology, and management expertise that transnational manufacturing firms had to offer. Increasingly over the course of the 1950s and 1960s, a different regulatory strategy was employed: Mexicanization, the requirement that firms be majority Mexican-owned, with foreign capital allowed only as a minority partner in a joint venture.[55]

A THEORETICAL APPROACH TO THE MEXICAN STATE

What makes the Mexican struggle with dependency in the twentieth century unusual in comparative terms is the fact of the revolution—a genuine social cataclysm that mobilized the lower classes to obliterate a regime that had enriched an elite closely tied to foreign interests while impoverishing the vast majority. Three themes have run through the foregoing account of events in Mexico following the revolution:

(1) Relative to the era of the *Porfiriato*, Mexico in 1960 showed both persistence and change in the character of its dependency within the world capitalist system. The global division of production and labor continued to place Mexico at a disadvantage in relation to the core areas of the world economy—the United States, Western Europe, and Japan—and its rate and direction of accumulation were externally conditioned by the expansion of these other economies. Mexico had, however, recaptured control over natural resources from foreign interests, it had established a domestic entrepreneurial class as well as institutions

[54] For a discussion of this preference, see Stephen Hymer, *The International Operations of National Firms: A Study of Direct Foreign Investment* (Cambridge: MIT Press, 1976); Raymond Vernon, *Sovereignty at Bay: The Multinational Spread of U.S. Enterprises* (New York: Basic Books, 1971); and Mira Wilkins, *The Maturing of Multinational Enterprise: American Business Abroad from 1914 to 1970* (Cambridge: Harvard University Press, 1974). The internationalization of the automobile industry will be discussed in chap. 3 in some detail.

[55] See chap. 6 for an assessment of the consequences of the Mexicanization policy.

37

and processes for domestic capital accumulation, and it had embarked on industrialization.

(2) Some of the changes in the character of Mexico's dependency resulted from events or processes in the world capitalist system—the depression and World War II, for example, stimulated industrialization—but many of them resulted from state action in which state power was used to restructure Mexico's relationship to the world capitalist system.

(3) The postrevolutionary Mexican state acted resolutely to promote economic growth and domestic capital accumulation, but it did little to alter the persisting inequality of distribution. In some ways, it even reinforced this inequality.

An explanation of the actions of the Mexican state must rest upon an adequate theory of the state in general, and such a theory, we believe, must have two characteristics: (1) it must conceive of the state as an *actor*—not necessarily a simple or a unified one, but at least as one having identifiable behavior of its own that sets it apart from other actors with which it may cooperate or conflict. Conceiving of the state as an actor means being able to explain why the state has the *interests* that it does and why it has the *power* that it does. (2) In giving an account of the interests and power of the state, it must show how these are shaped and reshaped *historically* within changing national and international *structures*, and it must allow for state action aimed at transforming these structures.

The reigning approaches to the state do not observe either of these requirements.[56] The behavioral/pluralist approach tends to conceive of the state as a more or less fluid and contentless shell, an arena where ever-changing group conflicts are fought out, bargains struck, and decisions made. The state does not exist as an identifiable and distinct actor. Various groups compete with one another to translate their interests and their power into state policy, but the state has no interests or power of its own. The emphasis tends to be on fluidity and multiplicity—of administrations, policies, decisions, laws—rather than on any stable or coherent state entity. At some times and places, this may be an accurate picture of how particular policies were made and implemented, but the problem with this approach is that it denies, a priori,

[56] A very useful review of recent approaches to the state is Theda Skocpol, "Bringing the State Back In: False Leads and Promising Starts in Current Theories and Research," working paper prepared for the Conference on States and Social Structures, Seven Springs Conference Center, Mount Kisco, N.Y., Feb. 25-27, 1982.

the possibility of a state actor with interests and power of its own, able to act irrespective of or even against outside pressures.[57]

Marxist approaches ascribe a capitalist character to the state (denying the pluralist conception of the state as contentless arena), but one variant, the instrumental, denies the state any interests of its own, while another, the structuralist, conceives of the state as having interests but can give no satisfactory account of how they are acquired. Neither deals adequately with state power.

The instrumental approach conceives of the state as an agency of the ruling classes. Thus, like the behavioral/pluralist approach, it sees the interests and power of the state as exogenously derived. But because the bourgeoisie (or its dominant faction) possesses disproportionate power vis-à-vis other classes and groups, its interests will prevail in essential matters. There is thus a coherence and a continuity to the state—the interests of the ruling class. The state has no interests or power of "its own, however."[58]

[57] The classic work of this genre is Robert Dahl, *Who Governs?* (New Haven: Yale University Press, 1961). One of a number of useful collections of criticism of the approach is William E. Connolly, ed., *The Bias of Pluralism* (New York: Atherton, 1969). An example of the analytical framework applied to Mexico is Robert E. Scott, *Mexican Government in Transition* (Urbana: University of Illinois Press, 1964). It was criticized in Brandenburg, *Making of Modern Mexico*, but Brandenburg's work emphasized the ruling elites in the "revolutionary family" and did not focus on the state. Susan Purcell and John Purcell bring this pluralist approach together with a bureaucratic politics approach which is explicitly critical of the conception of the state as actor. In their carefully researched article on political decision making in Mexico, they emphasize the policy incoherence of most ministries. Their explanation points to the character of the changing groups that staff these ministries and whose overriding concern is their own self-interest: "Ideology and policy position become free-floating resources to be espoused for both themselves and for strategic reasons, but never to be permanently appropriated." They emphasize that the "Mexican state is in reality a precarious association of ruling groups and interests" and that state institutions in Mexico have never developed "a life of their own." But while emphasizing (often quite correctly) the bureaucratic conflicts and policy incoherence during the Echeverría administration, they miss the historical coherence and consistency of the more deeply embedded orientations that constrain policy fluctuations over time. Susan Kaufman Purcell and John F. H. Purcell, "State and Society in Mexico: Must a Stable Policy Be Institutionalized?," *World Politics* 32 (1980):194-227.

[58] For example, Ralph Miliband, *The State in Capitalist Society* (New York: Basic Books, 1969), recognizes state autonomy but tends to stress the ways in which political leaders are influenced by pressures from business interests and their personal ties to members of the bourgeoisie. The emphasis is thus on the mechanisms by which ruling classes in capitalism constrain state action, and not on the state as an actor with interests and power. Instrumental treatments of the Mexican state are rare and unconvincing, because of the unusual separation of the capitalist class and the state managers and the paucity of mechanisms by which the ruling classes might directly exert their influence on the state. Furthermore, the Mexican state took actions which helped create the national bouregeoisie

The structuralist approach emphasizes the role of the state in "rationalizing" capitalism. Certain contradictions within capitalism (between finance and industrial capital, or between national and transnational capital, for example) create needs which the state satisfies, if only temporarily, in order to re-establish equilibrium. To do so, the state may act forcefully, at least in the short run, against the wishes of some fraction of the capitalist class. The structuralist approach, then, confers interests and power upon the state, but it lacks an explanation of why the state has certain interests and not others (there are many ways to rationalize capitalism), nor can it explain the extent of state power and its limits (some states may not have the power to rationalize capitalism, and social conflict may culminate in revolution). The central difficulty is one shared by all functionalist explanations: the identification of a "need" or "essential function" is not sufficient to account for how and why some actor or institution comes to satisfy it. Identification of the functions of a particular state is useful, but it is also important to explain historically how the state has come to take on these particular functions and how it does or does not acquire the power to carry them out. Under the structural approach, the state does have interests and power of its own, but the teleological account of their nature is not satisfactory.[59]

Closer to our central substantive concerns in this book, Alexander Gerschenkron has usefully identified an important comparative pattern in the process of industrialization. Rejecting the thesis that developing countries travel the same road toward industrialization as the more developed ones did, but trailing them by some decades, Gerschenkron argues that the industrialization process in later-developing countries required, among other things, "the application of institutional instruments for which there was no counterpart in an estab-

in the first place, and thus it would be difficult to explain such actions by reference to its influence. The Mexican state has, however, served the interests of this class and, we will argue below, such orientations still exist, deeply embedded within major state institutions.

[59] See, for example, Nicos Poulantzas, "The Problem of the Capitalist State," in Robin Blackburn, ed., *Ideology in Social Science* (New York: Vintage, 1973), pp. 239-258, and Louis Althusser, "Ideology and Ideological State Apparatuses," in his *Lenin and Philosophy and Other Essays* (New York: Monthly Review Press, 1971), pp. 127-186. A good example of such an approach to the Mexican state is Juan Felipe Leal, *México: Estado, burocracia, y sindicatos* (Mexico City: Ediciones El Caballito, 1976). Leal provides a useful description of the role of the Mexican state in encouraging and maintaining capitalism and in acting as a capitalist itself when the private sector did not, but his explanations are often functionalist in character. The "constitution of the state," for example, is presented as a "condition required by late and subordinate capitalist development" (p. 90).

lished, industrial country."[60] Whereas capital formation was accomplished in Great Britain through the exertions of individual capitalists, later industrializers, such as France and Germany, required investment banks for the same purpose. Those beginning still later, such as Russia, needed the yet more powerful institutional means of the state itself— i.e., its taxation powers—to generate the needed investment capital. Although Mexico, Argentina, Brazil, and Chile entered into manufacturing not with producer goods but with previously imported consumer goods, these "late late industrializers" faced still greater problems: catching up to compete internationally meant developing products and processes that were even more costly, risky, and technologically sophisticated than Gerschenkron's late industrializers had had to develop.[61]

In Mexico, such problems were exacerbated by the devastation wrought by the revolution and the lack of an entrepreneurial class capable of leading industrialization in the immediate postconflict years. The state therefore took on a particularly strong leading role. The delineation of a historical pattern which Mexico fits, however, is not sufficient to explain the interests and power of the state. The unwillingness or inability of private-sector actors in Mexico to solve the problems of late late industrialization there created "needs" which the state met, but that does not explain the state's willingness or ability—*its* interests or power—to meet them. Gerschenkron's approach, like the Marxist-structuralist one, is flawed as an explanation by its functionalist or teleological character.[62]

Weber's definition of the state, because it is nonteleological, is a useful starting point for a historical-structural approach. Stressing the means peculiar to it, rather than the particular ends it serves, Weber defines the state as "a human community that [successfully] claims the monopoly of legitimate use of physical force within a given territory."[63]

[60] Alexander Gerschenkron, *Economic Backwardness in Historical Perspective* (Cambridge: Harvard University Press, 1966), p. 7.

[61] The differences between Latin American and Eastern European late late industrializers are elaborated in Albert Hirschman, "The Political Economy of Import-Substituting Industrialization in Latin America," *Quarterly Journal of Economics* 82 (1968):1-32.

[62] For a fuller discussion of this point, see Bennett and Sharpe, "State As Banker."

[63] H. H. Gerth and C. Wright Mills, *From Max Weber: Essays in Sociology* (London: Routledge and Kegan Paul, 1948), p. 78. Weber wrote (pp. 77-78): "Sociologically, the state cannot be defined in terms of its ends. There is scarcely any task that some political association has not taken in hand, and there is no task that one could say has always been exclusive and peculiar to those associations which are designated as political ones. . . . Ultimately one can define the modern state sociologically only in terms of the specific means peculiar to it . . . namely, the use of physical force."

The state is not simply an aggregate of individual officials, Weber recognizes, but an ongoing organization—an administration with a civil and military bureaucratic staff. Weber also recognizes that states come to serve ends or functions and inevitably favor some groups and disfavor others. But the social foundations of a particular state, its power, and the class interests to which it attends are all issues that need to be explained historically. This is exactly what we must do in the case of Mexico: identify the ends that this state has come to serve, and explain how these ends were taken on historically and how the state institutionalized the capacity to pursue them. An adequate understanding of the state must comprehend both its ends and its means.

To say that the state has interests and power "of its own" is not by any means to say that it is always "autonomous" of powerful economic classes or social forces. It is only to say that it is an organization with institutionalized dispositions and capabilities to act in certain ways. Because the state is a part of other national and international structures, its interests are likely to have been shaped in ways that lead it generally to act in concert with dominant classes or groups. Alternately, the state's power may be insufficient for it to act successfully against the wishes of these classes or groups.

Understanding how the state acquires its interests and power means understanding the state as an actor involved in national and international structures—a world capitalist system, a system of nation-states, a national economic and class system, and a particular culture. This approach is necessarily historical, because the state's experiences with other actors and structures will determine whether the state is coherent or fragmented in its actions and what specific interests, what power or weaknesses, it has. At the same time, the approach is inherently structural; it denies the voluntarism that sees the state as an actor that chooses and acts wholly freely, viewing the state instead as an actor whose interests and power are shaped by structures. It can transform structures, but only within limits that are themselves historically structured.

The Interests of the Mexican State

Elected officials and state bureaucrats may be influenced in what they do or avoid by pressures from interest groups or through the direct influence of a particular class or class fraction. The pluralist and instrumentalist Marxist emphases on the external factors that shape state action, while important, are seriously incomplete. Although, it is commonplace to speak of corporations as having interests, it is much less common to speak of a state as having interests, beyond the maintenance of a monopoly of force within a particular territory. We conceive of the interests of the state as "embedded orientations" which are institutionalized in the ministries and agencies of the state—in their habitual ways of diagnosing and remedying problems and in their organization of staff responsibilities and resources. Because of the complexity of the modern state, different orientations may be embedded in different ministries, with consequent possibilities of bureaucratic conflict in setting state policy.

The discussion in the preceding section highlighted a number of orientations characterizing the management of the economy that have come to be embedded in the fabric of the Mexican state: (a) a basic commitment to the pursuit of rapid economic growth along a path that places primary reliance on private-sector initiative; (b) a tutelary role for the state in overseeing this process of growth, including a readiness to have the state undertake, as a last resort, those projects deemed necessary by the state managers but that the private sector is unable or unwilling to carry forward; (c) promotion of domestic over foreign ownership of productive assets, but with a willingness to allow foreign investment where it may contribute to growth and domestic capital accumulation; (d) after 1940, a commitment to the development of a modern, domestic manufacturing sector in Mexico, along—at least until the late 1960s—an import substitution path; and (e) in the two decades after 1954, a commitment to *desarrollo estabilizador*, a set of orthodox fiscal and monetary policies aimed at high savings with low inflation, foreign-exchange convertibility, and financing of state projects through reserve requirements rather than through unsupported central bank credits. These orientations have been institutionalized in an increasingly complex array of ministries and agencies, principally the Ministry of Finance, the Bank of Mexico, NAFIN, and the Ministry of Industry and Commerce (before 1958, the Ministry of National Economy; after 1976, the Ministry of National Properties and Industrial Development). They have been broadly shared throughout this institutional complex, but there have been focused responsibilities. *Desarrollo estabilizador* has been primarily the concern of Finance, for example; import substitution, of Industry and Commerce; public-sector investments, of NAFIN.

The policies that have emanated from these orientations have guided Mexican economic growth in the twentieth century, but to say that they have been "functional" for growth is not sufficient—it risks teleology again. Just how has the Mexican state taken on these orientations or interests? We can identify three principal ways in which a state acquires interests: (1) Initial orientations are set down at its founding, particularly in establishing its social foundations. (2) These initial orientations are elaborated and altered as the state confronts new problems and devises strategies and builds capacities for dealing with them, although the institutionalization of the initial orientations constrains what is seen as a problem and what as an appropriate solution. (3) Major changes in state personnel bring new orientations or reformulations of old ones. Each of these, but particularly the second, requires some elaboration.

Orientations at Foundings. When the state is founded (or refounded after a social upheaval), those elements that have seized the political initiative can set the initial orientations of the state by devising an array of institutions embodying their ideological vision, by coalescing class alliances to form the social foundations of the state, and by formulating legitimations to transform their might into right.[64] In postrevolutionary Mexico, it was the "constitutionalists," small businessmen and commercial farmers, mostly from Sonora, who ultimately prevailed in the fighting and re-established civil war. The orientations with which they imbued key state institutions defined the basic strategy for economic growth: primary reliance on the private sector, with the state poised to intervene in cases of private-sector incapacity or reluctance. It was a decidedly nationalist orientation, but "anti-gringo" did not mean "anti-capitalist" or "pro-redistribution." These initial orientations set the character of the Mexican state and restricted all but marginal changes in orientation. Only if the state were captured and reconstituted by new classes could major changes in orientation be expected.

Elaboration and Revision. Over time, problems or crises arise which those managing the state see as necessary to confront and to solve. A problem does not "call forth" a particular response, however. Indeed, the definition of what is a problem and what is a proper response is shaped by the existing orientations. There is thus a continual interaction between the state and other actors and the structures within which they are acting. Viewing the structures around them through the lenses of already embedded dispositions, state managers define certain aspects of these structures or the situations arising from them as problematic, and they devise strategies to deal with these. Recurring problems will

---

[64] The stress upon social foundations as the basis for setting initial orientations is what some have meant in referring to the state as a "pact of domination." Fernando Henrique Cardoso, "On the Characterization of Authoritarian Regimes in Latin America," in David Collier, ed., *The New Authoritarianism in Latin America* (Princeton: Princeton University Press, 1979), pp. 33-57.

likely lead to the institutionalization of capabilities for monitoring and coping with them. As problems are defined and policy options debated, adopted, and implemented, the orientations of the state will either be reinforced or altered, though generally only gradually and on the margins. Structures may also be changed by state action, setting the scene for the emergence of new sorts of problems and for further state action.

In this conceptualization of state interests, how can we account for the general tendency of the state in capitalist society to promote the interests of capital or of particular fractions of capital? Even if members of the dominant class have a hand in the founding of the state, there will inevitably be a growing separation between state managers and the business community. In Mexico, that separation has been particularly pronounced. The initial orientations of the Mexican state were such as to promote the interests of a domestic bourgeoisie, but what has prevented the elaboration and revision of these orientations from drifting away from those initial orientations? There is no need to postulate mechanisms by which the private sector exerts direct pressure on state managers, even though these do exist in Mexico to an extent. Rather, the very position of the state in a capitalist economy makes it rational for state managers to promote the general interests of capital because of their own interests as state managers. In order for the state to continue to finance its own activities and to maintain necessary public support, a reasonable level of economic activity must be maintained. Regardless of ruling-class hegemony or direct influence, the rational state manager will not behave in a way that will too severely discourage the rate of private investment (and thus a reasonable level of business activity) by undermining "business confidence." Within these limits, state managers may take actions that in effect "rationalize" capitalism and resolve or dissipate class antagonisms so as to maintain economic stability and political order.[65] This mechanism may not lead the state invariably to do what the private sector wants, but it will tend to restrain the state from developing and institutionalizing orientations that harm the interests of capital. We need to keep in mind, however, that this

[65] This approach is persuasively argued in Fred Block, "The Ruling Class Does Not Rule: Notes on the Marxist Theory of the State," *Socialist Revolution* 7 (1977):6-28. Hamilton, *Limits of State Autonomy*, is also informed by a similar, nonteleological Marxist perspective. Both Block and Hamilton have been influenced by the work of Claus Offe; see, e.g., Claus Offe, "Structural Problems of the Capitalist State," in Klaus von Beyme, ed., *German Political Studies* (Beverly Hills, Cal.: Sage, 1976), pp. 31-57, and Claus Offe and Volker Ronge, "Theses on the Theory of the State," *New German Critique* 6 (1975):139-147.

general consideration does not account for the *particular* ways that the Mexican state has employed to make capitalism work in Mexico. Only a historical examination of the state, of the structures around it, and of the procedures it has institutionalized to identify problems and construct strategies for their solution will be able to account for the particular interests or orientations of the Mexican state.

An example of how the interests of the Mexican state have evolved since they were first set down may serve to make this discussion less abstract. Initially, the Mexican state reconstituted after the revolution was antithetical to foreign investment; through the late 1930s, it pursued a policy of steadily reducing foreign ownership in those sectors where it had predominated before the revolution—banking, railroads, electric power, and petroleum. Expropriation of foreign holdings put a strain on the state's fiscal resources, however, and threatened Mexico's standing in the international economic order, most dramatically in a showdown with the oil companies in 1938. Once industrialization began in earnest, moreover, exclusion of foreign investment threatened to deny Mexico access to needed technology. Thus, during the 1950s and 1960s, a different approach to direct foreign investment evolved: Mexicanization. Foreign investment would be permitted but only in minority holding. In time, this policy itself created a problem. Mexicanization was tending to strengthen the hands of a few powerful economic groups, each of which had become the majority partner of a number of transnational manufacturing firms in their Mexican subsidiaries. Mexicanization then began to be used by the state managers more as a threat in the bargaining for other concessions (exports, location outside the federal district, or jobs) rather than as an end in itself.[66]

Changes in Personnel. Just as those who constitute or reconstitute the state set its initial orientations, so, too, can major changes in state personnel alter the state's interests, at least to a degree. In Mexico, the most important changes in personnel come with each sexennial change in the presidency and a concomitant large-scale turnover among the officials charged with the formulation and implementation of policy. Each presidential administration tends to have its own character or shading. Particularly since 1934, however, the increased institutionalization of the state and of the PRI has militated against significant redirection of state policy simply through change of personnel. It is extremely unlikely that a group representing a different coalition of

---

[66] For an elaboration of the state's evolving dispositions toward foreign investment, see Bennett, Blachman, and Sharpe, "Mexico and Multinational Corporations."

class forces could now capture the state through these normal political channels and alter its character in any dramatic way.

In the ministries concerned with economic growth in Mexico, there has been an unusual continuity of outlook, in part the product of certain enduring features of the national and international political economy and of constraints set by dispositions previously embedded in these state institutions, but in part also a product of continuity in personnel and of deliberate attempts by these ministries to inculcate a common perspective. While there is considerable restaffing in these ministries and related agencies, it is far more a reshuffling than a wholesale replacement. An economist may spend a *sexenio* in the Bank of Mexico, then one in the Finance Ministry, then several in NAFIN. In this institutional complex, there has been a longstanding preoccupation with the training of young *técnicos*. Promising young people are frequently employed in one of these institutions for a few years, then sent to the United States or Europe to complete their formal education, then returned for final shaping at the hands of senior officials. All this makes it very unlikely that a dramatic change in state policy could occur simply because of a change in presidential administration, but smaller changes frequently do take place this way as senior positions are assumed by a group with a slightly different approach within the broad outlines of established policy.

The Power of the Mexican State

To understand the state as an actor, we must understand not only its interests but also its power, its ability to implement the policies it formulates. The power of any actor, but particularly of the state, is difficult to examine in the abstract. It is always issue-specific, depending on the particular goals that the state is pursuing; and it is always relational, depending on the power of other actors or social groups who support or oppose its actions. Power is a matter of *who* is trying to do *what* to *whom*. At a very general level, we can say that the power of the Mexican state depends on certain internal characteristics of the state and on how the state is situated within national and international structures (political, economic, social, and cultural) in which other actors, its allies and opponents, also play a part.

Internally, two kinds of factors are particularly important: the cohesion or organizational unity of the state, and the skill or technical capability of its officials. In Mexico, the state has been strong in both these senses for several decades. Its evolution since the postrevolutionary chaos of the 1920s and early 1930s has given the president great authority over the civil bureaucracy, the military, and the PRI. The vast power of the president to make his own appointments at the beginning of each *sexenio* enables him to staff key positions with officials who are loyal not only to the state—as opposed to a particular class—but who are loyal to him personally. This loyalty is enhanced by the relatively great separation of the political elite from the business elite. Few top state officials are drawn from the dominant economic groups, and their career patterns differ substantially.

In those ministries charged with management of the economy, officials have become increasingly well-trained, both as a result of careful recruitment and retention efforts and as a result of internal education programs, particularly within the Bank of Mexico and the Ministry of Finance. As these ministries have grown in technical skill, they have also grown in complexity. New centers of bureaucratic power have been created, often diminishing the power of others. In the early 1960s, the Ministry of Industry and Commerce was reorganized and its functions were enlarged at the expense of the once all-powerful Ministry of Finance. The power of both was curtailed somewhat in the 1970s with the creation of the Ministry of Planning and Budgeting. While such changes have developed rival power centers with competing interests and personality clashes, the president can still impose unity, ultimately replacing recalcitrant ministers if necessary.

The power of the Mexican state is affected not only by its own resources and capabilities but also by its relationships to other actors within national and international structures. Its relationship to domestic classes is particularly important, but it is also true that the Mexican state has had a major hand in shaping the class structure and in organizing its own relationship with various social classes.[67] Cárdenas's moves—and later efforts of a similar sort by Luis Echeverría Álvarez (1970-1976)—relied on the mobilization of the peasant and labor classes. Votes from labor and peasantry (notwithstanding some tampering) are crucial in sustaining the electoral monopoly of the PRI. Political power has been used to organize these lower classes in such a way that they can be drawn on as a power base from time to time while minimizing the risk of their making demands upon the state that

[67] In his book on the state in Peru, Alfred Stepan emphasizes that the state "is the continuous administrative, legal, bureaucratic and coercive systems that attempt not only to structure relationships between civil society and public authority in a polity but also structure many crucial relationships within civil society as well." Alfred Stepan, *The State and Society: Peru in Comparative Perspective* (Princeton: Princeton University Press, 1978), p. xii. Skocpol, "Bringing the State Back In," also stresses the importance of understanding how the state itself structures society, rather than conceiving of the state as simply a product of social forces that exist independently of it.

have to be met. Corporatist mechanisms (control of union funds, permission to strike, selection of leadership, co-optation, selective repression) have directed and limited peasant demands, ensuring relative political stability and an economic climate conducive to investments, while at the same time forcing these classes to pay a disproportionate share of the costs of economic growth.

It is the national bourgeoisie, and the private market organization of production and consumption which form the foundation of its power, that most circumscribe the state's ability to carry forward its social and economic policies. It was state action, beginning in the 1920s, that helped create this class and the private market, but the very success of that endeavor led to a significant limitation of state power. Particularly important in any economy which places primary reliance on private-sector initiative are the abilities of the bourgeoisie to withhold investment and to export capital. The Mexican state may sometimes use its power to resolve conflicts among or between classes, or to act against particular economic groups, but its power is always limited by the necessity of maintaining "business confidence."

This structural relationship is the major source of capital's ability to constrain state action, but there are also instrumental mechanisms by which the power of the national bourgeoisie can be directly exerted upon the state apparatus. These include formal channels—such as the peak organizations of the private sector, industrywide organizations, and business-government advisory committees—and informal channels for direct negotiation, influence, and bribery.[68] Nevertheless, the separation of the political elite from the business elite strengthens the state's ability to formulate and implement policies that may run against the interests of the bourgeoisie.[69]

The state has developed the institutional power to direct and regulate investment by the national bourgeoisie into projects that it deems im-

[68] All businesses in Mexico must belong to the national chambers of industry (CONCAMIN) or of commerce (CONCANACO). Specific industry organizations—such as AMIA, the Motor Vehicle Manufacturers Association—frequently exercise more influence in their particular area of concern than the national chambers do. On influence and corruption, see Vernon, *Dilemma of Mexico's Development*, p. 18, and Hansen, *Politics of Mexican Development*, pp. 124-127.

[69] On the separation of the business and political elites, see Peter Smith, *Labyrinths of Power: Political Recruitment in Twentieth-Century Mexico* (Princeton: Princeton University Press, 1979). Others have pointed out, however, that while there is little recruitment from business into the government, there is the reverse: a pattern whereby government officials "retire" into private business, frequently brokering relationships with the state. See Hamilton, *Limits of State Autonomy*, chap. 1; and Lorenzo Meyer, "Historical Roots of the Authoritarian State in Mexico," in José Luis Reyna and Richard S. Weinert, eds., *Authoritarianism in Mexico* (Philadelphia: ISHI Press, 1977), p. 14.

portant. Toward that end, it uses its own fiscal resources (tax revenues, earnings from state enterprises, and domestic and international borrowing), and its administrative skill in employing these to encourage, co-opt, subsidize, or nationalize various enterprises and to make its own investments through public-sector banks, particularly NAFIN. State power also resides in import controls (permits and tariffs), tax subsidies, and reserve requirements, which allow the state to direct investments into areas it designates as crucial. Sophisticated fiscal and monetary tools created by the Ministry of Finance, the Bank of Mexico, and more recently the Ministry of Planning and Budgeting have given the state an important degree of control over macroeconomic conditions. Ownership of enterprises that produce key inputs (electricity, petroleum and natural gas, railroads, irrigation works, fertilizer, steel) has given the state significant potential leverage in industrial policy.

Finally, the power of the Mexican state to carry out its economic and social policies has also been shaped by international structures. In this chapter, we have reviewed the struggles of the Mexican state to reshape the character of dependency resulting from international structures of trade, finance, and investment. Financial dependency has compelled the Mexican state to be steadily conscious of the judgments of international banks, both public and private, and of foreign governments. The character of trade dependency has been altered considerably with industrialization, but the need to have sufficient exports to pay for its imports—even if these are now producer goods to a large extent—continues to be a significant constraint on the actions of the state. Direct foreign investment has also limited state power, as transnational corporations took dominant, often oligopolistic, positions in leading industrial sectors. Because the behavior of these corporations in Mexico has often been governed more by their global strategies and the conditions of the world market conditions than by conditions in Mexico, the ability of the Mexican state to regulate their behavior has been limited.

Eager to exercise greater control over the activities of the transnational corporations, the Mexican state has sought new sources of power for dealing with them. Its efforts to alter the trade and investment behavior of the transnational automobile companies, and to change the structure of the market and of ownership in the automobile industry, have been important parts of this search. We can more concretely specify a framework for treating the power of the state in its bargaining with transnational corporations if we first examine transnational corporations as actors, with interests and power of their own, in the world automobile industry and in Mexico.

·3·

TRANSNATIONAL CORPORATIONS IN THE
WORLD AUTOMOBILE INDUSTRY

The Automobile Industry in Mexico in 1960

As early as 1925, still in the halcyon days of the Model T, the Ford Motor Company took advantage of the restoration of internal peace in Mexico, government tariff reductions, and low labor and transportation costs to establish an assembly operation in Mexico City. General Motors followed suit in 1937, on the eve of the oil expropriation. Both of these were, from the beginning, wholly foreign-owned subsidiaries.[1] In 1958, these two firms accounted for more than half the vehicles sold in Mexico (see table 3.1).

The rest of the industry at the time—aside from a small number of cars that were imported fully assembled by a variety of European manufacturers—was comprised of ten other assembly operations that were wholly or majority Mexican-owned. The most important of these was Fábricas Auto-Mex, created in 1938 by Gaston Azcárraga to assemble vehicles under a license from Chrysler. Azcárraga had been a distributor first for Ford and then for GM, and he had unsuccessfully explored with each of them the possibility of his setting up a firm to assemble its vehicles in Mexico. Only Chrysler would agree to such an arrangement. Fábricas Auto-Mex continued to be wholly owned by the Azcárraga family until 1959, when Chrysler bought a third of the stock (see chapter 6). In 1960, Fábricas Auto-Mex accounted for about a quarter of sales in the Mexican market.

Willys Mexicana was typical of the smaller Mexican-owned assembly operations. It was founded in 1946 by Antonio Sacristán, a Spanish Republican who had fled to Mexico and who had created a *financiera* called SOMEX (Sociedad Mexicano de Crédito Industrial) to undertake industrial and commercial investments. For a time, Willys Mexicana had its vehicle, the Jeep, assembled in Mexico by other firms, but in 1953 it constructed its own assembly facility, and within a few years it was also assembling Austins, Datsuns, and Peugeots for other Mexican importers/distributors. Several of the other Mexican-owned firms sim-

---

[1] C. Sanchez Marco, "Introduction to the Mexican Automobile Industry" (Paris: OECD Development Center, Industrialization and Trade Project, 1968).

TABLE 3.1

SALES OF AUTOMOBILES BY MAJOR FIRMS IN MEXICO, 1958 AND 1962

		1958 SALES		1962 SALES	
Plant	*Make*	*No.*	*%*	*No.*	*%*
Automotriz	Volvo	0		519	
Internacional[a]	Jaguar	75		2	
	Total	75	0.3	521	1.3
Automotriz O'Farrill	Hillman-Minx	435		280	
	Sunbeam	0		9	
	Singer	0		6	
	Total	435	2.0	295	0.7
Automoviles Ingleses	Morris	0	0	159	0.4
Citroën Distribuidora de Mexico	Citroën	0	0	255	0.6
Diesel Nacional	Fiat[b]	2,101		0	
	Renault	0		6,097	
	Total	2,101	9.5	6,097	15.3
Equipos Superiores	Austin	256	1.2	145	0.4
Fábricas Auto-Mex	Valiant	0		2,334	
	Plymouth	2,839		1,429	
	De Soto	497		2	
	Dodge	1,752		1,156	
	Chrysler	234		0	
	Simca	0		118	
	Fiat[b]	0		2,274	
	Total	5,322	24.1	7,313	18.3
Ford Motor Company	Ford 200	0		3,946	
	Ford	4,327		2,519	
	Mercury	609		4	
	Lincoln	39		0	
	Edsel	115		0	
	Franceses	509		0	
	Ingleses	69		1	
	Alemanes	3		1,245	
	Total	5,671	25.7	7,715	19.3
General Motors	Chevrolet	3,854		3,393	
	Pontiac	432		6	
	Oldsmobile	316		0	
	Buick	285		0	
	Cadillac	115		0	
	Opel	648		4,884	
	Vauxhall	616		6	
	Total	6,266	28.4	8,289	20.8
Planta Reo De México	Rambler[c]	171		0	
	Toyopet	0		1,239	
	Total	171	0.7	1,239	3.1
Promexa	Volkswagen[d]	0	0	2,442	6.1
Representaciones Delta	Mercedes-Benz	387		2,769	
	Auto Union–DKW	0		686	
	Total	387	1.8	3,455	8.7

TABLE 3.1 *(cont.)*

		1958 SALES		1962 SALES	
Plant	*Make*	*No.*	*%*	*No.*	*%*
Studebaker-Packard	Packard	23		0	
	Studebaker	861		0	
	Total	884	4.0	0	0
Volkswagen Interamericana	Volkswagen[d]	472	2.1	845	2.1
Willys Mexicana	Rambler[c]	0	0	1,160	2.9
Total, all makes		22,040	99.8	39,930	100.0

SOURCE: Unpublished data provided by AMIA

NOTE: This table does not include sales by firms that imported already-assembled vehicles into Mexico. However, such sales had been restricted by 1962.

[a] Until 1969, Automotriz Internacional was called Jaguar Automotriz.

[b] Diesel Nacional began producing Renaults in addition to Fiats in 1960. In the same year, Fábricas Auto-Mex began assembling Fiats as well. Thereafter, Diesel Nacional produced only Renaults and Fábricas Auto-Mex produced Fiats until 1965.

[c] Planta Reo ceased producing Ramblers (an American Motors car) in 1958. In 1960, Planta Reo commenced assembling Toyopets (Toyota), and in the same year Willys Mexicana began assembling Ramblers.

[d] Promexa took over the sale of Volkswagens in Mexico in the middle of 1962.

ilarly assembled vehicles both for their own distribution and for distribution by others.

During much of the decade of the 1950s, government tariffs and import quotas in effect prohibited the importation of any vehicle into Mexico except as a "completely knocked down [CKD] kit" for assembly in Mexico. Toward the end of the decade, however, when the Mexican market was still dominated by vehicles of the U.S. Big Three but smaller vehicles were beginning to be exported from Europe, the Mexican government allowed the import of assembled European cars in order to help establish a market position for these smaller, cheaper vehicles that could challenge the U.S. makes.

From the standpoint of sales, the automobile market in Mexico in 1960 was as modern, at least at first glance, as that of any other country. Nearly anything that was available to be purchased anywhere in the world was available for purchase in Mexico. Mexican consumers could choose from among no fewer than 44 makes and 117 models. These consumers represented only a fraction of the population, however: the 15 or 20 percent who constituted the upper and upper-middle classes. Even after the introduction of smaller cars, most of the automobiles offered for sale in Mexico were the latest models of the high-priced U.S. and luxury European vehicles. Advertising by the firms was modeled after ad campaigns in the United States, emphasizing styling, status, and speed. But what was "free choice" for the minority of the population with the wherewithal to exercise consumer sovereignty was irrational from the standpoint of the majority. In an underdeveloped country with scarce resources, money was being poured into purchases of privately owned cars for a small number of people, while mass transportation remained woefully inadequate. There was no cheap, mass-produced vehicle designed with the transportation needs of most Mexicans in mind.

From the standpoint of production and industrial growth, the automobile industry in Mexico also presented a dual aspect. Most of the vehicles sold in Mexico were "made in Mexico," by twelve firms, only two of which were foreign-owned. But these vehicles were only assembled in Mexico; the components were made elsewhere. An executive of one of the firms exaggerated in saying that "we imported everything but the air in the tires," but it is the case that only simple "hang-on parts" for which there was also a replacement market were manufactured in Mexico for original equipment: tires, batteries, spark plugs, and the like. The other components were sold to the Mexican firms in CKD kits. While most of the firms may have been Mexican-owned, all of them relied upon a foreign transnational firm to supply them with these kits and with technical assistance to assemble, market, and service the cars made from them.[2]

Thus, it is possible to see a particular pattern of dependency in and around the automobile industry in Mexico in the early 1960s:

(1) Foreign design, technology, and parts. All the automobiles sold in Mexico were designed elsewhere, in developed countries—the United States, the western European nations, and Japan. They were designed for the economic and geographic conditions in those countries and for mass markets heavily influenced by advertising. Perhaps the appropriateness of that kind of industry for consumers even in those countries is arguable, but it certainly was not appropriate in Mexico. A high degree of product differentiation and annual model changes made no sense for a developing country with a small market and scarce resources.

(2) Limited industrialization. Half the vehicles sold in Mexico came from firms that were Mexican-owned, but none of these vehicles were

[2] Guillermo S. Edelberg, "The Procurement Practices of the Mexican Affiliates of Selected United States Automobile Firms" (Ph.D. diss., Harvard University, 1963).

manufactured in Mexico in any meaningful sense. The foreign-owned firms (Ford and GM) were unwilling, in the existing circumstances, to move beyond the simple assembly of imported kits toward more extensive manufacturing operations. The domestically owned firms, had they been willing, would not have been able: the transnational auto firms from which they obtained designs, technology, and parts would not have granted them the necessary licenses for domestic manufacture, and they could not have competed successfully with firms that continued to import all their components. This limitation on industrialization amounted to an opportunity forgone. In the developed countries, auto manufacturing had been a centerpiece of industrial growth, providing stimulus to many other industries, and it had been a source of much employment (as many as 10 percent of all jobs, by some estimates). In Mexico, the auto industry was not performing any of these functions. The source of the problem was external—the character of global competition among the transnational automobile firms.

(3) Exclusion of the mass population. What was an item of mass consumption in the developed-country markets was an item of luxury consumption in Mexico: Only the wealthiest fifth of the population could buy automobiles. This was not merely a problem of poverty—of the majority being unable to afford a product available to a more affluent minority. Beyond that, the automobile industry tended, in Mexico as elsewhere, to favor patterns of urbanization and suburbanization that were particularly suited for those who owned vehicles and unsuited for those who did not.

In summary, rather than speak of a Mexican automobile industry, it is more accurate to speak of the automobile industry in Mexico. The character of production and consumption of motor vehicles sold in Mexico was shaped outside of Mexico, in the core countries of the world capitalist system that were the homes of the transnational automobile firms. How the subsidiaries and licensees of these firms behaved in Mexico was conditioned by the firms' place in and relationship to a world automobile industry. To understand this pattern of dependency, and to understand the possibilities and limits for state action to change it, we need to understand more about the structure and dynamics of that industry.

Evolution of the World Automobile Industry

In 1960, the global automobile industry consisted of about twenty major firms, based principally in the United States and western Europe and together accounting for about 90 percent of the motor vehicles sold in the world. These firms were the survivors of a process of concentration in their respective home-country markets over the course of the preceding decades, and each was more or less far along toward being transformed into a transnational corporation with not only sales but also manufacturing operations in several different countries.

Concentration in the Developed-Country Markets

The United States. In the early years of the twentieth century, nearly 200 companies were manufacturing and selling automobiles in the United States. By 1927, three-quarters of them had disappeared. By 1960, fewer than ten survived; one of them accounted for about half of the motor vehicles manufactured in the United States and three of them for over 90 percent (and for over 98 percent of the automobiles). This trend toward concentration was the result of changes in technology and in demand, in part shaped by the auto firms themselves, that forced many firms to merge or to close and that raised such substantial barriers to entry into the industry that no new firms attempted it from the time that Kaiser made an unsuccessful effort following World War II until Volkswagen built a U.S. manufacturing plant in the mid-1970s.

The shift to higher-powered four-cylinder engines after World War I, and technical changes associated with axles and transmissions, raised production costs and forced out some firms; but Ford's reliance on a single standard model, the Model T—with the low-cost, mass-production methods that this permitted—was the most important factor in transforming the industry. Ford's price dropped from $950 in 1909 to less than $300 in the early 1920s, while its market share soared from under 10 percent to over 55 percent, and in a rapidly growing market.[3]

Ford's production techniques set the standard for the industry, but its domination of the market was soon challenged by GM and later by Chrysler. GM had been organized by William Crapo Durant, who controlled it and more than twenty other automobile and accessory companies by 1909. In the 1920s, GM began to offer a variety of makes and models to compete against Ford's single model. Ford was slow to respond to this strategy of product differentiation; it did not offer its Model A until the end of the 1920s, nor a V-8 engine until 1932. GM overtook Ford with a 43 percent market share in 1931, and it has retained that position of dominance ever since. Chrysler, formed in

---

[3] Ralph F. Lanzillotti, "The Automobile Industry," in Walter Adams, ed., *The Structure of American Industry* (New York: Macmillan, 1971), pp. 256-301.

1925 through a process of merger and acquisition, followed GM's product and marketing strategy, and by 1937 it, too, had overtaken Ford.

By 1930, GM, Ford, and Chrysler had established complete dominance of the U.S. motor vehicle industry. Their position was based upon the cost advantages of mass-production techniques but also, and increasingly, on the product-differentiation strategies that GM and Chrysler had first employed. The pattern of annual model changes introduced in the 1930s made it still more difficult for other firms to achieve the economies of scale necessary to remain competitive in price.[4] The pressure took its toll. Limited to a 10 percent market share before World War II, the independents surged ahead in the immediate postwar period, but as the pent-up demand was satisfied, they disappeared through merger or failure. By 1960, the only remaining independent manufacturer was American Motors.

Europe. Western European countries had motor vehicle industries with large numbers of firms as early as the United States did, and during the 1920s and 1930s these industries underwent a parallel process of concentration. In the early 1920s, Great Britain, France, and Germany each had dozens, even hundreds, of firms, but by the end of the decade the numbers had declined drastically and in each country three firms accounted for about 70 percent or more of production.[5] For the most part, the reasons for concentration were the same as those in the United States: the cost advantages and increased barriers to entry resulting from the scale economies that accompanied mass-production techniques.

The process of concentration in Europe was hurried along, however, by the competition these firms faced from U.S. manufacturers, particularly Ford and GM. These two companies had begun foreign sales at an early date, and by 1929 U.S. companies were exporting 536,000 vehicles and assembling another 200,000 abroad. The U.S. market was growing much more quickly than the European markets, with the result that the U.S. firms had a significant cost advantage. This not only provided a further impetus toward the adoption of mass-production techniques, but it also led to governmental efforts at defending the

[4] H. G. Vatter, "The Closure of Entry in the American Automobile Industry," *Oxford Economic Papers* 4 (1952):213-234; John A. Menge, "Style Change Costs As a Market Weapon," *Quarterly Journal of Economics* 76 (1962):632-647; and Lawrence J. White, *The American Automobile Industry since 1945* (Cambridge: Harvard University Press, 1971).

[5] D. G. Rhys, *The Motor Industry: An Economic Survey* (London: Butterworth, 1972), and Louis T. Wells, Jr., "Automobiles," in Raymond Vernon, ed., *Big Business and the State* (Cambridge: Harvard University Press, 1978), pp. 229-254.

fledgling national industries. Had political power not been exercised at this point, the U.S. Big Three might today dominate the international industry to a greater extent than they do.

Although protection policies varied from one country to another, the basic mechanisms were tariffs or import quotas. In many cases, though, the U.S. companies circumvented the barriers by setting up local assembly plants or acquiring domestic manufacturers. Ford established assembly operations in the United Kingdom in 1911, in France in 1913, and in Germany in 1929. Chevrolet (a GM company) acquired Vauxhall in Britain in 1925 and the ailing Opel in Germany in 1929. To protect against these tactics, tax systems that discriminated against U.S. cars were instituted in several countries; Italy, where Fiat was becoming increasingly powerful as the only major auto-manufacturing company, forbade all direct foreign investment in that industry.[6]

Even more so than in the United States, the years following World War II in Europe were years of recovery and conversion from war production. Competition among the firms stiffened as pent-up demand began to be satisfied, and demand took on a new shape after the formation of the European Economic Community. By 1965, internal tariffs within the EEC had been reduced to about 30 percent of their original levels, and trade in motor vehicles had increased nearly fourfold over its volume in 1958; a substantial interpenetration of markets had taken place. Competition in the European markets was further intensified by a new wave of foreign investment from the United States. Ford bought out the minority shareholders in its British subsidiary in 1960, and Chrysler, which hitherto had lacked a foothold in Europe, gained a minority position in Simca (France) in 1958 and in Rootes (Great Britain) in 1964. It later gained majority control of both companies.[7]

During the 1960s, the successful European firms increased the variety of their models and the frequency of model changes. Most of them had built up their positions by mass-producing a single model over a number of years, but now they shifted to the patterns of product differentiation that prevailed in the United States. Renault offered one model in 1961, ten in 1971; Volkswagen, slow to abandon its reliance on the redoubtable "Bug," expanded its range through the takeover of Auto Union and NSU, increasing its number of models from two in 1960 to eight in 1971.[8]

---

[6] Wells, "Automobiles," pp. 232-237.

[7] Sanchez Marco, "Mexican Automobile Industry."

[8] Rhys Jenkins, *Dependent Industrialization in Latin America: The Automotive Industry in Argentina, Chile, and Mexico* (New York: Praeger, 1977), pp. 16-47.

The moves toward a greater variety of models required firms of larger size, and this added one more source of pressure for concentration. A wave of mergers took place in the European industries, often abetted by government policies. These policies tended to favor the emergence of a single "national champion"—Fiat in Italy, British Leyland in Great Britain, Renault in France, Volkswagen in Germany—as governments sought to insure that at least one national firm would survive the increasingly keen international competition. As Jenkins has observed, competition tended "toward a situation in which each major producing country has one nationally-owned firm dominating the market, competing against a number of smaller foreign subsidiaries."[9]

Some of the same pressures that encouraged concentration also encouraged a search for export markets beyond Europe, in areas that had formerly been the preserve of the U.S. Big Three, such as Latin America. The increased size, efficiency, and marketing capability of the surviving European firms made possible the mounting of such an international challenge.

Japan. In Europe, a process of extreme concentration in the automobile industries occurred as it had in the United States, though in Europe the process was reinforced by government policies. In Japan, where an internationally competitive national auto-manufacturing industry also emerged, the government played an even greater role.

The Japanese industry developed much more slowly than in the U.S. and Europe. Until well into the 1950s, manufacture of commercial vehicles was much more important than production of passenger cars. As the major truck manufacturers (Toyota, Nissan, Diesel Jidosha—later Isuzu—Mitsubishi, Hino, Prince Jidosha, and Fuji subsequently moved into automobile production, they faced major competition from imports, particularly from the United States. In 1953, Japan had imported 23,719 cars, more than three times the domestic production.[10] Some of the Japanese producers sought licenses from European manufacturers for CKD assembly and technical assistance to begin the manufacture of components: Nissan tied up with Austin, Hino with Renault, Isuzu with Rootes, and Mitsubishi with Willys. Toyota alone elected to develop its passenger car, the Toyopet, independently.

In the early 1950s, the Japanese government began moving to insulate the industry from foreign competition. Domestic manufacture

[9] Ibid., p. 20.
[10] William Chandler Duncan, *U.S.-Japan Automobile Diplomacy: A Study in Economic Concentration* (Cambridge, Mass.: Ballinger, 1973), p. 146 n. 2.

of parts was mandated, and foreign investment was excluded. These government actions were crucial in reserving the consumer demand that was to grow rapidly during the 1960s exclusively for Japanese firms. Between 1961 and 1970, sales of passenger vehicles rose from 12 percent to 50 percent of total motor vehicle sales. Fewer than 100,000 automobiles were produced in Japan in 1959; over 4,000,000 were manufactured in 1972.[11]

The Japanese industry began not only later but also as a much more concentrated industry than in the United States and Europe. Yet it became still more concentrated, again with the government taking a strong hand. The government was interested in promoting international trade, and the auto industry was a potential source of exports. However, pressures (particularly from the United States) to liberalize trade barriers threatened to destroy the industry before it was strong enough to compete internationally. The Ministry of International Trade and Industry (MITI) judged, at least as early as 1961, that if the Japanese motor vehicle industry were to compete successfully abroad and withstand increased domestic competition from foreign firms, it would have to be "reorganized." Relying more on "administrative guidance" than on legislated sanctions, MITI encouraged the emergence of two major groups around Nissan and Toyota. By the early 1970s, these two groups accounted for 70 percent of domestic and 90 percent of export sales. Not all of the firms responded as hoped to MITI's shepherding, and the rapid expansion that the Japanese industry enjoyed through the 1960s and early 1970s made it possible for some of the smaller, independent companies also to survive and grow. Honda and Fuji (Subaru) remained wholly independent, but three others moved to defend themselves against Nissan and Toyota by linking up with U.S. companies as minority partners: Isuzu with GM, Mitsubishi with Chrysler, and Toyo Kogyo (Mazda) with Ford.

The reorganization of the industry and the growth of the domestic market permitted scale economies and cost reductions. The industry was well-positioned for the export drive that began in the mid-1960s. Export sales grew from 100,000 units in 1965 to 4,352,817 in 1977. While these exports were actively encouraged by the government, they also took on increased importance for the firms as the domestic market began to be saturated. Foreign sales were to be the source of future growth and profitability.

[11] These and subsequent figures on the Japanese automobile industry are drawn from ibid., pp. 84-100.

Emergence of the Transnational Companies

Before 1955, there was not so much a world automobile industry as a series of national automobile industries in the major industrialized countries of North America, Europe, and Japan. Firms in these various national industries did sell vehicles abroad, but mostly in countries that lacked domestic automobile manufacture. There was little direct foreign investment in the industry, the major exceptions being the investments of Ford and GM in Europe.

World War II devastated the automobile industries of Europe and diverted the U.S. industry from passenger-car production. The immediate postwar years were ones for rebuilding and for meeting pent-up consumer demand, but early in the decade of the 1950s, the larger firms, pressed by the same forces that had led to concentration in the national industries, began to look for opportunities abroad. For the first time, there began to be significant interpenetration of one another's home-country markets. The formation of the EEC led European-based firms to offer their vehicles for sale throughout the continent. In about 1955, Volkswagen began to ship vehicles to the U.S. market, which lacked a manufacturer of small cars; Renault and other European firms followed suit. In the middle of the decade of the 1960s, firms in the Japanese industry began to export vehicles, first to the United States and then to Europe. While there were increasing sales in one another's home-country markets, there were no new foreign investments in the major producing countries except for Chrysler's attempt to match the Ford and GM investments in Europe by acquiring Simca and Rootes.

By the later 1960s, a fully formed world automobile industry had replaced the national automobile industries of the United States, Great Britain, France, Germany, Italy, and Japan. This industry exhibited the same tendency toward increasing concentration that had been manifested in the national industries. By 1972, two firms, Ford and GM, accounted for over 40 percent of total world automobile sales, and the largest eight for about 85 percent (see table 3.2). The world auto industry was an oligopoly.

This concentration was the consequence, in large part, of the great economies of scale that had come to characterize mass motor vehicle production and the large amounts of capital that such production required. In 1968, Bain estimated that the minimum capacity of an integrated auto plant that could realize the lowest possible per-unit

TABLE 3.2

The Ten Largest Auto Makers
in the World, 1972

Manufacturer	Sales (millions)
General Motors	7.8
Ford	5.6
Chrysler	3.1
Fiat	2.2
Volkswagen	2.2
Toyota	2.1
Nissan	1.8
Renault	1.3
British Leyland	1.1
Peugeot	0.7

Source: *Business Week*, November 24, 1973, p. 38

costs was 300,000 vehicles per year.[12] However, an automobile is a complex product, and it must be kept in mind that scale economies vary considerably among the components and steps of motor vehicle production. Scale economies tend to be largest for stamped, exterior sheet-metal parts, next largest for the forging and machining of engines, and so on down through parts of simple fabrication in small batches. But no firm could survive that did not take full advantage of scale economies for all component manufacture and assembly. The importance of scale economies prevented the entry of new firms into the industry—Bain estimated a new firm would need an initial investment of $250-500 million with perhaps another $150 million in break-in losses, all with substantial risk of failure[13]—and drove out existing firms incapable of achieving sufficient sales volume.

Concentration was not dictated simply by technological necessity, however. The competitive practices that came to characterize the global oligopoly furthered the process. For while the world automobile industry was not uncompetitive—certainly there was no evidence of overt collusion—it was selective in its forms of competition. The firms eschewed price competition in favor of product differentiation and model proliferation (including annual model changes). As global competition intensified, the European firms tended to imitate the competitive practices of the U.S. manufacturers; as has been noted, for

[12] Joseph Bain, *Industrial Organization* (New York: John Wiley, 1968), pp. 284-287.
[13] Ibid.

62

example, Volkswagen acquired Auto Union and NSU so that it could diversify its product line, and it quickened the pace of its model changes. Since scale economies apply, for the most part, to individual models, this kind of competition tended to increase the minimum sales volume necessary for a firm to remain viable.

By the late 1950s, the auto-manufacturing companies—or at least those that would survive—could see that the markets of future significant sales growth were in the developing countries, and they began to compete for toeholds in the larger of these markets, Mexico among them. Concentration, high barriers to entry, and product differentiation had accorded the major auto firms power to drive out weaker firms, to exclude new ones, and to exact higher prices and profits from consumers.[14] As the now-transnational firms extended their reach to the developing countries, several questions were raised: Could their market power be translated to the new setting? How, and with what consequences?

Opening of the Developing-Country Markets

In the third world, there was a distinct and stable pattern of market spheres following World War II. European firms tended to dominate vehicle sales in their former colonies while U.S. firms dominated sales in Latin America. The latter conducted assembly operations but no appreciable manufacturing activity. Ford had set up subsidiaries to carry out assembly in all the major Latin American countries, beginning with Argentina in 1916. GM and Chrysler had followed suit, although the latter was more inclined to license local firms to assemble its vehicles.

When Volkswagen invaded the U.S. market in the mid-1950s, it began to contest Latin American markets as well. In contrast to the limited opportunity for future sales growth in Europe, it saw an open market niche in the Americas for the sale of small vehicles. Thus, rather than seek a larger share of the European market through price com-

---

[14] It has been estimated that U.S. consumers paid an extra $1.6 billion (or $170 per vehicle) in 1972 for the costs of model changes (most of this going for cosmetic restyling rather than for genuine improvement in performance, fuel efficiency, or safety) and $2.1 billion (or $230 per vehicle) in monopoly overcharges by the U.S. Big Three: Bradford Snell, *American Ground Transport: A Proposal for Restructuring the Automobile, Truck, Bus, and Rail Industries* (Washington: Government Printing Office, 1973), pp. 13-14. Snell argues that the consequences of market power in the hands of the Big Three go even further, to the deliberate shaping of public transportation policy to suppress competition with motor vehicles. In the late 1920s, GM, together with Standard Oil of California and Firestone Rubber, engineered the replacement of over 100 electric local transit systems with GM-supplied bus systems in forty-five cities: ibid., p. 32.

petition or new products, it looked abroad for new markets. Renault, Fiat, Mercedes, and others were not slow in following.

For these new entrants into the Latin American markets, as for the well-established U.S.-based firms, the preferred strategy was to supply assembled vehicles or CKD kits for local assembly rather than to undertake domestic manufacture. Exports of vehicles or kits would mean longer production runs for the firms in their home-country plants. Centralized production would allow them to benefit from scale economies in parts manufacture and to offer a wider array of models in all the markets they contested. Domestic manufacture in Latin American countries would have denied them these advantages and would have subjected them to higher production costs in these relatively small markets, making it more difficult for them to compete against the continuing imports of their rivals.

However, while domestic manufacture in the Latin American markets was initially irrational for the transnational auto firms, it lay within the power of the governments of these countries to make it rational. The Latin American markets had become a key competitive battleground of the world automobile industry. Governments controlled access to these markets; firms could be threatened with exclusion unless they undertook domestic manufacture. How significant a threat this was can be gathered from the facts that eleven firms began domestic manufacture in Brazil after it imposed minimum local-content requirements in 1956, and that when Argentina did the same two years later, twenty-one firms began domestic manufacture.[15] The experiences of these two countries would be studied closely by Mexican government planners.

The automobile industries in Latin America (and elsewhere in the third world) can be seen as proceeding through three stages: (I) a pre-industrialization stage, in which vehicles are imported into these countries already assembled or as kits to be assembled by licensees or subsidiaries of foreign manufacturer; (II) an import-substituting stage, in which some significant degree of local manufacture of vehicles for sale in the domestic market is undertaken; and (III) an exporting stage, in which a country begins to export vehicles or components to developed and developing countries.[16] Because of differences in level of devel-

[15] Douglas Bennett and Kenneth Sharpe, "The World Automobile Industry and Its Implications for Developing Countries," in Richard Newfarmer, ed., *Profits, Progress and Poverty: Case Studies of International Industries in Latin America* (Notre Dame: University of Notre Dame Press, 1984).

[16] For an elaboration of these stages, see ibid. For other efforts to delineate stages in the internationalization of the world automobile industry, see Jack Baranson, *Automotive*

opment, in size of effective markets, and in government policy, some countries have moved through these stages earlier than others. Brazil and Argentina began the transition from stage I to stage II in the late 1950s, a few years before Mexico did. In turn, Chile, Colombia, Peru, Uruguay, and Venezuela trailed Mexico in this transition by a few years. Brazil, Argentina, and Mexico arrived on the threshold of stage III around 1970—but that gets us ahead of our story.

In 1960, Mexico stood poised at the beginning of stage II. The structure and dynamics of competition in the world industry set limits on and shaped opportunities for the domestic manufacture of autos in Mexico. In 1960, Ford, GM, and Chrysler dominated vehicle sales in Latin America; in Mexico, they each accounted for about 25 percent of the market (see table 3.1). European firms had been selling vehicles in Latin America for a decade at most; Volkswagen and Renault each held about 5 percent of the Mexican market. Japanese makes were virtually unknown in Latin America (as they were in the United States at that time); a small Monterrey-based assembler called Reo had just begun to introduce Toyota vehicles to the Mexican market. But over the half-decade prior to 1960, the number of makes and models available in Mexico had been increasing: a kind of deconcentration was taking place as European-based firms challenged the U.S.-based firms. The Mexican automobile industry consisted of about a dozen assemblers. All but two of them were domestically owned, but all were closely linked to transnational automobile firms through purchases of kits and parts and through technology agreements. The only domestically manufactured parts were those sold principally for replacement. In the strategies of the transnational automobile firms, Mexico was a market of increasing importance but not a site for manufacturing. It was in this context that the first conflict took place between the transnational corporations (TNCs) in the automobile industry and the Mexican state. To understand the nature and outcome of this and other conflicts, it is important to understand the interests and power of the TNCs.

A HISTORICAL-STRUCTURAL APPROACH TO TNCs

The interests and power of TNCs, like those of the state, are constrained and conditioned by the principal structures in which they are enmeshed, but how they perceive their interests and utilize their power

---

Industries in Developing Countries (Washington: World Bank Occasional Staff Papers, no. 8, 1969); Jenkins, *Dependent Industrialization*; and Gerald Bloomfield, *The World Automotive Industry* (Newton Abbott: David and Charles, 1978).

within these limits is, to a substantial degree, a matter of their own choice. The structures that condition the actions of transnational corporations include those of the international regimes of trade, finance, and investment and those of the political economics of the countries in which they operate, particularly of their home country; but except in unusual circumstances, the most important of them is the global structure of the industry in which they operate. Industrial-organization theory furnishes an approach to industry structures that allows us to view the interests and power of transnational corporations in a historical-structural manner. Its leading ideas were implicit in the overview of the world automobile industry presented earlier in this chapter.

This approach argues that the structure of an industry shapes, but does not strictly determine, the conduct or behavior of the individual firms that comprise it. This conduct, in turn, eventuates in a "performance" for the industry as a whole, which can be assessed against certain norms. First elaborated in the United States and principally used so far for analysis of the U.S. economy, industrial-organization theory is concerned with the causes and consequences of deviations from a hypothetical competitive equilibrium in a geographically constrained market. Such deviations confer market power on some firms, undermining the beneficent performance that would follow from a perfectly competitive structure. Monopoly and oligopoly are the "deviant" industry structures that have been most carefully studied in the U.S., and industrial-organization theory has been the intellectual foundation of antitrust policy.[17]

The structure of an industry refers to the number of firms, the form of ownership and control, and the height of barriers to entry. As has been pointed out, mass-production technology in automobile manufacture dramatically increased economies of scale, leading to increased concentration in national automobile industries and raising a significant barrier to the entry of new firms. The surviving oligopolistic firms erected additional barriers through proliferation of models, advertising aimed at establishing product uniqueness and brand loyalty, and frequent model changes.

The conduct or behavior of firms includes the products they offer

---

[17] On industrial-organization theory, see Bain, *Industrial Organization*; Walter Adams, ed., *The Structure of American Industry* (New York: Macmillan, 1971); D. F. Greer, *Industrial Organization and Public Policy* (New York: Macmillan, 1980); F. M. Scherer, *Industrial Market Structure and Economic Performance* (Chicago: Rand McNally, 1980); A. P. Jacquemin and H. W. de Jong, *European Industrial Organization* (New York: John Wiley, 1977); and R. E. Caves and Masu Uekusa, *Industrial Organization in Japan* (Washington: Brookings Institution, 1976).

and the prices they charge. In the case of the automobile companies, the oligopolistic structure of the national and later of transnational industry made it rational for the firms to avoid price competition where possible and to compete instead by efforts to differentiate their products from one another and to establish consumer loyalty to their particular models. They did not collude—there has been no international cartel in automobiles—but they each realized that mutual forbearance would yield benefits to all of them.

Finally, the performance of an industry includes its efficiency, its rate and type of innovation, and its profitability. Mass-production technology made auto manufacture highly efficient, but the product-differentiation strategies pushed innovation toward "extras" and styling changes rather than toward fundamental engineering improvements. The industry consistently yielded profits that were higher than those normal in other industries.

Unlike more orthodox, neoclassical perspectives, industrial-organization theory sees industry structures as historical, not given, phenomena. It holds that these structures shape the conduct of firms but that these structures have themselves been created through the conduct of firms and of the state. (Analysts using this framework have frequently recommended state action—"trustbusting"—to alter an industry structure.)

Some modifications need to be made in this approach, however, if industrial-organization theory is to help us understand the causes and consequences of the conduct of TNCs in Mexico. They are required by the transnationality of the firms and the setting of a developing country.

(1) Because TNCs operate simultaneously in several different markets, it is not only a national market structure which shapes their conduct. In explaining the behavior of the automobile firms in Mexico, sometimes it will be the structure of the world automobile industry that is important, sometimes it will be the structure of the automobile industry in Mexico, and sometimes it will be both.

(2) Ownership needs to be given more searching consideration as an element of industry structure. Industrial-organization theory tends to take private ownership for granted, neglecting the possibility that publicly owned firms (more common in developing countries than in the United States) may behave differently from privately owned ones. Even in the case of private ownership, wholly owned subsidiaries of transnational firms may act differently from domestically owned firms that merely license technology from TNCs, and both may act differently from companies jointly owned by a TNC and a domestic entrepreneur.

(3) In a developing country, efficiency, innovation, and profitability are not the only important performance standards. Industrial growth, the creation of employment opportunities, and the transfer of technology are also matters of concern.

(4) These first three points have implications for the state's industrial policies. On the one hand, such policies must take into account a wider range of performance criteria than they would in a developed country. On the other hand, the "global reach" of transnational corporations extends well beyond the jurisdiction of the state. There are aspects of industry structure and of firm conduct that state action cannot hope to affect. Operating in several different markets, TNCs can even play one government off against another. Regulatory policymaking thus requires bargaining with the firms, bargaining in which the home-country governments of the TNCs may also become interested parties.[18]

In examining the ways in which industry structure conditions the behavior of firms, it will be useful to consider separately how industry structure shapes the *interests* of the firms and how it shapes their *power*, and this will be done in the next two sections of this chapter. The final section will consider the consequences of TNCs, introducing a number of propositions, drawn principally from dependency theory, about the performance of industries in the developing countries in which they operate. This discussion is a necessary preliminary to the task in chapter 5, which will be to develop a framework for understanding how the state and the transnational firms employ their power to resolve conflicts of interest.

The Interests of the Auto TNCs

So long as the TNCs had only assembly facilities in Mexico, the relevant industry structure shaping their interests was that of the world automobile industry. The firms' investments in Mexico—even those of Ford and GM, with their wholly owned subsidiaries—were too insubstantial for the structure of the industry in that country to affect their interests to any appreciable degree. Consequently, the TNCs' attitudes toward their Mexican operations were shaped by how they viewed Mexico (and other similar markets) within the context of their global strategies. While in some industries TNCs may have looked to developing countries as sources of raw materials or as potential production sites with an

---

[18] Industrial-organization theory describes state action but does not seek to explain it. We do seek to explain the actions of the Mexican state as well as of the transnational auto firms; for our approach to the explanation of state action, see chap. 2.

abundance of cheap labor, in the automobile industry these were not significant considerations. Instead, the automobile TNCs viewed Mexico primarily as a rapidly growing market, in which present, and especially future, sales were or could be of some importance.

The automobile industry fits a wider pattern identified by Hymer, Kindleberger, Caves, and others, who see the surge of direct foreign investment in the 1950s and 1960s as a form of oligopolistic expansion.[19] Challenging the orthodox view that direct foreign investment is analogous to portfolio capital flows, they have argued that TNCs, in the imperfect markets of their home countries, possessed certain monopoly advantages, such as patented technology, well-differentiated products, and access to capital. Their foreign investments stemmed not (as neoclassicists assumed) from higher marginal rates of return abroad in perfect capital markets, but rather from the better returns that these monopoly advantages could yield in new, foreign markets in comparison with further applications at home.

In the automobile industry, the maturation of markets in developed countries portended declining sales growth for the firms at home. Rather than develop wholly new products to sell in these markets or to engage in price competition to win a larger share of these slower-growing markets, these oligopolistic firms preferred to use their accumulated advantages in motor vehicle manufacture to gain increased sales and earnings in the new developing-country markets. The large scale economies of prevailing technology and the firms' product-differentiation strategies disinclined them to manufacture in those countries. However, despite their preference for export sales of vehicles or kits, they were willing to invest in local manufacture if the alternative were loss of access to these markets.

Interdependence among the members of the oligopoly—the mutual recognition that the actions of one could have a perceptible effect upon all of them—not only led the firms away from price competition but also provided a spur to direct foreign investment. Frederick Knickerbocker has argued that firms in "product-pioneering" manufacturing oligopolies tend to engage in defensive investments: each of them matches the others' foreign investments in order to minimize its own risks. An investment in a developing country by one TNC thus triggers a defensive "oligopolistic reaction" of similar investments by other firms

[19] Stephen Hymer, *The International Operations of National Firms: A Study of Direct Foreign Investment* (Cambridge: MIT Press, 1976); Charles P. Kindleberger, *American Business Abroad: Six Lectures on Direct Investment* (New Haven: Yale University Press, 1969); and Richard E. Caves, "Industrial Organization," in J. H. Dunning, ed., *Economic Analysis and the Multinational Enterprise* (Praeger: New York, 1974), pp. 115-146.

in the industry.[20] In the Mexican auto industry, the first investments were prompted by the government's import-substitution policy, but as soon as one firm indicated a willingness to invest, the others scrambled to follow.

Once the transnational automobile firms had made investments in Mexico and had begun domestic manufacture, the structure of the industry *in Mexico* became important, in addition to the structure of the global industry. Two elements of this local structure demand attention: the structure of the *market* and the structure of *ownership*.

The structure of the market—the number of firms, the extent of vertical integration, and the degree of product differentiation (number of models produced by each firm, frequency of model changes, etc.)— was important because of the large scale economies brought by the TNCs to the Mexican industry. The technology of auto manufacture had taken shape under particular conditions in large, developed-country markets and had been both the cause and consequence of increasing concentration in those markets. It was now transferred, essentially without alteration, to a small, developing-country market. The local market structure then determined the degree to which each firm could take advantage of the economies of scale embodied in the prevailing technology. This, in turn, would be the most significant factor in the industry's efficiency in comparison with motor vehicle production in the major producing countries, and thus in the industry's position in the domestic political economy on the one hand and in the world industry on the other.

In neoclassical theory, a private firm is presumed to be a rational actor oriented solely to the maximization of profit. Only the logic of profit, not the age, sex, religion, nationality, or other attributes of the owner or manager, is expected to affect the behavior of the firm. This argument about the irrelevance of ownership is buttressed by another: competitive markets serve to constrain. Particular owners may have predilections that would lead them to stray from the dictates of profit maximization, but competition from other firms disciplines their behavior. They will either respond to the forces of the market or they will be driven into bankruptcy.[21] These are questionable assumptions on which to dismiss ownership as a key variable. The constraining hand

[20] Frederick T. Knickerbocker, *Oligopolistic Reaction and Multinational Enterprise* (Boston: Harvard University School of Business Administration, 1973); cf. Jenkins, *Dependent Industrialization*.

[21] It is not only neoclassicists who assert the irrelevance of ownership; for a similar argument by a *dependista*, see Arrighi Emmanuel, "Myths of Development versus Myths of Underdevelopment," *New Left Review* 85 (1974):61-82.

of the market is frequently quite limp, especially in a concentrated, oligopolistic market, and the characteristics of the owner may then indeed influence the conduct of the firm. In Mexico, ownership characteristics did affect the relationship between firms in the national industry and firms in the world industry. Two of these characteristics especially warrant consideration: (a) public vs. private ownership, and (b) transnational vs. national ownership. Both are aspects of industry structure to which industrial-organization theory (as well as orthodox economics) pays insufficient attention.

Public ownership gives rise to interests and opportunities that are different from those of private ownership. Publicly owned firms may be operated at a loss for an extended period of time to subsidize lower-class consumption, for example, or to provide cheap inputs for leading growth sectors. The policy goals of the state compete with the imperatives of profit, and publicly held firms can thus escape the constraining hand of the market. What these goals are, and whether they are far-sighted or shortsighted, depend on the political forces affecting the state-owned firms.

Similarly, a transnational automobile firm will have a different interest in a wholly owned subsidiary than it will in a licensee owned by local entrepreneurs. In the licensee it will see an opportunity for current earnings through sales of parts, technical assistance, trademarks, and the like. Because the licensee may terminate the agreement, the TNC cannot count on these very far into the future, however. With a wholly owned subsidiary, on the other hand, a TNC may be willing to forgo short-term earnings for the sake of increased market penetration and hence the possibility of greater earnings in the future. A joint venture in which ownership is shared between a TNC and domestic investors presents an intermediate case, one in which there may be tension between partners with different profit horizons.

Considering the matter in another way, the opportunities and resources of a nationally owned firm are likely to be circumscribed by the domestic market, while a transnational subsidiary will have opportunities and resources unlimited by national borders. The latter may, for example, receive injections of capital from its parent company to allow it to take aggressive advantage of new possibilities, or its earnings may be drained abroad because opportunities elsewhere are more promising.[22] If the structure of the automobile industry in Mexico

[22] It must be kept in mind that there are also limitations on the rationality of TNCs that stem from the national context in which they evolved and which continues to circumscribe their vision. See Evans's discussion of "bounded rationality" in his *Dependent Development*, pp. 36-37.

became important in shaping the interests of the transnational firms once they had made investments there, the structure of the world industry hardly ceased to matter. The kinds of models produced by the TNCs and the kind of production technology they utilized—in a word, their overall strategy, in which their Mexican subsidiaries or licensees were only one small part—were affected more by the structure of the world industry than by that of the industry in Mexico.

It must also be pointed out, however, that while the structure of the world auto industry induced similar interests among the dozen or so firms that comprised it, there was also variation among them. There were two principal sources of this variation. First, although they had all become international, they nonetheless bore the marks of their national origins. Until well into the 1970s, the U.S.-based firms continued to manufacture primarily large cars, whereas the European and Japanese firms focused more on smaller vehicles and were also less given to annual model changes. The Japanese-based firms elected to maintain more of their manufacturing capacity at home; they made fewer foreign investments and relied more on exports than did the European and U.S. firms.

Second, there have been identifiable strategy differences even among firms with the same national origin. Ford and GM insisted upon sole ownership of all their overseas operations, even assembly facilities; Chrysler did not. Volkswagen and Renault showed the same difference. Relative to GM, Ford showed much more interest in international operations and kept a higher profile in dealing with foreign governments. These and other differences among the firms had significant consequences for how they perceived and pursued various opportunities.

Finally, it should be noted that ownership characteristics are important because they affect not only the conduct of a given firm but the conduct of its competitors as well. A company that derives advantages over others from either public or transnational ownership alters the terms of competition in the industry.

The Power of the Auto TNCs

The structure of the market and of ownership in both the Mexican and the world automobile industry also shaped the power of the transnational automobile firms. Ownership confers power, but competitive markets (and government regulation) limit the discretion with which this power can be utilized.

The power of privately owned firms is based on their control over capital. Unless restricted by the state, corporations can follow the logic of profit in deciding when, where, and how to invest their capital. With the same qualification, ownership gives corporations the right to make decisions about what products will be manufactured, in what markets they will be sold, and in what manner; the technology and manufacturing processes that will be utilized in production; how and where raw materials and other inputs will be procured, and whether components will be manufactured by the firm itself or obtained from other enterprises; the building of new plants and their capacity and location; and wages and other conditions of employment.

Perfectly competitive markets significantly decrease the ability of owners to act as they please in these matters. Under perfect competition, firms must follow the dictates of the market or go bankrupt. Markets are almost never perfectly competitive, however, and one concern of industrial-organization theory is the ways in which deviations from perfect competition remove constraints from and increase the market power of firms. In the auto industry in developed countries, the high degree of concentration allowed the firms to coordinate pricing strategies; in the United States, for example, GM acted as a price leader.

Raymond Vernon's "product life-cycle" model of international trade suggests that the market power that the auto TNCs enjoyed in their home countries could not be transferred to the developing-country markets, or at least not for long. A product introduced by one firm may accord it a monopoly position, but only until patents expire and other firms master the requisite technology. TNCs may accelerate this erosion of monopoly by diffusing new products and technologies abroad. Over time, Vernon argues, production processes become more standardized, financial uncertainty is reduced, barriers to entry become less formidable, and local firms are able to capitalize on their superior understanding of the local market to challenge the position of the transnational firms. "Workable competition" results.[23]

While this possibility must be considered in the Mexican case, a glance at world auto industry suggests it to be an unlikely one. On the whole, concentration has been increasing in the world industry. Since the end of World War II, new firms have arisen to challenge the domination of the existing TNCs only in Japan (although others may soon appear in South Korea). Elsewhere, particularly in Latin America, locally owned firms have been driven out of auto industries, and increasing concentration has been the rule. Indeed, the possibilities must

---

[23] Raymond Vernon, *Storm over the Multinationals: The Real Issues* (Cambridge: Harvard University Press, 1977), pp. 91-98.

be considered that, in contrast to the Vernon hypothesis, the transnational automobile firms have been able to use the market power
derived at home to buttress their position in the new markets (through
cross-subsidization, for example), and that the same barriers to entry
have emerged in these markets that existed in the home countries.

Publicly owned firms are less subject to the forces of the market
(whether it be competitive or oligopolistic), and they give the state an
additional lever of control over privately owned firms in the industry.
Within certain constraints (for example, what kinds of products consumers will buy), public ownership provides the state with a much more
direct way to accomplish certain goals than do either government regulations or inducements to get privately owned firms to act in desired
ways. By 1960, the Mexican state had acquired firms in both the terminal and the parts sectors of the Mexican automobile industry, and
it would acquire more later, but it rarely used these as instruments of
industrial policy or as deliberate alternatives to private ownership.
These were firms the state took over as a last resort, and it has tended
to treat them as afterthoughts or even as embarrassments in the making
of policy (see chapter 6). The fact of state ownership nevertheless
creates certain possibilities for policy to which we need to be attentive,
even if they were never pursued.

Market power has to do with the power of firms vis-à-vis their competitors, their suppliers, and their customers, but their power vis-à-vis
the state is also an important consideration. The exercise of state power
can limit the exercise of private corporate power; on the other hand,
firms will try to exercise power over the state in order to arrange the
regulatory apparatus to their liking. The power relationships between
the state and the TNCs will be one subject of the next chapter.

THE CONSEQUENCES OF TNC BEHAVIOR

Industrial-organization theory assesses the performance of an industry
by comparing it to the hypothetical performance that would result
from a perfectly competitive industry at equilibrium. Efficiency in the
use of resources, technical innovation, and normal profits have been
commonly employed as standards of performance in the U.S. However,
while these may be useful for developed countries, they are not adequate for developing countries. Efficiency hardly ceases to be important
in this context, but the assessment of performance also needs to take
into account the range of manufacturing activities, the rate of growth,
and the equitability in the distribution of benefits. Such standards direct
attention to a number of the consequences upon which the dependency

perspective has focused, standards which can be grouped into two sets: (a) the consequences that the behavior of transnational corporations has for *distribution*, both international and domestic, and (b) the possible *distortions* of the fabric of society, the economy, and politics thay may follow from the involvement of transnational corporations.[24] It is with the latter that we will be particularly concerned.

Distribution

Within the dependency perspective, TNCs are frequently criticized for contributing to the maldistribution of income, both within developing countries and between them and more developed countries. While neoclassicists argue that TNCs create more new jobs than they eradicate, raise the demand for labor and hence its wages, and lower the return to capital (thus equalizing rather than concentrating incomes), *dependistas* hold instead that TNCs are principally to be found in—and even help to create—oligopolistic industries, in which the resulting above-normal profits redistribute income from consumers to producers.[25] Questions of income inequality within developing countries are certainly germane to the Mexican case: the upward redistribution of income in Mexico after 1940 helped create an upper-middle class affluent enough to purchase automobiles and thus sustain at least a small manufacturing industry. But the increasing inequality of distribution in Mexico was the result not primarily of TNC behavior (although they initially benefited from it) but rather of the growth strategy pursued by the Mexican state. The role of the TNCs in maintaining inequality will be more at the periphery than at the center of our attention.

A second distributional proposition, and perhaps the most frequently voiced criticism of TNCs in developing countries, that they take more money out of a country than they bring in: they "decapitalize"

[24] For an overview, see Theodore H. Moran, "Multinational Corporations and Dependency: A Dialogue for Dependentistas and Non-Dependentistas," *International Organization* 32 (1978):79-100; Thomas Biersteker, *Distortion or Development? Contending Perspectives on the Multinational Corporation* (Cambridge: MIT Press, 1978); and Richard Newfarmer, "International Industrial Organization and Development: A Survey," in Richard Newfarmer, ed., *Profits, Progress and Poverty: Case Studies of International Industries in Latin America* (Notre Dame: University of Notre Dame Press, 1984).

[25] For one careful elaboration, see Nathanial Leff, "Monopoly Capitalism and Public Policy in Developing Countries," *Kyklos* 32 (1979):718-738. For a discussion and criticism of neoclassical assumptions in the study of developing countries, see William R. Cline, "Distribution and Development: A Survey of Literature," *Journal of Development Economics* 1 (1975):359-400.

it, thus stunting national development. Moran formulates the hypothesis in the following terms:

> The benefits of foreign investment are "poorly" (or "unfairly" or "unequally") distributed between the multinational and the host, or the country pays "too high" a price for what it gets, or the company siphons off an economic "surplus" that could otherwise be used to finance internal development.[26]

In extractive industries such as oil, copper, and tin, a major issue for both the firms and the government is the division of rents arising from the sale of a scarce, naturally arising commodity. In a manufacturing industry such as automobiles, however, the matter looks somewhat different.

First, there are more complex channels by which TNCs can transfer money out of a developing country. There are returns in the form not only of repatriated earnings but also of sales of parts, technical assistance contracts, and rights to the use of patents and trademarks. This complexity not only makes it more difficult to address the question of fair gain for the firm; it also makes it extremely difficult to estimate precisely what that gain actually is. If Ford sells a station-wagon tailgate to its subsidiary in Mexico, what price should it charge? Because there is no price for such a part determined at arm's length in a market, the transfer price must be established administratively, wholly within Ford as a global corporation. How this price is set will affect the earnings of Ford's various operations. The higher the transfer price, the more of its earnings will Ford realize in Detroit and the less of them, will it realize in Mexico. By manipulating these transfer prices, TNCs can shift their profits to locations where, because of investment needs, exchange controls, or tax laws, it is most advantageous. The costs a subsidiary pays its parent for trademarks, licenses, and technical and management assistance can similarly be arranged to maximize global profits, even it if means book losses (or inflated profits) for a particular subsidiary.[27] A further difficulty, at least for the researcher, is that TNCs typically

---

[26] Moran, "Multinational Corporations," p. 80.

[27] The interests of the TNCs in using such mechanisms have been elaborated in a number of works; see, for example, Sidney M. Robbins and Robert B. Stobaugh, *Money in the Multinational Corporation* (New York: Basic Books, 1973), and John Stopford and Louis T. Wells, *Managing the Multinational Enterprise* (New York: Basic Books, 1972). One of the most comprehensive empirical studies is Constantine Vaitsos, *Intercountry Income Distribution and Transnational Enterprise* (Oxford: Clarendon Press, 1974). See also R. S. Barnet and R. E. Muller, *Global Reach: The Power of Multinational Corporations* (New York: Simon and Schuster, 1974).

make publicly available only consolidated financial statements, rather than separate statements for each subsidiary.

However, these difficulties in tracing the impact of TNCs on the international distribution of income are not the principal reason we do not concentrate on them in this study. While manufacturing industries do present more complex avenues for capital flows than do the extractive industries, they also reduce the importance of such international flows relative to other issues—the social, economic, and political distortions.

Distortions

There are five ways in which TNCs have the potential for distorting development.

(a) *Reluctance to invest in activities that promote industrialization and growth.* The full range of a manufacturing firm's activities may include production of components, assembly of finished goods, distribution and marketing, design, and research and development. While a transnational firm may undertake some of these activities in a developing country, it is likely to be reluctant to engage in all of them. This restraint may be rational for the firm in light of its global strategy, but it may not be so for the host country in light of its development program.

TNCs have frequently been criticized for being unwilling to locate R & D facilities in developing countries, thus prolonging technological dependence—the inability of a developing country to generate, on its own, the innovations and know-how needed for self-sustaining growth. As Newfarmer has put it: "Centralization of the R & D activities of the global company conflicts directly with the interests of the developing countries in domestic technological 'parity' or interdependence."[28] In

---

[28] Newfarmer, "International Industrial Organization." The alternative held out by the dependency literature is that of a national firm developing its own technology, perhaps first by licensing from abroad and then by upgrading its own capacity at home; see Newfarmer's discussion of the Japanese case, ibid., p. 60. For other discussions of technological dependence, see Osvaldo Sunkel, "National Development Policy and External Dependence in Latin America," *Journal of Development Studies* 6 (1970):23-48, and Celso Furtado, "The Concept of External Dependence in the Study of Underdevelopment," in Charles K. Wilber, ed., *The Political Economy of Development and Underdevelopment* (New York: Random House, 1970), pp. 118-123. For an empirical examination of issues concerning TNCs and technological dependence, see Jorge Katz, "Industrial Growth, Royalty Payments, and Local Expenditure on Research and Development," in Victor Urquidi and Rosemary Thorpe, eds., *Latin America in the International Economy* (New York: John Wiley, 1973), pp. 197-224. Much of this literature is reviewed in Evans, *Dependent Development*, pp. 172-194.

the case of Mexico, however, the TNCs showed in 1960 an even more
basic reluctance: to move beyond simple assembly to the manufacture
of motor vehicles. When that reluctance was overcome, toward the end
of the decade, another replaced it: an unwillingness to export vehicles
and components from Mexico.

(b) *Manufacture of inappropriate products and use of inappropriate processes.* Those investments that TNCs do make may involve the introduction of inappropriate products or production processes, if judged by
standards other than corporate profit and growth. Their disposition
to use capital-intensive technology is one possibility that has been ex-
tensively explored in the literature.[29] TNCs introduce—this claim goes—
the same technology they have developed in the high-wage, labor-
scarce situations of their home countries into the low-wage, labor-
abundant situations of developing countries, thus failing to help generate new employment opportunities. The products that the TNCs make
may also be inappropriate for the circumstances of a developing country. Moreover, their marketing efforts may significantly alter consumer
tastes, undermining the indigenous culture. In Mexico, the transnational auto firms introduced the same products and the same manufacturing processes that they had developed in their home countries;
we need to be attentive to whether these have been appropriate in the
Mexican context.

(c) *Denationalization.* Dependency theorists have argued that TNCs
displace local entrepreneurs or pre-empt opportunities that the latter
would otherwise take advantage of. This hypothesis is particularly important insofar as domestically owned firms act differently from TNCs
with respect, e.g., to the products they offer, their prices, their foreign-
trade behavior, or their disposition to reinvest earnings. In 1960, only
two of the twelve auto assemblers in Mexico were foreign owned; these
two controlled half the market, while the firms controlling the other
half were all domestically owned. There were hardly any parts-man-
ufacturing firms. Once domestic manufacture began, the terms of competition in the industry changed dramatically; the place that the TNCs
and the domestically owned firms come to occupy in these new conditions, and the consequences of this structure of ownership for the
conduct of the firms and the performance of the industry, are matters
of concern.

(d) *Alterations in local market structures.* TNCs may act differently from
domestically owned firms because their behavior is shaped in inter-

---

[29] For a review of the literature in this area, see Moran, "Multinational Corporations,"
pp. 87-88, and Newfarmer, "International Industrial Organization."

national market structures. But they may also have a hand in constructing a domestic market structure in ways that transform—and distort—the behavior of all the firms, whether transnational or national, that are producing and selling in this market. TNCs may reproduce the same barriers to entry and the same patterns of oligopolistic competition in developing countries that they are accustomed to at home. In these circumstances, domestically owned firms may come to act increasingly like transnationally owned ones. Public policy to alter this behavior might be aimed not at changing ownership but at changing the structure of the domestic market. In 1960, the market structure of the Mexican auto industry was still to be formed. Would it exhibit the same characteristics as auto industries in more developed countries—oligopoly, avoidance of price competition, aggressive product differentiation? Once it took shape, how susceptible would it be to efforts to restructure it?

(e) *Interference in political processes and structures.* TNCs may co-opt local elites or form alliances with elements of the national bourgeoisie to block government efforts at regulation. Alternately, TNCs may call on their home-country governments for assistance in bargaining with the governments of developing countries. Or, instead of seeking to exercise power directly over actors whose behavior they seek to change, TNCs may try to use political power to mold an industry's domestic or international market structure in ways that make the desired behavior more rational for the actors in question. Once such a market structure is in place, and the history of its formation forgotten, it no longer seems as if the TNCs are exercising power, because there is no overt conflict of interest: what is rational for them has also been made rational for national firms and the state.

When Mexican officials set out to transform the automotive sector in the early 1960s, they sought to overcome the unwillingness of TNCs to invest in manufacturing, but in doing so they were aware of the economic, social, and political distortions that direct investment by the TNCs might bring. While the TNCs and the state had certain interests in common, serious conflicts would arise over the ownership and market structure of the industry and over the conduct of the firms within that structure. In the next chapter, we will develop a framework for understanding the nature of these congruent and conflicting interests and for understanding the power available to the state and the TNCs in their bargaining encounters.

·4·

A FRAMEWORK FOR ANALYZING
STATE-TNC BARGAINING

In 1961-1962, in 1968-1969, and again in 1977, there were major episodes of bargaining between the Mexican state and the transnational automobile firms. Chapters 5, 7, and 9 each examines one of these encounters in some detail, but we first need to develop a general framework for analyzing them. In what has proven to be a seminal formulation, Kindleberger and Herrick conceptualized the relationships between TNCs and host-country governments as one of "bilateral monopoly": one buyer and one seller of an investment project:

> In a typical situation, a company earns more abroad than the minimum it would accept and a country's net social benefits from the company's presence are greater than the minimum it would accept . . . with a wide gap between the maximum and minimum demands by the two parties.[1]

Thus viewed, the outside limits of acceptability could be located by means of economic theory, but the precise terms of the investment would be a function of the relative bargaining strengths of the two parties. Through an analysis of the relative power of each actor, the character of the resulting investment project could be explained. Equilibrium analysis would give way to power analysis, economics to political science.

Growing out of this leading idea, a "balance-of-bargaining-power" approach has taken shape.[2] It has been usefully applied in studies of TNC–host-country-government relations, but it is marred by weaknesses that derive from its kinship to the behavioral/pluralist approach to power in American political science. It tends to take the agenda of bargaining as given, failing to explain why some issues and not others become subjects of conflict. In accounting for the outcomes of bar-

---

[1] Charles Kindleberger and Bruce Herrick, *Economic Development*, 3rd ed. (New York: McGraw-Hill, 1977), p. 320.

[2] See Moran, "Multinational Corporations" and *Multinational Corporations and Politics of Dependence*; Raymond Vernon, *Sovereignty at Bay: The Multinational Spread of U.S. Enterprises* (New York: Basic Books, 1971), chap. 3; and Raymond F. Mikesell, ed., *Foreign Investment in the Petroleum and Mineral Industries: Case Studies of Investor–Host Country Relations* (Baltimore: The Johns Hopkins University Press, 1971), chap. 2. For one of the few case studies of a manufacturing industry, see Gereffi, "Drug Firms and Dependency."

gaining, it tends to consider power as a characteristic of individual actors, overlooking the fact that power is rooted in political and economic structures that are both national and international in scale. Power is shown not only when one actor can directly alter the behavior of another (as behavioralists have it) but also when an actor can change the structures that shape the interests and the power of other actors. Finally, it tends to assume that actors are unitary individuals rather than complex organizations such as nation-states and transnational firms. Our discussion of bargaining will seek to remedy these weaknesses.

AGENDA SETTING

As Schattschneider reminds us, "All forms of political organization have a bias in favor of the exploitation of some kinds of conflict and the suppression of others. . . . Some issues are organized into politics while others are organized out."[3] An adequate account of bargaining must contribute to an understanding of which actors are included and which excluded, and why these actors do or do not raise certain issues.

One or more of three factors may be involved in the exclusion of an actor from the agenda-setting process. First, the actor may lack the resources to participate: time, expertise, money, or the like. In the making of industrial policy, for example, smaller businesses may be at a disadvantage relative to larger firms.[4] Second, institutional structures, particularly political ones, may deny access. While giving them a formal place in governance, for example, the structure of the PRI denies peasant organizations and labor unions a significant role in the making of policies that affect their welfare (see chapter 2). Finally, actors may "choose" not to participate because they fail to understand that their interests are being threatened or because past experiences, perhaps deeply embedded in their culture, have engendered fatalism or a feeling of helplessness before those with significant power.

Exclusion of an actor may limit the scope of a conflict: issues of interest to that actor may never be raised. However, it is also possible

---

[3] E. E. Schattschneider, *The Semi-Sovereign People* (New York: Holt, Rinehart and Winston, 1960), p. 71.

[4] An early criticism of certain pluralist theories was that they assumed that nonparticipation meant lack of interest, since the American political system was ostensibly open (offering free speech, freedom to organize, periodic elections, etc.) to any group that felt its interests threatened. A succinct criticism of this position in the case of blacks in Newark, New Jersey, can be found in Michael Parenti, "Power and Pluralism: A View from the Bottom," *Journal of Politics* 32 (1970):501–530.

some other actor may plead those interests. The postrevolutionary regime in Mexico, for example, has denied businessmen a role in official decision-making arenas, but the Mexican state has nonetheless attended carefully to the interests of the business community in making economic policy. In any case, those actors that are included in the bargaining will be the ones that define the agenda and therefore set the terms of the conflict. However, for two nearly opposite reasons, actors may fail to raise issues of importance to them.

First, if actors have divergent interests, and one of them believes that another has such a preponderance of power that defeat can be the only outcome, the weaker actor may simply not articulate the interest. In other words, actors will place on the bargaining agenda only those issues on which they believe there is some possibility of success.[5]

The other reason that actors may not raise issues is far more important for our study. In some cases, there is such a *convergence* of interests among the actors that there is no need to bargain over certain issues, those that fall within the scope of agreement. While there may be other issues where interests diverge, and which therefore do find their way onto the bargaining agenda, focusing solely on them would make the bargaining appear more conflictual than it really is by obscuring the tacit agreements.

The possibility that some interests may not be made explicit gives rise to a vexing question: How are we to know what an actor's interests are, and how are we to understand how and why they change?

To the behavioralist, this does not seem a difficult matter. The interests of actors are simply and only what they say they are. Actors know best what they want or need. By definition, actors cannot be mistaken about their interests, no matter what the consequences may be of actions that proceed from interests thus understood. We take a different view of interests, one that sees them as having objective as well as subjective components. We take our actors to have interests that may be unexpressed and perhaps even unrecognized but that are no less real on that account. Corporations that drive themselves into bankruptcy when some other course of action would have avoided that fate should be recognized as having acted against their real or objective interests. On the other hand, in a given situation there may be several courses of action that allow a firm to prosper, and in opting for one of them the firm is adding a subjective component to its interests; however, this is a long way from saying that a firm's interests lie in

---

[5] The *locus classicus* of this argument is Peter Bachrach and Morton Baratz, "Two Faces of Power," *American Political Science Review* 56 (1962):947-952.

whatever course of action it chooses. Taking interests to have both objective and subjective components allows us to argue that an actor can make mistakes about its interests, but such a claim must be based on an analysis of its basic purposes and of the structural contexts in which it finds itself.

This conception of interests directs attention to two important points: (a) that actors' interests are shaped by the structures within which they act, and (b) that power may be most effectively exercised by altering those structures. Interests may be "engineered" into convergence through the exercise of power. Steven Lukes has put the essential point well:

> A may exercise power over B by getting him to do what he does not want to do, but he also exercises power over him by influencing, shaping or determining his very wants. . . . is it not the supreme and most insidious exercise of power to prevent people, to whatever degree, from having grievances by shaping their perceptions, cognitions and preferences in such a way that they accept their role in the existing order of things, either because they can see or imagine no alternative to it, or because they see it as natural and unchangeable, or because they value it as divinely ordained and beneficial?[6]

An actor's preferences or interests can be influenced, that is—even determined—not through some mysterious process of mind control but rather through alteration of surrounding institutional structures in such a way that it becomes rational for the actor to have preferences of a particular sort.

That the interests of corporations are shaped by structures (and are therefore susceptible to change as structures change) is implicit in industrial-organization theory. In this approach, the interests of firms are treated as subjects for analysis, not merely as givens (see chapter 3). In the case of the state, matters are more difficult, because it lacks, a single, overarching goal, such as the maximization of profit, which would circumscribe what is rational. Our approach to the interests of the state also treats them as susceptible to change and to analysis, however. The interests of the state are set in the first instance by its social foundations—by the relationship of the state to the class structure. As these social foundations change, the interests of the state change. More specifically, the interests of the state appear as embedded orientations adopted in response to particular problems which are

⁶ Steven Lukes, *Power: A Radical View* (London: Macmillan, 1974), pp. 23-24.

thrown up for the state to solve, orientations which become institutionalized in particular ministries or agencies. These orientations will be elaborated and altered as surrounding structures pose new problems, for which the state devises new strategies and capacities. The institutionalization of orientations will constrain what is seen as a problem and what as an appropriate solution. (For a more detailed discussion, see chapter 2.)

DECISION MAKING

In the conflicts that emerged between the Mexican state and the transnational automobile corporations in the 1960s and 1970s, each actor brought its power to bear in the making and implementation of policy decisions. In analyzing state-TNC conflicts, the balance-of-bargaining-power literature usually conceptualizes power in much the same way as is done in the pluralist/behavioral framework: actor A has power over actor B to the extent that A can get B to do something B would not otherwise do.[7] Typically, the actors are seen as unitary and relatively free-standing with regard to one another. The power of each is conceived as arising principally out of the possession of certain resources that can be employed as sanctions (positive or negative) in efforts to alter the behavior of others. As Vaitsos puts it in describing power resources in state-TNC bargaining conflicts:

> The foreign investor offers capital, know-how (technological and managerial), some opportunities of commercialization, and, among other possibilities, that of a certain structure of industrial development. The host country offers access to the home market (particularly in the manufacturing sector), access to natural resources (as in extractive industries), and access to special comparative advantages (such as cheap labour).[8]

The balance-of-bargaining-power approach tends to be careless about specifying the scope and domain of power, whereas the pluralist/behavioral perspective insists upon their importance.[9] The power of an

---

[7] For an early statement of this conception, see Robert A. Dahl, "The Concept of Power," *Behavioral Science* 2 (1957):201-205.

[8] Vaitsos, *Intercountry Income Distribution*, p. 119.

[9] Dahl, for example, writes: "The domain of an actor's influence consists of the other actors influenced by him. The scope of an actor's influence refers to the matters on which he can influence them . . . Any statement about influence that does not clearly indicate the domain and scope it refers to verges on being meaningless." Robert Dahl, *Modern Political Analysis*, 3rd ed. (Englewood Cliffs, N.J.: Prentice-Hall, 1976), p. 33.

actor depends on who is trying to get whom to do what. A simple list of each actor's power resources is inadequate, for a given resource may figure significantly in one conflict but not in another.[10] The effectiveness of a particular resource in a particular conflict is a function of the identities of the actors and the nature of the issue.

To take an example that will be important throughout the three bargaining episodes analyzed in this book: The Mexican state's control over access to the domestic market was a significant power resource vis-à-vis the transnational automobile companies, but it would not have been so vis-à-vis the transnational mining firms. What first attracted Ford and GM to Mexico was not cheap labor but rather a growing market that had the potential to continue growing for decades ahead. Sales within Mexico would not have been nearly so important for the American Smelting and Refining Corporation or for Kennecott Copper, however. It was access to ore bodies that they could refine and sell abroad that attracted the mining companies to developing countries. Thus, what is a power resource with respect to one kind of firm may be irrelevant with respect to another.

As for the issues in state-TNC conflicts, we will be concerned with two basic kinds: issues of the behavior of firms (incorporation of local content, exports, prices) and issues of industry structure (number of firms, presence of foreign ownership). Speaking very generally, we will find that the power of the Mexican state to exclude particular TNCs from Mexico (an issue of industry structure) was greatly restricted by the ability of the firms to call on their home-country governments as allies, but that this was a less serious restriction when the firms' behavior was in question.

Internal Characteristics of Actors

The power of actors that complex organizations such as TNCs and the state can bring to bear in conflicts depends on certain of their internal characteristics. Specifically, the greater the organizational unity and

[10] Treating power as a resource transferrable from one context to another makes the error of treating power as analogous to money in being "fungible" or interchangeable; see, for example, Talcott Parsons, "On the Concept of Political Power," *Proceedings of the American Philosophical Society* 107 (1963):232-262. For a corrective, see David Baldwin, "Money and Power," *Journal of Politics* 33 (1971):578-614. For a recent and thorough review of the power literature that pays particular attention to the questions of fungibility and the context dependency of power resources, see David Baldwin, "Power Analysis and World Politics: New Trends versus Old Tendencies," *World Politics* 31 (1979):161-194.

the technical and administrative capacity of an actor, the greater will be its ability to translate its potential power into actual power.[11]

This study is concerned with the organizational unity or cohesion of the state more than with that of the TNCs.[12] The relative power of the ministries or agencies involved in the formulation and implementation of policy, and the relationships among them, affect the state's ability to carry out its policies. If one ministry dominates the policy-making process, the state is likely to be more effective than if there are several ministries of equal power, each responsible for its own sphere of policy. Bureaucratic conflict within the state not only makes unified action more difficult but also allows corporations to increase their power by playing one ministry off against another. There may also be divisions and factions within particular ministries, and the staffing of key positions and the organization and reorganization of administrative responsibility will be important as well in determining the internal cohesion of the state.

In addition, the power of the state to formulate and implement policies against the opposition of TNCs will depend on its general planning capacity, its administrative ability to monitor and control foreign capital, and the knowledge the state's officials have of a particular industry (for example, its prevailing technology and the character of competition in the international market). Conversely, a transnational firm's knowledge of the local market and of the political system, and its administrative ability to negotiate with or conciliate governmental ministries, will affect its power. The focus of this study again will be on the technical and administrative expertise of the state, although at

---

[11] The relative power of actors ought not to be gauged merely from the outcome of a conflict. Such a post hoc analysis of power tends to exclude any meaningful analysis of why a particular outcome occurred and forecloses the possibility that one actor had *potential* power it did not exercise. Potential power may not be employed in a conflict because of internal characteristics of the actor: lack of technical or administrative capacity or internal conflict among the actor's decision makers. One could argue that because of disorganization the state never had the power in the first place. Instead, our formulation focuses on the difference between a lack of power due to internal causes and a lack of power due to external factors. Dependency theory tends to explain the powerlessness of third-world states by the structure of dependence and the power of TNCs even though the actual cause, in some instances, is internal to the state. By examining the internal characteristics that prevent the state from actualizing its potential power, we can emphasize the important case of a more unified, more capable state.

[12] Organizational constraints within the TNCs, even though beyond the scope of this study, are important in understanding the ability of these actors to exercise power vis-à-vis third-world states. For a broad general discussion of internal organization, see Alfred D. Chandler, Jr., *Strategy and Structure: Chapters in the History of the American Industrial Enterprise* (Cambridge: MIT Press, 1962).

a number of points the abilities of the TNCs will also be important. How staff are recruited and trained, their past experience in the area, and their relations with *técnicos* in other industries, will all contribute to this technical and administrative capacity.[13]

Effects of Structures on Power

Structures may be defined as determinate patterns of institutionalized relationships among two or more actors which have a relatively enduring quality.[14] Structures set limits to action and open possibilities for action, and they condition action by shaping the interests and the power of the actors, though generally they do not strictly determine action. They are themselves created through and can be transformed by human action, but they are not quickly changed, particularly not by the efforts of any single actor.

In the events with which this study is concerned, four structures were especially relevant. First, there was the *automobile industry in Mexico*, its structural characteristics defined particularly by the form of ownership and by the market relations among the firms. It must be seen as "nested" within the *world automobile industry*, whose structure sometimes shaped the behavior of the firms more forcefully than did the structure of the industry within Mexico. Third, there was the *political-economic structure of Mexico* (already sketched in chapter 2); and, finally, the *political-economic structure of the world capitalist system*. These structures (a) permitted or limited the development of resources in the bargaining encounters, and (b) facilitated or inhibited the formation of alliances among the actors.

Deployment of resources.[15] Certain structural characteristics can be identified as being likely to affect the ability of actors to bring their resources to bear in a conflict. These were, at any rate, important in the conflicts between Mexico and the auto TNCs, though they are not necessarily generalizable to other situations.

[13] For a fuller discussion of these issues, see Moran, *Multinational Corporations and Politics of Dependence*; Stepan, *State and Society*, pp. 237ff.; and Constantine Vaitsos, "Power, Knowledge, and Development Policy: Relations between Transnational Enterprise and Developing Countries," paper presented at the 1974 Dag Hammarskjöld Seminar on the Third World and International Economic Change, Uppsala, Sweden, Aug. 1974.

[14] See Anthony Giddens, *Central Problems in Social Theory: Action, Structure, and Contradiction in Social Analysis* (Berkeley and Los Angeles: University of California Press, 1979), chap. 2.

[15] This section draws heavily on Stepan, *State and Society*, pp. 237-248, a discussion which provides a useful synthesis of previous work.

(a) *The existence of national alternatives to direct foreign investment.* A country like Mexico may need some of the resources that a TNC can provide, particularly investment capital, technology, or access to export markets. The more the state has a national alternative for meeting these needs, either by providing for them itself or by drawing upon the domestic private sector, the less need there is for TNC investment and the greater is the state's bargaining power.

(b) *The importance or priority in the national political economy of the sector in which the conflict occurs.* The more important the sector, the less the bargaining power of the state, especially if there are few national alternatives. The importance of the sector will depend in turn on the structure of the national political economy and on the industrialization strategy being pursued. Developing breakfast cereals, cake mixes, and instant drinks would not, for example, be as important for Mexico as developing an auto industry, with the effects its backward linkages would have on the entire manufacturing sector. Ford and GM might thus be expected to have more power than Kellogg's and General Foods, but how much more depends on the national alternatives available.

(c) *The importance of the investment for the firm.* The more important the investment is for the firm—and the fewer alternatives it has—the greater will be the power of the state to set terms on the investment (e.g., in connection with ownership or firm behavior). What makes an investment more or less important for a firm depends in part on the sector in which it is located. In an extractive industry, the firm may be concerned with such factors as the other sources of supply available, the opportunity cost of letting a rival firm control the natural resource in question, and the relative cost of extraction (which would depend on the infrastructure, the availability of trained personnel, the stability and wages of labor force, and so on). In a manufacturing industry, the issues will be different for a firm that is looking for an export base, and is thus primarily concerned with the cost and stability of labor, the availability or transportation cost of needed materials, and government tax and subsidy policy, from what they will be for a firm looking to the domestic market, which will be more concerned with the size and growth potential of the local market and how big a share it can count on (will it have a monopoly position? will the number of firms be limited?). The importance of the investment for the firm is further affected by the amount of money it has already invested, how much of this "sunken" investment it has recuperated, and how easily this investment (machinery, for example) can be removed. Finally, the competitive position and global strategy of a firm vis-à-vis other firms in the international market will also affect the importance of the investment for the firm (see below).

Because the importance of an investment to a firm changes over time as it realizes earnings and depreciates the value of its sunken cost, the relative bargaining power of the TNC relative to the state will also vary over the life of an investment. In studies of natural-resource industries, for example, analysts have observed that the TNCs seem to have the greatest bargaining power at the moment of new investment. Once the investment is committed, it takes years before it can be recuperated, and it is hard to withdraw easily. The bargaining power of the state tends to increase, then, after the mining or oil company has made its initial investment.[16] This would not be the case in the auto industry, however, because of the many differences between mining and manufacturing.

(d) *The character of competition in the international industry.* As mentioned above, the importance of a particular investment to a firm is affected by the firm's competitive position in the international industry; in the same way, its ability to withhold a particular investment when bargaining with a government depends on the willingness of its rivals to withhold their investments. Keen international competition allows the state to play one corporation off against another, weakening the bargaining power of any one firm. On the other hand, if firms in an industry can collude over investment or entry, the state has less bargaining power. In different state-TNC conflicts, different aspects of competition in the international industry are important.

(e) *The position of the state in the international political economy.* In general, the state's ability to bargain with TNCs (or with their home-country governments, should they be brought into the conflict) will depend in part on how well it can resist or prevent economic or military sanctions. How well it can resist economic sanctions will depend on its place within the world capitalist system—not simply its overall need for access to foreign markets, international finance, and investment, but the possibility of turning to alternative trading partners, lending institutions, or sources of investment if particular governments or institutions apply sanctions. The more the state develops a credible range of alternatives, the more it can resist sanctions. Such alternatives will depend not only on its economic resources—Does it have an important export like oil? Is its economy growing? Does it have a good "investment climate"?—

---

[16] See, for example, Moran, *Multinational Corporations and Politics of Dependence*, pp. 153-224; Vernon, *Sovereignty at Bay*, pp. 46-59; and Raymond F. Mikesell, "Conflict in Foreign Investor–Host Country Relations: A Preliminary Analysis," in Mikesell, *Foreign Investment*, pp. 29-55.

but also on its diplomatic negotiating skills. A state may also be able to resist economic sanctions if it can threaten sanctions against economic assets important to the other actor—denying exports of strategic commodities, for example. How well a state can resist military sanctions—"destabilization" by an agency of a foreign government or by exile forces, naval blockades, and so on—is an even more complex issue, and one beyond the scope of this study.[17]

Formation of Alliances. Three sorts of alliance that TNCs might form warrant mention: those with local business elites, those with their own home-country governments, and those with the local government.
  (a) *Alliances with local business elites.* As Moran points out,

> both dependentista and non-dependentista theorists tend to argue that there is on some core issues and at some points in time, a fundamental "reactionary alliance" between foreign investors and host country business groups, landowners, or other conservative groups. It is implausible not to expect these elites to share an abhorrence of radical social change that would destroy them all, and to work together to prevent such an upheaval from taking place.[18]

However, there are other conflicts, which do not involve threats to capitalism in general (state efforts to prevent denationalization of local industries, for example) and in which local capital may ally itself with the state against the TNCs. The kind of alliances thus depends on the interests in conflict, and these interests depend on the way in which the relationships among the actors are structured by the national and international political economy and the national and international market in the industry.[19]

---

[17] A number of issues concerning the international position of the state are discussed in Stepan, *State and Society.* Stepan also makes the important point that the kind of response by a developed state will depend on general considerations of international security. "If the developed state values the maintenance of a security alliance with the Third World state, it might not apply economic sanctions and might even encourage its nationals to maintain economic links. However, if the Third World state is defined as a strategic enemy, strong sanctions might be applied to discourage nationals from doing business, even though such nationals might want to engage in business for economic reason." Ibid., pp. 245-246.

[18] Moran, "Multinational Corporations," p. 93.

[19] For a general discussion of the conditions under which alliances between TNCs and a national bourgeoisie may form, see ibid., pp. 93-95. For other discussions of alliances between TNCs and local elites, see Moran, *Multinational Corporations and Politics of Dependence,* pp. 190-197, and Tugwell, *Politics of Oil.*

(b) *Alliances with foreign governments.* The TNCs may be able to bring the power of their home-country governments to bear in a conflict with a third-world state. When our story opens in 1960, an alliance could be taken for granted between the U.S. government and U.S.-based TNCs, but by 1980 the positions both of the government and of the TNCs had changed (though in quite different ways), and the possibilities for alliance then depended much more on the particular issues at stake.[20]

(c) *State-TNC alliances.* We ought not preclude the possibility of alliances between a TNC and the government of a developing country—something that may seem absurd if the analysis of bargaining between them attends only to manifest conflict. A state may be able to exert pressure on domestic private-sector firms (to induce them to export, for example, or to reduce prices) by using TNCs as competitive alternatives. Under certain circumstances, a third-world state may be able to use TNCs as allies in bargaining with the governments of advanced countries (see chapter 12). Another possibility is that transnational firms may ally themselves with one government ministry in opposing policy proposals advanced by another ministry—which may have its own TNC allies (see chapter 9).

Use of Power to Alter Structures

Power is exercised not only when the behavior of individual actors is altered but also when the structures that shape the interests and power of actors are changed. The behavioral/pluralist and balance-of-bargaining-power approaches have a decidedly individualistic conception of power. Power is viewed as a bilateral relationship between individual actors that are abstracted from all other relationships. In state-TNC conflicts, the state is seen as trying to get the TNC to act differently than it otherwise might—for example, to make new investments, pay higher taxes, or increase exports. Power is thus seen as a more or less immediate cause of an actor's change of behavior, and the target of an exercise of power is an individual actor. However, this neglects another way in which power can be used. Actor A may seek to change the behavior of Actor B by changing the *structures* that shape the latter's

[20] For an analysis of the divergence of interests between the U.S. government and U.S.-based TNCs, see Robert Gilpin, *U.S. Power and Multinational Corporations* (Princeton: Princeton University Press, 1977). Cf. Peter Evans, "Shoes, OPIC, and the Unquestioning Persuasion: Multinational Corporations and U.S.-Brazilian Relations," in Richard Fagen, ed., *Capitalism and the State in U.S.–Latin American Relations* (Stanford: Stanford University Press, 1979), pp. 302-336.

power and interests. A state may, for example, try to change the structure of a local market (e.g., the number of firms in it) in order to alter the forces that shape the behavior of other actors. The causal nexus between action and response will be less immediate and direct.

A change of structure may lead to a change in the behavior of actors by affecting either their power or their interests. Just as A may be able to affect B's power by changing the structures in which B is acting (a possibility that has already been discussed), so also A may be able to create a structure in which B finds it "rational"—i.e., in B's interest—to act as A would like. If one does not look historically at A's role in the creation of this structure, but simply at the actions of B, one would see no visible conflict, since B's interests would be congruent with A's. It would even seem that no power had been exercised. For this reason, the exercise of power in this form is the most subtle but also perhaps the most important.

IMPLEMENTATION OF POLICY

Following agenda setting and decision making is the third stage in the bargaining process, *implementation*. Because there are usually several ways of carrying out a decision, and because actors who lose out at the decision-making stage cannot be counted upon to desist from trying to alter or undermine the outcome, bargaining and the exercise of power continue through the implementation of a policy.

For the most part, implementation of a policy comes through a series of smaller decisions. Consequently, the most appropriate conceptual tools for understanding implementation will generally be those that have been considered under agenda setting and decision making: why particular issues are raised for decision, and by whom, and why these issues are settled as they are through the play of interest and power.

In the course of the implementation of policy, the state is set for a new round of bargaining. The policies that are implemented and the ways in which they are implemented, will give rise to new structures—new patterns of ownership or new barriers to entry, for example. These new structures will, in turn, alter the nature and importance of the interests of the actors, thus creating new patterns of conflict and accommodation—new agendas for bargaining. The new structures will also alter the power the actors can bring to bear in the new conflicts. While particular actors may seek to alter structures to their liking, there may also be unintended consequences of action that result in structures of a sort that no one anticipated or wanted. Simultaneous efforts by various actors may produce enduring structures conducive to behavior and outcomes regretted by all. We have chosen to study the historical development of three major conflicts between the Mexican state and the transnational automobile corporations precisely in order to improve the understanding of this dialectical relationship between structure and action.

·5·

THE FIRST BARGAINING ENCOUNTER, 1960-1962

When Adolfo López Mateos took office as president of Mexico in December 1958, his chief economic policy makers set themselves the task of creating an automobile manufacturing industry in Mexico. The conflict that ensued pitted for the first time the Mexican state against foreign corporations in a manufacturing sector.

Initial planning was accomplished by an interministerial committee with representatives from the Ministry of Industry and Commerce, the Ministry of Finance, the Ministry of National Properties, and the Bank of Mexico. It was chaired by Carlos Quintana, a high official of NAFIN, the state industrial development bank. NAFIN staff provided technical support for the study. In 1960, after considerable research (including visits to countries like Brazil and Argentina, which had recently initiated the manufacture of automobiles), but without much consultation with the firms then assembling automobiles in Mexico, the committee submitted a detailed report.[1] The report of these economic *técnicos* constituted the government's initial policy position.

The intent of the proposed policy was to create an efficient, majority Mexican-owned manufacturing industry to replace the numerous small firms, some of them foreign-owned, that were then assembling vehicles from imported kits. Such an industry was expected to provide a broad stimulus to the rest of the economy by spurring demand for raw materials and a host of manufactured parts.

The NAFIN report contained quite specific recommendations for the market and ownership structure of the new industry:

(1) There would be no more than four or five firms manufacturing automobiles.
(2) Each auto producer would be limited to the manufacture of one model, with few extras. Model changes would be permitted only every five years. Luxury vehicles would be forbidden; the emphasis would be on compact cars.
(3) Auto producers would be limited to the machining and assembly of the engine, and the assembly of the vehicle. Parts supply firms independent of the auto producers would manufacture components.

[1] Nacional Financiera, "Elementos para una política de desarrollo de la fabricación de vehículos automotrices en México" (NAFIN, 1960).

94

(4) Standardization of parts across vehicle producers would be encouraged.

(5) Both the auto producers and the parts firms would be joint ventures with transnational automobile firms, but with majority ownership in Mexican hands. (The report hinted at the possibility of excluding foreign ownership altogether by having wholly Mexican-owned firms license technology and designs from the transnational auto firms, but hardly anyone thought this feasible.)

Ford and GM led the opposition to the NAFIN report. Their wholly-owned assembly operations together accounted for over half the vehicles sold in Mexico at the time. Their global interests made them reluctant to commence manufacture in Mexico, because it was more profitable to supply their assembly operations from their existing home-country facilities. They opposed restrictions on the number of models and the frequency of model changes because such restrictions would threaten their global competitive strategies, which were based on product differentiations. Majority Mexican ownership would run counter to a basic operational procedure of both companies: complete ownership of all foreign subsidiaries. They were not opposed in principle to a limit on the number of firms—so long as *they* were not excluded. Indeed, this became the most important issue. When the dust finally settled, the Mexican state had succeeded in achieving only some of its initial goals.

The conflict between the Mexican state and the transnational auto firms raises two broad areas for analysis. First, why were some issues on the bargaining agenda and others not? Second, why did the bargaining result in the outcomes it did?

AGENDA SETTING

In the bargaining that followed upon the NAFIN report, leading up to the issuance of a government decree in 1962, the interests of the TNCs flowed directly from the structure of the world auto industry (see chapter 3). They wanted access to a rapidly growing market, but they wanted to serve it with a minimum of disruption to their established global competitive strategies. They sought to offer the same broad array of makes and models in all the markets they sold in, and they preferred to maintain the manufacturing facilities for these makes and models in their developed-country bases, shipping vehicles in knocked-down kits to export markets around the world and thereby extending their production runs. The interests of the state generally proceeded from the orientations that had been institutionalized after the revolution: primary reliance on the private sector, government entrepreneurship as a last resort, preference for Mexican ownership and import-substituting industrialization (see chapter 2).

Among López Mateos's first steps had been a reorganization of the government ministries. He created a new Ministry of National Properties to manage the state's holdings in a growing number of industries. He also changed the name of the Ministry of National Economy to the Ministry of Industry and Commerce (Secretaria de Industria y Comercio or SIC) and invested this ministry with significant power by giving it control over tariffs and import licenses, the principal instruments of import-substitution policy. These had been under the jurisdiction of the Ministry of Finance (Secretaria de Hacienda y Crédito Publico), which nevertheless remained a powerful ministry, since it still had control over the budget, taxation, and fiscal subsidies and incentives.

Antonio Ortiz Mena was named minister of finance, Eduardo Bustamante became minister of national properties, and Raúl Salinas Lozano was appointed minister of industry and commerce. In the previous administration, Salinas Lozano had worked in the financial studies section of the Ministry of Finance, and he brought with him to the new ministry a number of his colleagues. Plácido García Reynoso became his deputy minister, and Jorge Espinosa de los Reyes and Roberto Flores were charged with the responsibility for industrial policy as director and subdirector, respectively, of the directorate of industries.

Having been trained in the central institutions of economic policy (the Ministry of Finance, the Bank of Mexico, and NAFIN), the new team in the Ministry of Industry and Commerce was imbued with the same basic orientations that had already been guiding economic policy, but its members brought with them a more aggressive and nationalistic posture. They were concerned that the first surge of import substitution—the "easy phase"—was nearing exhaustion. They were convinced that strong state action would be necessary both to rekindle industrial growth and to preserve or to recapture Mexican ownership of productive assets. This group had already engineered the state purchase of the electric-power industry and the Mexicanization of the mining industry. Both had been predominantly foreign-owned, and the new Mexican ownership had led the way to significant growth.[2]

[2] For a good general discussion of the different stages of import-substitution industrialization, see Villarreal, "Import-Substituting Industrialization." On nationalization of the electric-power industry and Mexicanization of the mining industry, see Wionczek, *Nacionalismo mexicano*.

Inclusion and Exclusion of Actors

On the governmental side of the bargaining, the new Ministry of Industry and Commerce was accorded the major role, but the Ministry of Finance also had a significant part. The ministerial reorganization had opened the possibility for some conflict between these two, however, for although they shared basic goals, they had different responsibilities. Moreover, Finance was smarting over its loss of control over tariffs and import licenses, and the two ministers, Salinas Lozano and Ortiz Mena, did not care for one another. Consequently, NAFIN was used as a coordinating mechanism to bring the various ministries together to do the basic planning, though it would be up to SIC to draft the final decree and carry through on its implementation.

A major role for state enterprise in the industry, either as an instrument of regulation or as a producer, was never seriously considered, nor was the development of an expanded public transportation network as an alternative to increased production of automobiles. Diesel Nacional, the state-owned automobile and truck firm, was not included in the bargaining, and the Ministry of National Properties and the Ministry of Communications and Transportation were almost completely excluded. Auto-industry policy was being viewed through the lens of industrial growth rather than as a transportation problem. The goals of policy were investments, jobs, foreign-exchange savings, and increased technical competence, not more adequate transportation for the broad mass of Mexicans, urban and rural.

The manufacturers had scarcely been consulted when the NAFIN report was being prepared, and only Ford, GM, and Fábricas Auto-Mex among them had the sunken capital, internal connections, and stake in the market to make participation in the subsequent bargaining both possible and vital to their interests. The absence of European and Japanese TNCs meant that the decree, when it eventually appeared, would be more responsive to the particular concerns of the U.S. firms than it might otherwise have been. Not until after the decree was issued did European and Japanese firms begin to bargain with the Mexican state over whether they would be allowed to manufacture in Mexico.

Ford asserted itself in the bargaining over the terms of the decree much more fully and forcefully than did GM. Edgar Molina was the general manager of Ford's Mexican subsidiary. He had been general manager of Ford's Argentine subsidiary when Argentina adopted local-content requirements in 1959. Fresh from that experience, Molina—a U.S. citizen but born in Guatemala—befriended Salinas Lozano and set about "educating" the SIC minister to make sure that the government's policy in the automobile industry would be as much to Ford's liking as possible. GM, on the other hand, kept a low profile, expecting that whatever was good for Ford would be good for GM, and that whatever Ford could gain in bargaining GM could lay claim to as well.

Of the three companies, however, Auto-Mex had the easiest access to the government. Its president, Gaston Azcárraga, was a Mexican entrepreneur and headed the largest Mexican-owned firm in the industry. Moreover, he and Salinas had been classmates at Harvard. Like Molina, Azcárraga had frequent discussions with the SIC minister during the year and a half before the decree appeared.

Azcárraga appears to have been the only member of the national bourgeoisie to have been party to the bargaining. None of the other Mexican-owned assembly operations were at all sizeable, and there were not many significant Mexican-owned parts-supply firms in the industry. The interests of the national bourgeoisie were voiced in the bargaining, however, not so much by Azcárraga as by the Mexican government. The government insisted from the beginning upon majority Mexican ownership of both the terminal and the parts supply industry.

Labor was not included in the bargaining, and no other actor, not even the government, articulated its interests.[3] This is not surprising in view of the role that had been allocated to labor in the Mexican political economy since the 1940s. Although labor is officially part of the PRI, the corporate structure of the one-party system has been largely a way of maintaining a stable, docile labor force through mechanisms of sanction and co-optation. Organized labor has not been an active participant in economic planning, it has lacked the independent organization to demand such participation, and those who have designed industrial policy have seen only reason to discourage its participation. These circumstances say much about the class foundations and legitimation of the Mexican state. Labor is a pillar of the PRI, and the state is constitutionally charged with representing the interests of labor; the bourgeoisie is officially excluded from the PRI, and the state presents itself as protecting labor and peasants from the exactions of capital; yet in the making of automobile policy—one example among many

[3] For detailed discussions of the role of labor in the Mexican auto industry, see Ian Roxborough, "Labor in the Mexican Automobile Industry," in Richard Kronish and Kenneth S. Mericle, eds., *The Political Economy of the Latin American Motor Vehicle Industry* (Cambridge: MIT Press, 1984), pp. 161-194, and Kevin J. Middlebrook, "International Implications of Labor Change: The Mexican Automobile Industry," Jorge I. Domínguez, ed., *Home and Abroad* (Beverly Hills, Calif.: Sage, 1982), pp. 133-170.

others—the state represented the interests of the national bourgeoisie, not those of labor.

It is difficult to say with any certainty what an organized, independent labor movement might have sought in bargaining over auto-industry policy. It might have urged that the automobile sector not be selected as a centerpiece of industrial growth, since other sectors might have generated more employment per dollar of new investment, and without the social costs of auto-centered development. Labor is the one actor that might have advocated a larger role for public enterprise or more attention to the transportation needs of those unable to afford automobiles.[4]

Inclusion and Exclusion of Issues

The Mexican state took the initiative in setting the agenda for the bargaining leading to the 1962 auto-industry decree. In considering its approach to that agenda, four matters warrant consideration: the choice of the automobile industry as a target, the role of the public and private sectors, the role of the TNCs, and the regulatory strategy. The state's position on each of these arose fairly straightforwardly from longstanding economic policies. Few issues were barred out of fear of the power of the transnational automobile firms.

Choice of the Automobile Industry. The state's continuing commitment to growth through import substitution led directly to the choice of the automobile industry as the target sector. By the late 1950s, further growth along that path required one of two courses of action: either the domestic market for nondurable consumer goods would have to be expanded, or domestic manufacture of consumer durables and capital goods would have to commence. Government action could have sought to redistribute income in order to widen the domestic market, but the López Mateos administration, like all Mexican administrations since Cárdenas, had no interest in challenging the class structure that constituted the social foundation of the Mexican state. Instead, his administration took as given the current structure of demand in Mexico, one which gave much greater weight to the wants of middle- and upper-class consumers, and it looked for opportunities to initiate domestic manufacture to satisfy these wants. From this perspective, the automobile industry seemed a nearly perfect candidate. Automobiles

---

[4] For a discussion of the role of labor in formulating auto-industry policy in Chile, see Jenkins, *Dependent Industrialization*, pp. 234-239.

constituted a large item in the country's import bill—over 10 percent of all merchandise imports.[5] Despite the limited size of the domestic market, domestic manufacture of automobiles could quickly become a significant proportion of manufacturing GDP. It would bring large new investments and employment opportunities. Most importantly, it would stimulate many other sectors of the economy because of its unusually long backward and forward linkages. There would be a boost to the metalworking, glass, steel, paint, and aluminum industries. Policy makers hoped that, as it has been in the United States and Europe in earlier decades, a domestic automobile industry would be an engine of industrial growth that would pull the rest of the economy with it, the centerpiece of a surge of industrialization that would move Mexico into a phase of self-sustained growth. Development of public transportation facilities might also have spurred industrial growth, but the import-substitution strategy did not identify this as an option because import substitution takes its signals from the current structure of demand as expressed through the market.

The choice of the auto industry left open a number of options for development of the industry—options for the roles of the state and of TNCs and for the regulatory strategy to be employed.

Public versus Private Ownership. The Mexican state owned one automobile firm. Diesel Nacional (DINA) had been founded in the early 1950s by private entrepreneurs, but it had been taken over by the state in 1958 when bankruptcy threatened (see chapter 6). Under private ownership, DINA had assembled cars and trucks under license from Fiat. Victor Manuel Villaseñor, López Mateos's appointment as DINA's director, terminated the agreement with Fiat and negotiated a new one with Renault. DINA could have been the cornerstone of a wholly or predominantly state-owned industry. It could have been one of several state-owned firms manufacturing motor vehicles, or even the sole manufacturer; or privately owned firms could have been allowed but in a way that made DINA the industry leader. A state-owned manufacturing industry, however, would have been contrary to the orientation of the Mexican state in favor of private-sector entrepreneurship, with the state conceived only as assisting or bailing out failing firms (as it had with DINA). Moreover, DINA had performed poorly since being taken

---

[5] This is not to say that reducing imports was the primary motive for promoting the domestic manufacture of automobiles; indeed, the state planners knew that it would require imports of machinery and intermediate goods. Nevertheless, it would reduce other imports somewhat, and it would allow foreign exchange to be put to better use: for building an industrial base rather than for the purchase of motor vehicles.

over by the state. With the exception of Villaseñor (who was never a party to the planning or the bargaining), no one considered a major role for DINA or for public ownership in the auto-manufacturing industry.

Role of the TNCs. Although the state planners assumed *private* ownership of the industry, *foreign* ownership was not taken for granted. Economic nationalism—a preference for Mexican ownership—was a deep commitment of the Mexican state, and it was strongly felt by the officials of the López Mateos administration. In the case of the automobile industry, however, the administration chose only to *limit* foreign ownership. It did insist, at least initially, that the firms in both the terminal industry (the manufacturers of finished vehicles) and the parts-supply industry (the manufacturers of component parts) have majority Mexican ownership. But it did not exclude foreign ownership altogether, to create a wholly nationally owned industry as did the Japanese and later the Koreans.

The reason for this again lay in the import-substitution strategy. What propelled this strategy was the burgeoning demand of consumers for modern U.S.- or European-style vehicles. Even if it were technically feasible to produce cars of Mexican design, it would have been extremely difficult to win acceptance for such vehicles from the car-buying public in Mexico, which was a politically potent segment of the population. Thus, if foreign ownership were to be completely excluded, some of the transnational automobile firms would have had to be willing to license their technology and designs without having any accompanying equity stake. Renault had shown itself willing in this regard, but most of the transnational auto firms—including all of the U.S. Big Three—had not. Besides, with the possible exception of Fábricas Auto-Mex (which already had minority foreign equity) and DINA, there were no existing Mexican firms with the experience for beginning automobile manufacture under license. On the other hand, the presence of established auto manufacturers would provide guidance and technical assistance for the new parts industry. Hence, the absolute exclusion of foreign ownership was rejected. Instead, the state's position was that both segments of the industry were to be "Mexicanized"—allowing direct foreign investment by TNCs but reserving a dominant position for Mexican capital.

Regulatory Strategy. Although the *técnicos* who first formulated the government's policy in the auto industry accepted the assumption that industrialization would rely on markets and private ownership (national and transnational), they did not share with neoclassical economists an awe of markets. They understood that markets are human creations, not sanctified natural entities, and that markets are structured by the exercise of private and public power. Like their predecessors, they believed that the state should regulate the behavior of firms in the market place and that this demanded an appropriate industry structure.

The principal concern of these planners was not the dangers of oligopoly (as it might have been in the United States). They recognized that oligopoly had become a characteristic of the international structure of the industry and that its consequences—in particular, a reluctance to engage in price competition—would be a problem for Mexico no matter how many transnational automobile firms they allowed in Mexico. Indeed, one of their major objectives was to *limit* the number of firms operating in the domestic industry. Even assuming rapid growth, the market for motor vehicles in Mexico would remain very small relative to the volume of production needed to match the scale economies prevailing in the international industry. To gain efficiency and keep production costs as close as possible to those in developed countries, the planners sought to prevent the fragmentation of the Mexican market among too many producers. In the judgment of those who prepared the NAFIN report, four or five was the maximum number that could rationally be accommodated.

The concern with efficiency led to other proposals. Even though they realized that proliferation of models and annual model changes had become well-established modes of competition in the international industry, the state planners nevertheless wanted to limit both the number of models that each producer could manufacture and the frequency of model changes, for the sake of extending production runs.

The level of mandatory locally manufactured content was a related issue. If the components with the greatest scale economies continued to be imported, there would be less manufacture in Mexico, but more overall efficiency. Costs and prices in the industry would stay closer to international levels. There was then a difficult trade-off between industrialization and efficiency. However, the more the Mexican government succeeded in limiting the number of firms, the number of models, and the frequency of model changes, the larger the production runs of each model and thus the higher the level of mandatory local content could be without risking great inefficiency.

A critical choice for policy makers was whether to set the local-content level so high that the stamping of exterior body parts (hoods, fenders, doors, roofs, etc.) would have to be done in Mexico. This operation has a very large economy of scale. Argentina and Brazil had set their level of local content sufficiently high (95-99 percent) to require that exterior body stamping be done domestically, and they had also mandated that models be frozen for several years, but they had not limited the number of manufacturers to any appreciable degree, nor had they shown much concern with inflation or with the cost of vehicles relative to prices in developed countries. Moreover, unlike Mexico, neither had a common border with the United States nor an extensive tourism industry which brought consumers an awareness of and a desire for the current models in the United States.

The original NAFIN report recommended a central body-stamping facility, but this recommendation was predicated on the assumption that there would be no more than five models, each to be produced for five years. When it became clear that it was not feasible to impose such rigorous restrictions, the idea was abandoned. In the end, the level of local content was set at 60 percent of the direct cost of production. This was the existing domestic-content requirement for firms in any industry that wanted to partake of tax subsidies and other incentives under the Law of New and Necessary Industries, a central instrument of import-substitution policy. This level would require domestic manufacture of the engine and of the other major components of the power train (clutch, transmission, axles, etc.), but it would allow exterior body stampings to be imported. Once the industry was well established, planners hoped, the level of local content could be raised to mandate domestic manufacture of the exterior body parts.

Finally, to establish a beneficent industry structure, the Mexican government sought a clear separation between the terminal automobile manufacturers and the parts-supply firms. The auto manufacturers would be allowed to assemble vehicles, machine engines, and manufacture any parts they had been manufacturing before the decree. Everything else would be manufactured by a parts-supply industry that was to be created. Reserving a place for new Mexican entrepreneurship was one consideration behind this position, but efficiency was another. Preventing the terminal firms from manufacturing their own components held out the possibility of having only one or two manufacturers of each component. This might require, it was realized, some standardization of parts among the automobile producers, but greater efficiency in manufacturing operations would be the result.

The Response of the Firms

A number of the issues raised by the state planners gave rise to sharp conflicts with the transnational automobile firms. There were, however, others on which there was a substantial convergence of interests between the Mexican state and the transnational automobile firms.

Convergence of Interests. While the TNCs might have been critical of some aspects of the economic-growth policies that Mexico had been pursuing, the basic outlines of the state's strategy were very much to their liking: It was a capitalist strategy, which placed primary reliance on private-sector investment and held the state in readiness to offer whatever was needed—investment incentives, tax subsidies, infrastructure projects—to facilitate rapid industrial growth. The highly inegalitarian class structure that state policies had nurtured guaranteed the TNCs a market among the middle and upper classes for the relatively expensive products they were manufacturing and a stable, low-wage labor force to employ in manufacturing them. They had little interest in promoting public transportation. Finally, the TNCs were of course quite pleased that the Mexican state did not seek to exclude foreign investment altogether from the automobile industry. Without this fundamental convergence of interests, the bargaining would have taken quite a different shape, or perhaps it would not have taken place at all.

Issues in Conflict. First of all, the TNCs were not eager to begin manufacturing motor vehicles in Mexico. It would necessitate sizeable investments, as well as the deployment of capable executives—always a scarce resource. There would be difficult problems in obtaining raw materials and parts. Some necessary raw materials were not locally available in sufficient quantity or at acceptable quality. A parts industry would have to be created from scratch—a responsibility they would presumably have to shoulder. Further, the Mexican industry still looked too small to support domestic manufacture. Even if they could pass along the costs of inefficiency to Mexican consumers, they would still have lost some volume from their home-country production, at a time when they were looking to increase these volumes to achieve greater economies of scale.

Yet, although all the TNCs would have preferred to continue to import and assemble, none of them wanted to oppose domestic manufacture, a posture that might lead to their exclusion from the Mexican market, ceding it to competitors. Thus, their short-run reluctance to commence domestic manufacture was seriously tempered by their long-run concern to preserve access to a sizeable future market. Their attitude toward domestic manufacture soon became a question not of whether but of how much.

A second conflict was over the level of local content. While all firms would have preferred to minimize the mandatory level, the U.S.-based

TNCs (which were the most influential in the bargaining) had a particular interest in not being required to manufacture body stampings domestically or to freeze models for several years. Because they relied more than their European (and later Japanese) competitors on annual model changes, domestic manufacture of body stampings would have greatly increased costs and put them at an even greater competitive disadvantage. They objected forcefully to the high local-content levels envisioned in the NAFIN report, and even more so to the central stamping plant.

Thirdly, Ford and GM voiced strong opposition to the proposal that all firms in the terminal industry be Mexicanized. They feared that if they gave in to the Mexicans on this issue, they would find themselves facing similar requirements all over the world. Proposals to limit the number of models, that each firm could manufacture, to freeze models, to standardize parts, and to prohibit the terminal firms from manufacturing parts were also opposed, for they would constrict the firms' ability to use in Mexico the competitive strategies that they had come to employ elsewhere in the world. Finally, and most significantly, there was the issue of the number of firms. All of the TNCs saw the need for limiting the number—but each one of them wanted to be sure that *it* was not shut out of the Mexican market.

DECISION MAKING

The auto-industry decree that was promulgated in August 1962 mandated the beginning of domestic manufacture of motor vehicles.[6] The required level of local content was set at 60 percent, and the vertical integration of the producers was limited by permitting them only to assemble vehicles and engines, machine the engines, and manufacture those components that they had been producing prior to the decree. The chief weapon of the decree was a provision that a firm could not import any parts unless its application to do so was approved by SIC. Failure to approve such an application was tantamount to exclusion from the industry, since it was taken for granted that all the firms would use some imported content in their vehicles. Thus, the most important issue in the continued bargaining between the state and the TNCs became the inclusion and exclusion of firms, and we will focus on this issue in analyzing the actors' exercise of power.[7]

Like the state, each firm had an interest in limiting the number of

[6] For the full text of the decree, see *Diario oficial*, Aug. 23, 1962.

[7] Because of the passage of time and the dearth of written documents, the specific details of the bargaining are difficult to piece together, but interviews with the major participants have allowed us to reconstruct the broad outlines.

firms in the industry—as long as it was included. Fewer firms would mean a larger share of the market, but exclusion would mean no share at all. Thus, while some firms voiced the opinion that the number of firms should be limited, each did what it could to insure approval of its own import application.

The principal basis of the state's power to limit the number of firms lay in its ability to control access to the Mexican market. The Mexican state had developed the technical and administrative capability to exercise this control through many years of experience with the mechanisms of import-substitution policy—import quotas and tariffs (which had been imposed on assembled motor vehicles and kits since 1925).

Structure of the International Auto Industry

This basis of power would have been rendered ineffective if there had been an international cartel in the automobile industry, which could have withheld applications from all the transnational firms until the Mexican state agreed to take those firms that the cartel insisted upon. Mexico needed the TNCs because no domestic firm had the capability to begin manufacturing motor vehicles wholly on its own. But there was no international cartel in the automobile industry. On the contrary: the pattern of competition that had arisen within the structure of the international automobile industry served to strengthen rather than weaken the power of the Mexican state to control access to its domestic market.

In 1960, the Mexican market for automobiles was quite small; fewer than 100,000 vehicles were sold a year, only a tiny fraction of the annual sales of the major transnational automobile firms. What made the Mexican market attractive, however, was its future sales potential along with the declining growth of developed-country markets (see chapter 3). In the United States and Europe, vehicle sales would increasingly be only for replacement; there would be fewer sales to first-time buyers. In the larger developing-country markets (such as Mexico, Argentina, and Brazil in Latin America), sales could be expected to increase by 5 to 10 percent a year for several decades, because of growing populations as well as first-time purchases. In the view of the major transnational auto corporations, access to these markets was essential for maintaining their position in the global automobile industry. While U.S.-based firms had dominated Latin American markets before the mid-1950s, exports from the European firms to North and South America, spearheaded by Volkswagen, had challenged this hegemony. Latin America had become "a battleground in the competitive struggle within the automobile industry."[8] As long as these companies could serve the Mexican market by sending CKD kits for assembly there, that was their preferred strategy. But when Mexico threatened to forbid imports to companies that did not begin domestic manufacture, that strategy could no longer work.

In the world automobile industry, rivalry for new markets has led to what Frederick Knickerbocker has characterized as a "follow-the-leader" pattern of defensive investment: "Rival firms in an industry composed of a few large firms counter one another's moves by making similar moves themselves" as a risk-minimizing strategy. When one firm in the oligopoly makes an investment, other firms defend their positions by making similar investments. Knickerbocker has called the TNCs' proclivity for defensive investments a "trump card" for a less developed country (LDC). "When one member of the club makes a move, the others pant to follow; and by realizing this, the LDC is in a position to demand a high entrance fee."[9]

Because the move to domestic automobile manufacture in Mexico coincided with heightened international competition, the potential power of the Mexican state was enhanced—as long as one of the TNCs was willing to make the necessary investments. Early in the bargaining, Ford had expressed a willingness to commence manufacturing under the right conditions, and the others were then quick to indicate their willingness as well. When the decree stipulating domestic manufacture was promulgated, eighteen firms submitted applications.[10]

[8] Jenkins, *Dependent Industrialization*, p. 49.

[9] Knickerbocker, *Oligopolistic Reaction*, p. 1. Cf. Jenkins, *Dependent Industrialization*, pp. 40-42. For a discussion of oligopolistic reaction in another industry in Mexico, see Gereffi, "Drug Firms and Dependency."

[10] Gudger has placed great emphasis on the fiscal subsidies that Mexico offered to the transnational firms, implying that the attractiveness of the Mexican market was in large part created by government largesse: Michael Gudger, "The Regulation of Multinational Corporations in the Mexican Automotive Industry" (Ph.D. diss., University of Wisconsin, 1975). Gudger, however, overestimates the importance of these subsidies. He includes in his estimates the uncollected amounts of the so-called "special assembly tax," as well as the rebates on the amounts that were collected. This tax (on domestic value added), and the accompanying rebate, had been created prior to 1962, while the auto industry was still in the stage of assembly of imported kits. Government officials knew that the tax made no sense after manufacturing began; indeed, it would have been so high as to have made production prohibitive (given price controls). Instead of repealing it, however, it was kept on the books, possibly as a potential instrument of leverage over recalcitrant firms in the future. The tax has not actually been collected since 1962, and officials readily admit that it is not really a tax at all; see, for example, Emilio Sacristán Roy, "Apoyos del programa de fomento," in Cámara Nacional de Industrias de Transformación, *Memoria II: Segundo simposio de la industria automotriz mexicana* (Mexico City: CANACINTRA, 1980),

The eagerness of the TNCs to be included in Mexico's new auto industry thus enhanced the bargaining power of the Mexican state, and it could therefore have used the threat of exclusion to set high terms for entry. However, there were two reasons why it did not use this threat.

Actions by Home-Country Governments

Exclusion from the Mexican market was not a serious concern for certain firms because of their ownership status and their market position. Fábricas Auto-Mex, Ford, and GM dominated the Mexican market, and it was assumed that at least one manufacturer of large, U.S.-style vehicles would be included. Because Fábricas Auto-Mex was the only one of the three that was majority Mexican-owned, its application would presumably be favored. A strong desire to diversify Mexico's trade partners (to lessen reliance on the United States), together with a desire to ensure that smaller vehicles for less affluent consumers would be produced, argued for a firm linked to a European or Japanese producer of *autos populares*. The state-owned DINA, with its new licensing agreement with Renault, offered the possibility of a completely Mexican-owned firm producing such vehicles. DINA's shaky business history and the state's commitment to private-sector initiative, however, meant that government planners were unlikely to allow DINA to be the sole occupant of this market niche. Volkswagen had captured a significant market share in just a few years, and there was considerable respect within the government for its reliable technology and infrequent model changes. Moreover, Promexa, the firm that submitted the application to manufacture Volkswagens, was wholly Mexican-owned. Both DINA and Volkswagen were therefore likely to be approved. Finally, Vehículos Automotores Mexicanos S.A. (VAM), a Mexican-owned firm established in 1946 as Willys Mexicana that assembled (among other cars) the Jeep, a useful vehicle in rural areas, seemed sure to be approved.

An industry comprised of Fábricas Auto-Mex, DINA, Promexa, and VAM would have fit the general scheme of the NAFIN report: four firms,

---

p. 36. Thus, inclusion of this uncollected tax as a "subsidy" exaggerates the actual level of subsidies. Gudger estimates, for example, that in 1979, the total subsidies to the auto industry were 7,258.4 million pesos. A more accurate figure, excluding the uncollected special assembly tax, is 3,025.8 million pesos: Secretaria de Hacienda, Dirección General de Promoción Fiscal, "Informe de resultados de visitas de control efectuadas a las empresas de la industria automotriz terminal para la verificación del año modelo 1979" (Jan. 1981), table 7.1.

all majority Mexican owned, two linked to U.S.-based and two to European-based transnational firms, producing both small and large vehicles. The nub of the exclusion question, then, centered on three transnational automobile firms: Ford, GM, and later Nissan.

Ford and GM (but particularly Ford) began their efforts early to win themselves a place in the Mexican market and to shape the market structure to fit their global strategy. While the NAFIN report was being prepared, Ford submitted a two-volume study of its own, one volume outlining the possible shape of a manufacturing industry, the other setting forth a role for Ford within that scheme.[11] Molina, Ford's manager, met frequently during 1961 and 1962 with Salinas Lozano to try to make sure that the plan for manufacturing contained nothing that Ford thought unreasonable. Later, officials from GM joined in this effort.

Ford and GM pointed to the disruption and the damage to "national interests" that their exclusion would cause, particularly in view of the fact that between them they held half the current market. Replacement parts and service for Ford and GM vehicles already sold would become hard to find, the resale value of their vehicles owned by Mexicans would decline, and distributors would be put out of business and their employees would lose their jobs. The Mexican policy makers were unmoved: parts could be imported and service continued, distributors could shift to other makes and their employees could be relocated within the growing industry.

The two companies sought to mobilize support in the Mexican private sector, urging their distributors and the few existing parts-supply firms (mostly producing replacement parts) to make separate representations on their behalf. These firms were weak and unorganized, however, and their efforts were not taken very seriously. It was not possible for Ford and GM to forge an alliance with the national bourgeoisie by depicting the exclusion of some firms from the market as a general attack on private investment. The Mexican state's clear intention to Mexicanize the industry left no doubt about its commitment to the national bourgeoisie.

Ford and GM were able to muster a more formidable ally, however: the U.S. government. Salinas Lozano was informed by U.S. Ambassador Thomas Mann that the Department of State would look unfavorably on the exclusion of any U.S. firms that had been operating in Mexico. Other SIC officials were told that such exclusion would be

---

[11] Ford Motor Company, "A Study of Automotive Manufacturing in Mexico" (Apr. 1960) and "Proposal for Automotive Manufacturing in Mexico" (Apr. 1960).

viewed as a "not very friendly act." Precisely what was said is not as important as how anything said on this issue by the U.S. government would be understood. Its explicit backing of the position of Ford and GM meant that Mexican policy toward its automobile industry would be linked with and would affect what happened in other spheres of U.S.-Mexican relations. The Mexican government found itself facing sanctions beyond those that the firms themselves could have brought to bear. Given Mexico's dependency on the United States in matters of trade, finance, and investment, pressure by the U.S. government had to be taken seriously. Actions that might threaten trade or capital flows between the United States and Mexico or create the image of a bad investment climate had to be weighed carefully. Mexico's position in the international political economy in these years (well before the rediscovery of oil) was not a strong one.

In the midst of its formulation of automobile policy, the López Mateos administration was forcefully reminded of these limitations. In 1960-1961, relations with the United States took a decided turn for the worse following Mexico's refusal to submit to U.S. pressure to join in trade sanctions against the Castro government in Cuba. The U.S. government and press criticized the "left-wing" tendencies of the López Mateos government, a perception that had already been conjured up by a series of actions toward foreign investment which it had taken earlier. Shortly after coming into office, the López Mateos administration had nationalized the electric-power industry and implemented Mexicanization requirements in the petrochemical and mining sectors, moves that were branded as "socialist" by conservative Mexican business interests and by some TNCs operating in Mexico. The result was a flight of capital of about $200 million in 1960-1961. The Mexican government trimmed its sails, to a degree. When the U.S. government voiced its concern over the treatment of Ford and GM, some officials of the Mexican government felt a need for circumspection, lest policy in the auto sector threaten the wider growth strategy. Consequently, both Ford and GM were approved as wholly foreign-owned subsidiaries.

Once these foreign companies had been approved, it was politically impossible to deny the applications from three other wholly Mexican-owned firms—Impulsora Mexicana Automotriz (to manufacture the Borgward), Reo (Toyota), and Representaciones Delta (Mercedes-Benz and DKW)—whose production plans met the minimum requirements set down in the decree. Their applications were indeed approved as well.[12]

[12] Despite the general commitment to support Mexican entrepreneurship, there was

Finally, in late 1964, two years after the legal deadline for approval, Nissan was able to gain entry to the Mexican market as another wholly foreign-owned firm. Reo had collapsed toward the end of 1963. The Japanese government insisted that it should be replaced by a Japanese firm, and Nissan was its choice. The application was opposed by the technical staff of SIC, who argued that the industry was already too crowded. But the Japanese government had a lever that it was able to use: Mexico's dependence on Japan as an export market for its cotton.

In 1963, cotton was the single most important export commodity for Mexico, accounting for exchange earnings of $196 million—over 20 percent of Mexico's total.[13] About 70 percent of its cotton exports went to Japan, Mexico's most important trade partner after the United States. The overall balance of trade between the two countries ran strongly in Mexico's favor; in 1962, Mexico's trade surplus with Japan was more than $100 million. For a number of years, the Japanese government had been pressuring Mexico to increase its imports, even offering a loan of $100 million if there were some improvement in this regard.[14] The Japanese government threatened to cut purchases of Mexican cotton if Nissan's application were not approved. It was. Thus, of the eighteen firms that had applied for import licenses, eleven were approved (including International Harvester, which manufactured only trucks)—far more than had been envisioned in the NAFIN report.

Lack of Internal State Unity

The support that Ford, GM, and Nissan received from their home-country governments would have made their exclusion difficult and costly, but not impossible. There were alternatives that might have been pursued, either to force exclusion or to obtain terms of entry that would have been more compatible with the state's wishes regarding Mexicanization and product differentiation. The U.S. firms might have been played off against one another. One could have been approved and the other rejected, undermining U.S. government assertions of

---

resistance within the technical staff of SIC to the approval of these applications, because it would increase the number of firms well beyond the number considered desirable. Auto-Mex, DINA, Promexa, VAM, Ford, and GM were all approved in December 1962, but approvals for Impulsora Mexicana Automotriz, Reo, and Delta were held up a month.

[13] Raúl Salinas Lozano, *Memoria de labores, 1963* (Mexico City: Secretaria de Industria y Comercio, 1963), pp. 136-137. Moreover, taxes on these exports earned the Mexican government $15 million. *Comercio exterior*, May 1961, p. 287.

[14] *Comercio exterior*, Mar. 1963, p. 167.

discrimination against foreign investment by its nationals. Alternatively, Mexico could have approved both but insisted that they accept majority Mexican ownership or limit their production to a single compact model. In the case of Nissan, the government might have responded to the Japanese government's pressure by negotiating for substantial Japanese investments in some other industrial sector. The Japanese bluff might even have been called: as some Mexican officials, particularly in the Finance Ministry, were aware, Japan could not easily have found suitable alternatives for long-fibered Mexican cotton.

For the Mexican state to have tried such parries, however, it would have needed a high degree of internal cohesion among key ministries and between the *políticos* and *técnicos* within ministries. But among those involved in making auto policy in 1962, such cohesion was lacking. Three aspects of internal disunity warrant mention.

(1) The administrative reorganization of 1959 had given control over tariffs and import licenses, previously in the hands of the Finance Ministry, to the Ministry of Industry and Commerce. These would be the primary tools for compelling domestic manufacture of automobiles. The Finance Ministry, however, retained control of the other major instruments of industrial policy, tax rebates and subsidies. This division of responsibilities between two ministries made coordination essential, but rivalry between the two, exacerbated by personal animosity at the ministerial level, interfered with such coordination.[15] The Finance Ministry continued to resist the diminution of its control over import policy, and the resulting conflict between the two ministries was sometimes sharp enough to require presidential mediation.

Coordination between the two ministries at the technical level was much better. Both the director of industries in SIC and the subdirector worked closely with the director of the department of financial studies and his staff in the Finance Ministry, first in writing the NAFIN report and later in formulating policy. All three supported a more demanding automobile policy, along the lines of the original report. Lack of co-

---

[15] The lack of coordination was evident in the formulation of tax and subsidy policies for the industry. The decree of August 1962 was promulgated by SIC and dealt only with import licenses (the requirements for continued imports of parts). It was silent on the crucial question of fiscal incentives, which were in the domain of the Ministry of Finance. It was not until 1963 that the Ministry of Finance announced its policies on fiscal incentives for the new industry. Interview evidence indicates that there may have been deeper conflict over the character and level of the subsidies (Finance arguing that they should be lower) and over the restrictions in the decree (Finance arguing for greater restrictions on the number of firms).

operation between the ministers, however, undercut this lower-level unity.

(2) The coordination problem was compounded by a split within SIC between the technical staff in the directorate of industries and the *políticos* who served as minister and deputy minister. The *políticos* felt that moderation and compromise with the TNCs were necessary and outweighed the arguments of the *técnicos*. One reason, suggested in the interviews, for the reluctance of top officials to take a stronger position was their time horizon which was quite different from that of the *técnicos*. The change of president every six years brings with it changes in all major policy-making posts. An official is unlikely to retain the same position, though many move to other positions of importance.[16] Cabinet ministers are invariably the strongest candidates for selection as the next president, and their prospects will depend on, among other factors, the immediate political consequences of their actions in the present *sexenio*—the friends and enemies they have made, the controversies in which they have been embroiled, and the stands they have taken in them. There is a strong incentive to pursue risk-minimizing strategies and to judge policies narrowly in terms of their short-run consequences. The deleterious effects of admitting too many firms into the auto industry would not be felt immediately, but the effects of a frontal confrontation with Ford, GM, and the U.S. government, or with the Japanese government, would be. Only an unusual minister would have risked such a conflict, unless he had the full and explicit support of the president. The *técnicos*, on the other hand, occupied more stable positions and took a longer view.

In the specific case of Ford, another source of reluctance on the part of Salinas Lozano may have been the close personal relationship that had arisen between him and Molina, the Ford manager. Molina had reckoned that early support of the government's general idea of moving toward domestic manufacture, combined with a great deal of specific technical information and advice about the industry, would give Ford an inside track on approval and an overall policy regime congenial to its strategy. It was Molina who had a Ford team draw up the study of auto manufacturing in Mexico that was submitted to SIC in 1960, and in the ensuing two years he had frequent conversations with Salinas

---

[16] On *políticos* and *técnicos* in the Mexican political system, see Merilee Grindle, *Bureaucrats, Politicians, and Peasants in Mexico: A Case Study in Public Policy* (Berkeley and Los Angeles: University of California Press, 1977). On sexenio change and careers within the bureaucracy of the Mexican state, see Smith, *Labyrinths of Power*.

Lozano. The minister may have come to feel an obligation to Ford that was not felt by the *técnicos*.[17]

(3) Because of the degree of centralization of power in the hands of a Mexican president, firm and explicit direction from López Mateos might have forged the inter- and intraministerial unity necessary to proceed with a stronger automobile policy. Instead, López Mateos's involvement seems to have been episodic and ad hoc. Key officials were left on their own to make hard decisions, so that it was easier for them to pursue risk-minimizing strategies. Moreover, specific directives to "ease up" on the transnational firms and to give favorable consideration to applications from some Mexican-owned firms filtered down from the president himself at key points in the bargaining. In the context of the Mexican automobile industry, only resolute guidance from the president could have fended off the pressures that were brought to bear, and this was not forthcoming.

IMPLEMENTATION OF THE 1962 DECREE

The conflict over the 1962 decree was only the first round of an on-going struggle. Negotiations were carried on almost constantly as firms sought changes in government policy or special exceptions for themselves. Although other major conflicts took place later, this initial round was the most decisive encounter because it set the terms for all subsequent bargaining. It is important, therefore, that the state did prevail on a number of key issues. It compelled the TNCs not only to begin local manufacture but also to limit their production of parts, thereby encouraging the development of an independent local parts-supply industry. These limits on vertical integration were accompanied by an insistence that firms in the parts industry have majority Mexican ownership.

The growth of the industry in the years following the issuance of the decree was quite dramatic (see table 5.1). In 1962, the assembly plants employed about 9,000 people; four years later (as the firms came into full compliance with the terms of the decree), the terminal firms were employing 19,000 workers. In 1962, the total investments of the assembly plants were just over 1.5 billion pesos (12.5 pesos = $1); four years later, they were more than 4.5 billion pesos. The industry's total import bill in 1966 was approximately what it had been

---

[17] There were rumors of corruption in the relationship, but it must be noted that such explanations of bureaucratic behavior are frequent in Mexico, often have self-serving motives as their origin, and are almost impossible to verify. We take note of them only as rumors.

TABLE 5.1

Growth of the Mexican Automobile Industry, 1960-1970

	Number of Vehicles[a]	Number of Employees	Value of Wages and Salaries	Value of Investments	Value of Production
1960	54,742	7,072	186	1,356	1,781
1961	61,636	7,724	220	1,436	1,923
1962	64,082	9,021	239	1,654	2,118
1963	75,581	10,504	308	2,009	2,730
1964	93,323	13,547	421	3,108	3,756
1965	102,508	16,800	542	3,977	4,026
1966	113,605	19,067	709	4,651	4,920
1967	119,253	21,530	815	4,905	5,461
1968	145,466	21,994	959	5,248	6,557
1969	163,596	22,303	1,056	5,692	7,463
1970	187,953	23,825	1,174	6,282	8,581

Source: AMIA, *La industria automotriz de México en cifras* (Mexico City: AMIA, 1972), p. 69

Notes: The figures in this table refer only to those companies that were eventually approved for domestic manufacture: DINA, Fábricas Auto-Mex, Ford, GM, International Harvester, Nissan, VAM, and Volkswagen. The figures on values are in millions of pesos.

[a] For 1960-1965, sales; for 1966-1970, production.

in 1962, but because of a substantial increase in the number of vehicles produced (from 64,082 to 113,605), there was a marked decrease in the average value of imports per vehicle.

These figures refer only to the terminal firms, which constituted less than half of the industry. In the other segment of the industry, the manufacture of auto parts, total investment climbed from 2 billion pesos to 5.6 billion pesos between 1962 and 1966, and the number of workers increased from 29,000 to 52,000. The value of the components manufactured almost tripled, from 1.3 billion pesos to 3.8 billion pesos.[18]

The qualitative aspects of these transformations were perhaps more important, though more difficult to measure. The growth of the automobile industry sparked by the 1962 decree not only quickened the pace of industrialization and increased the country's capital stock; it also raised the technical sophistication of the manufacturing operations that were carried out in Mexico. The decree directly promoted the

[18] These figures are from a speech given by Minister of Industry and Commerce Octaviano Campos Salas in August 1967, as reported in *Comercio exterior*, Sept. 1967, pp. 812-813.

creation of a machine-tool industry, for example, and enhanced the country's foundry capabilities. The transfer of technology took a number of forms. It was embodied in the technical assistance rendered directly to the new auto-parts firms, in the technology contracts that were arranged, and in the training of personnel in engineering, quality control, accounting, and administration. Nor was this transfer limited strictly to the automobile industry. One benefit of having parts suppliers that were distinct from the terminal firms was that the manufacturing processes they learned could be applied to other product lines. And rather commonly, workers trained in special skills in the automobile firms were hired away by enterprises in other sectors.

The TNCs would have been unlikely to undertake this massive shift from assembly to manufacturing had not the state intervened to make it rational for them to make the investments required. But within the structure of constraints and incentives created by the government, the TNCs were largely responsible for the rapid development of auto manufacturing. Not only did they build the plants, but they also provided invaluable assistance in creating a Mexican auto-parts industry. Forced to achieve 60 percent domestic content but prevented from integrating vertically beyond the machining of motors and assembly, they were compelled to provide the nascent majority Mexican-owned parts industry with markets, technological assistance, and "matchmaking" services.

The new industrial policy for the automobile industry was not an unqualified success, however. Many difficulties ensued because the state had been unable to prevail on key issues in the bargaining. The failure to require Mexicanization of the terminal industry allowed the TNCs to retain important powers, which they used in opposition to policies of the state. The failure to limit the number of firms made it harder to mold an efficient industry. The problems created by the new structure of ownership and of the market are the subject of the next chapter.

·6·

THE CONSEQUENCES OF IMPORT
SUBSTITUTION

The initial intention of the López Mateos government was to create a fully Mexicanized auto industry—majority Mexican equity in both the terminal and supplier firms. Faced with the resistance of the two major wholly foreign-owned TNC subsidiaries, Ford and GM, and the likely disapproval of the U.S. government, the state managers dropped their proposal for Mexicanization of the terminal firms in the final version of the 1962 decree; only the supplier industry was required to be majority Mexican owned. Concerned to protect the firms with Mexican capital, the state managers instituted a policy of production quotas for each terminal firm. These quotas, not mentioned in the 1962 decree itself, had a precedent in the "assembly quotas" that had been in force before 1962. They had been designed to control the industry's level of imports for balance-of-payments purposes, but after 1962 they were put to different purposes: limiting the market power of the biggest firms and guaranteeing a minimum market share for the firms with Mexican capital, whose more restricted connections with the major TNCs would put them at a disadvantage.

Denationalization of the Terminal Industry

When the 1962 decree was promulgated, a dozen firms were assembling motor vehicles in Mexico, and it was from among these assembly operations that most of the firms approved to manufacture were drawn (table 6.1). Ford and GM, the original assemblers in Mexico (established in 1925 and 1935, respectively), were approved to manufacture automobiles as wholly foreign-owned firms (and International Harvester, also foreign-owned, was approved to manufacture trucks only). Seven other approved firms were wholly or majority Mexican-owned: DINA, Fábricas Auto-Mex, Impulsora Mexicana Automotriz, Promexa, Reo, Representaciones Delta, and VAM. The ownership situation soon changed dramatically, however. Ownership of the completely foreign-owned firms went unchanged, as did ownership of the only completely state-owned firm, DINA, but ownership in every firm with some degree of private local capital underwent a change. Three of these firms ceased operations and three sold a substantial portion of equity to the transnational firm with which they were affiliated (see table 6.2). In addition, one more foreign-owned firm, Nissan, was approved in 1964. Thus, the industry shifted from one in which there were nine firms, of which only two were wholly foreign-owned, to one in which there were seven firms, of which five were wholly foreign-owned. The only surviving majority Mexican-owned firms were ones in which the state was the majority shareholder. Private Mexican capital was completely driven out of the terminal industry.

This denationalization process was not simply a matter of the TNCS using their market power to force out national firms. Government

TABLE 6.1

STATUS OF PRE-DECREE ASSEMBLY PLANTS IN MEXICO AFTER 1962

Firm and Date of Formation	MODELS ASSEMBLED IN 1962		Site of Assembly Operation	Status after 1962 Decree
	Cars	Trucks		
Ford Motor Co. (1925)	Ford, Falcon, Taunus	Ford	Federal District	Approved
GM de México (1935)	Chevrolet, Pontiac, Corvair, Opel	Chevrolet, GM	Federal District	Approved
Automotriz O'Farrill (1937)	Hillman-Minx	(None)	Puebla	a
Fábricas Auto-Mex (1938)	Dodge, Plymouth, Valiant	Dodge, Fargo	Federal District	Approved
International Harvester (1944)	(None)	IH	Saltillo	Approved
Willys Mexicana (1946)	Rambler	(None)	Federal District	Approved
Automóviles Ingleses (1946)	Morris, MG	BMC	Xalostoc	a
Diesel Nacional (1951)	Renault	Diamond T	Ciudad Sahagun	Approved
Studebaker-Packard (1951/1953)	Lark	Studebaker	Tlalnepantla	b
Representaciones Delta (1955)	Auto Union, Mercedes-Benz, DKW	(None)	Federal District	Approved
Planta Reo de México (1955)	Toyopet	Toyota	Monterrey	Approved

SOURCE: Adapted from Edelberg, "Procurement Practices of Mexican Affiliates," p. 67
a Acquired by Promexa (Volkswagen), whose application was approved.
b Acquired by Ford.

policy also played a role. The efforts of the state to preserve Mexican equity proved far more successful in the auto-parts industry, however, than in the terminal industry.[1]

The Collapse of Reo

Planta Reo de México started as a Monterrey assembly operation under the direction of Hector Cortés. Until 1958, the plant assembled Ramblers, but in 1960 it entered the market with the Toyopet, a Toyota general-purpose vehicle. A Reo line of trucks was also produced. Be-

TABLE 6.2

OWNERSHIP CHANGE IN THE MEXICAN AUTOMOBILE INDUSTRY, 1962-1970

Firm	Ownership Status, 1962	Ownership Change, 1962-1970
Ford	100% foreign	(None)
General Motors	100% foreign	(None)
Fábricas Auto-Mex	33% foreign, 67% domestic	Chrysler increased equity to 45% (1968)
Diesel Nacional	100% domestic (state-owned)	(None)
Planta Reo de México	100% domestic	Ceased operations (1963)
Representaciones Delta	100% domestic	Ceased operations (1964)
Impulsora Mexicana Automotriz[a]	100% domestic	Ceased operations (1969)
Promexa[b]	100% domestic	100% equity sold to Volkswagen (1963)
Vehículos Automotores Mexicanos (Willys)	100% domestic	40% equity sold to American Motors, 60% acquired by Mexican government (1963)
Nissan Mexicana	100% foreign[c]	(None)

SOURCES: See text
[a] Renamed Fábrica Nacional de Automóviles in 1963.
[b] Renamed Volkswagen de México in 1963.
[c] Established in 1964.

[1] There have been very few sector-specific studies of denationalization or more broadly of changes in ownership patterns in developing countries. For a suggestive discussion of denationalization in the Brazilian pharmaceutical industry, see Peter Evans, "Foreign Investment and Industrial Transformation: A Brazilian Case Study," *Journal of Development Economics* 3 (1976):119-139. For a study of a portion of the same industry in Mexico that is particularly instructive on the failure of the state to prevent denationalization, see Gereffi, "Drug Firms and Dependency." For a discussion of denationalization in the Latin American motor vehicle industry, see Jenkins, *Dependent Industrialization*. Jenkins, however, fails to see the full extent of denationalization in the Mexican automobile industry, perhaps because much of it happened so quickly after the 1962 decree.

fore the 1962 decree, and even in the first few months following it, Reo looked like a capable and vigorous contender for a segment of the Mexican market.[2]

The firm's application to manufacture Toyota automobiles under the terms of the 1962 decree was approved on January 9, 1963,[3] but the operation was virtually stillborn: less than six months later, Cortés was under arrest and the manufacturing plans were in shambles. Cortés had had interests in a Monterrey *financiera*, Impulsora Monterrey S.A., and he used this banking institution as a ready source of capital for the investments needed to transform Reo from an assembly operation to a manufacturing plant. He used the bank's resources a bit too readily, however, and there came a day when the bank could not cover the claims for interest payments, withdrawals, and the like. There were complaints to the National Banking Commission, an investigation, and finally the arrest of six men. Cortés was convicted and served a prison sentence.[4]

The Collapse of Representaciones Delta

Representaciones Delta had been assembling the Mercedes-Benz and the Auto Union-DKW in the years before the decree. The firm was owned and operated by members of the Abed family. Officials of the government were particularly eager that the Mercedes be manufactured in Mexico, President López Mateos himself was known to have a decided fondness for the car. Before the final decree was promulgated, there apparently were conversations between government of-

[2] Aside from DINA-Renault, Reo was the only firm selling non-American cars with an assembly operation of any appreciable size. For other indications of Cortés's serious intentions, see *Auto noticias*, Jan. 17, 1961, where it is announced that Reo had just signed an agreement with Toyota to make auto bodies in Mexico, and an interview with Cortés, "Meta: Precios internacionales," *Auto noticias*, Feb. 23, 1963.

[3] *Comercio exterior*, Jan. 1963, p. 28. *Auto noticias*, Jan. 12, 1963, gives the date as Jan. 7. The notice in *Comercio exterior* said that among the factors leading to the approval, "in addition to the adequacy of the plans and proposals of this firm, was the consideration that it had already made considerable investments in the purchase of Japanese machinery for the fabrication of monoblocs and other parts for vehicles of this make, as well as the advantageousness of strengthening commercial relations with Japan—the country where the parent of this make is located—whose balance [of trade] has persistently been in Mexico's favor."

[4] Immediately after the arrest, *Auto noticias* reported the incident as follows, trying to put the best possible face on it: "It should be said that, according to information we have obtained, it is not a matter of fraud, as the press has tried to pass off this painful incident, but simply a violation of certain banking regulations." *Auto noticias*, July 13, 1963.

ficials and Daimler-Benz, the German company that manufactures Mercedes, in which the firm clearly indicated that it was not interested.

The application of Representaciones Delta to manufacture under the terms of the decree included plans to produce both the Mercedes-Benz and the DKW (which was also controlled by Daimler-Benz), even though the Abeds did not have the approval of the parent company to manufacture the Mercedes. "We have almost won over the Germans," they told SIC officials at one point, explaining that all they needed was approval of their import application and of the necessary quotas for parts, machinery, etc. The application hung fire for several months and was not approved until well after the first eight had been approved.[5]

That Delta's application was finally approved (some government officials of the time prefer to remember otherwise) was probably due in part to the desire of government officials to explore fully every possibility of having the Mercedes manufactured in Mexico, but it was almost certainly due as well to a "special friendship" that the Abeds had with President López Mateos. "The whole affair," one official of the period said in an interview, "was the kind of business arrangement of people who wanted to take advantage of a friendship with the president and make a lot of money." The Abeds were given approval to manufacture DKWs, and the hope apparently, was that Delta would do well enough with the DKWs to induce Daimler-Benz to give the go-ahead for Mercedes production. To facilitate this, Delta was given a special quota to continue importing Mercedes into Mexico.

A plant to make DKW engines was opened in León, Guanajuato, with great fanfare by President López Mateos in late October 1964, with a representative of Daimler-Benz looking on.[6] Things never got much further than that, however, for the firm was incapable of complying with the terms of the decree. It simply lacked the technical and managerial know-how to manufacture an automobile; even its pre-decree

[5] Despite this, the Abeds continued to talk quite confidently of being approved, and they even took out paid advertisements in the newspapers to that effect. This was too much for *Auto noticias*, which ran an article entitled "El caso insólito de Delta Motors" (The unusual case of Delta Motors) on Jan. 12, 1963. Apparently, this was the first time that Delta officials had said more than the facts warranted. In its issue of July 15, 1961, *Auto noticias* had editorialized against an unnamed firm for promising more than it could deliver and for using "Lagunilla" tactics (Lagunilla is the name of Mexico City's thieves' market, a place of vastly exaggerated claims). The reference was surely to Delta; see *Comercio exterior*, Sept. 1962, p. 596.

[6] See "Inaugura el C. presidente de la república Lic. Adolfo López Mateos la planta de Representaciones Delta S.A.—DKW en la ciudad de León, Guanajuato," special supplement of *Auto noticias*, Nov. 1964.

"assembly plant" had been little more than a glorified garage. Auto Union was willing to sell machinery and parts and furnish technical assistance to the firm, but it would not become more deeply involved than that. As Delta's incapacity (and false assurances) came to light, SIC began to rescind its import permits, and it finally gave the company terminal quotas to close up the operation.

The Collapse of Borgward

In its first incarnation, the Borgward was a German automobile manufactured in Bremen that, finding itself unable to compete in the increasingly severe competition among Western European makers, closed its doors in mid-1961. Later in that same year, the Borgward appeared on a list, published by SIC in anticipation of the 1962 decree, of those automobiles whose importation would no longer be allowed into Mexico.[7]

That the Borgward had a second, Mexican life, was largely due to the efforts of a politically well-connected entrepreneur named Ernesto Santos Galindo. His original intentions are somewhat cloudy, but in one early move he arranged for DINA and VAM officials to visit Germany to inspect the plant and its machinery, apparently hoping to act as mediator in the sale of the equipment. Neither company was interested, however, and no sale came about. Instead, in July 1962 about half the machinery, especially that appropriate for truck manufacture, was purchased by Barreiros, a Spanish truck firm, and Santos Galindo, together with a group of other Mexicans, bought the rest. The purchase price, according to one source who claims to have seen the actual documents, was 39.32 million pesos, but soon afterward, the machinery was revalued at 190 million pesos by the accounting firm of Coopers and Lybrand.[8]

Santos Galindo established a company, Impulsora Mexicana Automotriz—the name was later changed to Fábrica Nacional de Automóviles S.A., or FANASA—with himself as president and Gregorio Ramírez, an industrialist already deeply involved in a number of automobile-related firms, as vice-president.[9] The application of Im-

[7] *Comercio exterior*, Dec. 1961, p. 725.

[8] Victor Manuel Villaseñor, *Memorias de un hombre de izquierda* (Mexico City: Editorial Grijalbo, 1976), 2:350. According to a letter quoted by Villaseñor, the revaluation was accomplished on the basis of information provided by Santos Galindo rather than on the basis of any actual inspection of the assets. Other sources confirm in virtually all respects the details given by Villaseñor.

[9] Principal among Ramírez's holdings at this time were Trailers de Monterrey, which made trucks and buses, and Industria Automotriz S.A., which manufactured wheels and rims.

pulsora Automotriz was opposed by DINA and VAM (whose officials having seen the Borgward machinery and parts, could argue that the firm could only produce an obsolete automobile), and some SIC officials were skeptical of the firm's technical and financial viability, but it was awkward to reject such a patriotic venture—a wholly Mexican automobile. López Mateos apparently made it clear to SIC officials that the application was to be accepted, whatever defects it might have.[10]

The start of production, in a plant in Monterrey, was announced for late 1964, then for early 1965, then postponed and postponed again. Troubles had arisen, and they mainly had to be dealt with by Ramírez, to whom Santos Galindo sold most of the stock in the firm. One of the problems was financing. Ramírez had paid a highly inflated price to Santos Galindo and his friends for the original machinery, parts, and plans. Setting up the plant was also a considerable expense, and difficulties in obtaining the necessary parts exacerbated the problem. To keep going, Ramírez borrowed heavily from SOMEX, a development bank that the government had taken over in the early 1960s. The SOMEX loans, eventually totaling about 200 million pesos, were guaranteed by the Ministry of Finance (involving almost certainly the approval of the minister, Ortiz Mena, and the knowledge of the president), and they developed a certain self-perpetuating logic. Once SOMEX had extended substantial credit, there was no possibility of repayment until the firm began selling cars; so SOMEX would lend more to ensure that the firm could begin production.[11]

Finally, in August 1967, assembly of cars was begun at the Borgward plant, an odd pastiche of modern and pre–World War II machinery. Within two years, after turning out 1,884 cars, the firm had failed.[12] In addition to his other problems, Ramírez had made a mistake in

[10] A number of accounts give a role to Ernesto Uruchurtu, then mayor of the Federal District, who apparently intervened on behalf of the application with the president. Indeed, some observers believe that Santos Galindo was merely a front man for Uruchurtu.

[11] In order to maintain enough appearance of solvency to continue receiving loans, Ramírez needed to show that his assets were roughly in line with his accumulated liabilities. He seems to have accomplished this on more than one occasion simply by revaluing his assets. Once, for example, he had the blueprints separately appraised at 40 million pesos. By 1968, the equipment purchased six years before for less than 40 million pesos was being valued in the firm's books at 243 million pesos. Villaseñor, *Memorias*, 2:350. Assessments made after the firm had collapsed put the value of FANASA's total assets at between 50 and 100 million pesos (though no value was placed on the blueprints and spare parts); its liabilities at the end totaled over 40 million pesos.

[12] Villaseñor, *Memorias*, 2:351. Figures given by the Asociación Mexicana de la Industria Automotriz indicate that 2,613 Borgwards were sold between 1967 and 1970: AMIA, *La industria automotriz de México en cifras* (Mexico City: AMIA, 1972), p. 52. The difference in the figures most likely lies in the failure of Villaseñor's total to include Borgwards produced after FANASA had been taken over by SOMEX.

selecting the model on which to concentrate. He picked the most expensive one of the Borgward line, hoping to capture the market that Mercedes imports had once held—but Mercedes had never sold more than 3,000 vehicles in any one year. The cost of production of each Borgward was around 100,000 pesos, but they were sold to dealers for 44,000 pesos and to the public for 55,000 pesos. (The joke was told that Ramírez and a friend passed by a Borgward distributor and the friend admired the car in the showcase window; Ramírez, so the joke went, told him he'd sell him the car at cost, but the friend said no, he could get it cheaper from the dealer.) Ramírez abandoned the firm to SOMEX, his creditor, in return for a note absolving him of any further debt. DINA took over the operation, a subsidiary called DINA-MAN occupying the assembly plant, and a joint venture called DINA-Rockwell the machining plant.

The Takeover of Promexa by Volkswagen

When Volkswagens were first sold in Mexico in the 1950s, they were imported as wholly assembled vehicles. Distribution was handled by a firm called VW Interamericana, but this company had responsibilities for areas of the Caribbean and Central America as well. In January 1961, a separate firm, Promexa S.A., was set up to handle sales to the Mexican market. The principal shareholders in this new firm were Edmundo Krause, the moving force behind VW Interamericana, and Edmundo Stierle and Rómulo O'Farrill, two pioneers in vehicle assembly in Mexico, having interests between them in Automotriz O'Farrill, Automóviles Ingleses, and (previously) Studebaker-Packard. Immediately preceding the 1962 decree, Promexa seems to have arranged for Volkswagens to be assembled at the Automóviles Ingleses plant in Xalostoc, Estado de México.

Promexa submitted an application to manufacture Volkswagens under the terms of the decree. The application was one of the first six approved. In an interview immediately after the application was submitted, Promexa's general manager affirmed that the company had all the necessary licenses from the German firm to comply fully with the decree.[13] The firm bought out two pre-decree assembly plants, that of Autómoviles Ingleses in Xalostoc and that of Automotriz O'Farrill in Puebla, and began preparing for manufacturing operations. What happened over the course of the next year is not very clear; not much was

[13] *Auto noticias*, Sept. 1, 1962. For more details on Promexa's plans at this point, see *Auto noticias*, Sept. 29, 1962, and *Comercio exterior*, Oct. 1962, p. 671.

heard of Promexa between January 1963 and January 1964.[14] Then, in mid-January 1964, it was announced that Volkswagen AG, the German-based TNC, had purchased Promexa, and with this seems to have come a great acceleration of activity. The group running Promexa had apparently discovered that it did not have the wherewithal to carry through on its plans. At the same time, Volkswagen seems to have studied the situation more carefully than it had previously and was attracted by the possibilities it saw, but wanted full control of the firm.[15] The government evidently raised no objections to the takeover, even viewing the import-application approval as passing automatically to the new owners.

The Sale of VAM Equity

Willys Mexicana was created in 1946 and began by importing assembled Jeeps. Starting in 1949, it imported semi-knocked down kits, but because it lacked its own assembly plant, it paid other assemblers to put the kits together. In 1953, the company built its own plant and after that date assembled not only its own vehicles but also a variety of other makes. Around 1960, it began assembling American Motors cars as well. Later, it changed its name to Vehículos Automores Mexicanos S.A. (VAM).

VAM was at that time a wholly Mexican-owned corporation, with about 98 percent of its stock being held by SOMEX, then still a private industrial development bank. VAM's application to manufacture American Motors and Willys vehicles under the 1962 decree was one of the first six approved. Not only was its application backed by SOMEX, but since it was one of the largest assembly operations, the denial of its application would have had serious repercussions on employment. Nevertheless, after its application had been approved, two changes transformed its ownership status.

First, about 40 percent of the shares in VAM were sold to American Motors and to Kaiser Industries, which had acquired Willys. Officials of VAM did not want to be dependent on American firms for parts, product development, and technology unless those firms were sharing some measure of risk. Subsequently, Willys was sold to American Motors, which thus came to own all of the 40 percent of VAM that was in foreign hands.

---

[14] In an article reviewing the progress of the terminal firms toward complying with the decree (60 percent integration had to be achieved by Dec. 1964), *Auto noticias* (Jan. 4, 1964) reported that little was known of Promexa or its progress.

[15] *Auto noticias*, Jan. 25, 1964.

Second, SOMEX, dangerously overextended, was taken over by the Mexican government in 1963 (see below). VAM, which had started out as a wholly Mexican, privately owned firm, had become a joint venture of the Mexican state and an American corporation.

The Sale of Auto-Mex Equity

By the late 1950s, direction of Fábricas Auto-Mex had passed from the founder to his son, Gaston Azcárraga Tamayo. Even though the firm was virtually wholly owned by the Azcárraga family, the involvement of Chrysler in its management was very substantial. Chrysler seemed to want to keep close tabs on its licensee, one of its largest foreign operations, and the Azcárragas seemed not to want to entrust the direction of the firm entirely to Mexican management.

A change in Chrysler's global strategy toward the end of the 1950s led to a change in Auto-Mex's ownership status. In a sharp reversal of its strategy, Chrysler decided it needed to make direct foreign investments in order to survive in the increasingly stiff international competition. It therefore acquired a minority position in Simca, a French firm, in 1958, making it possible for Auto-Mex to introduce Simcas into the Mexican market the next year; and in 1964 Chrysler bought minority equity in Rootes, a British company. Later, it took over majority control of both.

Immediately following its decision to change strategy, Chrysler approached Fábricas Auto-Mex with an offer to buy out the Azcárraga family holdings. The Azcárragas refused several Chrysler offers but finally sold a one-third share in the firm to Chrysler. The Chrysler offer may have been financially irresistible or perhaps, given the degree of Auto-Mex's dependence on Chrysler for technology and CKD kits, the Azcárragas feared the consequences of an outright refusal. In any case, the sale proved to be only the first step in Auto-Mex's denationalization.

When the auto decree was issued in 1962, Fábricas Auto-Mex had one of the highest market shares in the industry, nearly 18 percent. In 1965, it moved into the top position, with more than 29 percent, and it was first or second in market share in each ensuing year of the decade. Clearly the firm did not suffer from any inability to produce or to sell automobiles. But it—and Azcárraga—did have financial problems. The firm had been listed on the Mexican Stock Exchange in 1959, the year of the sale of equity to Chrysler, and it thus became the only terminal firm with publicly available financial data. Its balance sheets showed earnings equivalent to well over $3 million in each of

1964, 1965, and 1966, but less than a third of that in 1967. In 1970, Auto-Mex lost over $5 million, and even more than that in the next two years (see table 6.3).

The key to Auto-Mex's financial difficulties lay in the nature of its relationship to Chrysler. While other auto companies treated their subsidiaries as branches of their U.S. or global operations, Chrysler regarded Auto-Mex as an independent firm. Chrysler expected to make profits on its sales of parts and technology to Auto-Mex that were higher than what Ford, for example, expected to make on sales to its subsidiary. The logic was clear: the earnings of the Ford subsidiary were part of Ford's global earnings, but the earnings of Auto-Mex went mostly to Azcárraga. Chrysler had to look for its returns through other channels. Consequently, Auto-Mex's cost structure was higher than Ford's or GM's, yet it could not charge more for its products or it would surely lose sales. The resulting squeeze ultimately put Auto-Mex in the red.

At the same time, Auto-Mex was driven into increasing indebtedness to Chrysler. According to data compiled by Jenkins, "In 1968 it had short-term debts to Chrysler of over 260 million pesos and in 1969 of 350 million pesos. In 1969, too, it contracted a long-term debt of 73 million pesos, which rose to a further 191 million in 1970."[16] Finally, Azcárraga felt he had no choice but to sell out to Chrysler altogether.

TABLE 6.3

ASPECTS OF THE OPERATIONS OF FÁBRICAS AUTO-MEX, 1963-1972

	1963	1964	1965	1966	1967
Number of vehicles sold	17,286	20,115	27,859	26,044	29,304
Number of employees	1,545	2,134	2,233	3,984	4,261
Sales (millions of pesos)	587	832	1,067	1,189	1,298
Earnings (losses) (millions of pesos)	29.9	45.9	46.6	41.9	15.5

	1968	1969	1970	1971	1972
Number of vehicles sold	29,197	35,542	38,703	35,326	40,102
Number of employees	4,261	5,123	4,527	4,011	3,982
Sales (millions of pesos)	1,417	1,565	1,828	1,599	1,763
Earnings (losses) (millions of pesos)	23.9	15.9	(64.8)	(117.4)	(91.3)

SOURCE: *Expansión*, May 16, 1973, p. 27
NOTE: Figures are for fiscal year ending Sept. 30.

[16] Jenkins, *Dependent Industrialization*, p. 167.

Before doing so, he did explore, nearly to the point of success, a possibility that would have kept the firm in Mexican hands; but those events form part of a larger story which must wait until chapter 7.

THE CAUSES OF DENATIONALIZATION

What has become apparent in this examination is the competitive inadequacy of the domestically owned firms when faced with the superior market power that total foreign ownership afforded the TNC subsidiaries. First, the subsidiaries had a ready source for the importation of those component parts not required to be manufactured in Mexico, as well as for the machinery for domestic manufacture. Second, as subsidiaries of large companies they benefited from the economies of scale that their parent firms enjoyed because of their position in the world auto industry, and they had access to the most modern technology. Third, they had the benefit of sophisticated administrative techniques in such areas as inventory control and personnel management. Fourth, they had superior access to financing. If capital was not available from their parent firms, they could borrow more readily, even in local capital markets, because they had the backing of a major corporation. And finally, they enjoyed all of these advantages upon the most favorable terms. The denationalization of the Mexican automobile industry took place largely because the domestically owned firms could not compete against such privileged positions.

The Mexican state did seek to prevent the decline of Mexican capital in the terminal industry. It tried to use the production quotas to countervail the superior market power of the TNCs and to assure local firms a minimum market share, but those were not the critical problems of the Mexican firms. The structure of ownership in the industry put the local firms at a disadvantage well before adequate sales volume became a concern; higher costs for imported components, obstacles to obtaining adequate financing, and lack of access to advanced technology could not be compensated for by a guarantee of minimum market share.[17]

---

[17] It should also be noted that the *rapidity* of the denationalization was in part the unintended consequence of another element of government policy: a requirement that the firms be in compliance with the 1962 decree by Nov. 1964, only twenty-seven months after it was issued. The TNCs could reach 60 percent domestic integration much more easily than the domestically owned firms: they had the experience and resources to win approval of their plans quickly, secure financing, order machinery, build new plant facilities, hire and train workers, develop quality-control procedures, and arrange for manufacture of components by supplier firms. Why was there such pressure for speedy

This analysis seems to confirm the hypothesis that TNCs pre-empt the development of an indigenous economic base by squeezing out local entrepreneurs in the most dynamic sectors. One might be tempted to conclude that TNCs are inherently more able to survive and better able to compete than national firms, at least in capital-intensive, high-technology, globally integrated industries like the manufacture of automobiles. However, an important caveat must be added: this conclusion is true only under certain structural conditions. Given the pattern of ownership that existed in 1962, with two wholly owned foreign firms approved to manufacture and with the competitive advantages they enjoyed, a structural bias was introduced that made denationalization almost inevitable. But this structure was not itself inevitable; the Mexican government might have created another pattern of ownership when it moved to create a manufacturing industry in 1962. It could have built into the structure a guarantee against denationalization and could have put at least some of the firms on a more equal footing. The effects of a different structure of ownership can be seen most clearly by looking at the different policy followed toward the parts-supply industry.

Preservation of Mexican Capital in the Supplier Industry

The 1962 auto decree forbade firms in the terminal industry to engage in the manufacture of parts, except for the machining of motors and the production of parts they had been making before 1962.[18] Moreover, in firms established to manufacture parts, foreign capital was not to exceed 40 percent of equity.[19] There was comparatively little opposition to this scheme, and that was a key to its success. The exclusion

---

compliance? The López Mateos administration was to leave office on Dec. 1, 1964. In Mexico, one concomitant of the practice of sexenial change (barring the reelection of a president after one term) is a norm that policies are carried to fruition—and taken credit for—by the administration that adopts them. In 1964, there was an extensive round of automobile plant openings, presided over by the president and well-publicized by the press.

[18] GM, for example, had been manufacturing springs, batteries, and spark plugs.

[19] Although Mexicanization of the supplier industry was not mentioned in the decree, it was clearly an aim of the state managers. It was made explicit by the minister of industry and commerce, Salinas Lozano, when he said, "Because this sector was unquestionably the one of greater dynamism and of greater social and economic consequence, and because investments were greater in it than in the terminal industry, it has been considered advisable to maintain a firm and unbreakable aim that its development be for the benefit of national investors and entrepreneurs." *Comercio exterior*, Aug. 1964, p. 548.

of the terminal firms from parts manufacture was not favored by the major firms, but neither was it strongly opposed. They would not be forced to give up their existing investments in parts manufacture (which were quite minimal, anyway); they were already accustomed to purchasing many of their components from independent parts suppliers in their home countries (Ford and Chrysler somewhat more so than GM); many of the most important parts whose production they wanted to control (especially body stampings) could be included in the 40 percent imported content allowed to them; and they were able to obtain from state officials a few significant concessions on other important parts that were to be locally made (for example, Ford, GM, and Volkswagen were granted permission to forge their own engine blocks).

Furthermore, in the parts industry there were very few entrenched subsidiaries of TNCs to offer opposition to Mexicanization, and the state was in a strong bargaining position vis-à-vis those seeking entry. With the terminal industry bound to 60 percent local content, there would be a guaranteed market for those transnational parts-supply firms who entered (many of them the traditional suppliers of the TNCs in the terminal industry in their home countries), and the Mexican state could offer a share of this market on its terms to those who wanted in. Transnational supplier firms accepted minority equity as better than no equity at all. From the very beginning, then, the state was able to create a pattern of ownership in the supplier industry that assured a stable role for Mexican capital.

The success of state policy in the parts-supply industry can be best explained by examining a few specific cases that illustrate how the state, the TNCs, and national capital worked together in this sector. Two distinct types of parts firms emerged. Type I consisted of a few large firms manufacturing major components. Some of them were subsidies of transnational parts producers, but with majority equity being held by one or another of Mexico's major investment groups, and they were typically monopoly suppliers of the parts they made. Type II consisted of a very large number of smaller firms manufacturing simpler, cheaper components. They were usually wholly Mexican-owned and operated in competitive product lines, generally with a technology license from a foreign manufacturer. The pattern of sponsorship also differed between the two types of firms. In Type I, a terminal manufacturer often played matchmaker between a transnational parts maker and a Mexican investment group, though in a number of cases the government helped locate or convince the Mexican investors that participated in the joint venture. In Type II, the terminal firms discouraged some potential parts makers but helped others by providing them with technology licenses and with teams of engineers to advise and assist in setting up manufacturing operations. Ford played a leading role in both types: it was the most active terminal firm in the matchmaking that created Type I firms, and it was aggressive in setting acceptable standards of price, quality, and timely delivery for the Type II firms.

Type I Firms

Transmisiones y Equipos Mecánicos (TREMEC). Even before the 1962 decree was issued, Ford had been searching for an American company that would be willing to undertake the manufacture of transmissions in Mexico. Clark Equipment, one of Ford's U.S. suppliers, finally agreed. Edgar Molina, the manager of Ford's Mexican subsidiary, found a Mexican partner in Bernardo Quintana, head of a company called Civil Engineer Associates (Ingenieros Civiles Asociados, or ICA). Quintana's brother Carlos had headed the group that wrote the 1960 NAFIN report, and Bernardo was a childhood friend of SIC Minister Salinas Lozano, who probably was responsible for introducing him to Molina. ICA was principally involved at the time in the construction industry (it later built Mexico City's Metro), but it was interested in opportunities to diversify into manufacturing. Discussions were initiated among Clark, ICA, and Banco Nacional de México, one of Mexico's two major banking complexes. Banco Nacional seemed inclined to try to dominate the venture, however, and so the other partners initiated a search for a different source of financing. The American and Foreign Power Company proved the ideal candidate.

American and Foreign Power had been one of two major foreign-owned electric-power companies in Mexico until it was pressured by the López Mateos government to sell its holdings to the Mexican government in 1960. In this and other key infrastructure sectors, the government's policy with respect to foreign investment was one of nationalization with compensation. The settlement made with American and Foreign Power was a handsome one, but it included a stipulation that the company reinvest in other projects in Mexico. The Clark-ICA proposal made an attractive investment. A letter of intent was signed in April 1964, and TREMEC produced its first transmission (though one that was merely assembled from imported parts) a few days before the end of the year.[20]

---

[20] It is unclear who brought American and Foreign Power into the arrangement, but most likely it was again Salinas Lozano; as minister of industry and commerce, he also

There would be room in Mexico for only one manufacturer of transmissions if an efficient scale of production were to be obtained. The Mexican government indicated that it would provide tax benefits and other stimuli to only one such firm. Ford had not consulted with the other terminal firms, however, in setting up TREMEC. As one of its executives said, "we just took the ball and ran." Later, arrangements were made for TREMEC to supply all four American terminal firms operating in Mexico. Adjustments were made so that certain standard-size transmissions would fit the vehicles of each manufacturer. Since Clark supplied transmissions principally to Ford in the United States, it was primarily the other firms that had to make adjustments; that was one benefit to Ford of its matchmaking activities. TREMEC did not, and could not, rely solely on Clark technology, however. It had to supply a full line of transmissions, for vehicles ranging from compacts to light trucks. Licensing agreements were signed with Borg-Warner and New Process as well as with Clark, and once the marriage had been made, GM joined Ford in providing technical assistance. TREMEC became the largest manufacturer of auto parts in Mexico.

Spicer S.A. Ford was also involved in the matchmaking that produced Spicer S.A., which became Mexico's second largest maker of auto parts. It was a joint venture of two existing Mexican firms, both of them associated with U.S. manufacturers. One was a subsidiary of the Dana Corporation, a diversified manufacturing company which produced a broad range of auto parts, including axles. The Mexican subsidiary of Dana was rather small and was not involved in axle manufacture. The other firm was a partnership between Perfect Circle S.A. and a powerful, growing Mexican group headed by Manuel Senderos and Carlos Trouyet. Perfect Circle made piston rings for the replacement market, and soon after the 1962 decree appeared, it announced plans to manufacture original-equipment piston rings and engine heads.

This plan was pre-empted by another, more ambitious one. Ford's Molina proposed that Dana, Perfect Circle, and the Senderos-Trouyet group form a company to manufacture automobile axles. Dana would provide the technology, the Perfect Circle subsidiary's piston-ring operation would provide the basic foundry capability, and Senderos-Trouyet would provide majority Mexican capital. Agreement was reached among the partners, and Spicer was born.[21]

---

served as chairman of the board of directors of the Federal Electricity Commission, the entity that had bought out the company. On the buy-out itself, see Wionczek, *Nacionalismo mexicano*, pp. 33-168.

[21] Spicer was only one of a number of important joint ventures in which the Senderos-

Eaton S.A. Other large, transnationally linked auto-parts firms were launched in Mexico with less mediation. The Eaton Corporation, for example, established a Mexican subsidiary in 1964 to manufacture truck axles without the participation of any major Mexican economic group. It was encouraged to set up an operation in Mexico by its habitual customers in the United States: Ford, GM, Chrysler, and International Harvester. Eaton studied the matter and decided to invest but to achieve Mexicanization by selling shares on the stock exchange. This enabled Eaton to maintain managerial control over the subsidiary by diffusing the majority Mexican ownership. This has not prevented some concentrated holding—one as large as 15 percent of the shares of stock—but through a series of informal agreements bolstered by legal rules concerning decisions of the board of directors, Eaton has maintained management control. By contrast, the Mexican shareholders are much more firmly in control of TREMEC and Spicer.

Wholly Mexican-Owned Firms. Two sizeable Type I firms emerged that were wholly Mexican-owned—Motores y Refacciones S.A. (MORESA) and Industria Automotriz S.A. Both are examples of Mexican-owned firms that originated before the 1962 decree and that successfully made the conversion from replacement to original-equipment manufacture. MORESA was founded after World War II to rebuild engines. In 1956, it began manufacturing pistons, at first to supply its own needs but later for the replacement market as well. In 1961, it sold off the engine-rebuilding operation to concentrate on piston manufacture. Approached by the terminal firms soon after the 1962 decree, MORESA moved into original-equipment manufacture, selling its first piston to a terminal firm in September 1964. At about the same time, it added valves and piston pins to its product line. MORESA had signed a technology agreement with Sterling Aluminum Products, the largest independent U.S. piston manufacturer, when it first began producing pistons. After the decree, it received technical assistance from several terminal firms in making the conversion from replacement to original-equipment manufacture. In particular, Ford helped in quality control, in tooling, and in dealing with various problems. It helped to get delivery on a crucial machine in five months instead of the eighteen

---

Trouyet group became involved through the opportunity provided by Mexicanization policy; Monsanto, B. F. Goodrich, Hercules, and Phillips Petroleum were other transnational firms with Mexican subsidiaries in which the group had significant holdings. Spicer was the first point of corporate contact between Dana and Perfect Circle. A few years later, however, the Mexican marriage was replicated in the U.S., as Dana acquired Perfect Circle.

months that normally would have been needed; and when this machine required repairs a month and a half after installation, Ford saw to it that the necessary parts were flown in and installed over a long weekend. Subsequently, MORESA developed its own technology; the Sterling license has been allowed to expire, and MORESA has been seeking to license its own technology. However, when MORESA began manufacturing pistons for Volkswagen, several years after the 1962 decree, Volkswagen insisted that the company take out a license with Malle, a German piston manufacturer. MORESA also holds several technical licenses for its other products.

Industria Automotriz was started in 1957 by Gregorio Ramírez, a Monterrey industrialist with a long history in the motor-vehicle industry. He founded Trailers de Monterrey, a bus and heavy-truck firm, after World War II, and he captained the ill-fated FANASA in the 1960s. Industria Automotriz originally made seats and springs. In 1960, with technology agreements from Budd and Goodyear, but apparently with no expectation of the decree that was soon to follow, it moved into the manufacture of rims and wheels as well. Subsequently, it has added some original-equipment and replacement stamped body parts. As with the other firms in the Grupo Ramírez, there is no foreign equity holding in Industria Automotriz.

Type II Firms

The terminal firms could count the parts they made themselves and the components they bought from the Type I firms toward their required local content, but they needed parts from the Type II firms as well if they were to reach 60 percent. Again led by Ford, they worked hard to bring these firms into being, but their efforts with these smaller firms tended to entail technical advice and assistance more than participation in organization. Ford set up several teams of "source development engineers," staffed by U.S. technicians, whose function was to help Ford's parts suppliers initiate and improve production.

As one example, a manufacturer of mufflers was visited by a Ford team, which saw a worker welding baffles on a crude bench fashioned from an oil drum. The owner was urged to purchase a proper welding bench; when he remonstrated that he lacked the necessary capital, the Ford engineers suggested he at least fill the barrel with sand. In the normal case, the assistance was more substantial: the candidate supplier firm would be advised on the manufacturing process to be employed, the selection and purchasing of machinery, the set-up of the shop floor, procedures for quality control, and the like. Sometimes Ford or GM would use its business contacts in the United States to speed up the delivery of a critical piece of machinery. Often a parts firm would be encouraged to seek a technology license from (if not a joint venture with) a transnational parts supplier. One small firm that had been manufacturing a variety of simple, stamped parts for the replacement market decided after the decree to concentrate on fan assemblies for original equipment. Ford encouraged the owner to form a joint venture with a U.S. fan manufacturer. Sporadic discussions were held for several years after the decree, but the Mexican manufacturer was reluctant, because the arrangements proposed by the U.S. company would grant it full control over day-to-day operations despite a minority equity holding. In this case, a marriage was never effected, but the owner was afforded a substantial education in fan-manufacturing technology in the course of his lengthy visits to the U.S. plant.

Quality control was stressed by the source development teams in their dealings with potential parts suppliers; they insisted upon maintenance of the quality standards prevailing in the international automobile industry. SIC made gestures toward setting its own technical standards, but when Ford opened a quality-control testing facility in Mexico City, Molina used the occasion to urge the adoption of SAE (Society of Automotive Engineers) standards, before an audience that included Salinas Lozano and other high SIC officials.[22] Together with several Ford-employed Mexican engineers, Molina hurried into existence a Mexican chapter of the SAE. Some argued that Mexico was too poor a country to afford standards as exacting as those of the SAE, but the latter's technical norms prevailed.

While making efforts to render technical assistance to some fledgling Mexican firms, the terminal firms tried to discourage others, on grounds of technical standards. A Mexican engineer copied an automobile horn he had purchased in Texas, but it did not meet the tests applied in Ford's new quality-control laboratory. A Mexican entrepreneur tried to interest the terminal firms in frames he was prepared to manufacture, having built a prototype in his garage by carefully copying another frame—its hole placements, its welds, etc. He was turned down, and the frame business was captured by Manufacturas Metálicas de Monterrey, a joint venture of several Monterrey industrialists and the A. O. Smith Company, the principal U.S. frame manufacturer. In such cases, the terminal firms seemed unwilling to believe that anyone but an experienced company could make acceptable parts; the Mexicans, on the other hand, complained that they were not being given

---

[22] "La política de Ford en relación con sus proveedores," *Auto noticias*, Nov. 23, 1963.

opportunities to learn the business and acquire the necessary experience.

Where Type I firms were concerned, the government helped locate partners for joint ventures and encouraged rationalization by providing tax exemptions and import protection to only one firm making a given part. With their attention focused on the development of the terminal industry and on these larger parts suppliers, government officials tended to overlook the smaller parts firms, at least initially. In the manufacture of some components, the field rapidly became overcrowded, leading to an outcry in some quarters for the smoothing hand of government policy. "Regulation or Chaotic Competition?," ran a June 1964 headline in *Auto Noticias*, a trade newspaper, making no secret of this publication's preferences in the matter.

In sum, the Mexican government succeeded in achieving and maintaining 60 percent Mexican ownership in all parts-supply firms, and without any direct government investment. Because no exceptions were allowed, the Mexican-owned firms were not at a competitive disadvantage with wholly owned subsidiaries of transnational corporations. There were to be problems emerging in this section of the industry, but they arose not from the pattern of ownership but from the market structure: the differences between Type I and Type II firms in their relationships with the terminal firms. These problems will be examined below, but first we need to consider how much of a difference Mexicanization has made. What was gained by successfully insisting upon majority Mexican ownership of the parts industry?

BENEFITS AND LIMITATIONS OF MEXICANIZATION

In the auto-parts industry, the government created a structure that gave TNCs an incentive to associate with or otherwise assist the national bourgeoisie in establishing a viable position. It is tempting to view the state's success in preventing denationalization in this sector as an important accomplishment for its Mexicanization policy—i.e., preventing foreign ownership from coming to dominate a leading industry. The significance of Mexicanization must be further explored, however, relative to the problems created by TNC ownership.

Mexicanization has clearly made a difference for national capital: it has protected national entrepreneurs—indeed, encouraged the growth of the Mexican private sector—by reserving a place for Mexican capital in the subsidiaries of TNCs. This difference is not to be overlooked. It may be the most important argument for Mexicanization. But do Mexicanized firms behave differently than wholly foreign-owned ones in

136

ways that further national development goals? There are three arguments favoring Mexicanization on these grounds.

The first is based on the assumption of an identity of interests: the interest of Mexican capital is also the national interest. If we remove the ideological freight of nationalism with which this argument is often loaded, this would seem to mean that "what is good for capital is good for the nation"—that firms guided by profit maximization put capital into those areas of production and commerce that best achieve growth and its attendant employment, wages, and tax base. Even putting aside the grounds on which this assumption might be contested, however, the argument does not distinguish between private Mexican and private foreign capital. What is good for GM might be good for Mexico, too: why should specifically *Mexican* capital make a difference?

The second argument claims not identical but parallel interests: the particular interests of Mexican capital are different from those of foreign capital in ways that run parallel to the state's definition of national interests. For example, Mexican capitalists might be more likely to reinvest their profits in Mexican industrial activities; their ties to Mexican industry, their knowledge of national investment opportunities, and their lack of global operations would make them less likely to send capital abroad. Mexican capitalists, more than TNCs, would thus further domestic capital accumulation and growth, two important national goals. But this argument rests upon some questionable assumptions. Many Mexican investors do not have strong ties to Mexican industry, and it is not clear that many of them find long-term investments in domestic industry more desirable than short-term, often more immediately lucrative, speculative investments or than investment abroad in foreign securities. There is one sector of the Mexican bourgeoisie, however, for which assumptions of preference for long-term domestic investment may be warranted: the major banking and industrial groups that control many of the largest financial and nonfinancial enterprises.[23]

There is another, related parallelism argument. Mexican owners might be more likely to be guided by what is rational for a Mexican firm than by what is rational for a TNC. Their concern for the profit and growth of their own companies will lead them to rationalize local operations rather than global operations. If a country's tax laws make it rational for a TNC to overvalue imports or undervalue exports through transfer pricing among subsidiaries or some form of "trian-

[23] See Vernon, *Dilemma of Mexico's Development*, pp. 20-21, and Cordero and Santín, "Los grupos industriales."

gular trade," it will do so. The resultant increase in its global profits will not help Mexico increase capital accumulation or reduce foreign-exchange outflows. The use of a particular technology may be more costly to a subsidiary—and drain off more foreign exchange—than some alternative, but if the TNC is selling the relevant machinery or raw materials, such a technology may be economically rational from its global standpoint. Mexican shareholders, however, anxious to max-imize the profit or growth of the Mexican subsidiary, will seek to min-imize the cost of machinery and raw materials. They also have an interest in resisting expensive payments for technology, royalties, and service fees; they will not undervalue exports or overvalue imports; and they will encourage rather than discourage exports.[24] To the extent that these interests keep capital and foreign exchange in Mexico, what is good for the Mexican capitalist is good for Mexico.

But there is a dubious assumption in this argument as well: that Mexican owners have the power to act on their interests. "Mexicanized" industries are not fully owned by Mexicans. There may be 51 percent Mexican ownership, or even 60 percent, as in the auto-parts industry after 1972. But 51 or 60 percent ownership does not necessarily mean that Mexican shareholders control the behavior of the firm. A common pattern in Mexico had been the use of *prestanombres*, Mexicans who "lent their names" to a TNC to be used as "owners," so that the company was only *de jure* Mexicanized. Although the loopholes allowing such practices have been closed and enforcement is now stricter, a TNC with 49 or 40 percent of equity can still maintain control over the corpo-ration if the Mexican stocks are divided (or "pulverized" as the cor-porate lawyers say) among many Mexican stockholders. Its position is strengthened by its control over technology, sources of raw materials, and international marketing channels. However, when a single large Mexican investment group owns majority equity, it is likely to achieve control. This has been the case in some of the largest auto-parts firms, such as Spicer and TREMEC.

There is a third argument that Mexicanization makes a difference: The state can more easily steer a Mexican-owned firm toward national industrialization goals than it can a TNC, since the former would not be so apt to have the support of a foreign government. Clearly this

[24] A number of authors who have analyzed the ownership policies of multinational corporations have pointed to these possible results of joint ventures in presenting the argument against local partners. What is rational for the local partner is seen as an obstacle to the global rationality of the firm. See Stopford and Wells, *Managing the Multinational Enterprise*, pp 99-124, and Michael Z. Brooke and H. Lee Remmers, *The Strategy of Mul-tinational Enterprise* (New York: Elsevier, 1970), pp. 263-269.

argument applies only to the case where Mexican owners actually do exercise substantial control over corporate policies, which is to say, where a major investment group is the majority partner. Even then, it is not at all clear that the Mexican government has greater control over a large domestic industrial and banking group than it does over a TNC. Their concentration of banking resources, control of finance capital, and broad horizontal integration give these groups tremendous economic power. Their connections with government ministries and the media and their understanding of channels of influence—including bribery and more subtle forms—may actually give them more political clout than a TNC. Furthermore, Mexicanization policy not only encourages the growth and economic power of these groups—they are the actors most likely to be able to take advantage of equity participation schemes—but it also forges an alliance between them and the TNCs with which they share interests in the same firms.[25]

In summary, the principal benefits of Mexicanization would seem to come where the Mexican shareholders are a large bank-industrial group that genuinely exercises control over the company. There are a number of such cases among the Type I parts-supply firms. In these cases, the benefits of Mexicanization arise when the Mexican owners, acting in their own interests, direct the firm in parallel with the national interests of Mexico. This form of Mexicanization is a double-edged sword, however; firms with economically powerful Mexican partners are probably less susceptible to government regulation than wholly owned subsidiaries of TNCs.

The most important benefit to the nation that might come from a Mexican-owned auto firm is the development of new technology of a sort that would make Mexico an autonomous center of automobile

---

[25] These problems with Mexicanization have not been lost on those in charge of administering foreign-investment legislation in the last decade. Indeed, officials of the Foreign Investment Commission in both the Echeverría and López Portillo administrations came to see that Mexicanization of a firm often meant *less* and not more control over its industrial behavior, and so they have tended to use Mexicanization primarily as a threat or a lever. TNCs, wishing to avoid Mexicanization, come to the commission with requests for new investments. The commission bargains with them for other industrial goals—export of manufactured goods, development of local technology, construction of plants in underdeveloped regions, and use of domestically made parts. If a firm decides to Mexicanize, it moves beyond the control of the commission, since it then no longer needs approval of its investment plans. It is, perhaps, an irony (some might say, a contradiction) of contemporary capitalism in Mexico that a policy to control foreign investment through Mexicanization works least well when a TNC Mexicanizes. These arguments concerning Mexicanization are spelled out in greater depth in Douglas C. Bennett and Kenneth E. Sharpe, "El control sobre las multinacionales: Las contradicciones de la mexicanización," *Foro Internacional* 21 (1981):388-427.

manufacturing. That would be a genuine, if partial, end to dependency. While such a prospect is unlikely in any joint venture (TNCS keep tight control over the development of new technology), it is especially unlikely in the Mexican automobile industry. It is the terminal industry, not the parts-supply industry, that sets the overall technological direction. If Mexicanization was to make this kind of difference, the terminal industry would have had to be the far more important target.

STATE OWNERSHIP IN THE AUTOMOBILE INDUSTRY

Private domestic ownership is one alternative to transnational ownership, but state ownership is another. While the Mexican state has not actively pursued state ownership as a deliberate strategy of industrial policy in the automobile industry (as it has pursued Mexicanization), it nevertheless did come to own a number of firms in the sector.

TABLE 6.4

STATE-OWNED FIRMS IN THE MEXICAN AUTOMOBILE INDUSTRY, 1980

Controlling Entity and Firms	Products
Nacional Financiera (NAFIN)	
Diesel Nacional (DINA)	Trucks and buses
DINA-Komatsu	Tractors
DINA-Renault	Cars
DINA-Rockwell	Truck and bus axles
Forjamex	Precision forgings
Siderugica Nacional (SIDENA)	Engine-block forgings
DINA	
Maquiladora Automotriz Nacional	Truck assembly
Motores Pertrins	Diesel engines
SIDENA	
Tracto-Sidena	Tractors
Altos Hornos[a]	
Rossini Rheem	Springs
Fundiciones de Hierro y Acero	Forgings
Sociedad Mexicana de Crédito	
Industrial (SOMEX)	
Borg y Beck	Brake parts
Bujías Champion	Spark plugs
Mexicana de Autobuses	Buses
Manufacturera Mexicana de	Auto parts
Partes Automotrices	
Vehículos Automotores Mexicanos (VAM)	Cars
NAFIN/SOMEX (joint)	
Macimex	Machine tools

SOURCE: Authors' interviews
[a] Altos Hornos is a steel-making firm, which is controlled by NAFIN.

Through the two major state investment banks, NAFIN and SOMEX, the state became the principal owner of companies making a variety of vehicles and parts (see table 6.4). It is instructive to consider how the state acquired these firms, how they could have been used as instruments of industrial policy, and what have been the impediments to their being used in that fashion.

Acquisition of Firms

The disposition of the Mexican government toward primary reliance on private-sector investment might seem to preclude any significant state ownership of manufacturing firms, but the government has also been willing to act as an investor of "last resort" when necessary (see chapter 2). Not only has the Mexican state made investments in infrastructure and in certain basic industries which had low profit expectations or very large capital requirements, but it has also stood ready to bail out Mexican entrepreneurs who found themselves bogged down in projects they could not carry through. The latter was the route by which the Mexican state acquired two terminal firms and most of its auto-parts firms.

DINA, the most important state-owned auto maker, was organized in the early 1950s by two private promoters, Bruno Pagliai and Luis Montes de Oca. On the basis of studies done by themselves, Fiat, and NAFIN, they proposed to manufacture diesel trucks in Mexico using Fiat technology. Private Mexican investors put in 10.5 million pesos, and Fiat was allocated 6 million pesos of stock as payment for its cooperation and technology, but that was still not sufficient capital for the venture, and the organizers turned to the public sector for help. In response, NAFIN subscribed 59.5 million pesos of stock.[26]

DINA started operations in 1954 but fared poorly. The Fiat truck was ill-adapted to Mexican roads and cargos, the firm was induced to buy expensive and unnecessary machinery from Fiat, and complex problems of distribution were not adequately dealt with. Efforts to improve sales and profits by assembling Fiat automobiles (1100s and 1400s), which were then popular in Mexico, proved insufficient. Even without these problems, the firms would have had difficulty surviving, since there was little protection at that time from imported vehicles. By 1958, the firm was nearly bankrupt and the private investors were eager to withdraw. NAFIN bought their shares and recapitalized the venture, and

---

[26] Villaseñor, *Memorias*, 2:243.

the Mexican state thus became the proprietor of a major firm in the nation's rapidly developing automobile industry.

In 1959, President López Mateos appointed Victor Manuel Villaseñor as director of DINA. Under his leadership (1959-1970), it emerged as a better-organized, more efficient, profit-making state enterprise. DINA began assembling Renault Dauphines in 1960, and Villaseñor then negotiated with Renault an arrangement to manufacture its car in Mexico; Renault was the only European firm willing to license manufacture without demanding ownership control. The plan was to begin production with domestic content valued at 24 percent of the CKD price. Thus, two years before the 1962 decree, this state-owned firm had become a leader in using local content and was in a favorable position when local content became a requirement. Villaseñor also revamped truck production, breaking the contract with Fiat and backing the design and production of a Mexican truck. Instead of an equity or full licensing arrangement with another truck-manufacturing TNC, he had a group of Mexican engineers work with a Detroit consulting firm to design a DINA truck. With the assistance of U.S. engineers and the cooperation of U.S. component manufacturers, they designed and road-tested the DINA 501, with a Cummins diesel engine (to be produced under license at the DINA plant) and mechanical components made by Rockwell, Spicer, Ross Gear, and Dana.[27] Villaseñor had first to overcome the opposition within the DINA board to making a Mexican truck, then to ward off an attempt by International Harvester to buy out DINA's truck facilities, and finally to convince the government to refinance operations, still suffering from the Fiat losses, before production of the eventually highly successful DINA truck was begun in 1964.[28]

Once established on firm ground, DINA continued to expand, often by serving as a "last-resort" entrepreneur. When FANASA went bankrupt and no other auto firms showed interest, DINA stepped in to utilize the firm's plant and equipment. Under contracts with International Harvester, and later with GM, it organized a subsidiary called Maquiladora Automotriz Nacional to assemble pickup trucks; and in a joint venture with North American Rockwell, DINA and NAFIN set up DINA-Rockwell to manufacture heavy-duty truck and bus axles. In other, more recent instances, DINA's acquisitions have gone beyond last-resort justifications. In acquiring Motores Perkins, its major competitor in diesel engines, it acted much like any private-sector firm seeking to protect

[27] The existence of competing component suppliers gave the Mexicans some bargaining leverage, which was used to get technical assistance in design development and to lower costs. Cummins, for example, offered a less expensive licensing arrangement than GM.

[28] Villaseñor, *Memorias*, 2:247-250, 262-263, and 324-333.

its market and its earnings.[29] Last-resort intervention may thus be the initial cause of state ownership, but once acquired, state firms are likely to take on a dynamic of their own.

The Mexican state acquired majority ownership in VAM, another terminal firm, by a similar route. The Mexican owner of VAM was the large private investment bank SOMEX. In early 1963, SOMEX found itself overextended. Its collapse would have meant not only the demise or disorganization of the over forty firms it owned, but also a crisis of confidence in the banking system. Instead, the state took over SOMEX and it became a public-sector investment bank, with the state at the same time acquiring equity in all the SOMEX firms. In addition to becoming owner of SOMEX's 60 percent share of VAM—American Motors had the other 40 percent—the state acquired a bus-manufacturing firm, Mexicana de Autobuses (MASA) and three auto-parts firms: Manufacturera Mexicana de Partes Automotrices (MEX-PAR), Bujías Champion, and Borg y Beck, the latter two joint ventures with U.S. TNCS (Champion Spark Plugs and Borg-Warner, respectively).

Another state takeover of a joint venture with a U.S.-based TNC was that of Rassini Rheem. Until 1962, this long-established firm, which manufactured leaf springs for the replacement market, was wholly owned by private Mexican investors. In a move toward the production of original equipment, 40 percent of equity was sold to Rheem International, a California conglomerate and a major leaf-spring manufacturer. A number of diversification moves overextended the company, and by 1969 it was deeply in debt both to Rheem International and to Altos Hornos, the state-owned firm that supplied its steel. The two creditors bailed out the Mexican private investors by creating a state-TNC joint venture.

State Ownership as an Instrument of Industrial Policy

State ownership could have been used to achieve goals that the private sector would not have achieved, even with vigorous regulatory efforts of a more traditional sort. A state-owned firm could wield significant

[29] Until the late 1960s, Fábricas Auto-Mex was the majority owner of Motores Perkins, a diesel-engine manufacturer. Mexicanization policy demanded that all automobile-parts manufacturers be 60 percent Mexican-owned. When Chrysler bought majority interest in Auto-Mex, Motores Perkins became, contrary to the law, foreign-owned. Rather than search for Mexican private investors to buy up Chrysler's share in Perkins, DINA (with the backing of NAFIN) immediately bought the firm. An important consideration was the desire of state officials to maintain control over diesel-engine production, given the importance of this sector to Mexico's development of efficient, low-cost trucking. But it was also clear that DINA was moving, quite rationally, to eliminate a major source of competition by an acquisition that would improve its market position.

market power. As an oligopolistic buyer or seller, it could force prices down among other members of an oligopoly by operating at lower profits or even at a loss. As a sole source of inputs for private manufacturers, it could raise or lower their costs of production. State ownership could give the state power to influence the degree of product differentiation, the kind of technology used, and other aspects of production, with less regard to profit maximization. As a shareholder in a private firm, it might be able to direct the conduct of the firm more effectively from within than it could with the use of regulatory tools. Finally, state ownership could give state officials inside knowledge of an industry that would be invaluable for reshaping industry structure or regulating firm conduct.

Although there have been a few instances of state ownership being used in one or another of these ways in Mexico, significant obstacles have tended to blunt its effectiveness. First, and most important, there was little predisposition among state managers to use state firms as policy instruments precisely because of the last-resort orientation toward public ownership. Firms were not acquired by the state *for* any forward-looking purposes. This was not an insuperable obstacle, however: there were officials both within key ministries and in state-owned firms who saw the possibilities.

Second, the mode of selection of managers for the state-owned firms was an impediment to their use as policy instruments. Villaseñor, for example, was not head of DINA because of his managerial experience: he had been a labor activist and a party intellectual. While he did prove skillful as a manager, and his twelve-year tenure in the position gave DINA needed continuity, the firm was not so fortunate in its subsequent managers. There were three directors under Echeverría, and two under López Portillo, most of the appointments being based on political considerations and each change bringing a disruption in management. Such problems were not inherent in state ownership, however. VAM, for example, has been an efficiently-run auto maker, and for two decades after its nationalization in 1962, Fernández Sayago, its director, used the same sound business and management principles that he had used as its director when it was a private firm. However, so long as DINA, the major state auto maker, was not on a solid business footing, it was difficult for either it or VAM to be a centerpiece of industrial policy.

Third, the position of the state-owned firms within the governmental apparatus made difficult the coordination that was necessary if such firms were to be used as policy instruments. The two major firms have been controlled by different state investment banks: VAM by SOMEX and

DINA by NAFIN. These banks have exercised considerable control over their firms' investment policies: expansions, new product lines, acquisitions. They have somewhat different orientations and vested interests, however, and this has created a certain rivalry. To make matters worse, a number of different ministries are involved with the state firms and with auto policy. Until 1976, the Ministry of National Properties, which has had a more nationalistic, pro–state ownership orientation, was formally responsible for all state firms, but policy coordination of the auto firms could not be centered there because auto policy itself was the responsibility of SIC, whose officials were often skeptical of the competence and the intentions of National Properties. Moreover, fiscal policy for the auto industry was handled by the Ministry of Finance, whose orthodox monetary and fiscal orientations were shared by neither SIC nor National Properties. NAFIN and SOMEX were controlled by Finance as well.

The administrative reorganization instituted by López Portillo did make all industrial policy the responsibility of the new Ministry of Patrimony and Industrial Development, but it was not until the late 1970s that consideration was given to consolidating the state-owned firms. Studies were undertaken to explore the possibility of creating a state holding company which would bring together all majority state-owned firms in the auto industry: VAM and DINA-Renault in cars, DINA and MASA in buses, DINA and SOMEX-Mack in heavy-duty trucks, DINA, Perkins, and SOMEX-GM in diesel motors, and the major parts firms (DINA-Rockwell, Rassini Rheem, Borg y Beck, Bujías Champion, MEX-PAR, etc.). The idea failed to materialize because of opposition within the government agencies, however. Neither state investment bank (NA-FIN or SOMEX) and neither state auto maker (DINA or VAM) wanted to lose control to the other in the new enterprise. Further, there was little support among the major ministries. Patrimony and Industrial Development was notably cool toward it; its officials were doubtful that the holding company would be able to coordinate operations smoothly and efficiently; they were worried about having a monopoly supplier of important products such as buses, trucks, and diesel engines, even if it were a state firm; and they were concerned about losing their own power. The only residual of the effort was that the Ministry of Patrimony and Industrial Development took a tentative step toward coordinating the state-owned firms by organizing a Coordinating Commission of the Para-State Automotive Industry, composed of the major firms (DINA, VAM, and MASA) and presided over by the minister of patrimony and industrial development.

The position of the state firms in the industry structure has been a fourth obstacle to their use as policy instruments. As two of the weaker firms in a seven-firm industry, DINA and VAM had only small shares of the market (despite state efforts to protect them with production quotas), and this made it difficult for them to achieve the scale economies which might have allowed them to exercise leadership in price or in domestic content.

Finally, the position of the state enterprises in the international industry has been yet another obstacle to their use as policy instruments. Both VAM and DINA were heavily dependent upon TNCs whose strategies were dominated by international, not merely Mexican, considerations. American Motors held equity in VAM; DINA, already dependent on Renault for technology and credit, in the late 1970s sold 40 percent of its equity to Renault. If their efforts to exercise leverage over other firms meant low profits, there would be opposition from the minority foreign partner. When consideration was being given to the merger of all Mexican firms into one large corporation, AMC and Renault resisted all plans that threatened their equity position and control.

THE NEW MARKET STRUCTURE

The new pattern of ownership that emerged after the 1962 decree combined with the large number of firms and products to create yet other problems. Three warrant attention: (a) inefficiency and the high cost of production, (b) tensions between the parts firms and the auto producers, and (c) rising import costs. The government tried to cope with all of these, but they proved somewhat intractable within the new structure.

Inefficiency and High-Cost Production

In Mexico, as in all the other Latin American countries that required domestic manufacture of automobiles, the costs of production were significantly higher than in the vehicles' home countries (see table 6.5). In Mexico, the costs were only about 50 percent higher than in the home country. This was significantly better than in Argentina (which had about the same size market), because of Mexico's lower level of mandatory local content, which allowed firms to continue to import those parts most expensive to produce locally, especially exterior body stampings. Brazil's costs of production were slightly lower than Mexico's, even with higher required local content, but it had a much larger domestic market. Chile, on the other hand, had approximately the

146

same level of local content but higher costs, largely because its domestic market was smaller.

The standard view of neoclassical development economists is that such inefficiencies are the natural result of import-substitution policies in consumer-durable industries.[30] The lower labor costs in less-developed countries do not compensate for the higher prices of raw materials, intermediate goods, and machinery, this view asserts. Furthermore, the smaller size of the local market prevents firms from taking advantage of the scale economies available in more developed countries; even in 1970, motor-vehicle sales in Mexico were less than 200,000 vehicles, still well below the annual output of a single integrated auto plant in the United States. Finally, the protection afforded to the local market encourages inefficiency by shielding producers from the rigors of international competition.

This presentation of the problem overlooks some important points—in particular, that, in Mexico, the emergent market structure of the automobile industry exacerbated the problems of inefficiency. What prevented the firms from taking full advantage of the scale economies in prevailing technology was not just the overall size of the Mexican

TABLE 6.5

ASPECTS OF AUTOMOTIVE PRODUCTION IN FOUR
LATIN AMERICAN COUNTRIES, 1970

| | REQUIRED LOCAL CONTENT | | | | | |
| | Number of Firms (1) | Percent (2) | Basis of Measurement (3) | Number of Vehicles Sold (4) | Index of Production Costs[a] (5) | Index of Selling Price[a] (6) |
Country						
Argentina	10	95	Value	219,599	194.9	209.0
Brazil	9	98-99	Weight	416,040	134.6	196.4
Chile	13	58	F.o.b. value	24,591	263.9	305.0
Mexico	7	60	Direct cost of production	189,986	152.6	152.1

SOURCES: Columns 1-4, Jenkins, *Dependent Industrialization*, pp. 67ff. Columns 5 and 6: United Nations, Economic Commission for Latin America, *Perspectivas y modalidades de integración regional de la industria automotriz en America Latina* (New York: ECLA, 1973), table I.25

[a] Production costs and selling price in country of origin = 100.

[30] See, for example, Leland J. Johnson, "Problems of Import Substitution: The Chilean Automobile Industry," *Economic Development and Cultural Change* 15 (1967):202-216; B. Munk, "The Welfare Costs of Content Protection: The Automotive Industry in Latin America," *Journal of Political Economy* 77 (1969):85-98; Baranson, *Automotive Industries*; and Jack Behrman, *The Role of International Companies in Latin American Integration: Autos and Petrochemicals* (Lexington: D. C. Heath, 1972).

market but also the fragmentation of this market among a large number of producers, the proliferation of models by the terminal firms, and their predilection for annual model changes. Two or three firms each producing only one model would have been able to achieve greater efficiency in production than seven firms each producing two or more models. Standardization of parts and freezing of models also would have improved the situation. It was exactly that kind of market structure that the Mexican state had tried to create in 1962. But its attempts to limit the number of firms were blocked by pressure from the TNCs that did not want to be excluded and by the U.S. and Japanese governments' support for "their" companies, and its attempts to restrict the number of models and to achieve a degree of standardization of parts were defeated by the producers—national as well as TNC—with a variety of appeals.[31] Thus, some of the inefficiency was not simply a problem of import-substitution industrialization, but was rather the result of conflicts among the Mexican state, the TNCs, and foreign governments.

Three principal remedies for inefficiency were explored by the government. SIC Minister Salinas Lozano hoped that competition in the industry would reduce the number of firms and rationalize the industry. The firms most likely to fail, however, were Mexican firms, and the government wanted to prevent that. Three of the smallest Mexican-owned firms did fail, but this reduced the number of firms from ten to seven, only a slight improvement. The TNC subsidiaries, on the other hand, were unlikely to fold simply because of competition in the Mexican market; they could use the earnings from their deep global pockets to subsidize their Mexican operations and preserve a position in a market that would continue to grow for a number of years.

Both Salinas Lozano and his successor, Campos Salas, tried to increase standardization of major components among the auto producers. Standardization was achieved among the four U.S.-based firms (Ford, GM, Fábricas Auto-Mex, and VAM) in their drive-train components, but nothing more. The other firms had such different specifi-

---

[31] Ford, for example, was initially allowed production of a full-sized Ford and the Falcon; GM was to produce a Chevrolet and an Opel; and Fábricas Auto-Mex, a Dodge and a Valiant. But in 1964, Ford gained special permission to produce its Mustang by going over the heads of SIC officials and convincing President López Mateos. Auto-Mex was able to win permission to produce a second motor, a V-8, that would allow it, a national firm, to offer more powerful cars than its TNC competitors. The Díaz Ordaz administration later extended permission to Ford and GM to manufacture second engines as well. The TNCs were also able to sidestep certain restrictions on vertical integration; for example, Ford, and later GM, were permitted to cast their own engine blocks, because they claimed that Mexican foundries could not handle the desired volume and quality.

cations that they could join neither the U.S. firms nor each other in the standardization of the drive train. Because the only components that it was obligatory to have produced in Mexico were those in the drive train, the auto producers had little interest in standardizing other parts. They could import any part they thought was being made in Mexico at too high a price.

Finally, price controls were employed, particularly by Campos Salas, in the effort to bring about greater efficiency. Prices in the industry had been controlled since well before the 1962 decree. The Salinas Lozano policy was to allow the firms to charge 6.5 percent over their costs.[32] Campos Salas steered a different course: prices were required to be the same as for the previous year's models, except for an increase allowed in 1966. Campos Salas believed that the auto producers would thereby be forced to achieve greater efficiency if they were to obtain a profit.

Campos Salas did succeed in holding the line on prices. Between 1965 and 1970, motor-vehicle prices remained stable, while other prices rose (see table 6.6). However, although price controls might have

TABLE 6.6

GENERAL INDEX OF WHOLESALE PRICES AND INDEX OF
WHOLESALE PRICES OF AUTOMOTIVE PRODUCTS, 1962-1976

	General Index[a]	Index for Motor Vehicles and Accessories
1962	100	100
1963	100.5	100.7
1964	104.8	103.2
1965	106.8	103.4
1966	108.1	109.3
1967	111.3	109.7
1968	113.4	109.7
1969	116.3	109.7
1970	123.2	109.9
1971	127.8	109.9
1972	131.4	110.2
1973	152.1	113.5
1974	186.3	116.6
1975	205.9	134.3
1976	251.7	172.1

SOURCE: Banco de México, *Informes annales*, various years
[a] Wholesale prices of 210 articles.

[32] This arrangement seems to have been a concession that Ford's Molina extracted in return for Ford's helpfulness in moving the industry toward domestic manufacture.

prevented the transnational firms from making excessive profits from their Mexican operations, they could not affect the major sources of inefficiency. These were rooted in the industry's market structure, and only a restructuring of the market could attack them.

Tensions between Parts Firms and Terminal Firms

The problem of inefficient, high-cost production was also common among the firms in the parts industry, many of which had just started new manufacturing operations or shifted to new product lines. Moreover, there were numerous and no doubt justified complaints from the auto producers concerning poor quality and slow delivery as well as high costs. Overcrowding and transnational ownership in the terminal industry tended to exacerbate the problems of the parts-supply firms, particularly those of Type II, in their dealings with the manufacturers.

It was pointed out above that standardization had been achieved for only a few parts. With each of the terminal firms requiring its own special designs, production runs for many components tended to be quite small. In a number of cases, the producers insisted upon setting up their own "captive" supplier firm—a practice common in the automobile industries of many developing countries.[33] Thus, the fragmentation of the terminal industry produced a corresponding degree of fragmentation in the supplier industry. Annual model changes not only shortened production runs still more but also forced supplier firms that were just learning new manufacturing processes to change their product designs frequently.

The 1962 decree specified only a few parts for mandatory domestic procurement; for most parts, it was left to the producers to decide which would be included in their 60 percent local content and which would continue to be imported. This led to a situation in which some auto makers were importing a component that other auto producers were procuring from a domestic supplier, thus preventing the supplier firm from achieving a maximally efficient use of installed capacity.

The Campos Salas team in sic tried to address this problem by declaring that it would prohibit the importation of a part if a supplier firm could show that it was able to produce the part for a price no more than a certain percentage above the price of the imported part. That generally proved difficult to demonstrate, however. Since many of the imports were intracompany transfers, a producer could arrange

---

[33] See Baranson, *Automotive Industries*, p. 47.

administratively to lower the price of a part it wished to continue importing, should the part come under threat of being placed on the "mandatory" list. Often, a supplier firm, lacking access to the CKD price list, had difficulty finding out the price of an imported part. Producers could protest the mandatory incorporation of a domestically manufactured part by insisting that it was not of proper design or quality, and since the producers controlled the design and technical specifications, that was a difficult claim to disprove.

The fact that price controls applied only to the producers, not to the parts firms, tended to sharpen the conflicts between them. The producers found it necessary to demand increased efficiency from their suppliers. They could exert only limited leverage on the Type I firms because these generally were monopoly suppliers of components that had to be obtained in Mexico (although the producers could appeal to the parts firm's transnational partner to keep a rein on prices in the interest of good relations elsewhere in the world). The producers had more options with regard to the smaller, Type II firms, however, because they could usually import the part in question. In some cases, this was a strong incentive to the parts firms to search aggressively for ways to lower costs and prices, but in others it made the parts firms so uncertain of their market that they were reluctant to make additional investments. For their part, the producers complained that the parts firms, particularly the smaller ones, were excessively cautious and interested only in short-term profits.

Rising Import Costs

By requiring local manufacture of 60 percent of the direct cost of production, the 1962 decree brought a dramatic decrease in the value of imports per vehicle. In 1965 and 1966, the industry's total import bill for components decreased absolutely, but then, as sales volume grew, the 40 percent that continued to be imported began to force up the total import bill. By 1968, it had nearly reached the 1964 level, and there was every indication of further increases (see table 6.7). In 1962, automotive imports had accounted for 13 percent of total merchandise imports; by 1968, that figure had risen above 10 percent again and was increasing. The policy of import substitution in the automobile industry had been adopted so that, among other reasons, the industry's share of total imports would be significantly reduced, but the situation was not getting any better and might soon be worse than it had been before.

The Díaz Ordaz administration tried to improve matters with a new use of production quotas. These quotas had been imposed in an effort to preserve a market share for the firms with majority-Mexican ownership, but, as was seen above, they were largely ineffective for that purpose. Now, however, firms were offered larger production quotas for increasing their local content beyond 60 percent or for increasing their exports. The results showed some success but not nearly enough to deal with the magnitude of the balance-of-payments problem. The Díaz Ordaz administration felt it had to take more vigorous action. There were two obvious routes: mandate higher local-content requirements, or compensate for increased imports by stimulating increased exports. The new structure of dependency in the industry posed serious obstacles to each route, however.

Increasing local content. The privately owned producers had no interest in increasing local content, for it still would mean lower exports to Mexico from their home-country plants, with shorter production runs, lower efficiency, higher costs, and lower profits there as the consequences. Moreover, the flow of components into Mexico afforded the TNCs a convenient avenue for using transfer pricing to realize profits where tax liabilities or other financial considerations made it desirable. Lower transfer prices would tend to shift earnings toward Mexico; higher transfer prices would shift them toward their home countries (though they would also decrease the firms' level of domestic content as measured in Mexico). An increase in mandatory local content would mean higher costs, and with stringent price controls, it was not at all clear that the government would allow these to be passed along to

TABLE 6.7

AUTOMOTIVE IMPORTS AND TOTAL MERCHANDISE
IMPORTS, 1960 AND 1965-1969

	MERCHANDISE IMPORTS (millions of pesos)		Auto-Industry Imports As Percentage of Total
	Total	Auto Industry	
1960	14,830.6	1,862.8	12.6
1965	19,495.1	2,423.1	12.4
1966	20,064.5	2,088.0	10.4
1967	21,823.2	2,127.6	9.7
1968	24,501.4	2,617.0	10.1
1969	25,975.4	2,692.3	10.4

SOURCE: AMIA, *Industria automotriz*, p. 67

152

consumers. The restrictions on vertical integration meant that the auto producers would probably have to find (or bring into being) new parts firms to manufacture the needed additional components in Mexico. To the auto producers, this could augur only a new set of headaches.

Indeed, the new market structure allowed the TNCs to argue that it was "not in the national interest" to require an increase in local content. They correctly pointed out that, given the large number of firms and the size of the market, raising local content beyond 60 percent would dramatically increase costs and prices in the industry. Not only would this contradict the anti-inflationary policy of *desarrollo estabilizador*; it might also depress sales and thus slow the growth of industry and employment. Moreover, the resultant higher costs also threatened to make vehicle exports from Mexico more difficult.

Thus, while the new structure in the industry—the excessive number of firms and their private, transnational ownership—was conditioned by the pressures exerted by the TNCs during the struggle over the 1962 decree, the structure now, ironically, made their arguments plausible, even compelling. The only reasonable way the government could bring about a substantial increase in local content—one large enough to ease the balance-of-payments problems caused by automotive imports—would be to rationalize the industry: to reduce the number of firms and the degree of product differentiation, allowing a greater efficiency that would decrease the costs of higher local content.

Import Compensation through Exports. Increased exports not only would generate needed foreign exchange to pay for imports, but also, by increasing sales volume, would make possible scale economies, greater efficiency, and lower prices, as well as increased industrial growth and employment inside Mexico. The immediate problem, however, was Mexico's inability to compete with the already more efficient, lower-cost plants in Europe, the United States, and Japan. Moreover, the possibility of attaining the international efficiency levels needed to export seemed to be foreclosed by the new structure of dependency in the Mexican industry. Finally, sales on the international market were not determined simply by price, quality, and availability; much of the international automotive trade consisted of intracompany transfers, parts made by and "sold" among the subsidiaries of the TNCs.

But this coin had an adverse side: foreign ownership of Mexican firms by the transnational members of the world auto oligopoly meant that these firms had the capability of promoting exports from Mexico to their other subsidiaries. That is what the government had in mind when it began to use production quotas as inducements to export.

However, the exports resulting from the extra quota were only a small fraction of the rapidly growing auto-import bill. There simply was not sufficient incentive for the transnational firms to engage in any large amount of exports from Mexico. The new structure of the auto industry in Mexico made costs much higher than they were elsewhere. Extra quotas for exports gave the firms extra sales in Mexico and thus modified their cost accounting, but only marginally. In 1968, no firm was eager to begin a serious export drive.

If the industry were rationalized by reducing the number of firms, the TNCs might have been more interested in exports. With fewer firms, those that remained—and their suppliers as well—might gain greater economies of scale. But there was another possible solution: perhaps quotas could be used not merely as an incentive to export, but as a *requirement* to export. If continued access to the Mexican market were made contingent upon some amount of exports, it might compel the TNCs to export in order to avoid being forced out of Mexico. The government's initial efforts to promote automotive exports by giving incentives had had disappointing results. But when Fábricas Auto-Mex/ Chrysler proposed a plan to achieve higher local content through industry rationalization, a second plan for mandatory compensation of imports with exports found favor with Ford. These two plans would emerge as the major alternatives in the second round of bargaining between the transnational auto firms and the Mexican state.

·7·

THE SECOND ENCOUNTER, 1969

In October 1969, representatives of the terminal firms were summoned to the office of Luis Bravo Aguilera, director of industries in SIC. A new automotive policy was read and explained to them.[1] It required each terminal firm to make a steadily increasing amount of exports to compensate for the imported content of its vehicles. Shortly afterward, there was a meeting of the terminal firms at the headquarters of the AMIA, their trade association. There were complaints about the new policy and even a few confessions of responsibility for having allowed this new requirement to take effect. But no attempt was made to have the requirement withdrawn or to make the government back down. Instead, the firms set about making plans to comply. Scarcely seven years after it had compelled the world's major automobile firms to commence manufacturing vehicles in Mexico, the Mexican government had pushed them a step further—into undertaking automotive exports. This policy was chosen over a radically different alternative, which would have merged all the Mexican-owned terminal firms into a single large, majority Mexican-owned corporation, reduced the number of firms in the overcrowded market, and pushed the Mexican auto industry further along the route of import-substitution industrialization. This chapter is concerned with how each of the various corporate and state actors came to support one or the other of these policies, and how the ensuing conflict was resolved in favor of the export policy.

THE GROWING INTEREST IN EXPORTS

The installation of the Díaz Ordaz administration in December 1964 brought the usual turnover among the personnel of the state ministries. Campos Salas became minister of SIC, although he kept Plácido Gracia Reynoso as his deputy minister. Bravo Aguilera became director of industries, the major role in developing automobile-industry policies, and Antonio Gallart was named his subdirector for the automobile industry. Their first concern was to complete implementation of the 1962 decree. They saw to it that the terminal firms came into full compliance with the decree's local-content requirements, they oversaw

[1] See "Compensación de importaciones de partes automovilísticas," *Comercio exterior,* Nov. 1969, p. 864.

the further development of the fledgling auto-parts industry, and they made sure that the parts firms were majority Mexican-owned. What they came to define as major problems, however, were the inefficiency of the new industry, the competitive disadvantages of the Mexican-owned terminal firms, and the resumed rise in the industry's import bill. They also feared that the spur to industrialization and employment from the decree had been spent; a new policy would be needed if there were to be further expansion of manufacturing activity in this sector.

One possible means toward that end was to increase domestic-content levels above 60 percent, a step that would also help cut imports. The Campos Salas team's analysis of the Argentinian and Brazilian industries made them leery of this route, however. The much higher domestic-content levels in those automotive industries had led to even higher costs and prices, given the relatively small scales of production, and the inflationary pressures that similarly high domestic-content levels would create in Mexico would be incompatible with *desarrollo estabilizador.*

The members of the new SIC team brought with them a skepticism toward import-substitution industrialization. Díaz Ordaz had not chosen people who would immediately and radically challenge the orientation toward import substitution so deeply embedded in SIC and other ministries, but they were inclined to be critical of a strategy that, in their view, had spawned inefficient, high-cost industries because the protection it afforded to firms allowed them to escape the bracing discipline of international competition. Now that an industrial foundation had been created by import substitution, they were inclined to search for appropriate industrial sectors where policy could be more focused *hacia afuera*—"toward the outside," i.e., toward world markets.

This general analysis coincided with a shift in academic thinking about the economics of development. As an academic discipline, economics based on a neoclassical model is organized around the idea of unimpeded markets as the best way of handling transactions. In development economics, this manifests itself as a marked preference for a liberal international-trade regime, free of tariff and nontariff barriers. The Great Depression served to weaken the hold of this approach on development planners in Latin America, and Raúl Prebish's subsequent analysis of the terms of trade between manufactured and nonmanufactured goods provided the core of a justification for import-substitution policy: the promotion of manufacturing industries in developing countries through the use of protectionist devices to insulate the domestic economy. In the mid-1960s, however, neoclassical ideas were once again finding favor among policy makers in the region. With manufacturing industries now established, a dismantling of the protectionist barriers was called for: efficiency and, if possible, manufactured exports, had to be increased.[2]

Exports from the Mexican auto industry were believed to have several desirable consequences. They would promote industrialization, create a more efficient industry both through greater production volumes and through the rigors of international competition, and offset the industry's growing import bill. On the other hand, the automotive sector had just embarked on its manufacturing stage; talk of exports might be premature. Two serious obstacles had to be faced.

One was the very inefficiency that an export strategy was supposed to overcome: the high cost of Mexican-made components made them uncompetitive internationally. This inefficiency was in part a product of the small, class-bound domestic market, but it was also in part a product of the fragmentation of this market among too many manufacturers. The second was that much of the world trade in automotive components was in the form of intracompany transfers at prices set administratively within a TNC rather than at arm's length in the marketplace. Even if Mexican-manufactured components could be produced at internationally competitive costs, they would not necessarily find a buyer. This second problem also represented a possibility, however. The transnational auto firms could provide an avenue for exports if they decided to supply some of their other international operations from Mexico; Mexican plants might become a source and not merely a recipient of these intracompany transfers. This would occur, however, only if the transnational auto firms could be convinced or compelled to undertake exports from Mexico. Having just been compelled to undertake domestic manufacture in Mexico, they were less than eager.

Nevertheless, while the Campos Salas team was overseeing final compliance with the 1962 decree, they were also looking for ways to induce exports from the automotive sector. They studied, for example, the U.S.-Canadian Automotive Products Trade Agreement, approved in

[2] The most thorough general statement of this argument is Ian Little, Tibor Scitovsky, and Maurice Scott, *Industry and Trade in Some Developing Countries: A Comparative Study* (London: Oxford University Press, 1970). As part of the OECD project which culminated in this volume, a study of the auto industry in Mexico was prepared: Sanchez Marco, "Mexican Automobile Industry." For other urgings of a shift to export promotion, see Bela Balassa, "Growth Strategies in Semi-Industrial Countries," *Quarterly Journal of Economics* 84 (1970):24-42, and Daniel M. Schydlowsky, "Latin American Trade Policies in the 1970s: A Prospective Appraisal," *Quarterly Journal of Economics* 86 (1972):263-289. See also Raúl Prebish, *The Economic Development of Latin America and Its Principal Problems* (New York: United Nations, 1950).

1965, which in effect created a free-trade zone between the two countries in automotive products.[3] A similar U.S.-Mexican agreement seemed impossible, however, without the strong backing of the U.S.-based TNCs. The Latin American Free Trade Association (LAFTA) provided another possibility. There were discussions between Mexico and other LAFTA countries concerning automotive trade, but nothing came of them.

The proposal that took the initiative and was at center stage in 1968 and 1969 was a plan sponsored by Gaston Azcárraga and Chrysler, which sought to merge the four surviving Mexican-owned firms (DINA, VAM, FANASA, and Azcárraga's Fábricas Auto-Mex) into a single Mexican-owned firm affiliated with Chrysler. Though it was seriously considered for more than eighteen months and was quite nearly approved, it received no attention in newspapers, trade publications, or government reports. Yet it shaped a context in which an export plan that otherwise would have been difficult to adopt, and that pointed the industry down quite a different path, was set into motion.

The merger plan sought to deal with the new structure of dependency in quite a different way than did the export plan. First, it sought to rationalize the market by reducing the number of firms. Second, it sought to reverse the expanding foreign ownership of the industry by creating a majority Mexican-owned firm (including public and private ownership) that would have control of over half the auto market. The export plan, on the other hand, left the market structure more or less intact and augured further denationalization. These consequences were not, however, the primary concerns of the corporate actors. A brief look at the politics of corporate and state conflict will lay the groundwork for analyzing how the two plans came to set the policy agenda in the late 1960s and how the export plan came to be approved and implemented.

THE RIVAL PROPOSALS

Azcárraga's proposal to merge with the three other Mexican firms had a certain logic. DINA, VAM, and FANASA were three of the weakest and slowest-growing firms in the industry, and none of them could count on substantial assistance from a transnational partner. DINA and VAM were owned by the Mexican government (though by different agen-

---

[3] See Paul Wonnacott, "Canadian Automotive Protection: Content Provisions, the Bladen Plan, and Recent Tariff Changes," *Canadian Journal of Economics and Politics* 31 (1965):98-115.

cies), and FANASA was so heavily in debt to the government that it could be considered as a ward of the state. A merger would rationalize the state's investments in the automobile industry by creating a single stronger, more integrated firm.

Azcárraga was not the first to consider such a possibility; Gregorio Ramírez had earlier proposed a merger of DINA, VAM, and FANASA in a letter to Ortiz Mena. However, the major position of Auto-Mex in the industry meant that Azcárraga's initiative would be taken more seriously.[4] Auto-Mex's interest was shaped by its position in the new industrial structure. Although Auto-Mex was a dramatically successful Mexican-owned firm, whose market share was usually first and never worse than second throughout the 1960s, its ownership status created difficulties in the competition with the wholly foreign-owned Ford and GM subsidiaries. Although Auto-Mex might sell as many vehicles as its transnational competitors, it could not realize the same profit margins as they could. Its prices were frozen at the same level as Ford's and GM's. And yet its costs were higher, because Chrysler (with only one-third of the firm's equity) would not sell parts to Auto-Mex at prices that were as low as the transfer prices that Ford and GM charged to their subsidiaries. If Azcárraga could consolidate all the Mexican firms under his management control, the combined production quotas would give the firm more than half the Mexican market, and the higher sales volume would then compensate for the lower profit margins. Higher production levels would also allow the incorporation of more domestically made parts, and the higher domestic content might be achieved without significantly increasing costs if the magnitude of purchases by the new firm allowed greater scale economies in parts production. This possibility, attractive to government officials interested in increasing domestic content, could also serve Auto-Mex's corporate interests. If Ford and GM were forced to match Auto-Mex's domestic-content level, they would lose the cost advantages of importing from their parent companies, while their smaller production volumes would not allow them to purchase domestically made parts at the same cost advantage that the new firm would have.

The merger scheme may have first emerged in discussions between Azcárraga and Campos Salas. Rather regularly, Azcárraga talked with Campos Salas to lay before him Auto-Mex's disabilities in competition with Ford and GM and to plead for special treatment. Campos Salas was reluctant to single out one firm for special treatment, but he might

---

[4] Merger discussions involving the remaining Mexican-owned firms were reported in *Comercio exterior*, Nov. 1967, p. 906.

take a different view if that one firm were the only Mexican firm facing several transnational corporations.

It was not Campos Salas, however, but Finance Minister Ortiz Mena that Azcárraga initially relied on for support of his scheme. Ortiz Mena, reappointed finance minister (an unusual step) by Díaz Ordaz, was interested in the plan in a way that Campos Salas (searching for an export route) was not. He and Azcárraga were friends; but more than this, as finance minister he was concerned about the industry's balance-of-payments situation and about its market structure, particularly with regard to the weak positions of the state-owned firms, DINA and VAM. Ortiz Mena might not have opposed an export solution, but such a proposal was not being publicly debated within the government at the time; it was simply an aspiration of SIC officials. In any case, the merger plan promised more domestic production, fewer imports, greater efficiency, and a restructuring of state enterprises.

Ortiz Mena, however, had to tread lightly. Automobile-industry policy was within the jurisdiction of SIC, and there had been clashes between the two ministers in the past over the control of import licenses. Moreover, there was a certain degree of personal antagonism between the two ministers, which may have been exacerbated by the emergence of both of them as candidates for the PRI nomination for president in the 1970 election. Proceeding carefully, Ortiz Mena took the merger idea to Rodrigo Gómez, director of the Bank of Mexico (the central bank). Nominally, the Bank of Mexico is an independent institution not involved in politics or policy making. An office within the Bank of Mexico was responsible for certifying the level of local content achieved by the terminal firms (to determine the amount of their subsidies), and that recommended the bank for the role it was to play.

A trust fund was established in the Bank of Mexico to carry out a study of the auto industry, particularly the balance-of-payments situation and the possibility of a merger of the Mexican-owned firms. Auto-Mex made a contribution to the fund, as did the Finance Ministry on behalf of DINA, VAM, and FANASA. A technical committee was appointed to oversee the studies, with Gómez as chairman and Ernesto Fernández Hurtado, second in command at the bank, as secretary. Eventually there were representatives from SIC, Finance, National Properties, and NAFIN. The committee's first step was to commission a study of the balance-of-payments problem. The report, prepared by a retired executive from one of the U.S. auto firms, argued that the problem could best be dealt with by increasing the level of local content, but that this would be difficult with so many firms in the terminal industry. The

160

solution lay either in reducing the number of firms or perhaps in standardizing parts.

Two other studies were commissioned: Auto-Mex, with Chrysler, and VAM, with American Motors, were each asked to submit proposals on the merger of the Mexican-owned firms in the industry. The VAM proposal was quite sketchy—"primitive," one official described it—and was never considered seriously by the technical committee. The Auto-Mex/Chrysler study was a more substantial affair. An office of Chrysler International was set up in Mexico City, and Eugene Cafiero (later president of Chrysler) and several dozen experts were brought in from the United States to staff it. The proposal they drew up was based on a machine-by-machine study of each Mexican company.

Although the details of the Auto-Mex/Chrysler proposal changed as the discussions progressed, and several drafts were submitted, what it essentially suggested was that the four Mexican firms would be merged into a single, integrated operation. A number of existing makes and models would be eliminated, some of them to be replaced by their Chrysler counterparts. Thus, DINA's Renault R-4 would be dropped in favor of Chrysler's European-origin Simca as the firm's subcompact, and Dodge trucks would replace DINA's. The Borgward, the Rambler, and perhaps the Jeep would be eliminated altogether. The new enterprise would retain the production quotas of all its component firms, amounting to fully half of the extant quotas (and thus about half the market share), and it would be in a strong position to earn extra quota allotments. With the high volume and the rationalized line of models, higher levels of local content would be attainable without significant increases in costs or prices, and the increased local content would cut imports and help resolve the balance-of-payments problem.[5]

There were sticking points in the ensuing discussions over the structure of ownership and management—the mix of national and foreign, public and private. At least one version of the proposal suggested that Chrysler, the Azcárraga family, and the government each have a one-third share in the firm, but some government officials insisted upon majority government ownership. Chrysler was willing to accept minority ownership in the venture (that was its status in Auto-Mex), but it wanted management control in its own hands, and this spawned other objections. Despite these disagreements, by January 1969 the

[5] At some point in the discussion, Auto-Mex and Chrysler broached the possibility of exports by this new corporation, a step which would increase production as well as generate needed foreign exchange. There was never a firm commitment to that step, however. Had there been, the merger proposal might have been much more interesting to Campos Salas and to SIC.

SECOND ENCOUNTER, 1969

technical committee had decided to accept the Auto-Mex/Chrysler proposal and to reject the VAM/AMC plan. A policy memo was prepared,
outlining those features of the proposal that were basically satisfactory
and those still requiring negotiation. At this point, however, another
merger proposal made its appearance, provoked by and in direct opposition to the Auto-Mex/Chrysler proposal.

The officials of DINA had not been invited to join the discussions of
the Auto-Mex/Chrysler plan.[6] DINA, however, was preparing its own
proposals. Sometime in 1967 or early 1968, in response to SIC's search
for exports, Volkswagen had suggested the possibility of making substantial vehicle exports to the United States under certain conditions.
Not to be outdone by its principal competitor in the small-car field,
DINA initiated a study to develop an export plan. In June 1969, when
the study was ready, Pierre Dreyfuss, president of Renault, came from
France to accompany Villaseñor in submitting it to Campos Salas and
Ortiz Mena. Ortiz Mena took the occasion to let Dreyfuss know that,
with the Auto-Mex/Chrysler plan all but approved, Renault would soon
be out of Mexico—a surprise to Villaseñor as well as to Dreyfuss. (DINA
had received a letter asking for detailed information about its operations, in connection with the planning studies for the merger plan, but
it gave no indication that the proposal was so far along.) The Auto-
Mex/Chrysler plan was outlined to them. They asked for, and were
granted, a fifteen-day period in which to prepare a counterproposal.

Villaseñor contacted Gabriel Fernández Sayago, the president of
VAM, who was only too willing to join the opposition, since the plan
was as much a threat to VAM as to DINA. Dreyfuss flew in a team from
France and Fernández Sayago summoned one from American Motors.
They did not know the details of the Auto-Mex/Chrysler proposal—a
copy had been denied to them—but they did have some idea of the
problems that the counterplan would have to solve if it were to have
a chance of heading off the other one.

Their hastily developed alternative suggested a merger in which the
government would have majority ownership in the new firm, with
Chrysler, American Motors, and Renault (and perhaps Azcárraga) each
having a minority share. Models from each of the three foreign firms
would be manufactured. Provision was made for the utilization of

[6] It is interesting to speculate on why this was so. It may have been to avoid the
predictable opposition of DINA's director, Villaseñor, to a plan that would dismantle DINA—
opposition that could have been damaging, given Villaseñor's outspoken nature. Others
have suggested that all plans other than the Auto-Mex/Chrysler one were merely window
dressing, to give an appearance of impartiality, and if so, there was no need to involve
DINA at this stage.

existing facilities: Jeeps and pick-up trucks would replace the discontinued Borgward models at the FANASA plant in Monterrey, and a new Renault model (the R-12) would be assembled at the Chrysler plant in Toluca, where there was considerable excess capacity. The rationalization that was to be achieved was in production facilities rather than in product lines.

This counterproposal was submitted to the technical committee, which then circulated another policy memo. It found (again) for the Auto-Mex/Chrysler plan as the basic proposal to be considered. By some accounts, this proposal came very close to being approved and implemented at this time, mid-July 1969. A copy of the second policy memo was leaked to the Villaseñor-Fernández Sayago group. Rather than responding with another counterproposal, they threw together a fiery eighty-page critique of the Auto-Mex/Chrysler plan, trying to show that it constituted a giveaway of the Mexican-owned firms to Chrysler control and a windfall to Azcárraga without any redeeming benefits to Mexico. Copies of the critique were liberally distributed, including one to President Díaz Ordaz himself.

A decision as important as this would ultimately have to find its way to the president's desk. As it turned out, Díaz Ordaz had the matter before him for decision at the same time that another proposal concerning the automobile industry required his attention. This was an export plan, the result of discussions between Campos Salas and Ford. Consideration of the one could not help but affect consideration of the other.

SIC was represented on the technical committee that was studying the merger proposals, but Campos Salas knew that the committee was seeking rationalization of the industry and increased domestic content rather than more exports. He was hardly disposed to leave auto-industry policy wholly to Ortiz Mena, however. Parallel to the merger discussions, Campos Salas and Bravo Aguilera conducted their own discussions with the auto makers, principally the foreign-owned ones, concerning the possibility of exports. The most extensive discussions, and ultimately the successful ones, were with Ford.

A few years earlier Ford had been outraged—sharp words had passed between its director, Molina, and SIC officials—when Auto-Mex was granted a basic production quota 7,500 units larger than Ford's and GM's quotas, in spite of Ford's cooperation and assistance in the formulation of the 1962 decree. Ford had since been looking for ways to obtain a quota equal to Auto-Mex's. It submitted several proposals to SIC for programs it would undertake in return for quota increases, but most of these were rejected as involving favoritism to a foreign-owned firm. Ford had previously been granted additional quotas, as well as the right to manufacture a second engine in Mexico, in return for exports of engines and assembly tools.

Many of Ford's new proposals to SIC were for further increases in exports, to be rewarded by further increases in its quotas, but Campos Salas approached Ford (and the other auto manufacturers) with a less attractive offer: additional exports to compensate for the *basic* quota rather than to earn *extra* quotas. But why would Ford be expected to agree to an export *requirement* instead of the incentive program it proposed? The advanced stage of the merger negotiations weighed heavily. A consolidated firm selling the full Chrysler line would have half the total industry quota, and Ford would have to compete with the remaining firms (GM, Nissan, and Volkswagen) for the other half. Moreover, Ford knew that the worsening balance of payments in the industry would compel the government to opt either for increased local content or for mandatory exports. It would be able to comply with a mandatory export requirement, but it suspected that other manufacturers would not. Auto-Mex, in particular, would have a hard time, since Chrysler, with minority ownership, might be less than enthusiastic in promoting exports. The firm envisioned in the merger proposals would have a similar difficulty. By agreeing to an export requirement, Ford could forestall the adoption of a merger policy less suited to its capability and strategy. The company's calculations were much like those made prior to the 1962 decree: accepting stiffer requirements would increase the rigors of competition, leading to greater gains for the stronger firms that could survive. SIC officials had sounded out several other firms on the proposal for mandatory exports, pointing out the need for some policy to deal with the balance-of-payments problem, but all the others had argued that the plan was impossible. SIC officials knew, however, as did Ford, that once Ford agreed, the other firms would have to agree as well, or face exclusion from the Mexican market.

Under the proposed scheme, each terminal firm would be required to earn its basic quota by compensating for its imports with a steadily rising percentage of exports. For 1970, exports would have to equal 5 percent of imports to earn the basic quota, and the figure would rise to 15 percent in 1971 and 25 percent in 1972. The expectation was that eventually each firm would compensate for 100 percent of its imports with exports, but the required levels for the years beyond 1972 were to be left to the decision of the new administration that would take office in December 1970. Exports beyond the required level would still earn quota increments.

Thus, by the late summer of 1969, two serious proposals had been developed, each backed by a powerful government minister and by a major automobile firm. Though there were uncertainties about each, they clearly marked out quite distinct futures for the automobile industry. In Mexico's centralized, presidentialist political system, decisions of this importance are ultimately made by the president. Díaz Ordaz chose the export plan. Surprisingly, the most persuasive voice in urging this course of action was that of Rodrigo Gómez, despite his participation in the development of the merger proposal. The president's approval of the export plan was not necessarily a decision to reject the merger, but its consequences were, as Ford hoped, just that. The merger proposal was already facing vigorous opposition from DINA and VAM. Without majority ownership and full management control, Chrysler would be unwilling to arrange for the newly mandated exports. The merger was no longer tenable under the new export requirements.

AGENDA SETTING

In this encounter, there were two distinct agendas, involving two somewhat overlapping casts of actors and two parallel tracks of bargaining and decision making that affected one another at several critical points. The decision that was reached was as much the choice of one agenda over the other as it was the settlement of the issues on either agenda. They embodied very different conceptions of the best route toward further industrialization in the auto industry, and they weighed quite differently the importance of Mexican ownership and of a reorganization of the market structure.

The Issues

In 1962, a single conception of development, import-substitution industrialization, had dominated the formulation of automobile policy. The bargaining agenda formed around that conception: where the government's interest in promoting import substitution conflicted with the companies' corporate strategies, issues found their way onto the bargaining agenda; where there was a convergence of interests between the government and the firms, there was no need for bargaining or for the exercise of power. The situation in 1968-1969 was more complicated, for export promotion was challenging import substitution as an overarching conception of the road to industrialization.

The merger of the Mexican-owned firms was the central proposal

165

on one agenda, but it was seen as a remedy for the difficulties with import substitution up to that point. The large number of firms had created high costs and inefficiency; the increasing volume of imported parts had worsened the balance of payments; and the terminal industry was becoming de-nationalized. Advocates of the merger proposal argued that it dealt with all of these problems: The creation of a single strengthened Mexican firm and the reduction in the total number of firms would open the door to more import substitution and thus to greater industrialization and some balance-of-payments relief, without sacrificing either efficiency or national ownership.

The export plan, on the other hand, would seek to relieve the pressure on the balance of payments by generating foreign exchange through export and to promote growth in the auto industry by widening its sales horizons beyond the inherent limitations of the Mexican market. It was much less concerned with strengthening Mexican ownership than was the merger proposal.

Both proposals sought to promote efficiency in the industry, but the first aimed to achieve it through structural reorganization, the second by exposing Mexican firms to the rigors of international competition. Both sought to resolve the industry's balance-of-payments problem, but the merger plan would do so only by clearing the way for further doses of import substitution (higher local content) in the future. There were also some clear differences between the two agendas in their attitude toward foreign ownership: the export plan offered no specific assistance to the Mexican-owned firms, if indeed it did not cede to the foreign-owned firms an additional competitive advantage. Consequently, the choice between the two agendas depended on which problems were seen as more pressing or more fundamental: efficiency or balance of payments, Mexican ownership or growth.

Virtually every issue that was raised or that could have been raised in 1962 found its way onto one or the other agenda in 1968-1969. Even some issues that seemed to have been settled, particularly the question of industry structure, were raised again. But when this second bargaining encounter was over, questions of market structure and ownership had been definitively answered, and the answers would be given in subsequent bargaining.

The Actors and Their Interests

Despite the substantial growth of the domestically owned parts industry and of organized labor in the auto sector, neither of these groups was included in the 1968-1969 bargaining. Labor was still co-opted and

166

controlled by the state and the PRI, and the parts firms were just establishing themselves and had not formed a cohesive bloc. The central actors again were the TNCs, and the state ministries, but they lined up very differently than they had in 1962, in large measure because of the way their interests had been affected by the implementation of the 1962 decree.

In 1962, the TNCs shared a common interest in gaining access to the Mexican market, although their existing operations in Mexico were so small as to scarcely affect their interests. By 1968, the terminal firms had made substantial investments in Mexico. However, they had made different strategic decisions about their approach to the Mexican market, and they had experienced varying degrees of success in following these through. Thus, their interests now diverged from one another to a significant degree. With the auto producers divided among themselves, AMIA, the industry's lobbying organization, could play no role. And because the division among the firms pitted two U.S. firms against one another, the U.S. government was also precluded from playing a role in support of its "national" interests. Similarly, the interest of various governmental ministries had diverged as a result of their different experiences since 1962. Unlike the first encounter, then, when the producers were lined up on one side of the issue and the government on the other, the second found both the firms and the government divided.

The implementation of the 1962 decree had changed the interests of the firms. Before the decree, failure to sell vehicles in Mexico was an opportunity cost; afterward, it was a real cost, a loss of return on invested capital. The character of competition was altered as well. Prior to 1962, the transnational auto firms sought to realize returns on their substantial home-country investments by increasing CKD exports for assembly in Mexico. After 1962, these firms had to make their Mexican investments pay off as well, and they had to maintain a proper relationship between manufacturing operations at home and abroad. Moreover, a degree of complexity was introduced into the relationship between domestically owned firms and the transnational auto makers with which they were linked. Three considerations in particular tended to differentiate the interests of the Mexican auto firms: their ownership status, their product and marketing strategies, and the nature of their manufacturing activities in Mexico in relation to their other principal markets and to their manufacturing facilities elsewhere in the world. The divergence of interests between the two principal corporate actors, Ford and Auto-Mex, was especially important.

Having been the firm most instrumental in shaping the 1962 decree to its own liking, and having captured a significant market share for itself over the ensuing six years, Ford was not eager for fundamental changes in industrial structure or policy. It did not like the over-crowded industry, but rationalization by merger would have threatened its market share. It would also have created a structure in which it would be logical for the government to raise local-content requirements, and Ford preferred to maintain as large a flow as possible of manufactured parts from its U.S. plants to Mexico. Much of the imported material consisted of stamped exterior body parts. These were the parts that gave cars their distinctive and recognizable styling, and they were changed annually by the American manufacturers during the 1950s and 1960s as a central element in marketing strategy. If local-content requirements were substantially raised, these parts could no longer be imported. Given the size of the Mexican market and the large scale economies on these particular parts, their domestic manufacture would have compelled Ford to choose between unattractive options: either to raise prices or to maintain model styles for longer than one year. Either choice would have reduced sales.

Ford also had an interest in avoiding mandatory exports. These would displace home-country production, most likely without any savings in production costs. Wage rates might be lower in Mexico, but this would not translate directly into lower production costs, because of lower skill levels and less labor discipline. Moreover, any savings in labor costs would be likely to be offset by smaller production capacities, higher material costs, and the costs of idling installed capacity in U.S. plants. Ford was willing to undertake some exports if extra quota were to be a reward, but mandatory exports without extra benefit was another thing altogether. Nevertheless, Ford preferred mandatory exports to higher local content if forced to choose. Mandatory exports would allow Ford to maintain its accustomed production and marketing strategies and to rationalize production among its various international operations. Higher local content would tend toward a situation in which Ford's Mexican subsidiary was a self-contained microcosm of the home-country plant, denying Ford many of the advantages of transnational operations—intracompany trade at administered transfer prices, centralized production of parts having great scale economy, etc.

Auto-Mex was much less happy with the status quo than Ford; it proposed the merger to regain competitive position. How it was disadvantaged by the existing structure is best seen by comparing its situation to that of Ford and GM. Because Auto-Mex's earnings were distinct from Chrysler's earnings, Chrysler insisted on higher margins for parts sales to Auto-Mex than Ford or GM did for transfer sales to their subsidiaries. Auto-Mex thus had an interest in replacing imports with domestic production if a sufficiently large volume of production could yield cost savings. The merger proposal, with its promise of a high aggregate quota, could make such high-volume domestic production possible. Meanwhile, if Ford and GM were forced to raise their domestic content, they would lose some of the advantages of cheaper parts imports from their parents at the same time that their lower volumes would not allow them to achieve the same scale economies that the new, larger Mexican firm could. For its part, Chrysler had an interest in maintaining a flow of parts sales from Detroit to Mexico, but even if the merger proposal would mean less imported content in each vehicle, the larger number of Chrysler vehicles to be sold in Mexico would more than maintain the total sales volume from Chrysler to Auto-Mex. Neither Auto-Mex nor Chrysler was interested in mandatory exports. Auto-Mex would not be able to find buyers for its exports on its own; it would have to rely wholly on Chrysler, thus diminishing its independence. Chrysler would have to be the principal buyer of any Auto-Mex exports, and virtually all of these exports would have to be parts for Chrysler cars. Such purchases would displace purchases of parts from wholly-owned Chrysler subsidiaries or from supplier firms with which Chrysler had long-standing relations. Chrysler could hardly be enthusiastic about having to rely on parts purchases from a firm that it did not control and that had no track record in manufacturing parts to Chrysler's international standards.

The other firms tended to stay on the sidelines during this conflict. The other wholly-owned subsidiaries of TNCs viewed things much as Ford did. Actors—even transnational corporations—do not always see their interests with clarity or foresight, however. Ford was perspicacious enough to see that a growing balance-of-payments deficit would force the government to choose between mandatory exports and higher levels of required local content, and it wanted to seize a pre-emptive role in the choice. The other TNC subsidiaries confined their efforts to telling the government that, because the industry was so new, neither step would be feasible in the near future.

It would be a mistake, however, to believe that the interests of the other TNC subsidiaries were identical to Ford's. GM's situation was most similar, because of similarities in ownership structure, product strategy, and geographies of production and marketing. Perhaps for that reason, GM was again willing to let Ford represent their common interests in Latin America. Volkswagen's position was different on two of these dimensions, however. With its home-country plant in Germany, Volkswagen's shipping costs were significantly higher than those of the U.S.

firms. Volkswagen did have a major plant in Brazil, but production costs there were not yet low enough to warrant importing parts from São Paulo rather than Wolfsburg. Because Brazilian local-content requirements were nearly 100 percent, the Brazilian market could not be targeted by the Mexican subsidiary for export sales, and (again because of freight costs) exports back to Germany would be more expensive than the U.S. firms' rail shipments across the U.S. border. Volkswagen did have export possibilities that the U.S. firms did not have—replacement parts to the U.S. after-market and assembled vehicles to Latin American countries without manufacturing programs—but these were not major opportunities.

If geographical factors made the export route less attractive to Volkswagen than to Ford, product-strategy and other considerations made higher local content more attractive to Volkswagen than to Ford or GM. As its advertising trumpeted, Volkswagen's reliance on the familiar "Beetle" obviated the need for a plethora of models and for annual model changes. The expensive body-stamping dies could be amortized over the firm's total production and over several years, and Volkswagen had already installed body-stamping equipment in Mexico. Consequently, Volkswagen was better prepared to meet higher local-content requirements without sales-crippling price increases. It cannot be concluded that Volkswagen's interests definitely lay more with higher local content than with mandatory exports, but only that its interests were less clear-cut. It did not lend its support to either side in the 1968-1969 bargaining, and over the next decade its position wavered more than that of any of the other firms.

The interests of the remaining firms can quickly be summarized. As the latest entrant, Nissan was preoccupied with gaining a foothold in the market, but its interests most resembled those of VW among the foreign-owned firms. DINA and VAM saw only extinction in the merger proposal and so both were eager to torpedo it. Being state-owned gave them a certain freedom from the rigors of balance sheets, so the export plan looked less forbidding to them than to Auto-Mex.

Like the firms, the government found itself divided. SIC and the Ministry of Finance backed rival plans. Such a split within the government was perhaps not inevitable, but neither was it surprising, in view of the embedded dispositions of the two ministries and the policy preferences of their principal officials. Both ministries had a continuing interest in the automobile industry as a centerpiece of industrialization, but they had different ideas about how to go about encouraging its development.

The Ministry of Finance had primary responsibility for the balance

170

of payments, for the fiscal incentives that would be given to firms to encourage them along a particular development route, and for the efficiency and profitability of state-owned firms. In view of these responsibilities, it is easy to see why the merger proposal was appealing to this ministry: it promised to strengthen the state-owned firms, it would not require additional fiscal subsidies, and it opened the door to increased local content and thus to some amelioration of the industry's drain on the balance of payments. However, the export plan also had its attractions: it offered immediate help to the balance of payments, and by diversifying exports it would strengthen Mexico's overall trade position, alleviating dependency to a degree. But the merger plan was brought to Finance Minister Ortiz Mena by Azcárraga, a friend and a leading Mexican entrepreneur, and when Finance backed the plan, it was the only proposal in view. The export plan probably would not have surfaced—Ford would not have been willing to agree to it—if the merger plan were not under serious consideration. It is also possible that Ortiz Mena saw in the merger plan a chance to steal a march on a rival minister, a possible competitor in the jockeying for the PRI nomination for the presidency. Ordinarily, the finance minister would not be the one to have primary responsibility for auto-industry policy, but the merger proposal, because it dealt centrally with the fate of state-owned firms, gave him the opportunity.

Import-substitution industrialization was the dominant conception in SIC when it was founded in 1959, but Campos Salas and his director of industries, Bravo Aguilera, brought with them an interest in moving certain manufacturing sectors toward exports. New investments and technology transfers for export production would spur industrialization, create jobs, and help with the balance of payments. Exports would also encourage scale economies and thus efficiency far more than a continued orientation toward the small domestic market would. It was difficult to promote exports from the inefficient industries that had been created by import substitution, but Ford's opposition to the Auto-Mex merger proposal gave the Campos Salas team the wedge they needed. If Ford could be persuaded to accept a mandatory export program (which would compel the other firms to follow), Mexico would gain access to international markets, for the TNCs had the marketing facilities and could make the investments necessary to sell components abroad without first achieving sufficient volume in the domestic market.

Both Finance and SIC had concerns about the auto industry which made them interested in a change of policy. To a large degree, these concerns overlapped, but there were differences of emphasis. Azcár-

171

raga set the drama in motion by taking his merger plan to Ortiz Mena, but it was the industry's drain on the balance of payments—something that worried both ministries—that propelled the government to act. "The little red lights were flashing," as one official said. Thus, two agendas, two plans, and two convergences of interest took shape, but not, it is important to note, at the same time. The merger plan constituted one convergence of interest, involving Finance, Auto-Mex, and Chrysler. When this plan had taken shape and appeared likely to be adopted, a second convergence of interests took shape, involving SIC and Ford. They were not incompatible plans, strictly speaking, but they became rivals.

DECISION MAKING

Two different questions about the decisions need to be answered: (1) Why was the export plan selected rather than the merger plan? (2) Why did the firms accede to the export plan once it emerged as the government's preferred policy?

Selecting the Plan

Several people interviewed argued that the export plan was chosen simply because it was superior—more rational. There is some truth to this. Major opposition within the state to the export plan would have been expected from those officials who had been working on the merger plan: Ortiz Mena and Rodrigo Gómez. When Ford's apprehensions about the merger led to the emergence of the export plan, however, Gómez and probably Ortiz Mena as well were impressed by it. The balance of payments had been a far more central concern of the Finance Ministry and the Bank of Mexico than protection of Mexican ownership or assistance to state-owned firms, important as these may have been, and the export plan was far simpler and promised more immediate effects on the balance of payments than did the merger. When the merger plan's most powerful supporters in the government quietly voiced their support for the export plan to Díaz Ordaz, it was almost inevitable that the president would approve it.

If the export plan offered more reliable results for the balance of payments, however, it did not promise as much for the protection of Mexican ownership or the rationalization of the industry. The choice between the two plans came down to a choice between views of which problems were the major ones facing the industry, and power was exercised in making that decision.

It is not possible to argue that the Ford-SIC coalition was inherently stronger than the Auto-Mex-Chrysler-Finance coalition. Indeed, the reverse was probably true. However, the latter coalition broke apart, because of internal disharmony arising from several sources. Even before the export alternative was proposed, the directors of the two state-owned firms that would be absorbed in the merger, Fernández Sayago of VAM and Villaseñor of DINA, attacked the merger plan as vigorously as they could. Their opposition was anticipated, but they were able to depict the merger as a giveaway of Mexican patrimony to a foreign corporation. A further source of difficulty with the merger plan was continuing ambiguity over exactly what Azcárraga and Chrysler were proposing with regard to ownership, valuation of assets, local content, exports, etc. Finally, there was the defection of the merger plan's most powerful supporters in the government.

When Díaz Ordaz approved the export plan, he may or may not have seen it as a direct alternative to the merger plan. It probably seemed clean and simple, promising relief for the balance of payments and expanded production without the political complications—in the form of internal opposition from major ministries or state firms—that would have been provoked by the merger plan. Discussion of the merger plan did continue for some months after the export *acuerdo* (agreement) was promulgated. Nevertheless, approval of the export plan sounded the death knell of the kind of increased rationalization that Azcárraga had backed. Azcárraga saw the handwriting on the wall. Knowing that Chrysler would not be willing to commit itself to the purchase of export parts from a subsidiary over which it did not have full control, Azcárraga realized his competitive position had been rendered untenable, and in 1971 he sold his equity to Chrysler under the terms of an earlier agreement. Mexican ownership of the terminal industry suffered another blow when Ramírez closed the doors of FANASA, turning the assets over to SOMEX, his major creditor. Futher denationalization of the industry was a definite consequence, though probably unintentional, of the approval of the export plan.

Acceptance by the Firms

Ever since coming to office in December 1964, Campos Salas and Bravo Aguilera had been trying to get the auto producers to export automotive products. The firms had been willing to do so only with extra production quotas as a reward: mandatory exports were not even considered until 1968. How, then, did the government get the firms to accept mandatory exports against their opposition? Once the export plan had been approved by Díaz Ordaz (and the merger plan effectively shelved), the bargaining situation reverted to that of 1962: the transnational firms versus the Mexican state. But the balance of power in the bargaining had now changed.

The sources of state power show elements of both increased strength and weakness. The Mexican government now had nearly a decade of experience in making and administering industrial policy for the automobile sector. This may have brought about some "learning," to the government's advantage, but if so, the *sexenio* change in December 1964 dissipated it to a significant extent. In 1962, the government had been internally divided. In 1968-1969, the government was even more seriously split before the export plan was adopted, but after adoption, it was unified and so was able to wield more of its potential power. On the other hand, promulgation of the export plan late in the *sexenio* was a source of weakness for the government: an opponent of the plan could hope that a new administration could be persuaded to take a different course.

On the side of the firms, oligopolistic competition remained the most important element in their potential power. The transnational firms continued to have control over the technical and managerial knowhow for manufacturing motor vehicles, and they also controlled world trade in automotive products. Had they resisted mandatory exports in unison, the Mexican state could not have prevailed. Ford's willingness to agree to mandatory exports, however, broke the circle, and by the logic of defensive investment the other firms then had to agree as well.

Although its officials deny this, Ford must have made the commitment, and made it when it did, in order to torpedo the merger proposal. It seems likely that the merger proposal would have been enacted in some form if Ford had not accepted the export plan and that Ford would not have accepted it had the merger proposal not appeared likely to come to fruition. Ford suspected that the industry's drain on the balance of payments would require government action of some sort—either mandatory exports or higher local-content requirements. Of these options, Ford preferred exports. It knew that acceptance of the merger plan would tip the scales heavily toward higher local-content requirements and create an industry structure (a single large Mexican firm) that would make it even harder for Ford to compete under such requirements. Conversely, Ford knew that if exports were required under the current industry structure, it stood a very good chance of doing as well as or better than any of the other firms.

Once Ford agreed to export, the other firms felt compelled to go along or risk losing their place in the Mexican market. Oligopolistic competition was a constant in the balance of power in the bargaining in 1962 and 1968-1969, though there were two factors that altered its force somewhat, in opposite directions. On the one hand, the firms had made investments in Mexico; being excluded now would have meant more than an opportunity cost. On the other hand, these investments in Mexico also meant that the firms had potential supporters among the labor organizations and the network of parts-supply firms that had been developed since 1962. That these were excluded from the bargaining strengthened the hand of the government. The balance of power was further shifted toward the government by the exclusion of foreign governments from the bargaining, because of the circumstances under which the export plan arose.

The export *acuerdo* was simple in the requirements it imposed: Each terminal firm had to compensate with exports a steadily rising percentage of its imports of parts and components. Sixty percent of these exports could be of products manufactured by the terminal firms themselves; the rest had to be exports arranged for their suppliers. The *acuerdo* thus succeeded in finding an export route different from what neoclassical theory envisioned and also different from the model of the Canadian-U.S. agreement. It placed the responsibility for exporting squarely on the transnational terminal firms. They would have to find products appropriate for export and solve any problems of international diplomacy, or else face exclusion from the Mexican market. But, while simple in concept, the export requirements would prove difficult to implement. The difficulties, however, would have to be dealt with by Díaz Ordaz's successor as president, Luis Echeverría Álvarez.

·8·

THE CONSEQUENCES OF EXPORT PROMOTION

Structural Consequences

When the Echeverría administration came to power in 1970, Guillermo Becker was named director of industries in SIC, a position he had already held at the end of the López Mateos administration. The export-oriented automobile policy that he inherited promised to generate foreign exchange to meet the country's import bill, spur further industrialization, and provide new sources of employment, which were all major goals of Echeverría. Becker and his team might not have chosen such a policy themselves—they were skeptical that the automobile industry was sufficiently well established to commence exporting—but they also saw considerable harm in reversing course so soon after the new policy had been promulgated. Instead, they chose to push ahead with implemention of the 1969 *acuerdo*. They formalized its provisions in a second auto-industry decree issued in October 1972.[1]

The new decree sought little change in the major characteristics of the structure of the auto: the large number of firms, the predominance of subsidiaries of TNCs, and the complete reliance upon foreign technology. If anything, these were to be turned to advantage. If TNC subsidiaries dominated the Mexican market, their control of technology and their global organizational networks could be used to provide access to foreign markets. In the process of effecting this orientation toward foreign markets, however, there were unintended consequences both for ownership and for the market structure which tended to tighten the grip of the TNCs on the Mexican industry, nor were the effects on the balance of trade those that had been intended.

Ownership

It has already been seen that Azcárraga and the other Mexican shareholders sold their holding in Fábricas Auto-Mex to Chrysler in 1971, for they believed their position was untenable once the export plan had been adopted. This removed essentially all private Mexican capital

---

[1] "Decreto que fija las bases el desarrollo de la industria automotriz," *Diario oficial*, Oct. 24, 1972. This new decree also consolidated and codified a variety of other policies toward the terminal and supplier firms that had been devised in the decade since the first decree.

from the terminal industry. The only remaining auto makers with Mexican equity were the state-owned firms, VAM and DINA, and they were doomed to being the weak sisters in the industry.[2]

Private Mexican capital could not be so easily displaced from the supplier industry because by law foreign equity in such firms could not exceed 40 percent. Nevertheless, the new policy worked to strengthen those firms with significant foreign equity in comparison with the wholly Mexican-owned ones. A small number of companies soon came to dominate auto-parts exports from Mexico. In 1975, although forty auto-parts firms made some exports, one firm, TREMEC accounted for 42 percent of the total value, and ten firms accounted

TABLE 8.1

EXPORTS BY MEXICAN AUTOMOTIVE-PARTS FIRMS, 1975

Firm	Foreign Participant in Equity	Total Exports, 1975 (pesos)	% of Total Exports by Automotive-Parts Firms
Transmisiones y Equipos Mecánicos	Clark Equipment	405,934,529	41.7
Equipo Automotriz Americana	[a]	149,079,048	15.3
Rassini Rheem	Rheem International	127,984,629	13.2
Whitaker	Whitaker Inter-America	25,296,050	2.6
Aralmex	[a]	24,911,289	2.6
Industria Automotriz	None	21,948,193	2.3
Manufactureras Metálica Monterrey	A. O. Smith	20,744,295	2.1
F.U.M.E.[b]	[b]	18,037,490	1.9
Automanufacturas	Budd	16,093,927	1.7
Mex-Par Blackstone	Blackstone	10,917,522	1.1
Total of top ten exporting firms		820,946,972	84.5
Total of all auto-parts firms		973,142,915	100.0

SOURCE: Unpublished data provided by SIC, and authors' interviews
[a] Presence of foreign participation in equity is known, but identity of participant is not.
[b] No information is available either about the meaning of the letters "F.U.M.E." or about whether there is foreign participation in the form's equity.

[2] Although neither DINA nor VAM did particularly well, they were able to survive because of their state ownership (100 percent in the case of DINA and 60 percent for VAM). Not only could they sometimes afford to lose money, but the state was also not eager to enforce export requirements on them to the point where they would be driven under. In the case of VAM, another factor was its particular market niche, producing cars between the Japanese and European sizes on the one hand and the U.S. Big Three on the other; its competition with other firms was therefore not so direct. Further, it was the sole producer of Jeeps, many of which were bought by government agencies.

for over 80 percent (see table 8.1). The parts firms that succeeded in generating a significant volume of exports were disproportionately those with substantial foreign equity participation. While only 39 of the 410 firms identified in a 1976 study as being auto-parts suppliers had foreign equity,[3] at least 6 and probably 8 or 9 of the 10 biggest exporters had substantial (though still minority) foreign equity participation. Superior technological capability might have given these firms a competitive edge, but there was another and equally important consideration: the transnational auto firms, having longstanding relationships with their major parts suppliers, preferred to buy from subsidiaries of those suppliers rather than from independent Mexican firms.

The denationalization in the terminal industry and the increased significance of foreign equity in the parts industry suggest that one result of the export policy was to shift the locus of key decisions concerning the industry outside of Mexico to a greater extent than before. This was true in the areas not only of sales but also of design and technology. So long as vehicles and components produced in Mexico were targeted strictly for the Mexican market, they could be tailored (by government regulation if not by the free choice of the firms) for Mexico. Models could be frozen over a number of years, and components could be standardized across makes and models. But now that components manufactured in Mexico were destined, in part, for international markets, design and technology would have to conform to the specifications of vehicles produced in and for the largest developed-country markets. Decisions concerning such specifications were made in Detroit, Tokyo, Wolfsburg, and Paris.

Market Structure

The export policy also had the unintended consequence of hardening the industry's overcrowded market structure.[4] The denationalization of Fábricas Auto-Mex and the integration of all the firms more fully into the world automobile industry meant further obstacles to any effort to decrease the number of firms through mergers. While the dynamics of the world industry might in the future bring about mergers, or withdrawals of firms from Mexico, the number of auto-making

[3] Fajnzylber and Martínez Tárrago, *Las empresas transnacionales.*

[4] With the elimination of FANASA in 1969 (see chap. 6), the number of firms had dropped from eight to seven, but FANASA was such a minor producer (it only made a few thousand cars during its entire existence) that its disappearance was insignificant in reducing the problems that arose from the number of firms.

firms operating in Mexico was now essentially outside the control of the Mexican government. Moreover, the export policy raised subtle threats to the restrictions on vertical integration that had been established in the 1962 decree to protect the Mexican-owned parts industry. Since exports tended to be predominantly parts rather than finished vehicles (see below), the terminal firms pressed for permission to manufacture parts (primarily for export but also for domestic use) that they had not previously been producing. They began to argue that only their direct control over the manufacture of such parts could ensure the quality, cost, and delivery characteristics necessary for export, and that if permission for such increased vertical integration were denied they might not be able to comply with the export requirements, leading to loss of investments and jobs. On such arguments, Chrysler won permission to manufacture condensers for air conditioners, and Ford to manufacture hubs and drums, components they had been forbidden to make under the 1962 decree.

Trade Consequences

The government especially expected to see beneficial consequences from the new policy in the industry's balance of trade. However, while exports did increase significantly, many of the firms failed to comply with the required compensation levels. At first, the pattern of noncompliance was sporadic: some firms failed one year, others the next, encouraging the view that the difficulties were temporary and company-specific, the sorts of difficulties to be expected in the transition to a new policy. Gradually, though, noncompliance became more general and officials began to realize that there were deeper problems, rooted in the structure of the world industry. The peripheral position of Mexico in the TNCs' global strategies meant that exports from Mexico would not be given priority when world recession reduced international motor-vehicle trade, as it did in 1974-1975. Because of this, and because the Mexican economy grew faster than the economies of the major developed countries after 1972, the industry's trade deficit increased. By 1975, there was growing concern among government officials that some corrective action was necessary.

Understanding the precise extent of the firms' export shortfall requires an understanding of the mechanism by which exports were mandated. After the 1962 decree, production quotas set limits on how many vehicles each company could manufacture. These quotas were enforced by state control over import licenses: no company could import more parts than were needed to fill their assigned quotas. But after 1969, the terminal firms had to earn their quotas through exports. Each terminal firm was to export, or to arrange with an independent parts-supply firm to export, automotive products to compensate for a percentage of its imported content. At least 40 percent of these exports had to come from the parts firms, a provision designed to ensure that the benefits from exports would be shared by Mexican-owned companies. Firms that failed to achieve the minimum level of required exports would be penalized by a reduction in their basic quota for the following year.[5]

The industry as a whole fulfilled its exports commitments in 1973 but not in 1972 or in the years from 1974 to 1976.[6] The greatest shortfall came in 1975, a year when the world industry was caught up in recessions in a number of major auto-producing countries. The clearest perspective on what was happening is provided by the industry's balance-of-payments record. In the first few years after the 1969 *acuerdo*, exports did increase, but imports grew at the same rate; the deficit did not grow, but neither was it reduced. Beginning in 1974, however, imports increased more rapidly than exports, and so the deficit rose again. (See table 8.2.) It was evident that the new policy was not working as expected. World market conditions were partly to blame, but there had been difficulties even before the global recession. An examination of the interests of the transnational auto makers and the structure of world auto trade in the early 1970s will reveal their sources.

At first glance, the automobile industry might seem to have been an unlikely sector for SIC officials to single out for export promotion; one would have expected such efforts to be pursued in industries that were

[5] The actual enforcement was slightly more complex. The 1962 decree had provided for the possibility that the auto makers could earn extra quotas if they exported; the new policy also provided that exports beyond the minimum required level would earn extra quotas. Both basic and extra quotas were calculated from the firms' commitments to export in the following year, so that they could plan their production schedules. Thus, if a firm failed to comply with its export requirements in a given year, the sanction of a reduced basic quota was imposed in the following year.

[6] These export commitments include both those required to earn the basic quota and those incurred to earn extra quotas. No one of the TNCs stands out as the chief noncomplier. Volkswagen had the largest shortfall relative to its commitments in 1972, but the largest export surplus in 1973. Ford's record steadily worsened after 1972; GM's tended to improve. But nearly all the firms—Nissan was the lone exception—did worse in 1974 than they had done in 1973. GM, VAM, and Chrysler managed some improvement in 1975, but Ford and Volkswagen (not to mention DINA) did so much worse that, overall, the industry's record was poorest in that year. Only Nissan completed the years 1972-1976 without an accumulated export shortfall.

more labor-intensive or that employed less sophisticated technology.[7] That the Mexican automobile industry was substantially composed of TNC subsidiaries may seem to have been another ground for looking elsewhere for exports. It has frequently been contended that TNCs restrain their subsidiaries from making exports that would be in direct competition with the parent firm.[8] It was precisely the presence of TNC subsidiaries that recommended the industry as a candidate for export promotion, however. TNC subsidiaries would have advanced technology and access to marketing channels—and thus the ability to export. It was hoped that the Mexican government's control over the domestic

TABLE 8.2

BALANCE OF PAYMENTS IN THE MEXICAN AUTOMOBILE INDUSTRY, 1969-1976

	Imports of Assembly Material[a] (1)	Exports of Auto Products[a] (2)	(1)-(2)[a] (3)	(2)/(1) (in %) (4)	Required Basic Level of Export Compensation (%)[b] (5)
1969	1,789.8	185.9	1,603.9	10.4	0
1970	1,913.3	320.6	1,592.7	16.8	5
1971	2,095.1	449.4	1,645.7	21.5	15
1972	2,401.8	699.7	1,702.1	29.1	25
1973	2,899.2	1,233.6	1,665.6	42.6	30
1974	4,109.5	1,555.2	2,554.3	37.8	40
1975	6,157.2	1,784.6	4,372.6	29.0	50
1976	7,426.5	3.072.3	4,354.2	41.4	60

SOURCE: Guillermo Salas Vargas, "Política industrial e industria automotriz en México, 1947-1979" (Master's thesis, El Colegio de México, 1980), p. 135

[a] Millions of pesos.

[b] Since most firms incurred export commitments beyond the required basic level, the extent of failure to meet export commitments was actually greater than a comparison of cols. 4 and 5 would indicate.

[7] Robert Boatler has noted that Mexico's manufactured exports have tended to come disproportionately from capital-intensive sectors: "Trade Theory Predictions and the Growth of Mexico's Manufactured Exports," *Economic Development and Cultural Change* 23 (1974-1975):491-506. Boatler's explanation focuses upon the higher productivity of Mexico's capital-intensive industries, but his discussion does not touch on the role of direct foreign investments by TNCs or on the role of government policies (such as the one under discussion here) in bringing about this higher productivity or in inducing exports.

[8] This is a subject on which there have been conflicting claims. A study by José de la Torre, for example, showed that, in 1966, "U.S. affiliates accounted for only 9.5 percent of Latin America's gross manufacturing value added, although their share of manufacturing exports was 41.4 percent": "Foreign Investment and Export Dependency," *Economic Development and Cultural Change* 23 (1974-1975):133-150. Fajnzylber and Martínez Tárrago reached different conclusions for Mexico, however; their research showed that the share of TNCs in total manufacturing production was approximately equal to their share in total manufacturing exports—about one-third: *Las empresas transnacionales*, p. 300.

181

market through the quota system would make them willing as well as able.

Recognition of the centrality of the TNCs to the export policy requires a different view of the terms of success of the policy from a view of the matter through the lens of neoclassical economic theory.[9] Neoclassical economics would proceed from the assumptions that there were many buyers and many sellers of automotive products and that transactions were substantially governed by market competition. From such a perspective, the ability of Mexican manufacturers to win a share of world trade in automotive products would depend on whether these manufacturers could match the cost, quality, and delivery capabilities of existing suppliers closely enough to be competitive. If exports were not forthcoming, the explanation would focus on inefficiency of production, defective workmanship, or unreliable delivery.

The assumptions on which this perspective rests, however, do not obtain in the world auto industry. This industry is an oligopoly comprising eight or ten major firms. In and of itself, this number might be sufficient for workable competition. Because these firms are transnational, however, and because of the way they have organized production, a high percentage of international automotive trade is *intrafirm* trade among each TNC's integrated subsidiaries, and much of the rest involves longstanding, close working relationships between the auto firms and their equally transnational suppliers of major parts and components. For many automotive products there is only a single buyer, and the contracts for these products are worked out in ways that are influenced by market forces less than the neoclassical perspective would lead one to suppose. The effects of these circumstances in Mexico can be seen in each of the three major categories of world automotive trade: trade in whole vehicles, in original equipment parts, and in replacement parts (table 8.3).

In the early 1970s, exports of whole vehicles from Mexico to other major developing countries in Latin America were limited by tariffs and other import barriers which these countries had established to protect their own auto-manufacturing programs.[10] Exports to developed countries, however, were constrained by the kinds of price considerations emphasized in the neoclassical approach. In the case of

---

[9] The argument of the next several paragraphs is presented in greater detail in Douglas C. Bennett and Kenneth E. Sharpe, "Transnational Corporations and the Political Economy of Export Promotion: The Case of the Mexican Automobile Industry," *International Organization* 33 (1979):177-201.

[10] For an overview of this process, see Bennett and Sharpe, "World Automobile Industry."

Mexico—especially with the industrial structure created in 1962—production volumes were too small to allow prices competitive with say, the U.S. market. Even if price were not a barrier, it was rational for Nissan, Renault, and Volkswagen to continue supplying the U.S. market from their home-country plants rather than from their Mexican subsidiaries. Larger production volumes at home allowed them to take full advantage of the scale economies that kept them competitive in the world industry (see chapter 3). Not until the late 1970s would this situation change, with the advent of worldwide sourcing and "world cars." It is not surprising, then, that in 1975 only 6.6 percent of Mexican automotive exports were of assembled vehicles, and nearly all of these came from sales by the European- and Japanese-based firms to small markets in Central America and the Caribbean.

Trade in replacement equipment provided a potentially open market because of the larger number of buyers (service stations, repair shops, dealers, auto-supply stores, etc.). For some parts, those of simple technology and broad suitability across makes, models, and years (e.g., wheel rims, windshields and wipers, shock absorbers, batteries), competitive price and quality might be sufficient to capture a share of the market, though established brand names may constitute a significant barrier. The difficulties are more considerable, however, for parts that must meet the design specifications of a particular make or model (product differentiation reaches into the aftermarket as well) or parts that embody sophisticated technology. In these cases, export sales would be possible only if the auto manufacturer were willing to license the necessary technology or designs. Granting such licenses to Mexican

TABLE 8.3

COMPOSITION OF AUTOMOTIVE EXPORTS FROM MEXICO, 1975

		PERCENTAGE OF EXPORTS THAT WERE:		
Firm	Total Value of Exports (000s of pesos)	Assembled Vehicles	Parts Made by Firm Itself	Parts Made by Auto-Parts Firms
Chrysler	708,401	3.6	75.8	20.6
Volkswagen	617,691	11.5	88.5	0.0
Ford	542,705	0.7	26.8	72.4
General Motors	344,649	0.0	45.9	54.1
DINA (Renault)	133,071	24.8	1.5	73.6
VAM (AMC)	128,790	0.0	0.2	99.8
Nissan (Datsun)	101,573	37.8	41.4	20.8
Total	2,576,880	6.6	55.6	37.8

SOURCE: Unpublished data provided by SIC

manufacturers might disrupt long-established relationships between the transnational auto firms and their regular parts suppliers.

The automotive parts exports considered most important by the Mexican government were original-equipment exports, and here non-market considerations were extremely important. Such trade is of two kinds, intracompany trade and purchases from independent parts suppliers.[11] In the first kind, the choice of the plant or subsidiary to produce a given part takes account of the costs of raw materials, production, and transportation (subject to the provisions of local-content requirements). The determination of these costs in turn depends on how certain costs (e.g., for R & D, production equipment, and technical assistance) are allocated within the transnational enterprise. Furthermore, intracompany pricing can be arranged to take advantage of varying tax rates in different countries or to accord with a variety of other considerations of global strategy. Because of these several degrees of freedom in setting costs and prices for internal transfers, the ability to manufacture original-equipment parts at competitive costs would not in and of itself be sufficient to win Mexico a share of this kind of world trade.

Even when parts are procured from independent suppliers, decisions are again influenced by considerations other than simply cost and quality. The transnational automobile manufacturers have long-term relationships with their major parts suppliers which they are eager to maintain and which might lead them to be reluctant to accept imports from Mexican firms. In those fairly frequent cases where a Mexican parts firm is a subsidiary of a U.S. (or European or Japanese) parts firm, drawn to Mexico in the early 1960s at the urging of one of the terminal firms, an arrangement might be made to obtain parts from the Mexican plant rather than the home-country plant. But this is unlikely to be an arms-length market transaction; something akin to an administratively set transfer price is likely to be involved.

The general conclusion, then, is that while considerations of cost and quality were important to the possibility that exports would be realized by the Mexican automotive industry, they were neither necessary nor sufficient to generate such exports. Particularly because of their oligopsony position, the transnational firms had and have con-

---

[11] White (*American Automobile Industry*, pp. 79-80) has argued that in the U.S. the pattern of independent parts suppliers arose because of a desire on the part of the major firms to spread risk. With its various divisions, such as Delco and AC, GM produces more parts in-house than Ford or Chrysler or the European manufacturers. The Japanese pattern is more complicated, because the independent parts suppliers tend to be associated with the same industrial groupings or families as are the terminal firms they supply.

siderable control over the patterns of world auto trade. They can take account of other factors that bear on their global profits or strategy, and they can set prices for intrafirm trade as they please to some extent. Consequently, whether Mexico could capture a significant share of world automotive trade would depend on the dynamics of the world automobile industry and on the place that Mexico occupied in the global strategies of the TNCs. These conditions make it possible to understand why the export promotion policy in the Mexican automobile industry failed to live up to expectations, particularly in 1974-1975.

For the first few years of the new policy, the transnational automobile firms tried to find opportunities to export from Mexico. Fixed investments in their home-country plants and elsewhere in the world constituted something of a limit: there would be costs if Mexican exports displaced production elsewhere. But around the edges of their global production schedules, various opportunities for procuring Mexican parts were sought and found. Where excess capacity could be located in Mexican plants, and where this capacity could be utilized at costs close to those of alternative sites, the TNCs used it to produce parts for export. Ford and GM, for example, followed this course in their Mexican engine plants.[12]

With manual transmissions becoming, at that time, less and less common in the United States, the U.S.-based firms felt able to convert their U.S. plants to the manufacture of automatic transmissions and obtain more of such manual transmissions as they still needed from Mexico. TREMEC, the largest Mexican maker of transmissions, quickly emerged as the country's major auto-parts exporter. When pollution-control legislation was passed in the United States, it was as cheap or cheaper to obtain some parts of "dirty manufacture" from Mexico—springs, for one important example—than to invest in pollution-abatement equipment for U.S. plants.

The lure of the Mexican market induced the transnational firms to produce additional exports, even when the costs of Mexican parts were higher than the costs of parts obtained from alternative sources. One interesting example was an arrangement worked out between Chrysler and one of its suppliers of major components, a U.S.-based TNC with a subsidiary in Mexico, for parts to be used in U.S. assembly operations. Because of raw-material and transportation costs, the Mexican-made

[12] It is worth recalling that to some extent these plants had been set up with an eye toward export production. Ford, for example, was granted permission to produce a second engine in Mexico only with a commitment to export a significant percentage of the total output; see chapter 6.

components were more expensive than the American-made ones, but Chrysler wanted them made in Mexico so that its subsidiary could comply with the export requirements. It arranged for its Mexican subsidiary to transfer funds to Chrysler's U.S. assembly operation to compensate for the increase in parts costs.

This was obviously not an arms-length transaction in an open, competitive market. Indeed, cost considerations argued against the transaction rather than for it. The exports were possible only because of the existence of parallel transnational networks. The parts-supply firm could allow its U.S. plant to "lose" the sales to its Mexican plant because its global sales (and profits) were not changed thereby. Chrysler could allow its U.S. plant to pay more for Mexican-made parts because it could have its Mexican subsidiary compensate its American assembly operation. The advantage to Chrysler lay in the fact that the exports earned Chrysler a higher production quota—and hence higher sales— in Mexico. In the judgment of the Chrysler management, the increased sales were worth more, in terms of increased profitability in the short run or market penetration in the long run, than the increased components costs.

To a significant extent, these opportunities for finding places for Mexican-made components in the global production of the TNCs came from the increasing sales in most major markets between 1969 and 1973. However, such opportunities became more costly when the world recession of 1974-1975 intruded and sent auto sales plummeting. Registrations of new vehicles dropped in the United States from 14.4 million in 1973 to 11.4 million in 1974 and 10.7 million in 1975, a decline of 25 percent. In the four major European producing countries (West Germany, France, Italy, and Great Britain), the slump was from 7.7 million in 1973 to 6.4 million in 1974, and in Japan it was from 5.0 to 3.9 million, although 1975 showed no further decline in Europe and even a slight rebound in Japan. Overall, total world auto production slipped from 38.9 million units in 1973 to 34.7 million in 1974 and 33.0 million in 1975.

The transnational firms looked differently at Mexico in this changed context. In and of itself, the Mexican market was no less promising. In fact, vehicle production in Mexico, virtually all of it for sale in the domestic market, rose from 285,570 units in 1973 to 359,947 in 1974 and dipped only slightly in 1975 to 356,624. But in a period of slumping world auto sales, exports from Mexico were accorded a lower priority. Cutbacks in parts production had to be made somewhere, and Mexico was too small a market in the global scheme of TNC operations to be exempted. The threatened sanction of losing a share of the

Mexican market was simply not significant enough in a global view of costs and benefits. The partial reorientation toward the world market had made the Mexican auto industry more vulnerable to the dynamics of the world industry and to decisions taken in the headquarters of the major transnational firms.

This vulnerability was made all the more evident when the Echeverría administration found itself unable to use the sanctions that were supposed to be imposed for failure to fulfill export commitments. If only one or two firms had failed to comply, it would have been relatively easy to enforce the penalties: quotas could have been reassigned from the noncomplying firms to the complying ones. But in a situation where nearly all the firms failed to comply, the penalty of quota reduction turned out to be a sword that cut both ways: it could not be wielded for fear of injuring the country as well as the firms. If production quotas were decreased, the terminal firms would no doubt be hurt in several ways: sales would decrease; unit costs of production would increase, given the loss of scale economies, thus cutting the profit margin on the units that could be sold under the smaller quota; and sales of parts from the parent to the subsidiary would decrease, thus decreasing the parent's earnings. But the harm to the country would be no less serious. Decreased production of vehicles would mean fewer jobs for Mexican workers in the terminal industry. Fewer parts would be bought from the supplier firms; their sales would also decrease, and their profits as well, and more workers would be laid off. Automobile manufacture was desired in Mexico because of the manifold consequences it would have in stimulating other industries; should quotas for all the firms be decreased, those linkages would transmit production cutbacks in firms throughout the industrial structure of Mexico. Having engineered an increased integration of the Mexican industry into the world automobile industry, the Mexican state now found it had much less power to influence the behavior of the transnational corporations operating within its borders.

CRISIS OF THE GROWTH STRATEGY

The increasing deficit in auto trade was viewed with great concern by government officials; indeed, Mexico's overall balance-of-payments situation was so rapidly worsening by the mid-1970s that remedial action was considered imperative. The balance-of-payments problem, in turn, was but one aspect of more general difficulties facing the Mexican economy, difficulties rooted in Mexico's dependent relationships to the world economy. The Echeverría administration attempted to address some of these by increasing agricultural and manufactured exports, by offering tax reform to lessen reliance on foreign borrowing, and by tightening the regulation of foreign investment. These efforts were thwarted, however, by the resistance of domestic capital and by a world recession which made stubborn structural problems even harder to resolve. The upshot was economic and political crisis at the end of the Echeverría *sexenio*. Attempts to fashion a new auto-industry policy were undertaken in this context.

When Echeverría had come to office in 1970, he had inherited an economy described in international development circles as "the Mexican miracle." Gross domestic product had grown at an average annual rate in excess of 6 percent a year, which, "as a sustained growth record," Fitzgerald has noted, "must be almost unequalled in the post-war third world."[13] Manufacturing had led the way as Mexico pursued its policy of import-substitution industrialization. State policies in the early 1960s had promoted growth past the easy stage of replacement of imported consumer nondurables. Sector-specific policies, particularly in the automobile and petrochemical industries, had sustained growth by initiating an extension of the industrialization process into consumer durables and intermediate goods.

By the end of the decade, however, signs of difficulty were becoming evident. Not only were there obstacles to further growth, but long-simmering distributional problems were threatening to come to a full boil. They took on an ominous political cast when a vigorous and critical student movement took shape and began to voice broad criticisms of the "Mexican miracle," pointing particularly to its failure to diffuse the fruits of growth to a large majority of the Mexican poor. Its spokesmen argued that government policies favored the industrial and agricultural elites at the expense of the lower classes and that the PRI controlled and manipulated the workers and peasants and had erected barriers to meaningful political participation—electoral fraud, a co-opted press, and the hobbling of other political parties. The student movement was dispersed, violently, in 1968, when government troops opened fire on a large demonstration in Tlatelolco, the Plaza of the Three Cultures, in Mexico City.[14]

The sustained growth of the three decades after 1940 had been accompanied by—indeed, had depended upon—extreme inequalities

[13] Fitzgerald, "State and Capital Accumulation," p. 264.

[14] At the time of the assault, Echeverría was minister of the interior, and his was the ministry chiefly responsible for security forces. Once he became president, he would have to concern himself with restoring the legitimacy of the regime in the eyes of students, workers, and peasants.

of wealth and income. Despite the constitutionally enshrined promises of the revolution, there had been little redistribution of land since the presidency of Lázaro Cárdenas. In the urban areas, unionized workers fared better than nonunionized ones, but because the unions were largely controlled by the CTM, one of the three corporatist sectors of the PRI, even the wage gains of the unionized workers tended to lag well behind increases in productivity. Moreover, job creation tended not to keep pace with the expansion of the work force, partly because of the capital-intensive nature of much of the industrial development.[15] Mexico was a society of inequality, and it was growing more so. As Roger Hansen concluded in 1971, "a large part of the bill for the past thirty years of rapid industrialization has been paid in terms of foregone increases in consumption by the large majority of Mexican society located toward the bottom of the income scale. Between 1940 and the early 1960s the rich in Mexico became richer and the poor poorer, some in a relative sense and some absolutely."[16] These distributional problems were being exacerbated by demographic trends—rapid population growth and heavy migration from rural to urban areas[17]—and they would become unmanageable if economic growth could not be sustained. Growth had been the shield against the pressure to redistribute in the past, but its continuation now seemed problematic.

By the early 1970s, there were indications that the strategy of maintaining growth by extending import-substitution industrialization into consumer durables and intermediate and capital goods had accomplished all that could be expected of it, assuming that income redistribution to widen the domestic market was a political impossibility. A set of interlaced difficulties had arisen in import-substitution policies, the financing of development, and the balance of payments.

From 1958 to 1969, the proportion of manufactured goods that were imported had decreased by 25 percent. Most significant was the drop in imports of intermediate goods: by 1969, these had decreased by 45

---

[15] Between 1950 and 1970, for example, industry increased its overall contribution to GDP fourteen percentage points (from 20 percent to 34 percent), but the proportion of the labor force employed in industry went up only seven points (from 16 percent to 23 percent): Gerardo Bueno, *Opciones de política económica en México: Despues de la devaluación* (Mexico City: Editorial Tecnos, 1977), p. 26.

[16] Hansen, *Mexican Development*, p. 71. Cf. Eckstein, *Poverty of Revolution.*

[17] The population was growing by 3.4 to 3.5 percent a year, a rate that would increase Mexico's population from 51 million in 1970 to 150 million by the year 2000. By 1980, the population of Mexico City was about 13 million (in 1940 it was 1.5 million) and inhabitants were being added at the rate of 750,000 a year. Charles F. Gallagher, *Population, Petroleum, and Politics: Mexico at the Crossroads*, North American Series, no. 19 (Hanover, N.H.: American Universities Field Staff, 1980).

percent and represented only one-fifth of the total supply. Substitution of capital and consumer-durable goods was important but less dramatic: imports decreased by 28 percent and constituted half of the total supply in 1969. Looking back at the situation a few years later, Villarreal observed that "the process of import substitution as an incentive for industrialization and growth had approached its upper limit—for a policy of substitution of capital goods is likely to imply increasing social costs."[18]

Import substitution posed growing difficulties for agriculture as well. An overvalued peso and the relative inefficiency of Mexican manufacturing raised the prices of key agricultural inputs and discouraged exports. Price controls on staples (corn, rice, beans), imposed to restrain wage demands from urban workers, led to stagnation in their production. Growth in the agricultural sector dropped from a yearly average of 8.2 percent in the 1940s (a decade in which a great deal of land was brought under irrigation) to 3.3 percent in the 1960s. By 1970, growth in agricultural production was not keeping pace with population growth, and Mexico had begun to import agricultural products, placing an additional strain on the balance of payments.

Compounding these difficulties were problems in the financing of development.[19] To recharge the economy, the Echeverría administration made large state investments in basic industries (steel, electricity, petrochemicals, and fertilizer), in capital goods (railroad stock, machine tools, and electrical equipment), and in rural infrastructure, and it encouraged the state-owned oil monopoly (Petróleos Mexicanos, or PEMEX) to intensify its search for petroleum. Between 1971 and 1975, the public sector increased its share of industrial investment from 20 percent to 80 percent. Over the same period, total government expenditures grew from 41 billion pesos to 145 billion pesos.[20]

To finance these public-sector investments as well as his limited social-reform initiatives, Echeverría sought to increase taxes. When this was blocked by determined opposition from the private sector, he resorted increasingly to domestic and foreign borrowing. Domestically, this meant increasing reliance upon high reserve requirements to finance the public-sector debt while expanding credit so as not to squeeze out private-sector access to investment capital. As the expansion of credit and the increased government expenditures led to increasing

[18] Villarreal, "Import-Substituting Industrialization," p. 74.

[19] The argument of the next several paragraphs draws heavily on Fitzgerald, "State and Capital Accumulation."

[20] Robert E. Looney, *Mexico's Economy: A Policy Analysis with Forecasts to 1990* (Boulder, Col.: Westview, 1978), p. 65.

inflation (it reached 23.7 percent in 1974), Echeverría showed less concern for fiscal orthodoxy than his predecessors; *desarrollo estabilizador* was abandoned. The government's foreign borrowing grew from 9.8 billion pesos ($784 million) in 1970 to 72.5 billion pesos ($5.8 billion) in 1976. The proportion of export earnings needed to service this debt rose from 25 percent to 37 percent.

The skyrocketing foreign debt was one element in a steadily deteriorating balance of payments. A second was the increasing outflow of repatriated earnings, technology payments, and royalties stemming from foreign investment: over $300 million by the late 1960s. Still another element was Mexico's trade position. Import-substitution policy had sought to break the classic pattern of dependency on exports of primary goods to pay for imports of manufactured consumer goods. While this was accomplished, a new form of trade dependency replaced the old one: continued growth in the economy now required imports of capital and intermediate goods, which thus made up 90 percent of total imports by 1970. Because any reduction in these imports would directly threaten production and employment (unlike imports of consumer goods), this new trade profile placed the Mexican economy in a particularly vulnerable position. And yet Mexico's ability to pay for these imports was deteriorating. Already worsening during the 1960s, the balance-of-trade deficit more than tripled between 1970 and 1976.[21] As a result, the overall balance-of-payments deficit on current account increased from $726 million in 1971 to over $3.7 billion by 1975.

The crisis of the Mexican growth strategy set a context for a reconsideration of automobile policy by the Echeverría administration and by the next administration, that of López Portillo. But the domestic policy debates took place in a changed international context, for this was a time when the structure of the world automobile industry was undergoing important changes.

RESTRUCTURING OF THE WORLD AUTO INDUSTRY

The 1950s and 1960s had seen the emergence of an international automobile industry out of the several national oligopolies. In the major producing countries, this transformation was accomplished through the interpenetration of the firms' home bases via direct investments and export sales. After Chrysler's acquisitions of Simca

---

[21] Thomas G. Sanders, *Devaluing the Peso: Background and Implications*, North American Series, no. 5 (Hanover, N.H.: American Universities Field Staff, 1982).

(1958) and Rootes (1964), each of the U.S. Big Three had subsidiaries in Europe. The European firms, in turn, came to face the U.S. firms on their home turf not through investments but through exports. With Volkswagen leading the way, European small cars captured 10 percent of the U.S. car market by 1959. The Big Three beat back that threat to some degree with the introduction of compact-sized vehicles, but a second import surge, this one led by Toyota and Nissan beginning in the late 1960s, gave a 15 percent share of the U.S. market to foreign firms by the mid-1970s and considerably more by the end of the decade.[22] In Europe, the process of economic unification around the European Economic Community led to increasing interpenetration of one another's home markets by the major French, German, and Italian firms (the British did not fare well in these maneuvers), and late in the 1970s, the Japanese began to establish a significant presence in Europe as well. Only the Japanese home market remained primarily a preserve of its national producers, but in the early 1970s the U.S. Big Three ventured into it, too, with minority investments in the Japanese industry's smaller majors (GM in Isuzu, Ford in Toyo Kogyo, and Chrysler in Mitsubishi).

In the developing countries, the emergence of an international automobile oligopoly took place through a series of defensive investments. Rather than cede the emerging markets in these countries to their competitors, the major auto firms had responded to local-content requirements with investments in domestic manufacturing facilities. In Latin America, Ford by 1976 had plants in Argentina, Brazil, Mexico, and Venezuela; GM had operations in those four countries and in Chile; and Chrysler matched Ford's four but also had plants in Colombia and Peru. The European majors were nearly as active as the U.S. Big Three: Volkswagen had plants in four countries, and Renault and Fiat in five each. In contradistinction to the U.S.- and European-based firms, Nissan and Toyota continued to insist on manufacture of all major components in their home-country plants whenever possible. Because of this strategy difference and because of their late arrival on the international scene, the Japanese majors had fewer foreign manufacturing subsidiaries, but even they were represented in this competition for markets. Nissan's entry into Mexico in 1964 was at the very beginning of Japan's appearance as a major world automobile producer. The other Japanese subsidiaries in Latin America (Toyota had three and

[22] For a discussion of the changing import share of the U.S. market, see Eric J. Toder, Nicholas Scott Cardell, and Ellen Burton, *Trade Policy and the U.S. Automobile Industry* (New York: Praeger, 1978), pp. 29-35.

192

TABLE 8.4

Total Vehicle Production in Latin America, by Firm, 1976 (units)

Firm	Argentina	Brazil	Chile	Colombia	Mexico	Peru	Venezuela	Total	% of Latin American Market
American Motors	—	—	—	—	22,669a	11,031	1,213	23,882	1.4
Chrysler	21,986	27,831	—	15,336	55,929		43,355	175,468	10.2
Citroën	15,839	—	1,764a	—	—	—	—	17,603	1.0
Fiat	44,444	8,350	1,439	4,023	—	—	4,510	62,766	3.6
Ford	33,954	171,931	—	—	45,497	—	52,317	303,699	17.7
General Motors	16,195	181,144	960	—	36,757	—	30,238	265,294	15.4
Mercedes-Benz	6,682	48,817	—	—	—	—	2,180	57,679	3.4
Nissan	—	—	—	—	30,624	5,453	4,856	40,933	2.4
Peugeot	16,121	—	1,557b	—	—	—	—	17,678	1.0
Renault	30,896	—	1,307b	15,998	36,894a	—	5,266b	90,361	5.3
Toyota	—	1,498	—	—	—	6,609	7,326	15,433	0.9
Volkswagen	—	529,636	—	—	70,398	9,628	3,000	612,662	35.7
Others	7,400	16,262	—	—	1,161	1,623	8,471	34,917	2.0
Total	193,517	985,469	7,027	35,357	299,929	34,344	162,732	1,718,375	100.0
Percentage	11.3	57.3	0.4	2.1	17.4	2.0	9.5	100.0	

SOURCE: R. N. Gwynne, "Latin America: The Motor Vehicle Industry," *Bank of London and South America Review* 12 (1978):471

NOTE: Uruguay, Ecuador, and Costa Rica also assemble small numbers of vehicles.

[a] Joint ventures with respective governments.

[b] One firm produces two different makes.

Nissan two) were chiefly in countries, such as Peru and Venezuela, which had moved toward domestic manufacture at a later date than Brazil, Argentina, or Mexico (see table 8.4).

A number of forces began to disrupt this structure of the world automobile industry almost as soon as it had taken shape as a competitive international oligopoly of about a dozen firms. First, the saturation of markets in the industrialized countries meant reduced rates of sales growth in those markets. This was most evident in the United States, where over 80 percent of all households already owned at least one passenger vehicle by 1970, but Western Europe and Japan were rapidly approaching the same situation (see table 8.5). One consequence was that automobile sales were far more vulnerable to fluctuations in the business cycle: if vehicle purchases were primarily for replacement of existing vehicles, they could more easily be postponed. Another consequence was that competition among the major auto firms was sharpened. They had come to expect another shakeout in the industry, which only half of them might survive, and they focused their attention all the more firmly on LDCs as markets of the future.

A second factor was the proliferation of inefficient manufacturing subsidiaries in developing countries. The wave of defensive investments by TNCs in the late 1950s and 1960s had left each firm with a large number of subsidiaries, each of them a small-scale replica of production facilities in their home country. The defensive investment dynamic had led to overcrowded industries, and this, coupled with the firms' strategies of model proliferation, meant that manufacturing op-

TABLE 8.5

NUMBER OF PERSONS PER REGISTERED VEHICLE IN
TEN AUTO-PRODUCING COUNTRIES,
1960, 1965, 1970, AND 1975

Country	1960	1965	1970	1975
United States	2.4	2.2	1.9	1.6
France	6.2	4.5	3.5	2.9
West Germany	11.2	5.3	3.8	3.2
Italy	21.3	8.4	4.8	3.4
Great Britain	7.2	4.9	4.1	3.5
Japan	67.9	15.1	5.9	3.9
Argentina	28.3	14.1	10.3	8.1
Brazil	58.7	40.6	27.0	16.2
Mexico	41.2	33.8	27.8	18.1
Chile	65.4	44.6	29.7	24.2

SOURCE: Motor Vehicle Manufacturers Association, *Motor Vehicle Facts and Figures*, various years

erations were necessarily inefficient. Of the seventy-odd automotive plants in Latin America, only Volkswagen's operation in Brazil reached annual production volumes that allowed it to take full advantage of available economies of scale. Because the international industry was becoming more competitive, and because LDC markets would be a major site for this competition, the auto TNCs were interested in finding ways to rationalize their global production.

A third factor that provoked a restructuring of the world industry was the rapid increase in the price of oil that was engineered by the Organization of Petroleum Exporting Countries (OPEC) in two jolts, one in 1973-1974 and another in 1978-1979. These price rises helped to bring on world recessions and contributed to inflation in the developed-country economies. The resulting stagflation exacerbated the saturation problems of the auto TNCs, and the reduced sales volumes drove some firms to the brink of bankruptcy. The OPEC oil-price shocks were particularly damaging to the fortunes of manufacturers of large cars. Concerns about the availability as well as the cost of fuel led consumers to shift their preferences toward smaller, fuel-efficient vehicles.

Nowhere was this more evident than in the United States, the home market for the manufacturers that had dominated the global production of larger vehicles. In the late 1970s, all of the U.S.-based manufacturers, though some more promptly than others, undertook massive investment programs to downsize their vehicles. These events were of decisive importance in establishing the constraints on and opportunities for actors in Mexico, since the United States was Mexico's major export market.

Government policies were a fourth factor in the restructuring of the world auto industry. Export subsidies from the Spanish government in the early 1970s encouraged Ford and other firms to make new investments there. Performance requirements that imports and domestic production be linked to auto-parts exports were adopted not only in Mexico but also in Brazil. In the wake of the first oil price shock in 1975, the U.S. government enacted a set of fuel-economy standards that mandated a steadily-increasing fleet-average fuel economy for the years 1977 through 1985, thus giving further impetus to downsizing.[23]

[23] In the view of some analysts, mandatory fuel-efficiency standards nudged the U.S. auto manufacturers to do what they were reluctant to do but what was necessary for their survival. The Big Three, this view claims, had historically favored larger cars, because of the higher profit margins they afforded; the upsurge of demand for small cars in 1973-1974 was seen as a passing episode, and this perception was strengthened by the recovery of the market for larger cars in the middle of the decade. Furthermore, the manufacturers

These subsidies and requirements affected costs, sales potentials, and access to markets and therefore influenced the global strategies of the auto TNCs.

In order to deal with these changes, the auto TNCs felt the need to rationalize their global production patterns and to minimize costs. During the 1950s and 1960s, the firms had principally looked to reduce costs by the fullest possible utilization of economies of scale in their home-country plants and wherever else they had manufacturing operations. In the 1970s, however, they began to pursue other strategies, including not only automation and the extraction of concessions from labor organizations, but also new international arrangements, such as joint production agreements and global sourcing. It was particularly these latter changes which had the effect of restructuring the world auto industry in ways that benefited Mexico's export-promotion programs.

One of the most immediate ways to cut costs was to bargain with labor for wage concessions and reorganization at the workplace, using the threat of domestic job loss, plant closings, or lost investment as a bargaining tool.[24] The development of microprocessors has made possible a longer-term strategy for reducing labor costs: an increase in the

---

overestimated the time they would have for making the transition to smaller cars. (There is normally a lag of about three years between the start of planning on a vehicle and the time when it is produced for sale, although under special circumstances this lag can be cut in half, as GM did in bringing out the Chevette.) Thus, without the pressure of federal requirements, the Big Three would have been even less prepared for the second oil price shock and would have lost even more of the U.S. market to Japanese imports. (The best rendition of this argument is Joseph Kraft, "Annals of Industry: The Downsizing Decision," *The New Yorker*, May 5, 1980, pp. 134-162. But see also "New Grand Prix for Auto Markets," *Citibank Monthly Economic Newsletter*, Nov. 1978, pp. 12-13.) There is an opposed point of view that contends that the U.S. car companies *were* disposed to downsize in the wake of the 1973-1974 shock but that U.S. energy policy, by holding down the price of gasoline, encouraged the American public to go on buying large cars. The same act that mandated the fuel-efficiency standards also slightly rolled back the price of gasoline (which was still under federal controls) and set a ceiling on how quickly it could rise. In this view, the Big Three were caught in a bind between a car-buying public that still wanted big cars and government requirements for increased fuel efficiency. Had the price of gasoline been decontrolled from the beginning, according to this view, the Big Three would have been prepared for the second shock with downsized, fuel-efficient vehicles. (See William Tucker, "The Wreck of the Auto Industry," *Harper's*, Nov. 1980, pp. 45-60.) Both of these views lead to the conclusion that U.S. government policy played a major role in the timing and character of the changes in the auto industry.

[24] The 1982 contract which the United Auto Workers signed with Ford, for example, cut $2 an hour per car from the company's labor costs over the life of the contract, amounting to $190 a car: John Holusha, "Ford's New Contract: Who May Win, Who May Lose," *New York Times*, Feb. 26, 1982, p. D6.

degree of automation. "Smart robots" can now be programmed to accomplish many of the tasks—welding, for one significant example—that had required human labor (skilled and unskilled) on the assembly line. This new technology was first utilized on a large scale by the Japanese manufacturers, as they expanded their production capacity, but the U.S. makers also adopted it as they retooled for downsizing and have extended its use since then.

Joint production agreements have been another method for reducing costs. Historically, the auto firms bought many of their components from common parts suppliers but did not purchase parts from each other or enter into co-production relationships. Over the past decade, however, they have elaborated a complex web of agreements with each other designed to move more quickly to incorporate new production technology, to share costs, and to minimize risks. Renault, Peugeot, and Volvo have a joint venture in northern France to manufacture six-cylinder engines, for example; Chrysler has purchased four-cylinder engines from Volkswagen and Mitsubishi; American Motors and Renault have begun production of Renault cars in the United States.

The most important strategy in the restructuring of the world auto industry has been global sourcing: the location of production facilities for components and subassemblies (e.g., engines and transmissions) in many different countries, so that production can be integrated on a regional or worldwide basis. It was this strategy that created an interest among the TNCs in the export of components from countries like Mexico. It took on great importance when the U.S.-based firms began downsizing in the 1970s. They had to make massive new investments (estimated at upwards of $500 billion for the Big Three over the years from 1978 to 1985) in order to manufacture the new cars and to modernize their production equipment at the same time. The establishment of manufacturing subsidiaries in dozens of countries over the previous two decades allowed the auto makers, especially GM and Ford, to select low-cost production sites and techniques in a global context. New, automated production facilities could be kept at home, close to the firm's centralized R & D capability, while labor-intensive manufacturing processes could be located in low-wage countries and "dirty" manufacturing processes in countries without strict pollution-control requirements. And the firms could take maximum advantage of host-country restrictions and incentives—playing one government off against another, for example—in making the new investments.

The necessity of making these new investments also presented the firms with an opportunity to rationalize their worldwide production network by reducing the duplication of facilities. Instead of producing the new engines or hubs or drums in each host country, they could be manufactured at only one or two appropriate locations (two would be better, to prevent supply interruptions in case of a strike or accident), parceling them out among the various subsidiaries. Each subsidiary would continue to have the same level of manufacturing activity, but each would undertake assembly operations only for the local market and the production of one or a few components for the whole transnational network, rather than the production of a full complement of parts for domestic use.

The result of global sourcing has been the "world car": a vehicle of a single basic design, tailored in small ways to fit local conditions, assembled in many different countries from components obtained from plants scattered around the world. While the U.S.-based firms pioneered the world car and have developed it most systematically, European firms with foreign subsidiaries (Volkswagen, for example) and smaller Japanese firms with links to the U.S. companies (Toyo Kogyo, for example, in which Ford holds 25 percent equity) have also moved in this direction.

Global sourcing has a number of consequences for the structure of the world industry and the interests of the TNCs. One is that the common design allows firms to achieve greater economies of scale both for component production and for assembly, which in turn raises even further the barriers to entry for other firms. Another is that it lowers the "barriers to exit." Large capital investments in facilities in the United States meant that it was difficult for firms to close their U.S. plants. However, if they can obtain cheaper capital abroad or get subsidies from foreign governments, it may be more rational to build a plant abroad than to continue to operate facilities at home, allowing them to withdraw from the U.S. market.[25] Global sourcing also makes the industrial policies of other countries very important in planning global strategies. The calculation of comparative production costs must take into account the deals that can be struck with the several governments. Finally, this restructuring of the industry has given transnational auto makers a common interest with governments in promoting export-oriented rather than import-substituting policies, for the latter would impede global rationalization of production while the former

[25] See the discussion of "exit barriers" in Robert B. Cohen, "International Investment Strategies and Domestic Reorganization Plans of the U.S. Automakers: An Essay on the Response of the U.S. Auto Firms to Changes in International Competitiveness in Auto Production and Their Impact on the U.S. Economy" (photocopy, Mar. 1982), p. 6. For the framework of his discussion, Cohen cites Willi Semmler, *Competition and Monopoly* (draft manuscript, New School for Social Research, Department of Economics).

would facilitate it. Thus, at the same time that Mexico was deciding to renew and strengthen its export-promotion program, the auto makers were moving toward global sourcing and were reconsidering the locations for the production of components. Although there would be conflict over the specifics of Mexico's performance requirements, the changes in the world industry created opportunities for export production in Mexico which had previously been lacking.

The transnational auto makers reacted differently, and at different times, to changes in the world auto industry. Particularly important for Mexico were the firms' reactions to changes in the U.S. market, which, because of its size and proximity, was the market upon which the Mexican export-promotion scheme would depend.

Neither Nissan nor Toyota, the principal Japanese-based firms, had established manufacturing subsidiaries in LDCs during the 1960s. Their capital investments had been concentrated at home, in new technology; they had been the first to utilize robots and other forms of automation on a large scale. As a consequence, they had the least need to make adjustments to the new structure. On the contrary, to a significant extent they had forced the reorganization of the world industry by their penetration of first the U.S. market and then the European.

Increased competition in the world industry, the OPEC price increases, and the stagnation of the world economy in the 1970s compelled the European producers to make investments in new product lines at a time when they had limited capital resources. To a greater extent than their competitors, they responded by entering into co-production arrangements for the manufacture of four-cylinder engines, transaxles, and other components to share fixed capital costs and to reduce risk. The increased value of European currencies relative to the dollar and the Japanese invasion of the U.S. market together served to reduce the sales of Volkswagen, Renault, Fiat, and other European firms in the United States, which had been a major export market for these firms for more than a decade. Consequently, a second response of the European-based firms was to explore ways of establishing manufacturing operations in the United States. Volkswagen, for example, opened a plant in Pennsylvania, and Renault entered into a joint venture with American Motors.

For the U.S.-based firms, downsizing was the major needed adjustment. But smaller models could be price-competitive with the Japanese imports only if new, automated production equipment was installed. Substantial investments were clearly required. If this strained the capital resources of the Big Three, it also provided them with the opportunity to implement global sourcing and the world-car strategy.

While all of the Big Three were slow to downsize, GM had both the interest and the power to move more quickly than its domestic competitors. It had suffered the most in the aftermath of the first oil-price increase—its share of the U.S. market fell from 50 percent in 1973 to less than 40 percent in the first quarter of 1974[26]—and its size gave it superior access to resources. GM management decided in December 1973 to manufacture the subcompact Chevette (developed by the German Opel subsidiary) in the United States for the U.S. market, and also to bring out a smaller Cadillac, thus responding to the import threat at both ends of its line. It took another two and a half years for GM to announce that it was undertaking an investment program of $15 billion to downsize its entire array of models by 1985. The first of these new vehicles, the compact four-cylinder front-wheel-drive X-body cars, were introduced into the U.S. market in April 1979.

Ford's approach to downsizing was more gradual. This strategy proved to be profitable until 1978, because of the recovery of the market for larger cars within a year after the first oil-price rise. But because Ford did not commit itself to large investments for refashioning and retooling its line until well after GM's decision, it was relatively unprepared for the second rise.

Chrysler moved most slowly of the Big Three, for reasons of strategy and capability. Smallest of the three, and already in ailing financial health at the beginning of the 1970s, it was least able to mobilize the resources necessary to downsize its line. Its lack of success in the years between the first and second shock drove it closer to the edge, from where even the introduction of its subcompact Omni and Horizon and the divestiture of its overseas subsidiaries, both in 1978, could not rescue it. When the second shock came, Chrysler had no choice, if it were to survive, but to plead with the U.S. government for loan guarantees to enable it to complete the downsizing and refurbishing of its line.

Ford, GM, and Chrysler were thus quite differently prepared for any reconsideration of auto policy in Mexico—a reconsideration that was inevitable in light of the difficulties of export promotion policy in 1974-1975 and the wider problems of Mexico's growth strategy.

[26] Kraft, "Annals of Industry," p. 134.

·9·

THE THIRD ENCOUNTER, 1977

The growing economic crisis in Mexico at the end of the Echeverría administration led top policy officials to review the 1969 *acuerdo* and the 1972 decree. Export requirements were not stemming the automobile industry's trade deficit. Guillermo Becker, the director of industries, and his staff began to consider a policy change. They were not, however, fully cognizant of the changes taking place in the world auto industry, and they assumed that the best alternative would be to raise the level of domestic content. While the initiative came from Becker and sic, much of the planning was done in the Interministerial Commission for the Automobile Industry, created by the 1972 decree and composed of representatives of sic and Finance. Discussions began in the fall of 1975.

THE DRAFT DECREE OF 1976

On March 8, 1976, the interministerial commission released a report outlining the parameters of a new policy.[1] Export promotion would not be abandoned, but the emphasis would once again be on import substitution. The level of mandatory local content would be increased to 80 percent by 1981, now to be calculated by a more stringent "cost of parts" formula. To keep higher local content from affecting domestic prices, there would be renewed efforts toward rationalization of the industry through standardization of parts and encouragement of mergers among the existing terminal firms. Export promotion would continue, however: the terminal firms would be required to compensate 100 percent of their now-to-be-reduced imports with exports. In addition, the terminal firms would be allowed to lower their local content to 70 percent if they would doubly compensate the additional imports with exports. The terminal firms and the various associations of parts manufacturers were invited to comment on this set of proposals.

This was the first time that the parts firms had been consulted in the formulation of automobile policy. These firms—there were now

[1] Secretaria de Industria y Comercio, Comisión Intersecretarial de la Industria Automotriz, "Programa para una nueva estructura de la industria automotriz mexicano (industria terminal y de autopartes)" (1976).

several hundred of them—were grouped into two trade associations along geographic lines. The Asociación Nacional de Fabricantes de Productos Automotrices (ANFPA) comprised firms in the general vicinity of Mexico City; the firms in Asociación Mexicana de Productores de Partes Automotrices (AMPPA) were those in the vicinity of Monterrey. The parts firms were still not a powerful political force, however. Neither ANFPA or AMPPA had anything like the resources of AMIA, the association of the terminal firms. AMIA had a staff as large as the SIC team for the industry; ANFPA had one badly paid director, and AMPPA did not even have that. Further, there were often significant differences of interest among these firms because of the considerable variety in size, technical sophistication, degree of foreign ownership, and (largely as a function of these three factors) export potential. Those firms, mostly ones with foreign equity, whose sales benefited from export requirements were anxious not to lose the gains they had derived from this policy; the many smaller firms that had found no export opportunities thought they would fare best with increased import substitution. ANFPA and AMPPA were able to work out a compromise, however. Working together through the auto-parts section of the Cámara Nacional de Industrias de Transformación (National Chamber of Manufacturing Industries, or CANACINTRA), to which all these firms were legally required to belong but which had played little role in the past, a compromise position was formulated which basically supported the government's plans to increase the level of mandatory local content as long as export requirements were retained as well.[2]

The terminal firms responded separately, not through AMIA, and their positions were divided between import substitution and export promotion. The responses also varied considerably in analytic quality and depth. Some were only a few pages expressing summary preferences, while Ford supported its preferences with tables and calculations running to hundreds of pages. Ford and Chrysler argued most strongly

[2] Aware that many terminal firms opposed any increase in local content, ANFPA, AMPPA, and CANACINTRA pointed out that there were parts currently produced locally for one or two terminal firms but still imported by others. Higher local content could be achieved, they argued, simply by having all the terminal firms obtain these components from domestic parts suppliers. CANACINTRA sent a questionnaire to 225 ANFPA and AMPPA firms, asking them to detail which additional components they could supply to the terminal firms. On the basis of the responses, the CANACINTRA report estimated that 69.2 percent average local content could be achieved by 1977 merely by taking advantage of existing capacity, and that 74.6 percent average local content could be achieved by 1978 by making only small investments and counting on no new technology or installations. See Cámara Nacional de Industrias de Transformación, Sección de Autopartes, "Incremento de la industria automotriz: Memoria de cálculos" (Apr. 1976).

for a continuation of the export-promotion policy. GM and Nissan also appeared to prefer the export strategy, but their responses showed more uncertainty about the possibilities for reducing the industry's balance-of-payments drain or for stimulating industrial growth along either route. DINA, lacking export possibilities, argued for higher mandatory local content. Breaking sharply with preferences it had expressed in the past, Volkswagen also argued for higher local content, as much as a mandatory 85 percent. Volkswagen had seen its export possibilities undercut by currency revaluations and by U.S. safety regulations that banned its Mexican-made Safari from the U.S. market (where it was called "The Thing"). Having already made investments in stamping presses and dies in Mexico, Volkswagen could increase its local content more easily than the other firms. DINA and Volkswagen were also the most forceful in urging a mandatory reduction in the number of models permitted. VAM, with the industry's most diversified product line, spoke most strongly against this.[3]

By June 1976, a draft decree returning the industry to a more import-substituting route had been drawn up in SIC and was ready for promulgation, but it never appeared. What defeated it was not corporate opposition but opposition from within the government, compounded by the political and economic turmoil that characterized the last six months of the Echeverría administration. This opposition came particularly from officials who had already been tapped to play key roles in the López Portillo government, which was to take office in December: Carlos Tello, José Andrés de Oteyza, and Julio Rodolfo Moctezuma Cid. They voiced some policy disagreements with the SIC draft, but in the main they argued that they should be the ones to promulgate the policy that they would administer, so that it would be clear whose policy it was.

---

[3] Ford's response presented the most detailed criticism of import substitution. Its study blamed the industry's balance-of-payments deficit on the parts firms and on the general characteristics of the Mexican economy rather than on the terminal firms. It argued that Mexico lacked the competitively priced raw materials and the metalworking industry needed for substantially increased local content, and that the parts firms were limited in their ability to pursue exports by high prices and by a lack of aggressiveness in seeking new customers. It urged corrective action targeted on the parts firms. Considering the foreign-exchange savings and the inflationary impact, Ford estimated that an export route would generate $1.00 of foreign exchange for each $0.60 invested and would lead to no increase in prices for Mexican cars, whereas 90 percent local content would require an investment of $2.50 for each $1.00 of foreign exchange saved and would increase the price of Mexican cars an average of 36 percent. Even that could be accomplished only by eliminating two of the seven firms in the industry and reducing the number of models offered by the remaining five firms from thirty-four to eighteen. Ford Motor Company, "Estudio sobre contenido nacional y generación de divisas por exportaciones" (May 1976).

Their arguments were probably less decisive than the onward rush of events. The last few months of the Echeverría administration were a time of crisis and sagging legitimacy. The president's policies had provoked determined opposition from domestic and foreign business: his attempts to raise taxes, his support of land reform, his sympathy to wage demands, and his expansion of the state sector raised fears of incipient socialism and led to a drastic reduction in private-sector investment. Coupled with the global recession of 1974-1975, this investment boycott brought growth to a standstill. Continuing inflation and capital flight forced Echeverría to devalue the peso on September 1, the first devaluation in a quarter-century. A few weeks later, he announced the seizure of 250,000 acres of land for redistribution to peasants. In these final months, political and economic chaos reached a point where rumors of coups and counter-coups were frequent.[4] It was not a propitious time for the introduction of a new auto-industry policy.

THE 1977 AUTO DECREE

When the López Portillo administration took office in December 1976, the June draft decree was scrapped. Less than seven months later, a new comprehensive policy for the auto industry was promulgated.[5] Instead of returning to import substitution, the 1977 decree pressed forward vigorously with export promotion.

The new decree showed a technical sophistication that far outstripped the decrees of 1962 and 1972. This one had clearly been prepared with the aid of econometric models, and it was replete with complex algebraic formulas. Its principal provisions were these: (1) The terminal firms would have to move steadily over the next five years toward a position where their operations generated no balance-of-payments deficit. Not only would they have to compensate with exports their imports of parts for vehicles assembled in Mexico (as the 1969 policy had required), but they would also have to compensate for their other foreign payments (for freight and insurance, technical assistance, replacement parts for their dealers, etc.) and for the imported

---

[4] In the judgment of many, Echeverría was inept, profligate, and given to needlessly inflammatory rhetoric, but Fitzgerald's assessment of the situation seems more balanced: "Contrary to popular opinion, the recent crisis is not merely a result of economic mismanagement of the economy by the Echeverría administration, but rather a long-run structural contradiction of the Mexican growth model." Fitzgerald, "State and Capital Accumulation," p. 282.

[5] "Decreto para el fomento de la industria automotriz," *Diario oficial*, June 20, 1977.

content of the parts they procured domestically. (2) The burden was placed squarely on the transnational auto firms in the terminal industry to generate these exports, and now half (instead of 40 percent) of the exports would have to come from firms in the supplier industry (which continued to be required to have a minimum of 60 percent Mexican ownership). (3) Certain special considerations would be given to the two majority Mexican-owned firms in the terminal industry, in recognition of their greater difficulty in finding export opportunities. (4) Terminal firms would have to operate with a level of local content slightly higher than previous policies had required. (5) The regulatory apparatus was changed substantially: price controls were eliminated, and in other ways there would be greater reliance on market constraints rather than on direct prescriptions of behavior.

In contrast to the preparation that had gone into the 1976 draft, the 1977 decree was promulgated with scarcely any discussions between the new administration and the industry. Both before and after the rules for implementing the decree were published on October 18, 1977, there were attempts by some of the terminal firms, led by Ford, to modify the terms of the new policy. The U.S. government joined in these efforts, but unlike the case in the first bargaining episode, the Mexican government stood firm behind its new policy.

AGENDA SETTING

Because the government took the industry so much by surprise, one might be tempted to assert that the bargaining agenda on this occasion was set simply and fully by the government: it established what issues would be items of concern. For a number of reasons, this would be a misleading view, however. First, some characteristics of the industry were now deemed as given, no longer susceptible to change. Most importantly, there were seven firms in the terminal industry, and while it was acknowledged that greater efficiency could be achieved with fewer firms, the domestic and international costs of forcing some of them out were considered too great. Rationalization of the industry had been on the agenda in both the 1962 and 1969 bargaining, but now it could not be seriously considered.

Secondly, the domestically owned supplier industry played a more prominent role than it had previously; it had begun to come of age. Representatives of labor, however, were, as in the past, not involved in the bargaining at any stage.

Finally, some issues never appeared on the bargaining agenda because there was again a convergence of interest between the firms

205

(particularly the transnational terminal firms) and the government. One such convergence in 1962 had set the industry along the road to import-substitution industrialization, but the experiences of the state and of the transnational auto firms over the intervening years led in 1977 to a convergence in a more export-promoting direction. But to see which issues became items of contention and which did not—to see how the bargaining agenda was formed—it is necessary to review the interests of each of the major actors.

The Interests of the Firms

In 1969, most of the automobile TNCs had been strongly opposed to export requirements that would force them to make new, otherwise unnecessary investments in Mexico in order to maintain their share of the Mexican market. In 1977, the restructuring of the world auto industry had altered their interests. The TNCs were compelled to make substantial investments in their global operations in any event; it was only a question of where to make them. In effect, the Mexican government was demanding that the firms divert some of their new investments to Mexico. The major concerns of the auto producers would be how much they would have to export, how soon they would have to reach the required level, and the extent to which they would be responsible for arranging exports for Mexican parts firms. They were also upset over what they viewed as preferential treatment for the two state-owned firms, DINA and VAM.

As already noted, an export orientation accorded well with the interests of the larger parts firms that were joint ventures between Mexican capital and TNCs (TREMEC, Spicer, Eaton, etc.). These firms had come to dominate parts exports from Mexico after the 1969 *acuerdo*, and higher export requirements (and the higher percentage of them that would now have to be obtained from independent parts firms) would mean a further increase in sales. For them, export promotion meant guaranteed access to the world auto market. Higher local content requirements would not help them at all, since their components were already being incorporated by essentially all of the terminal firms in Mexico.

The smaller parts firms, far more numerous and most of them wholly domestically owned, lacked the international market access afforded by a transnational partner and so had less chance of finding export opportunities. Many of them made components that were used by only one or two of the terminal firms, the others continuing to import. Although the June decree emphasized export promotion, the smaller

206

parts suppliers were relieved to find that it also provided for some increase in the level of mandatory local content.

The Interests of the Government

One of López Portillo's first steps after taking office was to carry out a significant reorganization of the ministries charged with planning and managing economic growth. The Ministry of the Presidency was strengthened and renamed to reflect its actual functions: Programming and Budgeting. The Ministry of Industry and Commerce was divided in two: a separate Ministry of Commerce was created, and the industry sector was joined to the existing Ministry of National Properties to create the Ministry of National Properties and Industrial Growth (Secretaria de Patrimonio y Fomento Industrial, or SEPAFIN). By these moves, better coordination of auto-industry policy was made possible. No longer would the direction of policy in the industry as a whole be the responsibility of one ministry while nominal control over the state-owned firms in the industry (DINA, VAM, and about ten parts manufacturing firms) was the responsibility of another.[6] SEPAFIN would now control all of the significant instruments of policy toward the industry except for tax rebates, subsidies, and other fiscal stimuli, which remained in the hands of the Ministry of Finance and Public Credit. When the 1977 decree was promulgated, it provided for an Interministerial Commission of the Automotive Industry, which included two representatives each from SEPAFIN, Commerce, and Finance and Public Credit.

López Portillo appointed José Andrés de Oteyza as minister of SEPAFIN. Natan Warman was named deputy minister for industrial growth, Ernesto Marcos became director of the General Bureau of Industrial Development, and Juan Wolffer became subdirector for the automobile industry. Other key ministerial positions went to Carlos Tello (Programming and Budgeting), Julio Rodolfo Moctezuma Cid (Finance), and Fernando Solana (Commerce).

This reorganization did promise better coordination of government policy, but it did not reflect any significant change in the goals or the strategies of policy. The central goals remained very much what they had been in 1962: stimulation of industrial growth, creation of employment opportunities, development of domestic technological capability, and improvement in the balance of payments. How best to

[6] However, these two areas were placed in the hands of different deputy ministers within SEPAFIN.

serve these goals remained basically a question of whether to orient the industry principally toward the domestic market (import substitution) or to face the industry outward, toward the international market (export promotion). The new team favored further emphasis on export promotion in key sectors, such as automobiles. Manufactured exports were seen by Oteyza, Warman, and their subordinates in SEPAFIN as crucial to the stimulation of industrial growth given the relatively small size of the Mexican market, still limited by the maldistribution of income. Although the automobile market had grown to about 300,000 vehicles a year by 1976, it was still small by international standards, and it was fragmented among a large number of manufacturers. A reduction in the number of firms by government action was nearly impossible after the failure of the rationalization attempts in 1968-1969. Export production would allow greater efficiency and expanded sales volumes as well as earning foreign exchange.[7] SEPAFIN officials were aware that the auto TNCs were embarking on huge investment programs; the moment seemed right for Mexico to make its bid for a share of the investments for the worldwide distribution of parts manufacture.

Early drafts of the 1977 decree had been even more resolutely export-promoting than the final version. The report that Ford had submitted to the Echeverría administration in May 1976 presented a persuasive, carefully supported case for a full-blown export strategy.[8] Moreover, Warman, Marcos, and Wolffer were at first quite taken with the U.S.-Canadian Automotive Products Trade Agreement of 1965 (APTA), under which Canada had had only a small (or no) balance-of-payments deficit in automotive trade with the United States. Two factors seem to have been responsible for restoring a measure of import-substitution strategy to the final decree. One was the lobbying of the parts firms, which argued that any relaxation of local-content requirements would lead to the destruction of the smaller ones among them. The terminal firms, they said, would import nearly all the parts of their vehicles, compensating for these imports with massive exports of a few parts manufactured by themselves or by the largest parts firms, the ones that already dominated parts exports. This line of reasoning

[7] For discussions of the rationale of SEPAFIN in formulating auto policy in the López Portillo administration, see Natan Warman, "Política de estímulos a la inversión," in Cámara Nacional de Industrias de Transformación, *Memoria I: Primer simposium de actualización operacional de la industria automotriz en México* (Mexico City: CANACINTRA, 1978), pp. 11-14, and Ernesto Marcos, "Orígen y objetivos de la nueva política automotriz," in ibid., pp. 60-63.

[8] Ford Motor Company, "Contenido nacional."

was supported by a more careful examination of the APTA. Before that agreement was signed, Canada had had an integrated auto industry of its own. The plants were owned by the major U.S. makers, but substantially all of the principal components of a vehicle were manufactured in Canada. Canada even had its own makes and models. In the ensuing dozen years, however, the Canadian plants had been more fully integrated into the U.S. auto industry. To a large extent, it had ceased to make sense to speak of a Canadian automobile industry—at least, that was the perception of the officials formulating the new Mexican auto policy. The prospect of a similar fate for the Mexican auto industry bespoke an unacceptable dependency on the U.S.

Consequently, the final decree retained a substantial local-content requirement, although it differed from the one that had been in force up until then. Local content would henceforth be calculated on the basis of the cost of parts rather than the cost of production. This meant that firms would no longer be permitted to include the costs of assembly as part of their domestic content.[9] The minimum level of local content would now be 50 percent for cars (65 percent for trucks), but because of the new basis of calculation, this was about 8 percent higher than it had been before. (The increase, it was expected, could be achieved simply by taking advantage of excess capacity in the supplier firms.) Furthermore, local content would now be measured on a per-model, not a per-plant, basis; firms would no longer be able to balance higher local content on one model with lower local content on another. A reduction in the number of models was expected to be the result. Finally, in addition to the required minimum level of local content, there would be a recommended level, which would rise to 75 percent by 1981. Firms could choose not to fulfill this higher recommended level, but if so, they would have to compensate for the difference in imports by a more than 1:1 ratio of exports; the hope was that this would be a prod for higher local content.

Notwithstanding the provisions designed to maintain a broad spectrum of auto-manufacturing operations in Mexico, the primary thrust

[9] Moreover, the cost-of-parts formula would use the CKD price list in the model's home country for the cost of all parts, even those manufactured in Mexico. Thus, the new formula would not be affected by changes in the exchange rate between the dollar and the peso, nor would it be biased against more efficient production in Mexico. Under the old formula, two producers who made identical vehicles and imported the same parts at the same cost could have different levels of local content if one manufactured its local-content parts at higher cost than the other: the less efficient manufacturer would have higher local content. Under the new formula, both manufacturers would have the same local content, because the cost of parts would be regarded as the same.

of the new decree was to require the transnational auto firms to undertake significantly increased exports from Mexico. While the precise export volume each firm would have to generate was determined by complex formulae, they rested upon a few straightforward principles. By 1982, each terminal firm would have to fully compensate its imports with exports, and in the intervening years the firms would have to make steady, prescribed progress toward this goal. Under the 1969 export policy, the firms were obligated to compensate only their imports of assembly parts. Under the new policy, the firms would have to compensate for all their foreign payments: for production equipment, replacement parts for their distributors, technology royalties, even the imported content of the parts they obtained from supplier firms. When and if the terminal firms fulfilled these export requirements, one of the government's primary goals for the industry would have been achieved: to make it, in the words of the 1977 decree, "a source of net foreign exchange generation in the medium term."

Several provisions of the 1977 decree were designed to protect and to strengthen Mexican ownership in the industry. Half of the exports of each terminal firm (an increase from the 40 percent of the 1969 policy) would have to be obtained from supplier firms (which by law had to be majority Mexican-owned). A qualification was introduced into the export-promotion formulae to decrease somewhat the exports that would be required of DINA and VAM. (In addition, the provision concerning the recommended level of local content gave these two firms an alternative way to fulfill the terms of the decree.) Finally, certain activities were reserved for majority Mexican-owned firms, most significantly the manufacture of trucks with diesel engines.

The 1977 decree also called for a substantial overhauling of the government's regulatory apparatus for the industry. Price controls and production quotas, both of which had been in place since 1962, were eliminated. The latter, however, were in a sense replaced by a new mechanism, the foreign-exchange budget. Each firm would be given a foreign-exchange allotment at the beginning of the model year. Imports and other foreign payments would be charged against this allotment, and exports would be credited to it. Each firm could produce as many vehicles as it wished so long as it maintained the required minimum local content and its foreign-exchange budget had a positive balance. The foreign-exchange allotments given to the firms would decrease year by year, falling to zero in 1982, the year when the firms were to achieve full compensation of imports with exports.

Firms in both parts of the industry continued to be eligible for a complex array of tax rebates, subsidies, and other fiscal stimuli, but if a terminal firm failed to meet its export obligations, it would be punished by forfeiture of these fiscal benefits and by fines rather than by reduction of its production quota (the penalty under the 1969 policy, which had proved difficult to apply). With some exceptions, import licenses were dropped in favor of tariffs, which were to be gradually lowered to encourage greater efficiency on the part of Mexican manufacturers. Broadly speaking, the new regimen sought to utilize more general rules, rather than ad hoc bargaining with each of the firms, and to utilize the constraints of the market (albeit a carefully structured one) rather than direct proscriptions to regulate the industry.

Selection of Issues

A few days before the decree was promulgated, the government announced the lifting of price controls, which had been a constant target of complaints from the terminal firms. As a consequence, the first reaction of the industry to the new policy was almost uniformly favorable.[10] But complaints soon began to emanate from the terminal firms again, particularly from Ford.[11] (The supplier firms seemed satisfied even after a second look.) A variety of issues were raised in the ensuing bargaining, but four issues emerged as especially important:

(a) Degree of compensation. The terminal firms argued that the levels of exports required of them were too high, particularly the obligation to compensate for the imported content of parts they obtained from domestic suppliers. "That's carrying the joke too far," one executive said.

(b) Timing. The terminal firms complained that the new policy required them to generate exports too quickly. Increased exports required new investments, they said, and it would take several years to plan them and bring them to fruition.

(c) Sourcing. The terminal firms objected to being required to obtain half their exports from independent, majority Mexican-owned parts firms, over which they had no control.

(d) Discrimination against foreign-owned firms. A number of provisions in the new decree seemed to favor the Mexican-owned firms

[10] The manufacturers had applied for price increases averaging about 19 percent, but when price controls were ended they raised prices by an average of only 13 percent. It is possible that the price controls had been serving as an informal mechanism of price coordination among the firms and that the ending of the controls introduced a small measure of price competition among them.

[11] For one published indication of this opposition, see "Closer Look by Firms at Mexican Auto Decree Turns into Frown," *Business Latin America*, Aug. 3, 1977, pp. 247-248.

in the industry. DINA and VAM would have lighter export burdens, and certain activities were reserved for Mexican-owned firms (Ford was particularly upset at the provision allowing only Mexican-owned firms to manufacture trucks with diesel engines).

Serious discussions took place on these four issues after the decree was published and even after the clarifying and implementing regulations appeared four months later.[12] Why were these the major items of contention between the firms and the government? Why were other issues not on the bargaining agenda? And why were these issues of more concern to some of the firms than to others?

Some issues were not raised because the government knew they would be too strenuously opposed by the firms. Most important among these were the number of firms in the terminal industry and their foreign ownership. Both of these issues had been on the bargaining agenda in 1962 and 1969, but in neither episode had the government been able to reduce the number of firms or to insist upon majority Mexican ownership for firms in the terminal industry. Now, with the terminal firms deeply entrenched in Mexico, these issues were too costly to raise. Instead, they were treated as givens to be taken account of in formulating other provisions.[13]

Other issues were not raised because of a convergence of interests between the terminal firms and the government. Nothing in the decree challenged the basic principles of the Mexican growth strategy over the previous half century: primary reliance on private-sector investment and state responsibility for maintaining the conditions for capital accumulation.[14] The new decree sought, in effect, to induce substantial private-sector investments by both foreign and domestically owned firms. If the state was obtrusive in directing the general character of these investments, it also offered a variety of fiscal stimuli (as well as the lifting of price controls) to ensure a profitable return. The decree also came just six months after López Portillo had announced, as part of his "Alliance for Production," an agreement from labor leaders to

[12] "Acuerdo que establece las reglas de aplicación del decreto para el fomento de la industria automotriz," *Diario oficial*, Oct. 18, 1977.

[13] To be sure, the decree did provide a bit of encouragement for firms to Mexicanize (by providing special incentives for majority Mexican-owned firms) and to withdraw (by raising the costs of remaining in the Mexican market), but those were not the purposes of these provisions. One reason the government gave for excluding foreign-owned firms from diesel-truck manufacture was that diesel trucks were considered a capital good, and this was a sector being reserved for Mexican-owned firms.

[14] See Bennett and Sharpe, "State as Banker."

hold wage demands to 10 percent, well below the prevailing rate of inflation.[15]

Another convergence of interests concerned the export-oriented thrust of the new decree. The firms might complain about the volume, the timing, and the sourcing of the required exports, but these were objections to the manner in which export promotion was to be carried through, not objections to the overall direction of the policy. The firms might have preferred no new policy at all, but if the government felt a need to do something to promote industrial growth and reduce the auto industry's drain on the balance of payments, an export orientation was greatly preferable to an import-substituting one. It is not an exaggeration to say that the new decree compelled the firms to follow a route they were already traveling.[16]

On the other hand, the provisions concerning the extent, timing, and source of required exports obligated the firms to commit themselves to making substantial exports and therefore substantial investments in Mexico over a very short time span. Compliance would thus mean some diminution of managerial flexibility in siting component production around the world. Whatever fairness there might be in Mexico's requirement of 1:1 export compensation, extending this to include compensation of the imports of the parts firms seemed too much. The terminal firms would have to more than double their exports by 1982, and half of these increased exports would have to be procured from parts firms in Mexico.

Each of the terminal firms had its own particular problems with regard to these issues. Renault and American Motors, minority partners in joint ventures, were reluctant to purchase substantial amounts of exports from DINA and VAM. Lacking major assembly facilities outside Japan, Nissan would incur high transportation costs in sending its parts exports back to its home country. Volkswagen, having achieved an unusually high degree of vertical integration, would have particular difficulty in satisfying the requirement that 50 percent of exports come from parts firms. Chrysler faced the prospect of losing its diesel truck line (it had been granted the right to install diesel engines in trucks before its Mexican-owned equity had been sold in 1971, and it was

[15] For a discussion of labor in the Mexican automobile industry, see Middlebrook, "International Implications."

[16] The domestic-content requirements were somewhat higher than in the earlier decrees, but the minimum required level was well below that proposed a year earlier by the Echeverría administration, and the firms were allowed the flexibility to choose between exports and higher local content above the required level.

currently the only foreign-owned firm to be engaged in that kind of production).

Why, then, was it Ford that was most vocal in opposition? Ford's traditional leadership position in the Mexican industry is one possible explanation, and it is the one offered by Ford executives themselves. Ford had taken the lead in the bargaining over the 1962 decree, and it was Ford that made the offer that led to the 1969 *acuerdo*; it seemed logical that Ford should again take the lead in 1977. There are short-run situational factors that might have played a role as well. Ford believed that the future in trucks lay in diesels. Its management had been engaged in extended negotiations to win approval to manufacture diesel trucks in Mexico. It had just turned down one offer from the government as requiring too many concessions. But the new decree foreclosed the possibility altogether.

There is a deeper, more structural explanation, however, growing out of Ford's predicament in 1977 in adjusting to the changes in the world auto industry. GM had made a corporate commitment to down-size its entire U.S. line more than a year before the Mexican decree appeared. By June 1977, its planning for new models and production facilities was sufficiently advanced that it could immediately begin determining which components it could make in Mexico. Ford, however, had opted for a slower, wait-and-see attitude toward downsizing.[17] When the 1977 decree appeared, with its apparent obligations to make large investments and export commitments, Ford had a much less clear basis for deciding quickly what Mexican-made parts would best fit into its global production network. Ford was in no position to enter into discussions with parts firms, and the volume and timing of the exports required pressed the company very hard. At the same time, it was in difficult straits in the U.S. market because of the Japanese challenge and GM's quicker response in downsizing. The Mexican auto decree now threatened Ford in a market in which it had long been dominant and which it had counted on as a source of strength at a time when it could scarcely stand another threat.

BARGAINING

The bargaining that took place over the 1977 decree followed rather than preceded its promulgation and took place along two fronts: between the Mexican government and the transnational auto firms, and between the Mexican government and the U.S. government.

[17] See "Big Car Battle: General Motors Moves to Shrink, Lighten Full-Sized 1977s, Steps Up Competition," *Wall Street Journal*, Oct. 29, 1976.

*The First Front: The Terminal Firms and
the Mexican Government*

Soon after the decree was issued, the AMIA held a series of urgent meetings, followed by joint meetings between AMIA and government officials, between corporate and government officials, and between Mexican managers and their home offices. Several chief executive officers flew to Mexico for high-level talks, including some with López Portillo himself. These meetings sought not only to clarify the decree but also to influence the content of the forthcoming regulations. There were attempts to win exceptions of various sorts—Volkswagen, for example, is reported to have offered a much higher level of export compensation in return for permission to manufacture all of its exports itself rather than procure 50 percent from parts suppliers—and attempts to soften or slow down implementation. In various ways, the firms sought to convince the Mexican government that the terms were excessive: that they called for too much investment, or that they called for it too fast, or that they allowed the terminal firms too little control over the manner of their compliance.

In all these discussions, Ford led the opposition. "GM and Chrysler stood in back of Ford," one industry executive said, "which is not to be confused with backing Ford." The tenor of the opposition was set in a visit by Henry Ford to Mexico just a few days after the decree appeared. Ford had a half-hour meeting with López Portillo late one afternoon that touched on a number of concerns—how inflationary the new decree would be, how short the deadlines were, etc.—and finally got into the issue of the discrimination in prohibiting foreign-owned firms from installing diesel engines. According to Ford's account of the meeting, López Portillo said there would be no discrimination: Mexico needed diesel trucks and the Ford company could install the engines if it wished. (According to another account, Ford misunderstood: López Portillo had told him that there was no discrimination because Ford had only to Mexicanize to be able to manufacture diesel trucks.) That evening there was a dinner at the home of Minister of Commerce Solana, attended by Ford, SEPAFIN Minister Oteyza, and other officials responsible for automotive policy (none of whom had been present at the meeting between Ford and López Portillo). During the conversation, Ford casually mentioned that López Portillo had given the firm permission on diesels. Oteyza remonstrated that that was impossible: the decree was very clear on the subject and it bore the president's signature. Ford was urged by his staff to proceed quietly on the issue by writing a letter to the president reminding him of what he had said and asking him about what Oteyza had said. But at a press conference just before leaving Mexico, Ford was asked what he thought of the new decree, and he launched into a public tirade against its discriminatory features. The gauntlet had been thrown down.

The company's strategy was to seek a softening of the new policy in the regulations, but it stood to succeed only if none of the other transnational firms first announced plans for new investments to begin complying with the decree. It threatened, more than once, to pull out of Mexico if the decree were not changed, but both sides understood this to be posturing. Ford alone could not force a change; concerted action was the key to winning concessions. So long as the transnational terminal firms showed a unified front, the government would feel pressure to modify the decree, but if one of them "broke the circle," the government could play them off against each other, threatening those that refused to comply with exclusion from the Mexican market. The new policy was troublesome for the other terminal firms, but they preferred to keep a low profile. Nor could Ford find other allies inside Mexico: there seemed to be no opposition to the decree within the government, so ministries could not be played off against one another, and because the parts firms were on the whole quite pleased with the new policy, the government could not be painted as antibusiness in an effort to mobilize more general private-sector opposition. Ford did find an ally elsewhere, however: the U.S. government.

The Second Front: The U.S. Government and the Mexican Government

The U.S. government was brought into the fray along several paths. Ford (and perhaps the other U.S. firms) discussed the decree within the Motor Vehicle Manufacturers Association, the industry's lobbying arm in the United States, which in turn raised the various issues with the Departments of Commerce, State, and Treasury. Henry Ford himself contacted Secretary of State Cyrus Vance and Ambassador to Mexico Patrick Lucy. There were discussions of the decree at meetings of the export promotion committee of the American Chamber of Commerce of Mexico attended by the managers of the U.S.-based terminal firms and by officials from the economic and commercial section of the U.S. embassy.[18] Reports of these meetings were sent to the Departments of State and Commerce.

[18] The American Chamber of Commerce of Mexico has been a significant organization for TNCs located there and the auto firms have played leading roles within it. When the 1977 decree appeared, William Slocum, GM's general manager, was the immediate past

The timing and the character of the U.S. government's response was certainly influenced by these direct and indirect approaches, but it is important to recognize that the government had concerns of its own, independent of the TNCs, which might have drawn it into the conflict even if they had decided they could live with the policy. In fact, it appears that officials of the Commerce Department took some initiative in contacting the U.S.-based firms to learn their positions on the decree shortly after it was promulgated. The government's concerns revolved around three issues: trade, investment, and labor.

An important backdrop for the trade question was the condition of the U.S. balance of payments in the late 1970s. Because of the rising price of oil, increased world competition in manufactured goods, and declining productivity in the United States, a balance-of-trade surplus of $9 billion in 1975 had turned into a disturbing cumulative deficit of $75 billion over the next three years.[19] While trade with Mexico was hardly the cause of this deficit, the new auto policy did seem to portend a worrisome current in world trade: the use of government subsidies and industry-specific performance requirements to generate exports. To the Commerce Department, this seemed to be unfair to manufacturers based in the United States. "The Mexicans have realized that if they are going to expand industry, they've got to force exports; and with our geographic proximity, we'll get the brunt of such moves," one official said in an interview. "Mexico believes that the United States has the responsibility to absorb their production no matter how bad the quality is."

To the Treasury Department and the Bureau of Economic Affairs of the State Department, the Mexican decree appeared as a fundamental challenge to the free-trade regime the United States had been sponsoring since World War II. Before taking his post as assistant secretary of the treasury for international economic affairs, C. Fred Bergsten had written of the danger of "coming investment wars" as governments got more involved in the management of trade.[20] The espousal of free-trade principles by the Bureau of Economic Affairs, headed by Under Secretary of State for Economic Affairs Richard Cooper, put it at loggerheads with those sectors of U.S. business that were seeking protection from imports. But those same principles placed it in tacit alliance with the transnational manufacturing firms that wanted as few constraints as possible on transactions among their international subsidiaries. Free-trade principles seemed threatened by

president and thus an ex officio member of its board, and the general managers of both Ford (Lynn Halstead) and Chrysler (Jack Parkinson) were elected members of the board.
[19] *Fortune*, June 4, 1979.
[20] D. Fred Bergsten, "Coming Investment Wars?," *Foreign Affairs* 52 (1974):135-152.

the new Mexican automotive policy in two ways. First, Mexico was mandating a sectoral balancing of its trade position, by requiring each individual firm to compensate its imports with exports, rather than seeking a trade balance across the whole economy via the play of international market forces.[21] Moreover, it was imposing these performance standards in an industry that would not have been expected to operate at a comparative advantage in Mexico. This suggested a second issue: that, since Mexico could not be genuinely competitive in international automotive trade, it must be subsidizing exports. Treasury and State concluded that certain of the fiscal stimuli being offered the firms were, in fact, export subsidies. This raised the possibility of placing countervailing duties on U.S. imports of automotive products from Mexico.

Within the Bureau of Economic Affairs, the Office of International Finance and Development, under Deputy Assistant Secretary of State Charles Meissner, was more concerned with investment than with trade issues. The lighter export burden for domestically owned firms and the exclusion of foreign-owned ones from diesel-truck manufacture were cited as examples of discrimination against U.S. investors. It is a distinct possibility that Ford complained as loudly as it did about the diesel-truck question because it knew that this would engage the State Department's longstanding concern with this issue.

Finally, there was a fear that the new policy would take jobs away from U.S. workers. The Labor Department itself did not get involved in this issue as strongly as might have been expected (apparently it checked with but heard no urging to action from the UAW), but the State Department—e.g., the Policy Planning Staff—did voice a concern over the potential threat to U.S. labor.

Beyond these specific issues, the State Department (particularly Policy Planning and the Mexico desk) had to look out for the broader context of U.S.-Mexican relations. Questions of illegal immigration and of oil and gas sales would need to be weighed in deciding how to proceed. The complexity of the bilateral relationship was recognized by the two governments in the creation of a Consultative Mechanism in May 1977. The question of auto-industry policy was one of the first issues the Consultative Mechanism was called on to deal with; it was assigned to the subgroup on industry, investment, energy and minerals in the economic working group.

---

[21] It was an insult added to injury, on this view, that the terminal firms would have to compensate for the imports of their suppliers and to compensate by more than 1:1 if they did not achieve the recommended level of local content.

Two things should be noted about these interests of the U.S. government. First, they were rooted in its orientations toward international economic affairs. The Mexican auto decree could have raised the ire of the U.S. government by the way it affected free trade and investment, even if the firms had not sought its assistance. There was, in other words, a degree of convergence of interests between the U.S. government and the U.S.-based transnational auto firms that led both of them to challenge the decree.

It is also important to see that the U.S. government response arose from the diverse concerns of the Departments of State, Treasury, Commerce, and (to a lesser degree) Labor. These various interests ran parallel to one another with respect to the decree, but they were by no means identical. On the contrary, opposition to the decree within the government rested on a potentially fragile alliance. However, under the aegis of the State Department, the different agencies were brought together to confront the Mexican government at a special meeting of the Consultative Mechanism in November 1977. The U.S.-based firms were also invited to send representatives, but they declined; perhaps they wanted the Mexicans to see that the U.S. government had its own concerns with the new policy and was not simply acting at the behest of the Big Three.

At this meeting, department officials presented their queries and their points of objection. The Mexican position was defended by Warman and Wolffer from SEPAFIN. Concerning investment discrimination, they observed that exclusion of foreign firms from selected activities was a longstanding policy of the Mexican government; the discrimination was against all foreign-owned firms, and yet only the U.S. government had objected. In addition, they contended that firms without foreign capital had an intrinsic disadvantage in exporting, and Mexico certainly did not want to discriminate against Mexican-owned firms. The charges concerning export subsidies were denied: they were held to be merely an inference based on erroneous estimates of costs and of labor productivity in Mexico. The only tax rebates being given to the firms were CEDIS (*certificados de devolución de impuestos*)—rebates of domestic taxes—and why should Mexico export its domestic taxes? Finally, concerning performance requirements and sectoral compensation, Warman and Wolffer acknowledged that Mexico did have plans to extend this kind of policy to other sectors, but only to those with reasonable export possibilities. They sympathized with those who wanted greater trade liberalization, but Mexico needed some compensating mechanism. The country still had a huge trade deficit in the automotive sector. If this were reduced, perhaps more progress could be made in the direction of true liberalization.

There were quite different assessments of what happened at the meeting and quite divergent conceptions of what was supposed to follow from it. On the U.S. side, the Bureau of Economic Affairs saw a number of possibilities for future negotiations to get the Mexican government to modify the volume or the sourcing of the exports that were to be required and to allow market forces to play a larger role in bilateral auto trade. It was joined by others in the State Department and in the Treasury Department who saw a chance to develop a more general U.S. policy toward performance requirements and export subsidies. At a minimum, everyone on the U.S. side hoped the Mexicans would hear a strong warning not to extend the policy to other sectors.

The Mexicans believed the meeting had been an occasion for explaining and clarifying policy rather than as the beginning of a series of negotiations. After the meeting, they considered the policy no longer an issue of bilateral discussion, an attitude that angered the Mexico desk and the Bureau of Economic Affairs when reports to this effect came back from the U.S. embassy in Mexico. There was some eagerness to pursue the matter further, but events on the first front made this more difficult.

The Closing of the First Front

After the November 1977 meeting of the Consultative Mechanism, the U.S. subsidiaries in Mexico found themselves on the receiving end of stern admonitions from the Mexican government to discontinue efforts to mobilize U.S. government pressure. Such efforts would only be "counterproductive." "The decree is here to stay," SEPAFIN told Ford pointedly. "This kind of reaction could lead to real conflict. We could go back to price controls." The message was clear: the firms needed smooth relations with the Mexican government in the coming negotiations over the interpretation and implementation of the decree. Even if the government were unwilling to change the basic policy, there might be flexibility or leniency in meeting deadlines and targets. The managers of the Mexican subsidiaries may have been chary all along of headquarters' attempts to bring in the U.S. government, but now they were eager to dissociate themselves from those moves. As one executive put it:

> We here in Mexico have taken the position that, because of the idiosyncrasies of the Mexican government, it would be counterproductive to have the assistance of the U.S. government in settling

our "differences" with the Mexican government. What's more, we don't think we need that assistance. People who would do us a good turn in the U.S. government are not as well acquainted with the situation as they might be. There might be an honest intention to help, but they could create a nasty situation.

The message was relayed from Mexico to Detroit and from Detroit to Washington. The U.S.-based firms, too, distanced themselves from the U.S. government's efforts to change the decree.

Another event in November completely altered the bargaining between the firms and the Mexican government: GM announced the start of an investment program designed to generate sufficient export volume to comply with the decree. The first step was to expand a subsidiary in Mexico, a *maquiladora* called Conductores y Componentes de Juárez that made automotive wiring systems in Ciudad Juárez. (A *maquiladora* is an "in-bond" assembly plant, which is permitted to import components duty free from the United States, assemble the product in Mexico, and export it back to the United States with only the value added in Mexico subject to U.S. import taxes.) That was just what the Mexican government needed to get the other firms to comply. Indeed, after the decree appeared, the government had entered into discussions with each·of the firms, trying to find one that would be willing to make the first move, in the belief that matching defensive investments would then be made by the other firms.[22]

In both 1962 and 1969, the firm that made the first move had been Ford. In 1977, however, after negotiations in Detroit, Paris, Wolfsburg, and Tokyo, it was (to the surprise of many) GM that stepped forward. Already launched on a massive investment campaign to downsize its U.S. models and to reorganize its global production facilities, GM was well positioned to make such a move. If the other firms were less prepared, then "breaking the circle" could win for GM an increase in its market share. In the past, GM had been a quiet firm in the Mexican industry, reluctant to do business in an aggressive way ("Talk about a clam," an executive in a rival firm said). Its strategy had now changed, however. GM had decided to seek to dominate Ford as much abroad as at home. While GM had been the market leader in the United States for several decades, Ford had traditionally had the stronger foreign operation, selling more vehicles outside the United States than GM. With the industry restructuring that began in the mid-1970s, GM saw the chance to make its move. All over Latin America, it began to be more aggressive. It decided there was little prospect of future growth in Argentina, so it withdrew from that country altogether. But in Brazil,

---

[22] For discussion of the defensive-investment dynamic, see chap. 3.

Venezuela, and Colombia, it made large new investments in the late 1970s. Following a corporate reorganization in 1976, when its Mexican subsidiary was transferred from its Overseas Operations to its North American Assembly Division, Mexico became a prime candidate for a share of the investments needed to downsize the company's U.S. models.

GM's announcement of the plan for a *maquiladora* in Ciudad Juárez was only the first shoe, and a small one at that. In February 1978, GM President Elliot Estes dropped the other one. He announced plans to build four large new plants in Mexico, one for assembly and one for engine manufacture to be located in the north, close to the U.S. border (Ramos Arizpe, Coahuila, was eventually designated as the site), and two additional plants in Ciudad Juárez to make engine parts.[23] These investments were expected to expand GM's exports from about $10 million in 1977 to $150-$200 million in 1983, and thus to allow GM to capture a much larger share of the Mexican market.[24]

Once GM had made its move, the other firms quickly followed suit. In March 1978, Ford and Volkswagen announced plans to expand production capacity both for export and for the domestic market.[25] Later, Chrysler began development of a four-cylinder-engine plant (also in Coahuila), American Motors announced plans to export more manual transmissions to the United States, Nissan indicated it would increase exports of engine parts to Japan, and so on. Ford discovered that acceding to the requirement that 50 percent of its exports come from Mexican-owned parts suppliers could be the solution to compliance with the decree without having to draw on scarce capital resources from the United States. It entered into several joint ventures with large industrial groups in Mexico: one with Grupo Alfa to make aluminum cylinder-head castings, one with Vidrio Plano de México to make automotive glass, and one with Valores Industriales S.A. (VISA) to make plastic parts. In each of these, Ford was to have only minority equity but would maintain a voice in management.

The Quieting of the Second Front

Because the U.S. government had its own objectives, the auto firms' withdrawal of support for U.S. government action did not necessarily

---

[23] "Una nueva inversión de General Motors," *AMIA Boletín*, no. 159 (Mar. 1979):1.

[24] Motor Vehicle Manufacturers Association, "Views of the Motor Vehicle Manufacturers Association of the U.S. on the President's Report to the Congress on North American Trade Agreements," Feb. 6, 1981, table 2.5.

[25] "Programa de expansión de Ford" and "V.W. inicia su nueva inversión," *AMIA Boletín*, no. 160 (Apr. 1979):1.

mean that pressure on Mexico on this front would automatically cease. For the U.S. to maintain effective pressure, however, particularly through the Consultative Mechanism, interdepartmental unity and co-ordination were essential. But the coalition within the U.S. government that had presented a unified front at the November meeting began to fall apart just a few weeks later. The Commerce Department—widely regarded as faithfully representing the auto industry's wishes within the government—became less than eager to push the case against Mexico when the companies signaled that they would rather handle the matter on their own. Those in the State Department who were primarily concerned with investment questions also felt less urgency once the firms had indicated it would be healthier for U.S. investments if pressure were withdrawn. Elsewhere in the State Department, there was a feeling that other bilateral issues, particularly the question of natural-gas exports to the United States, required a lower-key approach on the auto-industry decree. The Bureau of Economic Affairs, however, continued to argue that there should be some follow-up, even if a coordinated policy position could not be formulated. Its officials felt that acquiescing in the use of performance requirements in this instance would lead to their use by other countries and in other sectors. They therefore considered it an issue of principle.

In February 1978, a diplomatic note was sent to the Mexican government. It had been drafted by the bureau, with the Mexico desk signing its assent. One State Department official said of this note:

> Unable to formulate a position, we still had to do something. The companies drew back, but we had already gone out there in November and had these talks with the Mexicans. So we decided to just slap the Mexicans on their wrists. This was the purpose of the February note. It was a blunt but technically worded note. We repeated our criticisms and said that we hope you will change this. Period.

The note raised questions about the full range of issues—investment discrimination, performance requirements, and export subsidies—and hinted broadly at the possibility of countervailing duties (for the full text, see appendix A). The note was also meant to be a warning not to extend performance requirements or export subsidies to other sectors. The same official said: "If Warman had further plans in other fields—which he indicated he had—he should not go ahead with them. We had to hit them with a rock and show them that we would tramp all over them if they tried it again."

Mexican officials, thinking the issue closed, were taken aback at the sharpness of the note. They were surprised again when nothing followed. Ambassador Lucy made no mention of the issue in his periodic meetings with government officials. In the spring of 1978, on the occasion of Secretary Vance's visit to Mexico, Under Secretary of State Cooper did bring up the decree again in a meeting of the Consultative Mechanism, but the joint communiqué that came out after the meeting made no mention of the matter. For the time being at least, pressure from the U.S. government had ceased. Unlike the case in 1962, the Mexican government had stood firm in the face of opposition from the TNCs and the U.S. government.

Elements of Bargaining Power

Why did the bargaining in 1977 turn out so differently from that in 1962? First, the conflict between the TNCs and the Mexican government was not very severe. Rather, there was a basic convergence of interests with regard to the export-promoting orientation of the new policy. The conflict was only over the manner in which it was to be carried out.

On those issues where there was genuine conflict—the degree, timing, and sourcing of the required exports, and discrimination against foreign-owned firms—the explanation lies in changes in the power of each of the major actors and their ability to exercise it. For the Mexican state, one important and relatively new element of bargaining power was technical expertise. Despite the disruptive effects of the *sexenio* change, the new team dealing with auto policy had not only access to the accumulated data and reports of fifteen years but also extensive training in and experience with economic planning and with the auto industry. Mexico had moved well along the "learning curve."[26] A second element was intragovernmental unity. In 1962, disagreement between ministries weakened the government's bargaining position; in 1977, the ministries presented a common front. "The TNCs thought if they pushed hard something would break," one SEPAFIN official said. "They shopped around in different ministries but this time it didn't work."[27]

---

[26] On this notion, see Moran, *Multinational Corporations and the Politics of Dependence.*

[27] Once the decree was in force, government unity was further strengthened by the way the decree's regulatory apparatus was constructed. It was based on general rules applicable to all of the companies on a more or less automatic basis. The two earlier decrees had given considerable discretion to the government in the treatment of individual cases, particularly in the determination of production quotas, and this case-by-case determination allowed the coherence of the decrees to be nibbled away. An ad hoc provision for one firm would lead to cries of inequity from other firms and demands for individual

The primary basis of power for the Mexican state neverthless remained what it had been since 1962: its control over access to the Mexican market and the eagerness of the firms not to be excluded from it. But this power was now reinforced by a changed context. The discovery of large oil reserves in Mexico promised a booming domestic economy and thus made the firms all the more eager to have a share in it; and since the firms were reorganizing their global production networks, Mexico took on added importance to them as a low-wage production site close to U.S. assembly plants.

The primary basis of power for the transnational auto firms also remained what it had been since 1962: their control over automotive technology, managerial expertise, capital, and (a newer element) access to international trade opportunities. But these elements of power could be effective only if the firms stood together to refuse these assets to Mexico except on their own terms. A threat, such as the one by Ford, to withdraw from the Mexican market raised the specter of unemployment, dealership closings, and disruption for parts suppliers and consumers. But it was not a credible threat, both because the government suspected that no firm would in fact withdraw (part of the government's learning since 1962 was an appreciation of the power of the defensive investment dynamic) and because, with seven firms operating in Mexico, the government would have gladly accepted the short-run disruption of a withdrawal for the long-run benefit in rationalization of the industry.

Unified action has generally not been possible for the auto TNCs, in Mexico or elsewhere. The oligopoly shuns price competition, but it is fiercely competitive in many other ways. In all the strategy sessions at AMIA, joint action to withhold investment was never even discussed. In view of the increased market share that one firm would obtain from complying with the decree; in view of the fact that new global investments had to be made by all the firms, anyway; and in view of the increased attractiveness of Mexico as a production site, one firm was almost certain to try to comply, thus triggering defensive investments by the others. Finally, no antigovernment alliance was possible with domestic entrepreneurs in the supplier industry; the decree was simply too favorable to their interests.

---

relief. The elimination of production quotas (and price controls), and the establishment of foreign-exchange budgets—which were set simply and automatically by export earnings and past performance, and which the firms were relatively free to allocate for production as they saw fit—avoided this bargaining for special advantages. In areas where there was ambiguity or special circumstances, the government took care to make determinations or exceptions applicable on a common basis.

The remaining element of power for the TNCs was the possibility of mobilizing their home-country governments to bring pressure to bear on Mexico. Historically, the power available to the U.S. in dealing with Mexico has been enormous. In this instance, trade relations were used as a bargaining instrument. About 70 percent of Mexico's exports are directed to the United States and over 60 percent of Mexican imports are of U.S. origin. In its efforts to have the 1977 decree altered, the United States could and did threaten countervailing and anti-dumping duties, as well as new legislation restricting imports from Mexico. But its power was limited by the oil-import difficulties it was then facing and by the recent discovery of vast reserves of petroleum and natural gas in Mexico, all controlled by PEMEX, the state-owned oil company. These reserves, outside the control of Middle Eastern countries and located so close to home, were a new bargaining chip, which would henceforth demand serious consideration before the United States played its otherwise strong hand.

Mexican oil and gas notwithstanding (and even though negotiations for the sale of natural gas to the United States were actually underway in late 1977 and early 1978), the United States still sought to flex its economic muscles in November 1977 and in the ensuing months. The efforts failed, however, because of disunity within the U.S. government, fostered in part by the withdrawal of TNC support for its assistance. The Mexican government had convinced the firms that reliance on U.S. government pressure was counterproductive, a point emphasized when GM, seeking its own advantage, broke the circle.

·10·

EXPORT PROMOTION IN AN ERA OF
OIL AND DEBT

The 1977 decree reaffirmed the Mexican government's commitment to an export-oriented strategy in the automobile industry. As with the 1969 *acuerdo*, its implementation has crystallized a situation of dependency characterized by two major problems. One is a conflict over how much of the benefits of new export markets would flow to firms in the nationally owned parts industry and how much to the foreign-owned auto makers. The other is that the Mexican auto industry is vulnerable not only to fluctuations in the world market but to the vagaries of U.S. government trade policy as well. These problems have unfolded, however, in a context quite different from that in which the 1969 policy was carried out.

Oil and the New Economic Context

The Echeverría administration had ended in political and economic crisis. Inflation was soaring, growth had stalled, and, amid angry charges and countercharges between business and government officials, the private sector had ceased investing. Increasingly, its funds went to banks in the United States or to dollar-denominated accounts in Mexico. Three months before he left office, Echeverría devalued the peso, something that had not been done in more than two decades.

López Portillo's immediate strategy was a stabilization program very much attuned to the conditions set down by the International Monetary Fund in extending a loan to Mexico in the wake of the devaluation. His administration pledged to cut government expenditures, particularly for social services; to stimulate domestic savings and create more jobs; and to restore equilibrium to the country's balance of payments. In an effort to restore the confidence of the private sector, López Portillo dubbed this economic strategy *desarrollo compartido*—shared development. He negotiated investment commitments from the private sector in return for commitments that labor would accept wage restraints tantamount to reductions in real wages.[1] The costs of this

---

[1] For a detailed discussion, see Laurence Whitehead, "Mexico from Boom to Bust: A Political Evaluation of the 1976-79 Stabilization Programme," *World Development* 8 (1980): 843-864.

program were thus not distributed equally; the lower classes paid heavily. The program "worked" in the narrow sense: inflation was reduced, although not back to the 1973 single-digit levels maintained under *desarrollo estabilizador*. The consumer price index increased 29.1 percent in 1977, but only 17.4 percent in 1978 and 20 percent in 1979. Real growth in GDP was renewed: from a rate of 1.7 percent in 1976, it rose to 3.2 percent in 1977 and 6.6 percent in 1978.[2]

It was not just the stabilization program and *desarrollo compartido* that made this growth possible, however, for Mexico had joined the privileged circle of oil-rich countries. Soon after taking office, López Portillo acknowledged the existence of substantial proven reserves, the size of which was upgraded every few months, sometimes every few weeks. Echeverría had spoken of only six billion barrels of proven reserves in 1976, scarcely enough for Mexico's own needs. By January 1979, the figure stood at forty billion barrels.[3] PEMEX, the state oil monopoly created after the 1939 expropriation, embarked on a crash program to develop oil and gas fields, pipelines, refineries, and port facilities. Oil promised state revenues, foreign exchange, cheap energy for domestic manufacturers, and easier credit for the private sector— not just release from the crisis, but the foundation for a new surge of growth. The confidence of domestic and foreign investors was soon restored, and Mexico became a favored borrower in international lending circles.

Mindful of the mistakes that other oil-rich countries had made, López Portillo's economic team undertook to ensure that oil revenues would make a substantial and lasting contribution to broad economic development. For the first time, a serious plan for economic development was devised, with targets for individual sectors.[4] Continued industrial growth was seen as crucial. State officials wanted to avoid a "petrolized" economy, with inflation and an overvalued currency making exports uncompetitive abroad, export of traditional and new manufactured goods replaced by export of petroleum, and massive imports of consumer and capital goods (that could otherwise be produced domestically) causing trade deficits and weakening local industry. Nor would the expansion of petroleum production alone create the 800,000 new jobs needed annually. The government sought to "sow petroleum"

[2] Ibid.

[3] See George W. Grayson, "Mexico's Opportunity: The Oil Boom," *Foreign Policy*, no. 29 (1977-1978):65-89, and Alan Riding, "Taming the Mexican Passion for More," *New York Times*, Sept. 12, 1982, p. 3.

[4] Secretaría de Patrimonio y Fomento Industrial, *Plan nacional de desarrollo industrial, 1979-82* (Mexico City: SEPAFIN, 1979).

in order to "grow industry"—i.e., to transform oil into jobs. To do this, it was disposed to follow much the same basic development strategy that it had followed in the past: primary reliance on private-sector investment, state financing or ownership of industrial projects that the private sector was unwilling or unable to undertake, and tolerance of a highly unequal distribution of benefits—indeed, a disavowal of Echeverría's redistributive rhetoric and policies. However, there were some changes, too. For the first time in postrevolutionary Mexican history, there was public recognition of the limits of land reform, and there were efforts to promote increased agricultural production, even at the expense of redistribution.[5]

Under López Portillo, there was an even greater stress than there had been under Echeverría on liberalizing trade and promoting manufactured exports. Tariffs were reduced and licensing protection lessened in an effort to encourage particular industrial sectors to become more efficient and internationally competitive. This stronger commitment to export promotion as a route to industrial growth informed the auto-sector policy promulgated in June 1977, just six months after López Portillo took office and before the importance of oil reserves and their potential contribution to industrial growth were fully realized. With increased oil production, the determination to promote manufactured exports was intensified. Recognizing that oil reserves would some day be exhausted, state officials deemed it crucial to solidify Mexico's position as an exporter of auto parts now, while oil was plentiful, if Mexico were to establish a strong and lasting position as an industrialized country in the international economic system.

Between 1978 and 1981, four million new jobs were created in oil, public works, and industry. New foreign investment increased from $327 million in 1977 to $1.6 billion in 1981. Real growth in GDP reached 8 percent in 1979 and stayed at that heady rate in 1980 and 1981. Increasingly, however, difficulties in the new growth strategy became apparent. Trade deficits and foreign debt began to get out of hand, despite the oil wealth. Under these conditions, the failure to "balance" trade in the auto sector—to fully compensate imports with exports—became a worrisome problem. The difficulties of export promotion in the auto sector were part of the larger troubles of the Mexican economy, rooted in its dependent position within the world capitalist system.

Despite the efforts taken to forestall them, Mexico found itself with

[5] For a discussion of one such effort, the Sistema Alimentaria Mexicana, see John J. Bailey and Donna H. Roberts, "Mexican Agricultural Policy," *Current History*, Dec. 1983, pp. 420-424.

all the symptoms of a "petrolized" economy. Heightened expectations on all sides outstripped oil revenues, and with the developed world growing much more slowly, Mexico found itself with skyrocketing imports, increasing foreign debt, and accelerating inflation. Imports of the intermediate and capital goods (oil-drilling equipment, machine tools, etc.) needed for the rapid industrial expansion, coupled with imports of consumer goods stimulated by the new oil wealth, drove Mexico's import bill from $5.9 billion in 1977 to $23.1 billion in 1981. To pay for these and for increased government spending on infrastructure and social services, the government decided to increase oil production and exports to levels originally thought unwise. Toward that end, it resorted more and more to foreign borrowing, with the oil reserves serving to reassure the lenders. By the end of the *sexenio*, Mexico had $80 billion in foreign debts, more than any other developing country.

The pace of the expansion and the increased borrowing fueled an inflation that exceeded 100 percent by 1982. As the peso became increasingly overvalued, Mexican manufactured goods became less and less attractive in foreign markets. The resulting decline in non-oil exports was worsened in some sectors by growing domestic demand, which often left little to export. In 1977, oil accounted for 21.5 percent of total export earnings, but this proportion rose to 43.3 percent in 1979 and 68.7 percent in 1981. Efforts to stimulate manufactured exports faltered. As imports and the trade deficit increased, oil production and exports were again boosted to sustain growth. But this demanded still more borrowing and imports, further fueling inflation and weakening efforts at export promotion. Two external circumstances tightened the vise: the softening of oil prices after 1980, because of slack international demand, and exceptionally high interest rates, stemming from U.S. monetary policy.

By early 1981, the government was taking steps in some sectors— autos among them—to reduce imports, but matters continued to worsen. Many Mexicans began to purchase dollars as a hedge against a possible devaluation, which itself increased the pressure for devaluation—and it finally took place in February 1982, the peso going from 26 to the dollar to 49. Panic and capital flight were renewed in August, and the government responded with limited exchange controls.

Before López Portillo left office in December 1982, full-blown financial panic had set in. In August 1982, the government suspended payment of principal on its foreign debt. In his last State of the Union address on September 1, an angry López Portillo announced a further devaluation, the imposition of the exchange controls, and the nationalization of the country's banks. He denounced as traitors the *sacadó-lares*, those who had been converting pesos to dollars and sending the money out of the country. As in 1976, hysterical rumors circulated in the capital suggesting that a military coup was imminent. In fact, the transfer of power took place without incident, but the new president, Miguel de la Madrid Hurtado, like his two predecessors, found himself with an economy in shambles and a political system with damaged legitimacy.

Exchange controls were surprising enough, but López Portillo's eleventh-hour nationalization of the banks sent shock waves through Mexico and international financial circles. The creation of a privately owned banking sector had been the first and most critical step in the resuscitation of the Mexican economy after the revolution. These banks had been the point of crystallization for the dozen or so major bank-industrial groups, each with extensive holdings in manufacturing, mining, commerce, and finance. At first glance, nationalization of the banks appears to be a sharp break with the broad development strategy that Mexico had been following since the 1920s, a renunciation of one of the state's most deeply embedded orientations. At a second look, however, it appears more like an attempt to restore the continuity of the development strategy.

The Mexican state's initial commitment to reliance on the private sector had been coupled with an insistence that the state determine the general direction of development. So long as the national bourgeoisie was in its infancy and adolescence, there was no question of who was in control. But as the private sector grew in strength, it became both willing and able to demand more autonomy. The manner in which the state financed its own activities gave the national bourgeoisie powerful leverage when the two disagreed. Since the state depended upon bank deposits and reserve requirements, the national bourgeoisie needed only to cease channeling its savings through Mexican banks (or to denominate them in dollars) to starve the state of financial resources. López Portillo's outburst at the *sacadólares*, followed by his nationalization of the banks, was an attempt by the state to reassert its tutelary role by capturing the commanding heights of the economy. Thus, nationalization was not so much a change in the rules of the game—primary reliance was still to be placed on private-sector investment—as a move to re-establish the primacy of the state in setting the basic direction of the economy.

The six years of the López Portillo administration had seen recession and austerity change to economic prosperity and then back to recession. It was in this roller-coaster context that the 1977 auto decree was implemented. Considering it to be a crucial element of industrial policy, state officials put considerable effort into carrying it through. Yet, despite its success in generating investments and exports, the trade deficit in the automotive sector grew so large that it became a significant factor in the overall balance-of-payments problem and the ensuing economic crisis. Conversely, the worsening economic situation in the last two years of the López Portillo administration magnified the problems in the automotive sector.

EFFECTS OF THE 1977 DECREE

The principal aims of the 1977 auto decree, like those of the preceding decrees, were to further industrial growth and to lessen the industry's drain on the balance of payments. In that light, the investments announced by the transnational auto makers in the months after the decree was promulgated occasioned great optimism on the part of state officials. Ford, Chrysler, and Volkswagen all followed GM in developing plans for new engine plants that would export to the United States. With the restructuring that was taking place in the world auto industry, each firm's investments were made with an eye to demarcating a precise place for Mexican production in its global production and sourcing strategy. Because engines were the major components whose manufacture for domestic installation was allowed to the auto producers, and because raw-material availability and labor-cost considerations were favorable, engines (particularly four-cylinder engines for the new downsized autos for the U.S. market) and engine parts quickly emerged as the most important components that Mexico would supply. A 1980 estimate based on the announced plans of the major auto makers put the number of engines to be shipped to the United States in model year 1983 at 1,575,000, over twice as many as would be installed in vehicles sold in Mexico.[6] But the auto makers also said they would make investments in the production of other components for export, such as wiring harnesses (GM), hubs and drums (Ford), and injection-molded plastic parts (also Ford). Overall, the U.S. Department of Commerce reported, capital expenditures by foreign-majority-owned affiliates of U.S. firms in the transportation equipment industry in Mexico (principally Ford, GM, and Chrysler) increased from $31 million in 1978 to $405 million in 1980.[7]

[6] Arthur Andersen and Co., University of Michigan, and Michigan Manufacturers Association, *The U.S. Automotive Industry in the 1980s: A Domestic and Worldwide Perspective* (photocopy, 1981).

[7] *Survey of Current Business*, Mar. 1980 and Mar. 1981.

While these investments could not be expected to generate exports until the new manufacturing facilities came on line, the auto makers were expected to increase their volume of exports from the facilities constructed under the earlier decree, as well as from the parts industry. Exports did begin to increase significantly, from 4.7 billion pesos in 1976 to 13.5 billion in 1978.[8]

Not everything was rosy, however. One problem that concerned the Ministry of Finance was the level of fiscal subsidies that the program was using as an incentive to go along with the threat of denied access to the domestic market if export volumes were too low. The industry had been receiving subsidies since before 1962, but they were not declining, as Finance had hoped they would. More serious were two problems that had arisen in the earlier efforts at export promotion and that now reappeared. One was that the transnational auto makers resisted the requirements that half their exports come from the auto-parts firms. The other was the growing trade deficit in the industry. Although these were not new problems, they unfolded differently now because the context, domestically and internationally, had changed significantly.

The Problems of Denationalization and Displacement

Both the 1962 and the 1969 policies had unwittingly furthered the denationalization of the terminal industry. The renewed emphasis on export promotion in the 1977 decree took this yet a step further. DINA, the last completely Mexican-owned auto maker, faced with the need to gain the access to international markets that only a transnational firm committed to exports could provide, split apart its truck and auto operations, selling 40 percent equity in the latter to the newly created Renault Mexicana. The Mexican government did not particularly regret this turn of events; indeed, some officials in SEPAFIN encouraged DINA to sell an even larger equity share, to impel Renault to have an even stronger export commitment.[9] The desire to gain access to TNC-

---

[8] Cámara Nacional de Industrias de Transformación, *Memoria I: Primer simposium de actualización operacional de la industria automotriz en México* (Mexico City: CANACINTRA, 1978), p. 151, and Cámara Nacional de Industrias de Transformación, *Memoria II: Segundo simposium de la industria automotriz mexicana* (Mexico City: CANACINTRA, 1980), appendix table 5.

[9] Similarly, SEPAFIN opposed a proposal initiated by Chrysler to have the state buy majority equity in Chrysler's very profitable Mexican operation, because it might undermine export possibilities.

controlled export markets effectively canceled out the concern over foreign ownership of the auto-manufacturing firms. (See table 10.1.)

The protection of the nationally owned parts industry remained a priority, however. Because of the legal requirement that parts firms be 60 percent Mexican-owned, the issue here was not so much one of preventing the denationalization of individual firms as it was the displacement of the parts firms by the foreign-owned auto makers. The López Portillo administration sought to block this displacement in two principal ways: by limiting the vertical integration of the transnational auto manufacturers and by requiring them to meet 50 percent of their export compensation with components manufactured by the parts industry. Not only would this maintain the Mexican firms' export sales; it would also induce the TNCs to facilitate development of the Mexican parts industry—helping them market their parts and improve their production costs, delivery, and product quality. But it was the requirement of export compensation itself that developed the pressures that threatened to displace the Mexican parts companies.

Because much of world auto trade has been composed of intrafirm trade among TNC subsidiaries or long-term arrangements between TNCs and their major parts suppliers, the transnational auto makers controlled access to the export market. They pointed to that market's demands for competitive price, international quality standards, and timely delivery (especially on motors, which would be the bulk of their

TABLE 10.1

OWNERSHIP CHANGE IN THE MEXICAN AUTOMOBILE INDUSTRY, 1970-1980

Firm	Ownership Status, 1970	Ownership Change, 1970-1980
Ford	100% foreign	(None)
General Motors	100% foreign	(None)
Fábricas Auto-Mex[a]	45% foreign, 55% domestic (private)	Chrysler increased equity to 99% (1971)
Diesel Nacional[b]	100% domestic (government)	Renault acquired 40% equity (1978)
Vehículos Automores Mexicanos	40% foreign, 60% domestic (government)	Mexican government increased equity to 94% (1977)
Volkswagen	100% foreign	(None)
Nissan Mexicana	100% foreign	(None)

SOURCE: Authors' interviews

[a] Renamed Chrysler de México in 1971.

[b] Auto manufacturer renamed Renault Mexicana in 1978; DINA continued as truck manufacturer.

exports) to argue against limits on vertical integration and for the right to source exports from their own plants. Reminders of the failure of the auto-parts industry to provide adequate supply for exports during the years immediately following the 1972 decree underscored the TNCS' arguments.

To the degree that the government was counting upon exports from the automotive industry, it thus found itself with interests similar to those of the auto TNCS. Yet the state's disposition to protect the national bourgeoisie, together with some pressure from the parts industry, pushed officials in the opposite direction.[10] This same dilemma had emerged in the implementation of the 1969 export policy. Then, the government had been largely unprepared to deal with it; it responded in a reactive fashion, granting the auto makers permission to manufacture for export some components not previously open to them, and also allowing noncompliance with export commitments. This time, the government took a more aggressive stance: it positioned itself between the terminal and the supplier firms to set into motion a program of "concerted planning"; it gave the parts firms additional subsidies for new investments; and it worked out a detailed compromise position in the crucial area of engine manufacture, which allowed the auto makers some, though only a little, additional vertical integration. The government was determined to have both exports and a domestically owned parts industry.

Concerted planning. The auto makers argued, often with reason, that their export programs were being held up by inadequate supply from the parts industry. They blamed the problem on a putative lack of

[10] By 1980, the parts firms, though still not a strong political force, were better organized than they had been in the mid-1970s. Their two trade associations, ANFPA and AMPPA, were presenting unified positions to the government regarding the auto-makers' attempts to encroach on the parts industry. The two associations had even begun to merge into a single organization, the Consejo de la Industria Nacional de Autopartes (INA), which was intended as a rival to the powerful and well-staffed terminal-industry association, the AMIA. The initiative in this merger was taken by a number of long-time stalwarts in the parts industry, especially Héctor Vázquez Tercero, who in 1980 became president of the auto-parts section of CANACINTRA; Sebastian J. Aguinaga, president of ANFPA; and Carlos Zambrano Plant, president of AMPPA. Many of the parts-industry's demands were presented forcefully at a meeting (characterized by both sides as "often violent") between industry representatives and the Interministerial Automobile Industry Commission on June 20, 1980. The result of the pressure exerted by the parts firms was not to win state protection and encouragement—key state officials were already inclined in that direction and would have acted in favor of the national parts industry in any event, as they had done in the past, before any industry or organization existed—but rather to improve the terms of protection: the commitments to concerted planning, the subsidies, and the limits on vertical integration.

entrepreneurial spirit among the Mexican suppliers: despite good profitability, investments in the auto-parts industry were only 10 percent of the investments by the auto makers between 1977 and 1979. The auto makers therefore wanted permission to produce parts for export without being bound by the limits on vertical integration or the stipulation that 50 percent of their exports be sourced from the parts industry. If such permission were not granted, they said, the government should not penalize them for failing to meet export requirements.

The auto-parts firms were indeed slow in responding to the export program, but they asserted that there were bottlenecks beyond their control, such as problems in obtaining adequate supplies of raw materials. Furthermore, the 1976 devaluation, the ensuing recession, and the high cost of money deterred them from making large investments. Most importantly, the parts firms blamed the auto makers for creating a situation of uncertainty which discouraged investments by failing to place orders far enough in advance, abruptly changing orders, and demanding new components without sufficient notice. This conflict between the auto makers and the parts firms had simmered since manufacturing began under the 1962 decree, but with the new export promotion drive, the stakes became much higher.

To deal with this problem, SEPAFIN instructed the terminal and supplier industries to work out a mutually agreeable form of planning, which SEPAFIN would then formalize and administer. In the resulting "Concerted Planning Resolution,"[11] the terminal firms were required to place orders (specifying quantity, part number, and delivery date) twelve months before the beginning of each model year. Two-year notice was required for the overall product mix and for identification of new and discontinued parts. Accepted orders would be registered with SEPAFIN. Only if a parts firm failed to deliver would restrictions on imports be waived for the terminal firm.

Subsidies. In another move to ease supply bottlenecks and strengthen the national parts industry, the government offered the industry a special package of incentives.[12] The parts industry was also encouraged to take advantage of two subsidy programs that had recently been established for all majority Mexican-owned firms. The Certificates of Fiscal Promotion (Certificados de Promoción Fiscal, or CEPROFIS), established in 1979 as part of the National Industrial Plan, granted sub-

---

[11] "Resolución sobre planeación concertada de la industria automotriz," *Diario oficial,* Oct. 3, 1980.

[12] "Programa de fomento para la industria nacional fabricante de autopartes," *Diario oficial,* Jan. 21, 1980.

stantial fiscal credits (a form of tax exemption),[13] and on any new installations the parts firms could benefit from a reduction of up to 30 percent in their energy costs. In addition, the parts firms would be granted subsidies on tariffs for imports of raw materials and parts not available in Mexico. These subsidies were not offered to the foreign-owned auto makers.

Vertical integration. Even with the concerted-planning and subsidy programs, the structure created by the 1977 decree still made it rational for the TNCs to manufacture parts themselves to fulfill their export requirements. If the TNCs had or developed export capabilities superior to those of Mexican industry, Mexico's need for exports would create pressure to relax the 50 percent export rule, increasingly leaving exports to industries owned by TNCs. Such vertical integration would threaten to segment the market, confining the independent parts firms to production for the Mexican market (with the very inefficiencies of small-scale production that the decree sought to eliminate) while the terminal industry handled production for export. "The autonomy and independence sought for our economy," declared a high official early in 1980, "is founded on maintaining an auto-parts industry dominated by national capital. Horizontal integration may make export compensation difficult; it does, however, take priority and we ought to defend it at all costs. It is the only way our industry will be able to continue to have the fundamentally national character it has so long had."[14]

In August 1980, the government published its "Engine Resolution," which restricted vertical integration of the TNCs in the production of engines, the major export component. The resolution permitted the terminal firms to continue to machine engine blocks and to assemble and test motors (as they had been permitted to do since 1962), and to manufacture ten other specific engine parts. The manufacture of all other engine components, however, was expressly reserved for auto-parts firms.[15] Thus, engines manufactured for export (as well as those

[13] "Decreto que establece los estímulos fiscales para el fomento del empleo y la inversión en las actividades industriales," *Diario oficial*, Mar. 6, 1979. Under this program, a fiscal credit of 10 to 15 percent was given for new investments (outside of Mexico City, the exact amount depending on where the facility was located); of 20 percent for new employment created (except in the Mexico City area); of 10 percent for expanding installed capacity (except in the Mexico City area); and of 5 percent on the value of machinery and equipment bought that was made in Mexico.

[14] Sacristán Roy, "Programa de fomento," p. 39.

[15] Secretaria de Industria y Comercio, Comisión Intersecretarial de la Industria Automotriz, "Resolución sobre la producción de motores de la industria terminal," Aug. 27, 1980. The manufacture of twenty-five important engine components was reserved for

for domestic use) would have to contain many locally purchased components.

Unless the parts companies made new investments to increase their production, however, it would be impossible to enforce the limits on vertical integration or the 50-percent export requirement. Mexico's critical need for exports, combined with TNC control of access to export markets, gave the foreign auto manufacturers a strong bargaining position vis-à-vis the Mexican government. The chief executive of one U.S. auto maker outlined the logic that he believed was working in his favor: "We're making our investments in motors for export. If the parts industry cannot supply the parts, and the government won't let us make them, then the government can't insist on compensation when we're forced to import them. Either they make them or we make them, or we don't have to compensate for importing them."

The Problem of the Trade Deficit

The succession of policies in the auto sector since 1962 that had sought to spur industrialization in this industry (and in the other industries linked to it) had also aimed to lessen Mexico's trade dependency, first by import substitution and then, in the 1977 decree, by requiring exports to compensate for imports. If the 1977 decree were to be fully implemented, Mexico would become a significant exporter of automotive products, particularly to the United States. The path of implementation has hardly been smooth, however.

The 1977 decree initially appeared to be an unqualified success, as the major auto companies committed themselves to major investments in export-oriented facilities. Automotive exports did increase, but the firms were not altogether successful in meeting their commitments. In 1978, they all complied with the still comparatively small compensation requirements set out by the decree. In 1979, however, Chrysler failed to meet the requirements. For 1980, its tax subsidy was decreased by the amount of its 1979 subsidy that had not been justified by its exports. It then became clear that a number of the firms—including Ford, Chrysler, and Volkswagen, the three largest producers—would not comply in 1980. Meanwhile, the industry's overall trade deficit was growing steadily worse. Between 1977 and 1979, Mexico's auto-related trade deficit with the United States more than tripled (see table 10.2).

the national parts industry. A terminal firm could obtain special permission to produce up to three of these parts, but only if their total value did not exceed 15 percent of the total cost of parts for the engine and if the terminal firm undertook to assist parts firms in the manufacture of other components for engines to be exported.

In 1979, the auto industry's trade deficit of $862 million was nearly a quarter of the country's overall trade deficit ($3.66 billion), and in 1980, it was over a third ($1.4 billion out of $4.0 billion).[16]

Several factors were responsible for this situation. Exports were slow to develop, partly because of the lead time necessary to bring new projects to fruition; an investment undertaken at the beginning of 1978 could not be expected to yield exports until 1980 at the earliest. The quite opposite performance of auto sales in Europe and the United States on the one hand and in Mexico on the other was also involved. In Europe and the United States, 1979-1980 recapitulated the experience of 1974-1975: OPEC-induced increases in the price of oil engendered a slowdown in these economies that particularly affected automobile sales. Mexico's 1977 auto decree had been propitiously timed

TABLE 10.2

MEXICO'S AUTOMOTIVE IMPORTS FROM AND EXPORTS TO
THE UNITED STATES, 1965-1980
(millions of dollars)

	PASSENGER CARS		AUTO PARTS[a]		TOTAL[b]		
	Imports	*Exports*	*Imports*	*Exports*	*Imports*	*Exports*	*Balance*
1965	51	c	73	0.1	159	0.1	−159
1966	53	c	77	1	158	1	−157
1967	54	c	79	1	162	1	−161
1968	79	c	91	3	206	3	−203
1969	71	c	103	9	206	9	−197
1970	38	c	129	18	195	18	−188
1971	57	c	137	25	218	26	−192
1972	76	c	151	35	244	35	−209
1973	98	8	209	56	322	76	−246
1974	136	8	258	84	465	119	−346
1975	150	1	346	131	528	136	−392
1976	131	c	337	18	496	18	−478
1977	119	c	338	238	482	240	−242
1978	93	0.1	594	269	750	280	−470
1979	26	0.1	907	321	1056	327	−729
1980	18	c	937	242	1067	245	−822

SOURCE: "Views of the Motor Vehicle Manufacturers Association of the U.S., Inc., on the President's Report to the Congress on North American Trade Agreements" (Feb. 6, 1981), table 2.4 (derived from data of the U.S. Bureau of the Census)

[a] As defined by and prepared from the end-use classifications of the Bureau of Economic Analysis of the Department of Commerce.

[b] Also includes trucks, buses, and special-purpose vehicles.

[c] Less than $100,000.

[16] *Automotive News*, Jan. 11, 1982, quoting Deputy Minister of Finance Jesús Silva Herzog.

to acquire an increased share of world automobile production for the country, but because a recession followed the decree so closely, Mexico could not help but experience some effects from the production cutbacks in the TNCs' sourcing networks. Mexican automotive exports to the United States did increase in 1979 but fell in 1980. At the same time, auto sales were booming in Mexico, in large part because of the revenue produced by petroleum. Between 1977 and 1981, annual sales rose from 286,725 to 561,249 vehicles, an average increase of 19 percent a year. Since each vehicle had imported content, rising sales meant a rising import bill. In fact, domestic sales grew so quickly that firms had trouble keeping up in their domestic production; some even failed to fulfill their local-content requirements.

The López Portillo administration tried a variety of strategies to cope with the problem. The first was the penalization of Chrysler for failing to fulfill its export commitments in 1979. When it became clear that several other firms would not comply in 1980, however, the Interministerial Commission on the Auto Industry decided against using any of the sanctions that the 1977 decree made available, despite the fact that some of them—e.g., the reductions in subsidies—could be employed more easily than those of the 1972 decree. Instead, the commission chose to allow firms to postpone their export compensation, provided that the shortfall be made up in the future—and with interest.

Under a 1980 resolution, the auto makers were allowed to apply for an advance or a loan on the foreign exchange they would need for a particular model year, on condition that they presented detailed investment plans showing how, within two years, exports would be generated to "pay back" the foreign exchange that had been advanced.[17] Interest would be charged on the advance, but the interest would be lower if the plans involved exports from an auto-parts firm. To pay off these advances and to meet their future export commitments, the auto makers would have to increase substantially their level of exports. Sanctions would be imposed only if the firms showed a sustained unwillingness or inability to meet their accumulated commitments.

State officials chose this route of advances and future sanctions rather than immediate sanctions for a number of reasons. For one, they recognized that export shortfalls might be short-term and beyond the control of the auto makers—a consequence of world market con-

[17] "Resolución sobre anticipos y contabilización de divisas de las empresas de la industria automotriz terminal," *Diario oficial*, Aug. 27, 1980. The foreign exchange could be "paid back" by increasing exports, by increasing domestic content, or by making new investments with capital from foreign shareholders. (Investments made with capital from foreign lenders did not count for this purpose.)

ditions or of the time lag between investments and actual exports, for example. If the auto makers were indeed making export-oriented investments that would eventually yield compliance, then sanctions would be of little use. Advances were also another way of protecting the Mexican parts industry. A SEPAFIN official explained: "Ford and GM could, at any moment, have sent us fifteen auto-parts projects and said, 'Here—give us these if you want us to export. We'll do them right away. Or else don't sanction us for not exporting.' The advances give us a certain flexibility with the TNCs so the parts projects can be done by Mexican enterprises." Anxious to encourage the parts industry to make the needed investments rather than allow encroachment by the foreign auto makers, state officials were reluctant either to relax the limits on vertical integration or to apply sanctions against the auto makers when parts supply was the problem. By giving advances, they could avoid this dilemma.

The carrot of advances had other advantages over sanctions. Since an annual interest rate (about 20 percent in 1980) was being charged on the amount of foreign exchange advanced, the plans presented by the auto makers when requesting the advance had to be larger than they would otherwise be. Further, officials believed the advances would initiate a process of continual investment, rather than having just one big wave. Each year, the firms would have to present their investment plans for the next six years in order to qualify for advances. Officials hoped this would create a certain rhythm of investment and increase their information about and control over the process.

By late 1981, however, with Mexico's oil bubble in the process of bursting, the overall trade deficit and the share of automotive products within this deficit had become so worrisome that the López Portillo administration felt forced to take further, short-term measures. In October, the government stipulated that the volume of automobile production and the value of imported material for the 1982 model year were to be frozen at 1981 levels. Any production of vehicles not meeting the minimum domestic-content requirements was forbidden. Imports of deluxe components were prohibited, and no additional exchange advances were to be granted.[18] These rules were designed to be temporary, to last only until investments in export production by auto makers and parts suppliers came on line.[19]

[18] "Measures for Rationalizing the Trade Balance Deficit in the Automotive Industry," *Automotive News*, Jan. 25, 1982.
[19] Engine plants constructed by GM, Chrysler, and Ford were scheduled to begin exports in 1982 or 1983. Jack H. Parkinson, managing director of Chrysler de México, indicated that the effect of the 1982 import restrictions would be to accelerate current export

If the early wave of investment after the 1977 decree illustrates the possibilities of export compensation policies, the resort to these emergency measures dramatizes the dangers. They allow for the achievement of growth and efficient production despite small or overcrowded domestic markets, but they make a developing country vulnerable to the fluctuations of world markets and to the global decisions of transnational firms. The 1977 decree came at a time when Mexico had an opportunity to capture a long-term share of production in the sourcing networks of the transnational auto firms as they were being reorganized. In the short term, however, the timing was not so fortunate. Mexico experienced an oil-based domestic boom just after the decree, which led to surging domestic auto sales during a period when the major auto-producing countries—Mexico's principal export markets—were heading into recession. One consequence was a rapidly increasing trade imbalance for Mexico in the automotive sector. It appeared that Mexico would be forced to choose between tolerating large foreign-exchange deficits and cutting domestic production (and thus industrial growth). But the snowballing difficulties of the last months of the López Portillo administration, with their huge foreign debt, devaluation, and political crisis, removed the choice. As a condition of receiving an IMF stabilization loan, Mexico had to bring its trade deficit under control.[20]

PRESSURES FROM THE UNITED STATES

Mexico's export strategy for the automotive sector has depended heavily on the U.S. market. Anything that decreases sales to the United States has put pressure on the balance of payments and threatened the growth of the Mexican auto industry and the sectors linked to it. Recessions in the United States have been one cause of such decreases. Protectionist policies might be another. The problems plaguing the

---

programs and stimulate expansion of a domestic luxury-components industry: *Automotive News*, Jan. 11, 1982. Another U.S. auto executive predicted that "Mexico will become one of the world centers for worldwide supply of components. As economies of scale reduce costs and sourcing becomes worldwide, we'll see incredible growth": ibid., Jan. 25, 1982.

[20] In and of itself, the devaluation shows the vulnerability of the auto industry within Mexico's overall trade and financial dependency. On the positive side, the devaluation lowered the price of Mexican exports, making their Mexican plants and suppliers more attractive to the transnational auto makers. On the negative side, however, the devaluation of the peso left a number of companies holding large dollar debts which effectively doubled overnight. GM borrowed heavily from U.S. banks to finance its expansion. Ford borrowed in pesos most of the $42 million it spent to increase its assembly capacity from 72,000 to 93,000 units a year, but its new engine plant was financed primarily in dollars. *New York Times*, Oct. 7, 1982, p. D1.

U.S. auto industry in recent years have spawned a number of initiatives to restrict auto imports or to impose trade sanctions against countries, such as Mexico, that are viewed as engaging in unfair trade practices. With Mexico committed to an export-oriented policy, its auto industry is hostage to decisions that the United States makes about *its* auto industry.

The U.S. auto market has been crucial for the Mexican industry because it is the destination of an overwhelming proportion of Mexico's automotive exports. For the United States, however, these imports from Mexico are much less important. In 1980, they constituted only about 1.5 percent of its total automotive imports. Meanwhile, despite Mexico's export-promotion thrust, the U.S. trade surplus in automotive products with Mexico was continuing to grow.

Despite the relatively small volume, automotive imports from Mexico have become a significant issue in the debate about the future of the U.S. auto industry. As total imports of vehicles and of parts have taken a growing share of the American market, with attendant plant closings, unemployment, and near-bankruptcies, voices from labor, from auto and auto-parts firms, and from within the U.S. government have begun clamoring for measures to restrict the flow. In the restructuring of the world auto industry that began in the mid-1970s, production in the United States was displaced in part by imports of assembled vehicles from Japan and in part by imports of components by U.S.-based producers for incorporation in vehicles assembled in the United States. Imports from Mexico acquired their importance not because of their volume (which didn't begin to compare with the volume of Japanese imports) but because of the precedent that action on them might set. Mexico's 1977 export requirements were held to be an unfair interference with the market and a violation of the principles of free trade embodied in the General Agreement on Tariffs and Trade. They became the prime example of performance requirements. If other countries follow suit, the threat to U.S. manufacturing would become increasingly serious: U.S.-based TNCs would be compelled to export back to the United States, displacing production at home. Mexican policy makers thus experienced two kinds of reaction from Washington: (a) direct, bilateral pressure to soften or rescind the requirements of the 1977 decree, and (b) more general efforts to protect production in the United States, affecting other countries as well as Mexico.

The failure of Washington's efforts to change the 1977 decree (see chapter 9) was followed by over two years of relative silence, while Mexico proceeded with implementation. Increasingly serious difficulties in the U.S. auto industry eventually led to a renewal of pressure in the last months of the Carter administration. Some of the concern continued to emanate from within the government, from officials in State, Treasury, and Commerce who were concerned over the general question of performance rquirements, but there were also political demands—this time from labor as well as from industry—for the government to act. Several AFL-CIO unions (though not the UAW) joined with several firms (though none of the Big Three) to form the Labor-Industry Coalition for International Trade (LICIT). LICIT testified before Congress in opposition to performance requirements and threatened to bring suit claiming unfair trade practices against Mexico, Brazil, Australia, and Spain for their automotive export policies.

In October 1980, there were discussions of the Mexican automotive export requirements in Washington at a meeting of the bilateral consultative mechanism that had been established by Presidents Carter and López Portillo. SEPAFIN Deputy Minister Warman and Héctor Hernández, deputy minister of commerce, were told that U.S. labor was very concerned about the increasing automotive imports from Mexico. They were asked why Mexico could not revoke its policy now that the TNCs had made substantial investments in export production. Warman and Hernandez insisted that this was impossible: the United States still enjoyed a large trade surplus with Mexico in automotive products, and total manufactured exports from Mexico to the United States had been declining while manufactured imports from the United States had increased by nearly 50 percent. When Mexico's automotive exports exceeded imports, they said, Mexico would begin talking about changes in the decree.

Another meeting was held in December 1980. U.S. representatives from the Departments of Commerce, Labor, and Transportation told the Mexicans about pressures for sanctions from LICIT and other sources. The Mexicans again stood firm, even suggesting that Mexico and the United States ought to develop a coordinated policy in the automotive sector. Instead of simply reacting to investments and decisions already made, the United States could develop a plan for phased investment in Mexico for the production of certain components, in such a way as to allow the U.S. industry to become more efficient in other areas and to adjust in an orderly fashion.[21]

When the Reagan administration took office in January 1981, it renewed the expression of concern. In September, Secretary of Com-

---

[21] When the Mexicans were told that such planning would be virtually impossible in the U.S., one high official responded by offering "technical assistance"—amusing the Mexican contingent but angering the U.S. representatives.

merce Malcolm Baldrige and Special Trade Representative William Brock headed a large delegation to Mexico (including officials from the Departments of Energy, Transportation, Labor, Commerce, and Treasury as well as observers from labor and industry) that discussed a host of trade questions. One important item on the agenda was Mexico's auto-sector performance requirements. The U.S. government position was that Mexico was subsidizing its exports and that, instead of such unfair trade practices, Mexico should devalue the peso to make its goods more competitive. Although there was some talk of setting up a special committee on automotive exports, U.S. disapproval of Mexican policy was interpreted by the Mexicans as a lecture on the virtues of free trade rather than as a serious proposal for the resolution of differences.

It is not just the executive branch that has been worried. Members of Congress, particularly those from areas affected by auto-industry problems, have also been concerned about the impact of automotive imports. In early 1980, Senator Howard M. Metzenbaum, Democrat of Ohio, made public what he said were internal documents of the Ford Motor Company that proposed investment in a plant for four-cylinder engines in Mexico, which Metzenbaum said would be tantamount to moving a Cleveland plant to Mexico.[22] The senator claimed the plan showed "callous disregard" for workers and was "hypocritical" in light of Ford's concurrent efforts to have limitations placed on automotive imports.[23] He said he was releasing the information to dramatize the need for legislation he was drafting regarding plant closings. Ford neither confirmed nor denied the authenticity of the documents,

---

[22] The documents compared the costs of building four-cylinder engines in the U.S. or Mexico, and purchasing them from Japan. The Mexican cost was lower, but convincingly so only when Ford counted in the extra benefits of production in Mexico that resulted from government policy: tax subsidies and access—through performance requirements—to a larger share of the Mexican market. U.S. Senator Howard M. Metzenbaum, press release, Feb. 21, 1980.

[23] Ford's efforts, however, were very specifically aimed at imports of foreign-owned (especially Japanese) companies and not at imports of products manufactured by Ford subsidiaries. The Ford documents illustrate the company's concern not to appear hypocritical: "The juxtaposition of any such action with whatever push Ford may make to restrain Japanese imports needs to be weighed. The credibility of any effort we make to impose local content requirements or quotas on the Japanese could be undercut by our sourcing engines in Japan for Ford's U.S. cars. On the other hand, we could say, quite properly, that the competitive situation in the industry compels us to take advantage of some low-cost sourcing off-shore to keep up with other manufacturers." Exhibit 16 in Ford documents, in ibid. Nevertheless, Ford was also very desirous of keeping a low public profile; the documents detail a public-relations campaign to minimize publicity regarding these new investments.

but in June 1980, it announced plans to build a four-cylinder-engine plant in Mexico and to close an old plant in Ohio.

In late 1981, the Subcommittee on Foreign Trade of the House Energy and Commerce Committee renewed congressional interest. Its chairman, Sam Gibbons, Democrat of Florida, and several other members wrote letters to Special Trade Representative Brock urging legal action against countries that imposed export requirements on foreign-owned firms within their boundaries. One of these letters, that from William Brodhead, Democrat of Michigan, said:

> At a time when our domestic economy, and our auto industry in particular, are under such tremendous strain, we cannot continue to tolerate the lost jobs, production and sales which result from this unfair trade practice. . . . It is essential that action on this issue not await the outcome of prolonged negotiations, and that we convey to our trading partners swiftly and forcefully that we will not tolerate indirect trade barriers which violate principles of free trade and fair trade.[24]

Perhaps the most important congressional action, in terms of its implications for trade relations with Mexico and other auto-exporting countries, was a proposal for legislation establishing local-content requirements for U.S. manufacturers. It would mandate that 90 percent of all vehicles sold in the United States be manufactured in the United States. Such legislation, which has been strongly supported by the UAW, would severely threaten the growth of the Mexican auto industry by limiting access to its major export market. It is ironic that this proposal would have a developed country employ for defensive purposes precisely the same policy that a number of LDCs used to enter into auto manufacturing.

Until the economic crisis in the last years of the López Portillo administration, the Mexican government was able to fend off the relatively mild pressures put on it by the U.S. government to change its export requirements. In part, Mexico's ability to resist was the result of the skillful diplomacy of top officials in SEPAFIN, Commerce, and Finance. Their bargaining position was based on important changes in Mexico's relationship with the United States, however. Most important were Mexico's oil reserves and the increasing dependence of the United States on oil imports. Mexico could also count on the U.S.-based TNCs to help resist specific sanctions. The investments they have made in production for export from Mexico have given them interests in com-

[24] *Automotive News*, Jan. 11, 1982.

mon with the Mexican government in opposing U.S. trade restrictions, even though they also still object to certain elements of Mexican policy. Mexico's recent economic difficulties, however, have made it much more vulnerable to economic pressures from its northern neighbor. Mexican confidence has been shaken by its deteriorating trade position its debt-repayment problems, and the financial instability following devaluation and the nationalization of the banks.

Nevertheless, it is unlikely that Mexico will abandon its export strategy. Even if it relaxed some of its requirements, the substantial investments in export facilities made by the TNCs would probably sustain the export thrust for at least the next decade. Pressures from the United States might succeed in limiting the incentives that Mexico offers to encourage exports, but it is unlikely they will succeed in decreasing the flow of parts. Too many firms now have an interest in continuing this trade.

·11·

SUMMARY AND CONCLUSIONS

The organization and content of this book have been informed by an historical-structural approach which seeks to avoid both the implicit determinism and the voluntarism of more conventional approaches in American social science. It is founded on the straightforward premises that human beings make crucial choices which shape the course of their lives—they "make their own history"—but that these choices are constrained by structures, the historical products of the actions of previous generations, which shape what they want and limit what they are able to do. Structures are political, economic, social, and cultural institutions; they involve two or more actors, have an enduring quality, and are not easily susceptible to unilateral change. They are created through human action, but over time they come to take on a life of their own, to appear as "given" or "natural."

Structures, moreover, shape the interests and power of the actors (individuals, groups, classes, or organizations) that exist within them, often in ways that give rise to antagonisms and conflicts of interest. Actors may seek to use their power to alter their position within the structures or to change the structures altogether. The actions they take, and the structures they create or shape, will have consequences (not all of them intended, by any means) for all of the actors within them. Interests and power will be solidified or rearranged; new possibilities for action and new limits will appear.

The tasks of research in employing this method are to identify relevant structures, to explain how the interests and power of actors are shaped by these structures, and to identify the limits and possibilities for transforming the structures.

We have had a general concern in this book with the structure of the Mexican political economy, with the structure of the world capitalist system, and with the consequences of the relationships between the two for economic growth and equity in Mexico. We have focused in particular on one element in this relationship, the automobile industry, and on two actors, the transnational automobile corporations and the Mexican state. On the one hand, we have tried to show how these structures shaped the interests and power of the TNCs and to determine the consequences of their resulting action in Mexico. On the other hand, we have sought to explain how these structures shaped the in-

terests and power of the Mexican state and how they delineated the
limits and possibilities for using state power to compel the TNCs to act
in ways perceived to be more beneficial for Mexico.

TNCs AND THE STATE IN THE
HISTORICAL-STRUCTURAL APPROACH

Industrial-organization theory provides us with an understanding of
corporate behavior that fits well within the general outlines of the
historical structural approach. It holds that the actions of firms are
shaped by the structure of the industry in which they operate (the
degree of concentration, the barriers to entry, etc.). Industry structure
does not fully determine firm behavior, however; corporations pursue
different strategies within certain limits.

We have modified the framework of industrial-organization theory
in some important ways. First, we emphasize the form of ownership
as an important aspect of industry structure, rather than simply assuming domestic private ownership. Transnational and public ownership turn out to be important *structural* alternatives; the form of
ownership of a firm affects not only its own behavior but also the
behavior of all other firms in the industry. Although avoided by the
Mexican government, which placed primary reliance on private-sector
investment, public ownership can provide the state with an additional
and important instrument of policy. With transnational ownership, the
structure of the world industry becomes as important as that of the
domestic industry. These modifications allow us to give greater spec-
ificity to the insight of dependency theorists that external structures
(in this case, the world capitalist system) condition the internal ones
(the domestic economy of a developing country). We can show how
the negative consequences of TNC behavior in Mexico result from strategies growing out of the structure of the world industry.

Second, we emphasize the historical character of these industrial
structures. While at any particular moment the structure of the world
industry or of the Mexican industry might seem given or fixed, these
structures are subject to change, partly as a consequence of political
struggle or economic competition. They might have been different,
and, within certain limits, action might make them different.

This is closely related to a third point, the importance of the exercise
of power—by the state and by TNCs—to maintain or to change these
structures. In itself, this is hardly new for industrial-organization theory, many of whose proponents in the United States have been explicitly interested in antitrust legislation as a way of re-establishing

effective competition. Given the nearly inevitable pattern of oligopolistic behavior that arose from the structure of the world automotive
industry, however, trust-busting was not a feasible policy goal of the
Mexican state. Rather, the Mexican state sought a controlled oligopoly.
The contested issues of industrial structure were the number of firms
engaged in the industry in Mexico and the extent of domestic ownership.

Like transnational corporations, the state is an actor with interests
and power of its own, interests and power that are shaped by the
national and international structures in which it is enmeshed. In stressing this, we depart from other approaches to the state—pluralist, functionalist, and Marxist. On the one hand, we insist that the state is not
to be simply dissolved into a host of smaller components, each with
transitory, shifting intentions. On the other hand, we hold that there
is no essential character of the state that can be deduced from some
"function" which "needs" to be performed in society.

We conceive of the state's interests as embedded orientations: dispositions to act in particular ways that are taken on by, and institutionalized in, various state agencies in response to problems or opportunities that arise. Different orientations become institutionalized
in different ministries or agencies of the state, however, setting the
stage for conflict within the governmental apparatus. There has been
remarkable basic continuity in the orientations and policies of the Mexican state organizations charged with economic growth. Some of
these—primary reliance on the private sector, vigorous action by the
state to do what the private sector cannot or will not do—were formed
when the state was reconstituted on particular class foundations after
the revolution. Others have emerged in the course of pursuing economic growth: import substitution as a strategy for industrialization
in the 1940s, export promotion as both an extension of and a replacement for it three decades later. The changes in state personnel which
have come with the sexennial changes of presidential administration
have introduced minor variations within these policy continuities. Finally, to assert that the state has interests of its own is not to deny that
external pressure on the state by other actors can and does affect how
the state acts.

The power of the state depends on certain of its internal characteristics, particularly its organizational unity and its technical capability,
as well as on its position within national and international structures.
In addition, the state draws power from its particular social foundations—the class forces on which it rests. These introduce constraints
as well, however. In a capitalist economy, state policies that are det-

rimental to the investment climate risk such economic chaos that they are likely to be avoided. The context of dependency introduces further limitations: trade imbalances, international oligopolies, the power of other governments. An historical-structural approach to the state must attend both to these constraints and to opportunities for change within the structures and for transformations of the structures.

To analyze bargaining between the state and the TNCs, we have developed and employed a theoretical framework that focuses on congruences and conflicts of interest and on relative power. Two elements of this framework warrant emphasis. First, the congruence of interests in any bargaining encounter is as important as the conflict of interests. The sound and fury of a conflict tend to attract attention, yet it may be merely a minor spat among otherwise comfortable bedfellows. There may well be tacit bases of agreement among the actors, and some issues may never find their way into a bargaining agenda because, lacking a conflict of interests, there is no need to bargain over them. To focus only on issues of conflict may distort understanding of the relationship between the parties to the bargaining.

Second, power is exercised when one actor makes another act differently than it would otherwise, but power is also exercised (and perhaps more significantly) when an actor can so change institutional structures that other actors will be led to act differently without any visible conflict. The interests and the power of the state and of the TNCs are shaped by the structures in which they operate; altering these structures will lead actors to behave differently because their interests and power have been altered.

DEPENDENCY

One of the central purposes of this study has been to explore the effects of world capitalism on development and underdevelopment. While our historical discussions (especially in chapter 2) dealt with this question in a general fashion, they were meant principally to set a context for a more focused analysis of the impact of TNCs on Mexico, and the specific conclusions we draw about dependency are limited by this focus. Three aspects of our approach need to be stressed. First, the historical-structural approach to dependency challenges more deterministic approaches, which see underdevelopment as a necessary and mechanistically conditioned response to world capitalism, or which view internal phenomena simply as a consequence of external ones. Rather, as Cardoso and Faletto have put it, the relationships between internal and external phenomena form

251

a complex whole whose structural links are not based on mere external forms of exploitation and coercion, but are rooted in coincidences of interests between local dominant classes and international ones, and, on the other side, are challenged by local dominant groups and classes.[1]

Second, the concrete forms which the relationship between external and internal forces take need to be specified by identifying the interests and power of the actors involved in conflicts. Instead of talking vaguely about the "conditioning" of underdevelopment by world capitalism, we have tried to show precisely how particular external structures, such as the structure of the world auto industry, have affected the interests and power of particular actors, and how the behavior of such actors, because of their global strategies and international sources of power, has had negative consequences for Mexico.

Third, internal forces—in the present case, the Mexican state—may have the power to alter the effects of external actors and structures. They may do this by regulating the behavior of the external actors or, more powerfully and effectively, by changing the structures that shape the interests and power of those actors. At the same time, there are severe limits on what such state power can accomplish. Coincidences of interest between the state and transnational actors may protect the latters' interests by removing certain issues from the bargaining agenda. On the other hand, conflicts may create new opportunities, and changes in structures open and close possibilities, so that new antagonisms and new areas of common interest arise. In exploring the limits and possibilities of state action to change dependency relationships, and in exploring how such action eventuates in new forms of dependency, the historical-structural approach rejects both voluntarism and determinism, proceeding instead with an empirical examination of how "men make their own history," yet not "just as they please."

Within this framework, three conclusions of this study are particularly important:

(1) The interests of the transnational automobile corporations led them to pursue strategies that were injurious to Mexico, but the Mexican state was able to mitigate many of the negative consequences by exercising its own power.

(2) State policy tended to succeed when the structure of the auto industry, both domestically and globally, made the interests of the firms consistent with the goals of the state, but it tended

[1] Cardoso and Faletto, *Dependency and Development*, p. x.

252

to be ineffective or to yield perverse results when this was not the case. Thus, state action to set or to alter *industry structure* appears more likely to have the effects desired than state action to regulate the *behavior of firms.*

(3) The policies of the Mexican state were successful in changing certain aspects of the country's dependent relations with the world capitalist system so as to gain greater accumulation and growth, but such gains often created new forms of dependency and left untouched and may even have solidified some of the broader characteristics of Mexican dependency, particularly the highly unequal distribution of income and life chances.

Each of these conclusions demands some elaboration.

Conflicts between the State and the TNCs

In chapter 3, we presented a series of propositions, drawn principally from the dependency perspective, outlining the likely consequences of the actions of transnational corporations in developing countries. These propositions were concerned with the economic, social, and political distortions that TNCs may introduce into national development. The experience of Mexico shows that the interests of the auto TNCs often led them to pursue courses of action that were detrimental to Mexican welfare, but it also shows that the state was able to alter their behavior to make them contribute more to industrialization and economic growth. This latter is a point frequently overlooked by analysts of dependency. After a review of the consequences of TNC behavior and the ways in which it has been affected by state regulation, we will take up the question of why the state has been willing and able to rectify some injurious aspects of TNC behavior but not others.

Transnational corporations are frequently said to take more out of a country in profits and royalties than they put in as investments. This issue of intercountry income distribution is particularly important in extractive industries, such as copper and petroleum. While it may also be important in a manufacturing industry, the data are lacking for a judgment of whether the transnational auto firms have been net importers or exporters of capital from Mexico. But our concerns have been with larger and more qualitative questions. What have been the consequences of the auto TNCs for the character and extent of manufacturing activity in Mexico? Have they been willing to make investments in Mexico, and if so, in which activities? Have their products and manufacturing processes been appropriate to Mexican conditions? Have their investments augmented or displaced investments by domestic entrepreneurs? Does the industry that has taken shape with their investments have a structure that fits Mexico's needs? In what ways has their involvement altered political processes and political outcomes?

The Socioeconomic Arena

The socioeconomic consequences of the behavior of the auto TNCs and the effectiveness of Mexican industrial policy in altering it can be described under four headings: investments, technology and products, domestic market structure, and ownership.

Investments. The transnational auto makers were reluctant to make investments in Mexico of the sort that would have spurred industrialization and economic growth. Their reluctance stemmed from their global strategies in the international industry. In the early 1960s, they were unwilling to commence manufacturing vehicles in Mexico because it was more profitable for them to continue using installed capacity in their home-country plants to make kits of parts that could be assembled in Mexico. But what was rational for the firms was injurious to Mexico, particularly in view of its import-substitution industrialization strategy. It denied to Mexico the stimulation to industrial growth that automobile manufacture could provide through its linkages to other sectors, and it also denied to Mexico the technical learning that would come with auto manufacture.

In the late 1960s, the TNCs were unwilling to begin manufacturing for export because the Mexican industry had not yet achieved the cost efficiencies, product quality, or reliability of delivery that would make it rational for them to source parts from Mexico rather than from their other manufacturing sites. Again, what was rational for the firms was injurious to Mexico: Only through exports could the industry achieve efficiency given the small and fragmented domestic market; exports were needed to balance the flow of imports and reduce the loss of foreign exchange; and exports of manufactured goods were particularly wanted in order to end the previous reliance on exports of primary products.

In both of these cases, however, it was impossible for the Mexican state to alter the conduct of the TNCs. By threatening to deny them access to the Mexican market, a market they judged of considerable future importance, the state made it rational for them first to begin manufacturing vehicles in Mexico (as a result of the 1962 decree) and then to begin producing components for export (as a result of the 1969 *acuerdo*, reaffirmed in the 1972 and 1977 decrees).

Technology and products. The production technology employed by the TNCs was generally the same as that used in their home-country plants. The capital-intensive nature of this technology may have generated less employment than alternatives that would have taken greater advantage of Mexico's low-wage labor force, but it may nevertheless be judged appropriate by the standard that state officials used: the fact that it brought to Mexico the technology that would allow the new Mexican industry to reach international levels of efficiency.

The vehicles produced in Mexico were also the same as those the TNCs manufactured in developed countries; no effort was made to design or adapt a vehicle to Mexican conditions, particularly to the needs of the poorer part of the population for affordable basic transportation. Automobiles were thus produced only for buyers who resembled automobile buyers in the United States, Europe, and Japan. This is a general problem of import-substituting industrialization: it conforms to the existing, class-biased demand. What the upper and middle classes in Mexico wanted were the same models being offered for sale in the major producing countries. While advertising by the TNCs had a hand in shaping these tastes, the more important influences were tourism, television, foreign travel, and a long history of dependent development that had accustomed the privileged classes to imported manufactured goods.

The auto makers also used in Mexico the same product-differentiation strategies that characterized the competition among them elsewhere in the world. Again, what was rational for the firms was injurious to Mexico. Proliferation of models and annual model changes impeded the creation of an efficient industry by blocking standardization of parts and full utilization of available scale economies. The Mexican state tried to limit the number of models allowed each firm and to encourage standardization (e.g., of the power train among the four U.S.-based firms), but here it was only partially successful. The root of the problem lay in the structure of the market created when the Mexican state succumbed to the pressures of too many makers for access to the Mexican market.

Domestic market structure. The presence of ten firms in the Mexican market after the 1962 decree created a distorted structure that has hindered all subsequent regulatory efforts of the government. Mexican officials were well aware of the costs in inefficiency that would arise

255

from dividing a small domestic market among more than a few firms, but the transnational firms were so insistent upon access (and the Mexican state was irresolute enough) that the market was fragmented from the beginning. Besides reducing scale economies, this also hampered the state's ability to limit the number of makes and to achieve standardization of parts. Yet the oligopolistic character of the international industry deprived Mexico of any of the benefits that might arise from a domestic industry with such a large number of firms: price competition, innovation, or the elimination of weaker firms.

In 1962, the state attempted to shape a domestic market structure that would have made sense for Mexico, but again it had only limited success. In 1969, it considered but ultimately rejected a plan that would have rationalized the industry by merging a number of firms. Instead, it opted for an export-promotion strategy that has tried to circumnavigate these difficulties by escaping the limits of the small local market while leaving unchanged the structure of the domestic industry (table 11.1).

TABLE 11.1

Ownership Status in 1980 and Production of Firms in the Mexican Motor-Vehicle Industry, 1970, 1975, and 1980

Firm	Ownership Status, 1980	1970 185,031	1975 341,419	1980 456,372
Total production		*Percentage of Production*		
Chrysler de México	100% foreign	20.9	18.5	23.2
Diesel Nacional[a]	100% domestic (government)	9.7	9.4	4.3
Ford Motor Company	100% foreign	20.1	16.4	18.9
General Motors de México	100% foreign	14.2	11.0	8.4
Nissan Mexicana	100% foreign	8.4	9.1	10.4
Renault de México	40% foreign, 60% domestic (government)	[b]	[b]	4.7
Vehículos Automotores Mexicanos	6% foreign, 94% domestic (government)	7.1	6.8	6.0
Volkswagen de México	100% foreign	19.2	28.4	23.8
Others		0.4	0.4	0.4
Total		100.0	100.0	100.0

Source: amia, *Industria automotriz de México*, various years, and authors' interviews
Note: Data refer to cars and trucks weighing less than 13,500 kilograms and manufactured in Mexico.
[a] Manufactured only trucks after 1978.
[b] Company was formed in 1978.

256

Ownership. The re-establishment and maintenance of domestic control over resources and industry, and the creation of a strong Mexican private sector, were deeply embedded orientations of the Mexican state, which arose from a desire to prevent the recurrence of the pre-revolutionary distortions of the economy that came with foreign control of leading economic sectors. With these goals in mind, the Mexican government first explored the possibility of Mexicanizing the terminal industry, but it relented when faced with the firm opposition of Ford and GM, backed by the U.S. government. The state managers then sought to protect the domestically owned auto makers with a system of production quotas, in the hope of ensuring them a market share which they could retain against the superior market power of the TNCs. This effort failed because it did not address the inadequacies of the domestically owned firms in competition with the integrated subsidiaries of the TNCs (see table 11.2). The only domestically owned firms to survive, of the eight that had been in operation, were VAM and DINA, both of them state-owned and both of them among the weaker firms in the industry.

In the manufacture of auto parts, however, the state was able to structure the industry from the very beginning in such a way that there were no majority foreign-owned firms. However, while restrictions on vertical integration of the auto producers gave the auto-parts industry a degree of protection, it has faced steady pressure and encroachment from the terminal firms seeking to manufacture their own components.

TABLE 11.2

MARKET SHARES IN THE MEXICAN MOTOR-VEHICLE INDUSTRY,
BY OWNERSHIP TYPE OF FIRMS, 1962-1980

	PERCENTAGE OF VEHICLES SOLD IN:				
Ownership Type of Firms	*1962*	*1965*	*1970*	*1975*	*1980*
Majority foreign-owned[a]	51.2	57.0	62.2	83.7	85.0
Majority Mexican-owned, private[b]	31.0	30.0	20.9	0.0	0.0
Majority Mexican-owned, state[c]	17.7	13.0	16.8	16.3	15.0

SOURCE: AMIA, *Industria automotriz de México*, various years, and authors' interviews

[a] Ford, GM, International Harvester, Volkswagen (1965, 1970, 1975, and 1980), and Chrysler (1975 and 1980).

[b] Fabricas Auto-Mex (1962, 1965, and 1970), Planta Reo (1962), Representaciones Delta (1962), Promexa (1962), and FANASA (1965).

[c] DINA, VAM, and Renault (1980).

With export promotion, the threat of displacement has grown more acute.

Yet the consequences of Mexicanization for the regulation of TNCs, and for the national welfare do need to be questioned. Mexicanization has promoted the growth of a national bourgeoisie, but its effects on other goals, such as domestic capital accumulation and technology transfer, are unclear. It appears that Mexican-TNC partnership may have some advantages for these purposes.

The Political Arena

The actions that the transnational auto firms took to affect the political processes and outcomes were neither as distorting nor as deliberate as might have been predicted by the more deterministic of the dependency approaches. Two points can be made here concerning alliances with other actors and two concerning the industry structure.

Co-optation of local elites. The auto TNCs were not able to co-opt local elites or to form alliances with elements of the national bourgeoisie to block government efforts at regulation. In large part, this was because the Mexican state did not pursue courses of action that could be depicted as being against the interests of "capital in general"; indeed, it often acted to assist local elites vis-à-vis the TNCs. Once the terminal industry had been denationalized, the state acted frequently in ways that protected or promoted the interests of the parts makers (particularly the larger ones), because they were still Mexican-owned. This was done with little urging from the parts firms; only recently have they become a significant voice in policy making.

Alliances with home-country governments. The auto TNCs called on their home-country governments to assist them in bargaining with the Mexican state, and they responded, with some effectiveness in the early 1960s but less in the late 1970s. The U.S. government was able to prevent the exclusion of any U.S.-based firm in 1962, but it was unable to compel Mexico to modify its export-promotion program in 1977. The increased ability of the Mexican state to resist the pressures of foreign governments can be accounted for by its enhanced technical sophistication, greater internal cohesion, and new-found oil reserves, and by a gradual weakening of the hitherto unquestioned "natural" alliance between the auto TNCs and their home-country governments.

258

Local market structure. The structure of the automobile industry in Mexico limited the ability of the Mexican government to compel the firms to act as it wanted them to. This structure was created and has been maintained by the auto TNCs, but while the product differentiation that characterized it was deliberately brought into Mexico by these firms, the fragmentation of the market was not something desired by any of them, even though it may have resulted from their individual efforts to gain access. Each would have preferred to be one of fewer firms.

International structures. The auto TNCs did not structure the international industry to respond to their needs to the detriment of Mexico. There are international cartels, but the automobile industry is not one of them. Notwithstanding the lack of price competition among the firms (except, perhaps, very recently), the automobile TNCs did not collude with one another concerning the markets they would enter, the prices they would change, or other actions. Their behavior has been shaped by the structure of the international industry, but as individual actors they have done relatively little to transform that structure.

The Interests and Power of the Mexican State

The interests of the Mexican state vis-à-vis the transnational auto makers arose from the orientations that had developed since the revolution, and they were little influenced by pressure from domestic groups. These interests created conflicts with the TNCs over a number of issues, but just as significantly, there were important congruences of interests. In some instances the state fought dependency; in others, it was implicated in it.

Both the state and the TNCs favored an industrialization strategy that placed primary reliance on the private sector. The state encouraged private investment with loans, noninflationary fiscal and monetary policies, low taxes, and repressive labor policies. Although the Mexican state wanted to promote and protect domestic capital, it was never seriously opposed to the participation of TNCs in the auto industry. Finally, both the state and the TNCs favored the development of an auto industry, as opposed to, for example, an emphasis on public transportation.

On the other hand, the TNCs did not share the state's interest in furthering import substitution by replacing the assembly of imported parts with the domestic manufacture of these parts; nor did the TNCs have an interest in exporting from Mexico in the late 1960s and early

259

1970s (though this began to change in the mid-1970s). The state's efforts to Mexicanize the terminal firms were opposed by the TNCs, and they also resisted the efforts to limit the number of firms and to regulate firm conduct (product differentiation, prices, levels of domestic content, level and timing of export requirements, and global sourcing of patterns).

When the interests of the TNCs and the Mexican state conflicted, the state attempted to exercise power to control the behavior of the TNCs. Several observations can be made about the three major bargaining encounters between them that resulted, in 1962, 1969, and 1977.

(1) The greater the degree of competition for new markets among TNCs in an international industry, the greater the bargaining power of a state whose market they seek to enter. Throughout the period that we have studied here, the major basis of the power of the Mexican state was the rivalry among the auto TNCs, which made them eager for access to the domestic markets of the larger, faster-growing developing countries. They viewed these as the markets of future sales growth in the international industry and thus as a major key to surviving the intense competition in an industry that was growing ever more concentrated. A defensive investment dynamic has characterized the industry: When one firm makes a move, the others follow suit to avoid being excluded from a market. In 1962, this was the key to winning concessions from those firms that were allowed to begin manufacturing in Mexico. The Mexican state did not take full advantage of the eagerness of the firms or of the strength of its own position, however; it allowed in too many firms and exacted fewer concessions from them than it might have. Once the firms had begun manufacturing in Mexico, excluding any of them would have been difficult and costly, but the Mexican state has continued using the defensive investment dynamic, and with increased appreciation of its efficacy. Outright exclusion has been threatened at times, but more often the state used more subtle and flexible controls: until 1977, production quotas, and since then, foreign-exchange budgets.

(2) A major source of TNC power (and conversely, a weakness for the state) has been TNC control over prevailing technology in the automobile industry. This has been a source of power, however, only because of the state's need for the technology, and this need arose out of the strategy of import-substitution industrialization. Mexico's policy makers believed that a domestic auto industry was necessary to spur growth beyond the "easy stage" of industrialization, and they judged that TNC participation would be necessary to produce the kinds of vehicles that would sell in the Mexican market—a small market of

middle- and upper-class consumers long accustomed to U.S.- and European-style vehicles. Rivalry among the firms prevented them from bargaining in unison, however, and that more than compensated for the state's weakness. The state could and did play one firm off against another. In 1969 and in 1977, the TNCs' control over international trade in auto components and the state's need for exports—a need created by the problems connected with import substitution—gave the TNCs another source of power, but the defensive investment dynamic and the willingness of at least one firm to export (Ford in 1969, GM in 1977) allowed the state to prevail.

(3) The U.S. government regularly tried to influence the industrial policies of the Mexican government in the automobile sector on behalf of U.S.-based TNCs and U.S. trade. In the early 1960s, Mexico's ability to use the power provided by international competition was greatly weakened by fear that the U.S. government would act as an ally of the TNCs, and the U.S. government did make it clear that exclusion of U.S. firms would not be viewed kindly. Overt pressure was probably not as important, however, as the understanding among Mexican officials that the "business climate" and U.S.-Mexican economic relations might be seriously damaged if they succeeded in excluding U.S. firms. The Japanese government was similarly instrumental in preventing the exclusion of Nissan.

By 1977, however, the power of the Mexican state to resist pressure from foreign governments had increased. The Mexican economy and Mexico's position in the international system were much stronger, particularly because of the newly discovered oil reserves. When the U.S. government threatened trade sanctions, Mexican government officials confidently turned a deaf ear. The power of the Mexican state was further strengthened by the TNCs' new interest in global sourcing, which made them tacit allies rather than opponents of the Mexican government.

(4) While some dependency theorists focus almost exclusively on external factors—such as the powers of TNCs and of foreign governments—in explaining the limited power of dependent states, internal factors are important as well. Two warrant emphasis: the unity of the state, and its "learning."

Disunity within the state apparatus—interministerial conflicts compounded by personal rivalries—hindered the state's efforts at structuring the auto industry in 1962 and restructuring it in 1968-1969. In 1977, the state apparatus was far more unified, and so the government was much more successful in achieving its aims. This unity was facil-

261

itated by an administrative reorganization and strengthened further by the leadership exercised by President López Portillo.

In any case, the state's technical capability did increase steadily between 1960 and 1980: the state "learned." The sources of this learning were various. For one thing, the basic competence of state officials in the economic ministries and their understanding of the automobile industry grew with experience. Despite the considerable turnover of personnel with each sexennial change, many officials were continuously involved with auto policy over the entire period, even if not in the same posts. Second, the Mexican state learned from the experience of other countries. In 1960, officials studied the Brazilian and Argentine industries, and they continued to study their ups and downs over the ensuing two decades. The Canadian industry was examined carefully in the early exploration of export promotion. Finally, the Mexican state learned (for well or ill) from academic disciplines concerned with development. The 1969 *acuerdo* was influenced by the shift in development thinking from import substitution to export promotion. The 1977 decree showed the influence of increasing technical sophistication (such as the use of linear programming).

(5) The potential power of the Mexican state to control the auto TNCs was greatest at the point of the firms' initial entry, because of their eagerness to gain access to the market and because of the inchoate structure of the Mexican industry. After 1962, however, as the structure of the industry took shape and solidified, the potential power of the state tended to decrease in some respects. The situation in a manufacturing industry is very different from that in extractive industries—for example, copper mining.[2] In the latter industries, the power of the state is lowest at the point of initial investment. There is often little interfirm rivalry for making the investments needed to exploit ore deposits. However, the power of the state to capture additional revenue from the firms in taxes begins to increase once investments have been made, for it is then costly for firms to pick up and leave, and the state has the credible option of operating the facilities itself. Renegotiation of contracts in favor of the state is common.

In the auto industry, sunken investments have quite a different corollary. They link the firms much more tightly to the domestic economy. If a firm were to leave or be evicted, it would not be the only one to pay the cost: workers would lose their jobs, suppliers their purchase orders, dealers their products. Moreover, the state cannot credibly threaten to operate an auto plant on its own, since a continuing source

[2] Moran, *Multinational Corporations.*

of technical assistance is needed. Furthermore, in the automobile industry, sunken investments also mean a solidified industry structure,
which shapes the firms' interests in ways that make impossible some
actions the state may prefer. When seven firms had come to constitute
the Mexican auto industry, for example, domestic-content levels could
not be increased without significantly reducing efficiency and raising
costs.

Thus, after 1962 the new structure of the auto industry in Mexico
made it irrational or impossible for the state to compel the firms to act
in some ways. This raises the question of the strategies which the state
could use in regulating the TNCs.

STRATEGIES OF REGULATION

A second major substantive conclusion emerging from this work is that
state policy tended to succeed when the structure of the auto industry,
both domestically and globally, made the interests of the firms consistent with the goals of the state, and it tended to be ineffective or to
yield perverse results when this was not the case. The two aspects of
the structure that were of particular concern to the Mexican government were the structure of ownership and the structure of the market.
The effects that these structures had on the ability of the state to
regulate the behavior of the firms are clearest in two arenas: import
substitution versus export promotion, and denationalization.

Import Substitution versus Export Promotion

The automobile industry first became a subject of state policy within
the context of import-substitution industrialization. Import substitution had been the state's strategy for industrial growth; when it stalled
at the end of the easy phase, the auto industry was selected as the
mechanism for spurring further growth. As early as the 1960 NAFIN
report, concern was expressed that unless the Mexican market were
properly structured—with a limited number of firms and a limited
degree of product differentiation—an inefficient, high-cost industry
would result. In the bargaining over the 1962 decree, the state did
succeed in requiring that the vehicles produced by each firm incorporate 60 percent of domestically manufactured content, but it did not
succeed in limiting the number of firms nor did it succeed appreciably
in limiting the extent of product differentiation.

A high-cost, inefficient industry did emerge. Economists have argued
that inefficiency is a predictable consequence of import-substituting

263

policies, but in the Mexican automobile industry, inefficiency resulted at least as much from the fragmentation of the market among too many makers and models—a problem of industry structure rather than an inherent characteristic of import substitution.

The initial failure to properly structure the domestic industry had enduring consequences. Competition could not be expected to winnow out the weaker firms. Three Mexican-owned firms did collapse, but the remaining seven were able to rely on their transnational parents (or the state) to sustain them. In this situation, higher levels of local content were not rational for the firms, for it would have them substituting higher-cost locally made parts for cheaper imported ones, as well as displacing production in their home-country facilities. Nor was it rational for the government to require higher levels of local content; that would only make the industry more inefficient by leading to local production of components like body stampings that had higher scale economies than components already being manufactured in Mexico. A less fragmented market structure would have made further import substitution much easier to pursue.

In 1969, the Mexican state considered a merger proposal that would have restructured the domestic auto industry and made further import substitution possible, but it rejected the proposal and opted instead for a strategy of industrialization via export promotion. While import substitution had aroused little interest among the TNCs in increasing domestic content, because of the small and overcrowded domestic market, export promotion was expected to remove this structural limitation: the size of the international market would make scale economies possible and investment in export production rational. The very fact of the foreign ownership of most of the auto makers would give them access to the channels of international (mostly intrafirm) trade.

The structure of the international industry at that time, however, was not conducive to the attainment of these ends. Few TNCs then were interested in a strategy of worldwide sourcing that would have an important place in it for Mexico. Consequently, the increased volume of auto-related exports generated by the 1969 export requirements lasted only until the 1974-1975 global recession, when it became apparent that Mexican production had been accorded only a peripheral place in the TNCs' strategies. But when changes shook the international industry in the 1970s—the Japanese challenge and the move to energy-efficient cars—the TNCs became more interested in worldwide sourcing, and Mexico thus looked more attractive. The reaffirmation of the export policy in 1977 accorded Mexican production a much more secure place in the firms' reorganized sourcing patterns.

Two other points warrant emphasis. First, the unfavorable structure of the Mexican auto industry became, over time, a given in further policy deliberations—what a Mexican official called one of the *vicios de origen*, the "vices of the origination." Structures may be created by actors, but they can take on a solidity that makes them resistant to change. Second, while the structure of the market that emerged from the 1962 decree was far more accommodating to export promotion than to import substitution, the import-substitution policy nevertheless laid the foundation for export promotion. Much of the academic disputation over import substitution and export promotion poses these simply as alternative industrialization strategies. In the automobile industry in Mexico, however, export promotion would not have been possible without the dramatic alteration in structure that occurred because of import substitution.

Denationalization

In 1962, the state managers not only wanted domestic manufacture of motor vehicles to begin in Mexico; they also wanted the new industry to be predominantly Mexican-owned. The latter goal was much better served in the auto-parts sector of the industry than in the terminal sector. When the terminal firms were first approved for manufacture, eight of the ten were majority Mexican-owned. The two foreign-owned firms that were also approved, however, had distinct advantages in competition with the Mexican-owned firms: lower markups on imported parts and lower costs for technical assistance, for example. The result was rapid denationalization. By 1972, only two of the seven remaining firms were majority Mexican-owned, and these were both state firms. The competitive advantages of the TNC subsidiaries overwhelmed the production quotas which the state established to protect the domestically owned firms. A guaranteed share of the market could not bring the profits that were denied by the new structure of ownership in the industry.

The shift from import substitution to export promotion was also the death knell for private Mexican auto makers. Because of the structure of the international industry, domestically owned firms lacked export opportunities. Within this structure of ownership, it would have made no sense for the Mexican state to prohibit the acquisition of locally owned firms by TNCs. The state's basic interest in Mexican ownership was the fostering of a strong national bourgeoisie. But Mexican entrepreneurs were being driven bankrupt, and to forbid them to sell

265

out to TNCs would have prevented them from recouping anything on their investments.

In the auto-parts sector of the industry, however, the state was successful in requiring from the very beginning that all the firms be majority Mexican-owned. Transnational parts makers were put in the position of having to locate and encourage Mexican partners, and they were limited in the degree to which they could exercise the market power drawn from their global position to squeeze out independent firms.

By barring the auto producers from manufacturing most components, the state also attempted, with some success, to structure the relationship between the two sectors of the industry. This rule made it rational for the auto producers to standardize certain parts and to give technical assistance to fledgling parts firms, even without any specific requirement from the state that they do so. When the state began to mandate exports, it attempted to give further assistance to the parts companies by requiring that 40 percent (later 50 percent) of the exports be obtained from them. This requirement ran against rather than with the logic of interests engendered by the structure of the industry and thus introduced an element of tension into the relationship between auto producers and parts suppliers. The auto producers began to assault the barriers against vertical integration by insisting that they could export the required volumes only if they exported components of their own manufacture, for that was the only way to insure the quality, price, and timely delivery needed for international sourcing. Stated somewhat differently, the structure of ownership in the two sectors of the industry, and the structure of the relationship between them, made it increasingly difficult for the state to insist upon exports and to protect the position of the Mexican-owned parts firms.

Structural Alternatives

If the state failed in some respects to establish the industry's market and ownership structures in ways that were conducive to the attainment of its goals, were there alternative possibilities? There were three that might have made a substantial difference. One would have been aimed at the market structure, the other two at ownership.

Controlled oligopoly. What the authors of the NAFIN report intended was an industry that would have allowed the participation of TNCs, but of only a few of them, creating a less fragmented market and thus a more efficient industry. If the only firms approved had been ones that agreed to produce small cars and to extend model runs for several years, the industry could have achieved levels of efficiency that rivaled those of the major producing countries. This policy would have made exports more difficult, because the vehicles produced in Mexico (and the components for them) would not have been up to date, but the domestic market would have been larger, because of lower prices. Furthermore, as the domestic market grew, more frequent model changes would have become possible, opening the door to exports. In this strategy, strict state regulation would have been essential to control the firms, and it would have been important to have at least two firms that were international rivals, to allow the state to play one off against the other.

State ownership. Virtually from the beginning, the Mexican state owned two of the auto producers, VAM and DINA. Both had been acquired in the course of bailing out private Mexican entrepreneurs. Several parts firms had also been acquired in the same way. The Mexican state never made use of these publicly owned firms as instruments of industrial policy, however. Yet if the presence of one or two foreign-owned subsidiaries of TNCs could determine the structure of ownership in the industry, so too could the presence of one or two state-owned firms. They could have helped control prices by underselling the other firms; other firms would have to lower their own prices or risk ceding a larger share of the market to the state-owned firms. A state-owned firm could have been given a monopoly on the production of a particular kind of vehicle (small cars or light trucks, for example). By its purchases of components, a state-owned firm could have ensured a minimum level of sales for parts firms and could have taken the lead in standardizing parts. In short, a state-owned firm as an instrument of industrial policy could have taken the lead in establishing the terms of competition to be met by others, rather than struggling to react to the terms set by others.

National champions. The boldest option, essentially the one followed by the Japanese and the Koreans in building their automobile industries, would have excluded foreign ownership altogether. National firms, public or private, would have licensed technology from transnational automobile firms, at least at first, but the goal would have been the gradual development of local technology to the point where the national firms could go it alone. The industry would have developed more slowly, and exports would have been more difficult—indeed, they might have been impossible until the industry was ready to export whole vehicles at internationally competitive prices. On the other hand, an industry so structured would not have been under the same pressure to export, since the imported content of vehicles would have been very small. Keeping the number of firms down to just a few would also have been essential under this strategy, but restructuring of the market (through mergers, for example) would have been easier, since none of the firms would have been tied through equity to a transnational company.

The possibilities of carrying through any of these alternatives are difficult to determine in any definitive way. Creation of alternative structures for the auto industry was limited by structural elements in the national and international political economy that went far beyond the auto industry. In chapter 5, we analyzed the failed attempt to create a controlled oligopoly, a failure explained in part by threats from the U.S. and Japanese governments. State ownership was popular only among a handful of officials already involved with the state-owned firms; among the rest, the orientation toward private-sector investment was so deeply embedded that the state-ownership alternative was never seriously considered. The closest the Mexican government came to considering this option was the effort to merge domestically owned firms that was mounted in the late 1960s, and here conflicts within the state as well as opposition from some TNCs rendered the effort futile. The national champion alternative, by far the most radical, was not considered at all and would have faced even stronger opposition from the U.S. and other foreign governments, demanding that their corporations not be excluded. Such structural alternatives within the auto industry, were not impossible, but they would have been difficult to bring about.

DEPENDENCY AND STATE ACTION

The Mexican state had considerable success in establishing an auto industry in Mexico, one that generated exports within a decade of its establishment, and in making the auto TNCs do some things they would rather not have done. Mexico's dependent position in the world economy, however, could not be ended by actions in a single industry. While some structures of dependency in and around the auto industry were broken or weakened, others were tightened; and what was accomplished in the auto industry did little to transform the wider situation

268

of Mexican dependency, which itself alters the meaning of what had been accomplished in this one sector.

Dependency in One Industry

In 1960, dependency in the automobile industry in Mexico manifested itself in (a) limited industrialization (the reluctance of the TNCs to do more than assemble vehicles from imported kits), (b) exclusive reliance on foreign designs and foreign technology, and (c) the class-based constriction on the size of the domestic market. In the 1962 decree, the state set out to attack the first of these and to lay the foundation for a future effort against the second by creating a Mexican-owned domestic manufacturing industry. It did not seek to alter the third.

The implementation of the 1962 decree succeeded in creating a domestic automobile-manufacturing industry, but it was accompanied by rapid and substantial denationalization of the manufacturing firms. However, a separate parts industry was also born, and it remained, as intended, majority Mexican-owned throughout. The denationalization of most of the auto producers made it unlikely that Mexico would develop its own vehicle designs or production technology in the foreseeable future. The market structure of the new industry—an excessive number of firms and a high degree of product differentiation—was shaped less by domestic conditions than by the dynamics of competition in the world industry. Thus, there was substantial reduction of dependency, in the form of the beginning of domestic manufacture, but there were also denationalization, a distorted local market, and new restraints on industrial growth. While the gains and losses were not intrinsically linked, only stronger state action could have prevented the denationalization and market distortion that accompanied the move to domestic manufacture.

Similarly, there were gains and losses in the struggle against dependency during the next stage of the industry's development, the move from manufacture for the domestic market to manufacture for export as well. The implementation of the 1969 *acuerdo* succeeded in prodding the transnational automobile firms to make exports they would not otherwise have made, but it also furthered the denationalization of the manufacturers. The beginning of exports allowed the industry to escape the limitation of the small domestic market and to achieve greater efficiency, but the increased reliance on export markets brought its own particular form of dependency. Whereas the Mexican

269

market had been growing steadily, the world market was prone to cyclical ups and downs. When a world recession came in 1974-1975, automotive exports from Mexico dropped substantially. In the early 1970s, Mexican production was quite marginal in the transnational firms' sourcing plans, but a restructuring of the world industry in the middle of the decade, coupled with Mexico's reaffirmation of the export policy, began to accord Mexico a more secure place in these sourcing networks. On the other hand, because world automotive trade consisted so largely of intrafirm transfers within the TNCs, the door was closed even more firmly on the development of Mexican-designed vehicles or technology. Moreover, a source of friction was introduced into the relationship between the foreign-owned auto producers and the Mexican-owned parts firms. Again, the gains and losses were not indissolubly linked, but they were connected.

The Wider Fabric of Mexican Dependency

One enduring feature of Mexican dependency has been the poverty of the majority of its people. Dependency does not inherently mean that the United States is rich and Mexico is poor. Rather, it means that the structures and processes of growth in the world economy are centered more in the United States than in Mexico and that the way Mexico is tied into them serves to benefit only a minority. Without vigorous action to change this situation, the majority of the population will be excluded from the fruits of economic growth. The choice of the automobile industry as a target for industrialization was predicated on this pattern of inequality, and the development of manufacturing in the industry did nothing to alter it, if indeed it did not add a further obstacle to its amelioration.

In the strategy of industrialization via import substitution, the automobile industry was a sensible choice for a leading sector. This strategy, however, encouraged the development of manufacturing industries that tended to serve the needs of the wealthier segment of the population more than those of the poorer segment, and this tendency intensified as import substitution moved from consumer nondurables to consumer durables, from processed foods and toilet paper to television sets and automobiles. A basic premise of the strategy was that consumer demand for previously imported goods would be the driving force of economic growth: this demand would thenceforth be met by locally manufactured goods. The class structure in Mexico meant that

270

the small number of consumers from the middle and upper classes would have a disproportionate share of the income with which to express that demand, however. There was little effective demand for health services for the poor, for cheap housing, for public transportation, or even for inexpensive, nonstylish standardized cars. Effective demand, rather, was for stereo systems, microwave ovens, electric typewriters, and the current models of automobiles made in Detroit.

A major proposition of the dependency perspective on the consequences of TNC behavior is that they worsen the distribution of income within a developing country. If industrialization in the auto sector proceeded *because of* income inequality, what effect did the coming of TNC-dominated auto manufacturing have *on* this pattern of income equality? While state action did induce rapid growth in the auto sector, growth that helped the Mexican economy as a whole grow quickly in the 1960s and most of the 1970s, the fruits of that growth did not improve the distribution of income. Overall, the relative position of the poorest 60 percent did not improve, and may have worsened, between 1960 and 1980. Responsibility for this persisting inequality cannot be laid at the feet of the transnational automobile firms, but they did benefit from it. Inequality has been perpetuated in Mexico by the country's position in the world economy and by the capitalist growth strategy which the state has supported since the mid-1920s. Low corporate taxes, low income taxes, subsidies, limited social-welfare and land-reform programs, and wages that rose more slowly than inflation created a business climate that nurtured profits and reinvestments but that also reinforced the pattern of inequality. Not only did the auto TNCs—among other corporations—benefit from the tax subsidies and the low-wage work force; the pattern of inequality provided them with a growing minority of consumers affluent enough to afford new automobiles.

It is also important to see, however, that once automobile manufacturing began in Mexico, an additional obstacle to income redistribution was erected. No Mexican politician would ever allow himself to be quoted saying anything so blunt, but the basic point has been well expressed by a Brazilian minister of finance, Mario Henrique Simonsen:

A transfer of income from the richest 20% to the poorest 80% would probably increase the demand for food, but diminish the demand for automobiles. The result of a sudden redistribution

271

would be merely to generate inflation in the food producing sector and excess capacity in the car industry.[3]

Industrialization in the auto sector was shaped around a class-skewed pattern of inequality; it now serves to reinforce that inequality.

To blame the transnational auto corporations for this persistent inequality would be a historically shortsighted and unduly narrow allocation of responsibility, even if they did benefit from it and help to perpetuate it. But equally, it would be naive to conclude that the use of state power in this sector indicates that the Mexican state is willing and able to transform fully the pattern of inequality resulting from dependent development. A complete end to dependency would require both a social upheaval reorienting state interests and a use of state power far beyond that involved in the successful implementation of industrial policy.

[3] Quoted in Norman Gall, "The Rise of Brazil," *Commentary*, Jan. 1977, pp. 49-50.

POSTSCRIPT

Like his predecessor, Miguel de la Madrid Hurtado assumed the presidency of Mexico in the midst of an economic crisis. Unlike López Portillo, however, de la Madrid had no prospect of an early return to economic expansion.

When the oil boom came to an abrupt halt in 1982, it left Mexico with inflation running close to 100 percent and with $80 billion of foreign debt. The debt was not only a public-sector debt; many private firms had borrowed abroad to finance expansion during the boom. With the devaluation of the peso, many firms found themselves with debts that exceeded the value of their total assets. Stock prices on the Mexican exchange fell to a fraction of what they had been in 1980 and 1981.

In part compelled by the conditions of international loans for refinancing the debt, de la Madrid imposed a strict regimen but one familiar to developing countries in the midst of economic crisis: a sharp reduction in public-sector expenditures (especially social-service expenditures and subsidies for basic goods), restrictions on imports, and wage and price controls.

The crisis affected the automobile industry as much as any other sector. Sales of motor vehicles, which had jumped from 286,725 in 1977 (the last year of the previous crisis) to 561,249 in 1981, fell to 461,622 in 1982, and in 1983 they tumbled to 272,089. Firms that had borrowed to make major investments since the 1977 decree (particularly GM) found themselves not only with heavy debts but with excess capacity.[1]

In September 1983, less than ten months after it had come into office, the de la Madrid administration promulgated a new auto decree, the fourth major policy initiative since the beginning of manufacturing in the industry.[2] This decree seeks once again to reduce the industry's trade deficit, but what is particularly noteworthy is that it also seeks to address some of the problems of industry structure that emerged in the implementation of the 1962 decree and that had been treated as givens for many years.

Despite the success of the 1977 decree in compelling the auto TNCs

---

[1] Lydia Chavez, "Mexico Turns Sour for Detroit," *New York Times*, Oct. 7, 1982, p. D1.

[2] "Decreto para la racionalización de la industria automotriz," *Diario oficial*, Sept. 15, 1983.

273

to make investments in export facilities, the oil-boom years from 1977 to 1981 saw a growing trade deficit in the industry. Surging domestic demand meant increased parts imports; the same demand reduced the volume of parts available for export; and the United States and other industrialized countries were suffering from a recession that depressed auto sales. In 1981, the auto industry accounted for 58 percent of Mexico's commercial trade deficit. In an effort to reduce the deficit, the 1983 decree mandated higher local content. For automobiles, local content is to rise from the present 50 percent to 55 percent by the 1986 model year and to 60 percent by the 1987 model year. Similar increases are mandated for trucks and buses. The decree does not abandon export promotion—the firms are still required to compensate their imports with exports—but, like the never-promulgated draft decree of 1976, it relies less on exports and more on local content to deal with the trade deficit.

As has been stressed repeatedly in this study, the auto industry in Mexico has been bedeviled since 1962 by too many manufacturers (seven in 1981), too many makes (nineteen), and too many models (forty-seven). "Whereas Japan, the United States and the principal European countries produce an average of between 100,000 and 150,000 units per line," Héctor Hernández Cervantes, Mexico's minister of commerce and industrial development observed the day the 1983 decree appeared, "Mexico produced in 1981 an average of 13,000 units per line and this year will produce less than 7000."[3] The effect is both to reduce exports and to increase imports. Firms import parts for small-volume models because they cannot be manufactured domestically at competitive costs. Thus, reducing the number of makes and models makes possible higher levels of domestic content.

The new decree does not seek to reduce the number of manufacturers. (With Renault's acquisition of American Motors in the United States, however, VAM has disappeared as a separate firm, reducing the number of firms to six.) Instead, it sharply limits the number of makes and models allowed. For 1984, no firm can produce more than three makes or seven models; for 1985 and 1986, the limit is lowered to two makes and five models; and for 1987 and beyond, the firms are limited to a single make and five models. Firms can produce an additional model only if they can show that half the production would be exported and that the model would be self-sufficient in foreign exchange. Eight-

---

[3] Richard J. Meislin, "Mexico Set to Revamp Troubled Auto Industry," *New York Times*, Sept. 15, 1983, p. D1.

cylinder engines are barred altogether, and a quarter of each firm's production must be "austere" cars, equipped with no extras.

The severity of Mexico's current economic crisis makes it difficult to predict the consequences of these measures. The broader predicament of Mexico's dependency continues to condition the achievement of the government's goals in any single industry.

APPENDIX A

DIPLOMATIC NOTE FROM THE UNITED STATES TO MEXICO, FEBRUARY 1, 1978

The Embassy of the United States of America presents its compliments to the Secretariat of Foreign Relations and has the honor 'to refer to the decree regarding automotive production proclaimed by the Mexican Government in June 1977 and implementing regulations published in October 1977. The United States Government appreciates the opportunity afforded by the Ad Hoc Meeting of the Economic Subgroup of U.S.-Mexico Consultative Mechanism in November 1977 to discuss the potential effects of the decree and the implementing regulations on the U.S. economy and on U.S. firms. As noted by U.S. Government representatives on that occasion, the United States understands Mexico's desire to make its domestic motor vehicle industry more efficient. However, the United States Government believes that the decree and regulations could have a severe, adverse impact on U.S.-Mexican trade.

The Mexican decree essentially requires motor vehicle assemblers to cover all foreign-exchange costs through exports. A foreign-exchange allocation, based on a complex set of interlocking formulas, is assigned to each company of the terminal industry. Fifty percent of this allocation must be met by the export of finished vehicles and parts manufactured in the companies' own plants and the remaining fifty percent through the export of parts or components manufactured by the Mexican automotive parts industry.

The United States Government believes that the regulations are prejudicial to U.S.-owned firms in Mexico since the amount of the foreign-exchange allocations varies directly with the degree of Mexican capital participation. Such inequitable treatment is counter to longstanding U.S. policy opposing discriminatory treatment of foreign investors on the basis of nationality.

Linking foreign-exchange allocations with the export requirement, particularly the obligations to export parts or components manufactured by Mexican-owned firms, could result in a rapid increase of relatively high-cost Mexican exports to the U.S. market. U.S. manufacturers of parts (and the workers involved), losing orders as a result of the U.S. automotive industry's sourcing in Mexico to meet their export requirements under the decree, would likely seek remedial U.S. Government action. Inasmuch as Mexican parts are generally understood to be higher cost than U.S. parts, U.S. industry and labor could easily presume that any significant increase in parts from Mexico in the magnitude contemplated by the decree results from subsidies or dumping with consequent requests for countervailing or antidumping duties. If the disruption is great enough and/or existing U.S. legal remedies prove inadequate, there may be efforts by the affected U.S. firms and workers to seek remedies through new legislation restricting imports to Mexico.

The U.S. Government is also concerned that the Government of Mexico has the intention to institute similar programs in textiles, pharmaceuticals, and other industries. To the extent that these programs are implemented and affect Mexican exports to the United States, U.S. industry and labor in these sectors will react in the same manner.

These potentially disruptive effects on our trade relationship are of special concern since they stem from the policy of sectoral trade balancing embodied in the decree. Such a policy requires U.S. firms operating in Mexico to export Mexican products without regard to efficiency or cost advantages. Moreover, the implementing regulations compound these problems through the use of devices which artificially inflate the value of automobile component imports. Specifically, the foreign-exchange allocation is inflated by:

A) Including in the formulae the import content of locally procured parts and components;

B) Multiplying the value of imports by the difference between the required degree of local content and the actual degree of local content;

C) Including in the formulae multiplicative factors based on the degree of Mexican capital participation.

The United States understands Mexico's efforts to increase its exports of manufactured goods. If this is accomplished by more efficient production in Mexico, combined with efforts to remove barriers to trade on a mutual basis in the multinational trade negotiations, such a development would be perceived in a positive manner as being in our mutual interest. However, use of artificial and discriminatory devices requiring foreign-exchange balancing by sector can, in the view of the U.S. Government, lead to adverse effects on trade and investment flows between our two countries. The United States Government therefore respectfully requests that the Government of Mexico review the decree and implementing regulations to eliminate the discrimination against U.S. investors and the potentially disruptive effect on U.S.-Mexican trade. In connection with such a review we believe that it would be useful to have further consultations within the framework of the Subgroup on Energy, Minerals, Industry, and Investment, or the Subgroup on Trade.

The Embassy of the United States of America avails itself of this opportunity to renew to the Secretariat of Foreign Relations the assurances of its highest consideration.

APPENDIX B

INTERVIEWEES

As part of the research for this book, we conducted approximately 170 interview sessions with more than ninety people between 1975 and 1981. Our aim was to talk to every government official who had had any direct role in making or implementing policy toward the automobile industry between 1960 and 1980; to officials of each of the auto producers, particularly those whose experience went back to the early 1960s; and to officials of a broad spectrum of the parts manufacturers. Nearly everyone we wanted to see was available, and nearly everyone we approached agreed to be interviewed. Many of the interviews lasted two hours or more, and we reinterviewed a number of people a second, third, or fourth time—in some cases, even a fifth or sixth time. Particularly at the beginning and at the end of the research, we also conducted interviews with people in both the public and the private sectors on the general economic policies of the Mexican government and on the regulation of foreign investment. The interviews were not taped, but because we conducted them together we were able to write up detailed transcripts.

Following is a list of those interviewees who were directly concerned with the automobile industry. Industry officials are identified with the name of their firm or organization, but Mexican government officials are not identified with the name of a ministry or agency because most of them held different positions in different administrations.

MEXICAN GOVERNMENT OFFICIALS

Guillermo Becker	Carlos Quintana
Luis Bravo Aguilera	Gonzalo Robles
Gerardo Bueno	Juan de Dios Román
Jorge Espinosa de los Reyes	Emilio Sacristán Roy
Ernesto Fernández Hurtado	Raúl Salinas Lozano
Roberto Flores	Guillermo Salorio
Antonio Gallart	Rogelio Sánchez y García
Plácido García Reynoso	Rafael Urrutía
Adrian Lajous	Amado Vega
Augustín López Mungía	Natan Warman
Ernesto Marcos	Jaime Mario Willars
Hugo Margain	Juan Wolffer P.
Vicente Pedrero	

INDUSTRY OFFICIALS

Sebastián Aguinaga (Spicer)
Shoichi Amemiya (Nissan)

279

Guillermo Arroyo B. (ANFPA)
Gaston Azcárraga (Fábricas Auto-Mex)
Carlos Bandala (AMIA)
Randall Beatty (DINA-Rockwell)
Armando Carrillo (Volkswagen)
Francisco Casasus (Renault)
John Christman (American Chamber of Commerce of Mexico)
Ricardo Elizondo (Trailers de Monterrey)
Gabriel Fernández Sayago (VAM)
César Flores (AMIA)
Archie Frame (Eaton)
Roberto Rúiz García (DINA-Rockwell)
George Grobien (Troqueles y Matrices)
Francisco Gutiérrez (Mex-Par)
Pedro Haas García (DINA)
Mauricio Licona Enciso (Maquiladora Automotriz Nacional)
Claudio Mayoral (Chrysler)
Peter Meinig (Rassini Rheem)
Edgar Molina (Ford)
Abelardo Padín (Ford)
Bartolomeo Póvero Bordiga (DINA)
Gregorio Ramírez (FANASA, Trailers de Monterrey)
Ponce Robles (AMIA)
Pedro Rúiz (Borg y Beck)
Eduardo Sanudo Soules (Artículos Troquelados de Monterrey)
Ian Shaw (MORESA)
William Slocum (General Motors)
Saturnino Suárez (TREMEC)
Luis Javier Valdes (VAM)
Héctor Vázquez Tercero (consultant to the parts industry)
Victor Manuel Villaseñor (DINA)
Stanley D. Young (Manufacturas Metálicas de Monterrey)
Carlos Zambrano (Industria Automotriz, AMPPA)
Hans Zoebisch (General Motors)

U.S. GOVERNMENT OFFICIALS

Richard Ades (Commerce)
Edward Bittner (State)
Laurel Cooper (U.S. Embassy, Mexico)
Richard Feinberg (State)
Dennis Finnerty (State)

BIBLIOGRAPHY

A. BOOKS AND ARTICLES

Adams, Walter, ed. *The Structure of American Industry.* New York: Macmillan, 1971.

Aguinaga, Sebastián J. "Compromisos de la industria de autopartes." In Cámara Nacional de Industrias de Transformación, *Memoria II: Segundo simposium de la industria automotriz mexicana.* Mexico City: CANACINTRA, 1980.

Almond, Gabriel A., and James S. Coleman, eds. *The Politics of Developing Areas.* Princeton: Princeton University Press, 1960.

Althusser, Louis. "Ideology and Ideological State Apparatuses." In Louis Althusser, *Lenin and Philosophy and Other Essays,* pp. 127-186. New York: Monthly Review Press, 1971.

Arthur Andersen and Co., University of Michigan, and Michigan Manufacturers Association. *The U.S. Automotive Industry in the 1980s: A Domestic and Worldwide Perspective.* 1981. Photocopy.

Asociación Mexicana de la Industria Automotriz. *La industria automotriz de México en cifras.* Mexico City: AMIA, 1972.

————. *La industria automotriz de México en cifras, 1976.* Mexico City: AMIA, 1977.

Bachrach, Peter, and Morton Baratz. "Two Faces of Power." *American Political Science Review* 56 (1962):947-952.

Bailey, John J., and Donna H. Roberts. "Mexican Agricultural Policy." *Current History,* Dec. 1983, pp. 420-424.

Bain, Joseph. *Industrial Organization.* New York: John Wiley, 1968.

Balassa, Bela. "Growth Strategies in Semi-Industrial Countries." *Quarterly Journal of Economics* 84 (1970):24-42.

Baldwin, David. "Money and Power." *Journal of Politics* 33 (1971):578-614.

————. "Power Analysis and World Politics: New Trends versus Old Tendencies." *World Politics* 31 (1979):161-194.

Baranson, Jack. *Automotive Industries in Developing Countries.* Washington: World Bank Occasional Staff Papers, no. 8, 1969.

Barkin, David. "Mexico's Albatross: The U.S. Economy." *Latin American Perspectives* 2 (1975):64-80.

Barnet, R. S., and R. E. Muller. *Global Reach: The Power of Multinational Corporations.* New York: Simon and Schuster, 1974.

Bendix, Reinhard. "Tradition and Modernity Reconsidered." *Comparative Studies in Society and History* 9 (1967):292-346.

Behrman, Jack. *The Role of International Companies in Latin American Integration: Autos and Petrochemicals.* Lexington: D. C. Heath, 1972.

Bennett, Douglas, Morris Blachman, and Kenneth Sharpe. "Mexico and Multinational Corporations: An Explanation of State Action." In Joseph Grunwald, ed., *Latin America and World Economy: A Changing International Order,* pp. 257-282. Beverly Hills, Calif.: Sage, 1978.

281

Bennett, Douglas, and Kenneth Sharpe. "Agenda Setting and Bargaining Power: The Mexican State vs. the Transnational Automobile Corporations." *World Politics* 32 (1979):57-89.

———. "El control sobre las multinacionales: Las contradicciones de la mexicanización." *Foro Internacional* 21 (1981):388-427.

———. "The State As Banker and As Entrepreneur: The Last Resort Character of the Mexican State's Economic Interventions, 1917-1976." *Comparative Politics* 12 (1980):165-189.

———. "Transnational Corporations and the Political Economy of Export Promotion: The Case of the Mexican Automobile Industry." *International Organization* 33 (1979):177-201.

———. "The World Automobile Industry and Its Implications for Developing Countries." In Richard Newfarmer, ed., *Profits, Progress and Poverty: Case Studies of International Industries in Latin America*. Notre Dame: Univ. of Notre Dame Press, 1984, pp. 193-226.

Bergsten, D. Fred. "Coming Investment Wars?" *Foreign Affairs* 52 (1974):135-152.

Bernstein, Marvin. *The Mexican Mining Industry, 1890-1950*. Albany, N.Y.: State University of New York Press, 1964.

Biersteker, Thomas. *Distortion or Development? Contending Perspectives on the Multinational Corporation*. Cambridge: MIT Press, 1978.

Black, Cyril E. *The Dynamics of Modernization*. New York: Harper and Row, 1966.

Blanco, Alfredo Jaime. "Evaluación económica de la industria automotriz en México." Ph.D. diss., Escuela Nacional de Economia, Universidad Nacional Autónoma de México, 1971.

Block, Fred. "The Ruling Class Does Not Rule: Notes on the Marxist Theory of the State." *Socialist Revolution* 7 (1977):6-28.

Bloomfield, Gerald. *The World Automotive Industry*. Newton Abbott: David and Charles, 1978.

Boatler, Robert. "Trade Theory Predictions and the Growth of Mexico's Manufactured Exports." *Economic Development and Cultural Change* 23 (1974-1975):491-506.

Bodenheimer, Suzanne. "Dependency and Imperialism: The Roots of Latin American Underdevelopment." In K. T. Fann and Donald C. Hodges, eds., *Readings in U.S. Imperialism*, pp. 155-181. Boston: Porter Sargent, 1971.

Bonilla, Frank, and Robert Girlin, eds. *Structures of Dependency*. Stanford: Stanford University Press, 1973.

Brandenburg, Frank. *The Making of Modern Mexico*. Englewood Cliffs, N.J.: Prentice-Hall, 1964.

Brooke, Michael Z., and H. Lee Remmers. *The Strategy of Multinational Enterprises*. New York: Elsevier, 1970.

Brothers, Dwight, and Leopoldo Solis. *Mexican Financial Development*. Austin: University of Texas Press, 1966.

Bueno, Gerardo. "La industria siderúrgica y la automotriz." In *El Perfil de México en 1980*, pp. 83-99. Mexico City: Siglo XXI Editores.

———. *Opciones de política económica en México: Despues de la devaluación*. Mexico City: Editorial Tecnos, 1977.

Cámara Nacional de Industrias de Transformación. *Memoria I: Primer simposium de actualización operacional de la industria automotriz en México*. Mexico City: CANACINTRA, 1978.

———. *Memoria II: Segundo simposium de la industria automotriz mexicana*. Mexico City: CANACINTRA, 1980.

Campos Salas, Octaviano. "La industria auxiliar automotriz." *Mercado de valores*, June 1966, pp. 600-601.

———. "Mexico produce motores para automóviles." *Mercado de valores*, Feb. 1965, pp. 173-174.

Carballo, Marco Aurelio. "Frenazo a la industria automotriz." *Proceso*, May 23, 1977, 10-13.

Cardoso, Fernando Henrique. "On the Characterization of Authoritarian Regimes in Latin America." In David Collier, ed., *The New Authoritarianism in Latin America*, pp. 33-57. Princeton: Princeton University Press, 1979.

Cardoso, Fernando Henrique, and Enzo Faletto. *Dependency and Development in Latin America*. Berkeley and Los Angeles: University of California Press, 1979.

Caves, Richard E. "Industrial Organization." In J. H. Dunning, ed., *Economic Analysis and the Multinational Enterprise*, pp. 115-146. New York: Praeger, 1974.

Caves, R. E., and Masu Uekusa. *Industrial Organization in Japan*. Washington: Brookings Institution, 1976.

Centro de Investigaciones Agrarias. *Estructura agraria y desarrollo agrícola en México: Tenencia y uso de la tierra*. Mexico City: Fondo de Cultura Económica, 1977.

Chandler, Alfred D., Jr. *Strategy and Structure: Chapters in the History of the American Industrial Enterprise*. Cambridge: MIT Press, 1962.

Chilcote, Ronald, and Joel Edelstein, eds. *Latin America: The Struggle with Dependency and Beyond*. Cambridge, Mass.: Schenkman, 1974.

Christman, John H. "The Automotive Industry." *Business/Mexico, 1973*, pp. 123-130. Mexico City: American Chamber of Commerce, 1973.

Cline, Howard F. *Mexico: Revolution to Evolution, 1940-1960*. London: Oxford University Press, 1962.

Cline, William R. "Distribution and Development: A Survey of Literature." *Journal of Development Economics* 1 (1975):359-400.

Cohen, Robert B. "International Investment Strategies and Domestic Reorganization Plans of the U.S. Automakers: An Essay on the Response of U.S. Auto Firms to Changes in International Competitiveness in Auto

Production and Their Impact on the U.S. Economy." Mar. 1982. Photocopy.

Connolly, William E., ed. *The Bias of Pluralism*. New York: Atherton, 1969.

———. "On 'Interests' in Politics." *Politics and Society* 2 (1972):459-477.

Contreras Z., Bartólome. "El futuro de la industria de automotores en México." *Comercio exterior*, Jan. 1970, 52-55.

Cordero, Salvadore, and Rafael Santín. "Los grupos industriales: Uno nueva organización Económica en México." *Cuadernos del CES*, no. 23. Mexico City: Colegio de México, 1977.

Cordova, Arnoldo. *La ideología de la revolución mexicana: La formación del nuevo régimen*. Mexico City: Ediciones Era, 1973.

Dahl, Robert. "The Concept of Power." *Behavioral Science* 2 (1957):201-205.

———. *Modern Political Analysis*, 3rd ed., Englewood Cliffs, N.J.: Prentice-Hall, 1976.

———. *Who Governs?* New Haven: Yale University Press, 1961.

dos Santos, Theotonio. "The Structure of Dependence." *American Economic Review* 60 (1970):231-236.

Duncan, William Chandler. *U.S.-Japan Automobile Diplomacy: A Study in Economic Concentration*. Cambridge, Mass.: Ballinger, 1973.

Eckstein, Susan. *The Poverty of Revolution: The State and the Urban Poor in Mexico*. Princeton: Princeton University Press, 1977.

Edelberg, Guillermo S. "The Procurement Practices of the Mexican Affiliates of Selected United States Automobile Firms." Ph.D. diss., Harvard University, 1963.

Emmanuel, Arrighi. "Myths of Development versus Myths of Underdevelopment." *New Left Review* 85 (1974):61-82.

Espinosa Olvera, René. "Aspectos de la industria automotriz en México." *Foro Internacional* 15 (1974):116-127.

Evans, Peter. *Dependent Development: The Alliance of Multinational, State, and Local Capital in Brazil*. Princeton: Princeton University Press, 1979.

———. "Foreign Investment and Industrial Transformation: A Brazilian Case Study." *Journal of Development Economics* 3 (1976):119-139.

———. "Shoes, OPIC, and the Unquestioning Persuasion: Multinational Corporations and U.S.–Brazilian Relations." In Richard Fagen, ed., *Capitalism and the State in U.S.–Latin American Relations*, pp. 302-336. Stanford: Stanford University Press, 1979.

Fagen, Richard. "The Realities of U.S.–Mexican Relations." *Foreign Affairs* 55 (1977):685-700.

Fajnzylber, Fernando, and Trinidad Martínez Tárrago. *Las empresas transnacionales: Expansión a nivel mundial y proyección en la industria mexicana*. Mexico City: Fondo de Cultura Económica, 1976.

Felix, David. "Income Distribution Trends in Mexico and the Kuznets Curves." In Sylvia Hewlitt and Richard Weinert, eds., *Brazil and Mexico: Patterns in Late Development*, pp. 265-316. Philadelphia: ISHI Press, 1982.

Fitzgerald, E.V.K. "The State and Capital Accumulation in Mexico." *Journal of Latin American Studies* 10 (1978):263-282.

Frank, André Gunder. *Capitalism and Underdevelopment in Latin America: Historical Studies of Chile and Brazil.* New York: Monthly Review Press, 1967.

Furtado, Celso. "The Concept of External Dependence in the Study of Underdevelopment." In Charles K. Wilber, ed., *The Political Economy of Development and Underdevelopment*, pp. 118-123. New York: Random House, 1970.

————. *Economic Development of Latin America: A Survey from Colonial Times to the Cuban Revolution.* London: Cambridge University Press, 1970.

Gall, Norman. "The Rise of Brazil." *Commentary*, Jan. 1977, pp. 45-55.

Gallagher, Charles F. *Population, Petroleum, and Politics: Mexico at the Crossroads.* North American Series, no. 19. Hanover, N.H.: American Universities Field Staff, 1980.

García Reynoso, Plácido. "La exportación como factor de desarrollo económico." *Comercio exterior* (1968):389-392.

————. "La política mexicana de fomento industrial." *Comercio exterior* (1968):959-964.

Gereffi, Gary. "Drug Firms and Dependency in Mexico: The Case of the Steroid Hormone Industry." *International Organization* 32 (1978):237-286.

————. *The Pharmaceutical Industry and Dependency in the Third World.* Princeton: Princeton University Press, 1983.

Gereffi, Gary, and Peter Evans. "Transnational Corporations, Dependent Development, and State Policy in the Semiperiphery: A Comparison of Brazil and Mexico." *Latin American Research Review* 16 (1981):31-64.

Gerschenkron, Alexander. *Economic Backwardness in Historical Perspective.* Cambridge: Harvard University Press, 1966.

Gerth, H. H., and C. Wright Mills. *From Max Weber: Essays in Sociology.* London: Routledge and Kegan Paul, 1948.

Giddens, Anthony. *Central Problems in Social Theory: Action, Structure, and Contradiction in Social Analysis.* Berkeley and Los Angeles: University of California Press, 1979.

Gilpin, Robert. *U.S. Power and Multinational Corporations.* Princeton: Princeton University Press, 1977.

Glade, William P., and Charles W. Anderson, Jr. *The Political Economy of Mexico.* Madison: University of Wisconsin Press, 1963.

González Casanova, Pablo. *Democracy in Mexico.* New York: Oxford University Press, 1970.

Grayson, George W. "Mexico's Opportunity: The Oil Boom." *Foreign Policy*, no. 29 (1977-1978):65-89.

Greer, D. F. *Industrial Organization and Public Policy.* New York: Macmillan, 1980.

Grindle, Merilee. *Bureaucrats, Politicians, and Peasants in Mexico: A Case Study in Public Policy.* Berkeley and Los Angeles: University of California Press, 1977.

Gudger, Michael. "The Regulation of Multinational Corporations in the Mexican Automotive Industry." Ph.D. diss., University of Wisconsin, 1975.

Gusfield, Joseph R. "Tradition and Modernity: Misplaced Polarities in the Study of Social Change." *American Journal of Sociology* 72 (1967):351-362.

Gwynne, R. N. "Latin America: The Motor Vehicle Industry." *Bank of London and South America Review* 12 (1978):462-470.

Hamilton, Nora. *The Limits of State Autonomy: Post-Revolutionary Mexico*. Princeton: Princeton University Press, 1982.

———. "Mexico: The Limits of State Autonomy," *Latin American Perspectives* 2 (1975):100-101.

Hansen, Roger. *The Politics of Mexican Development*. Baltimore: The Johns Hopkins University Press, 1971.

Hellman, Judy. *Mexico in Crisis*. New York: Holmes and Meier, 1978.

Hirschman, Albert. "The Political Economy of Import-Substituting Industrialization in Latin America." *Quarterly Journal of Economics* 82 (1968):1-32.

Holusha, John. "Ford's New Contract: Who May Win, Who May Lose." *New York Times*, Feb. 26, 1982, p. D6.

Huizer, Gerrit. *The Revolutionary Potential of Peasants in Latin America*. Lexington, Mass.: D. C. Heath, 1972.

Hymer, Stephen. *The International Operations of National Firms: A Study of Direct Foreign Investment*. Cambridge: MIT Press, 1976.

Jacquemin, A. P., and H. W. de Jong. *European Industrial Organization*. New York: John Wiley, 1977.

Jaguaribe, Helio. *Economic and Political Development: A Theoretical Approach and a Brazilian Case Study*. Cambridge: Harvard University Press, 1968.

Jenkins, Rhys. *Dependent Industrialization in Latin America: The Automotive Industry in Argentina, Chile, and Mexico*. New York: Praeger, 1977.

Johnson, Kenneth. *Mexican Democracy: A Critical View*. Boston: Allyn and Bacon, 1971.

Johnson, Leland J. "Problems of Import Substitution: The Chilean Automobile Industry." *Economic Development and Cultural Change* 15 (1967):202-216.

Katz, Fredrich. "Labor Conditions and Haciendas in Porfirian Mexico: Some Trends and Tendencies." *Hispanic American Historical Review* 54 (1974):1-47.

Katz, Jorge. "Industrial Growth, Royalty Payments, and Local Expenditure on Research and Development." In Victor Urquidi and Rosemary Thorpe, eds., *Latin America in the International Economy*, pp. 197-224. New York: John Wiley, 1973.

Kindleberger, Charles P. *American Business Abroad: Six Lectures on Direct Investment*. New Haven: Yale University Press, 1969.

Kindleberger, Charles, and Bruce Herrick. *Economic Development*, 3rd ed. New York: McGraw-Hill, 1977.

King, Timothy. *Mexico: Industry and Trade Policies since 1940*. Oxford: Oxford University Press, 1970.

Knickerbocker, Frederick T. *Oligopolistic Reaction and Multinational Enterprise.* Boston: Harvard University School of Business Administration, 1973.

Kraft, Joseph. "Annals of Industry: The Downsizing Decision." *The New Yorker,* May 5, 1980, pp. 134-162.

Lall, Sanjaya. "The International Automotive Industry and the Developing World." *World Development* 8 (1980):789-812.

Lanzillotti, Ralph F. "The Automobile Industry." In Walter Adams, ed., *The Structure of American Industry*, pp. 256-301. New York: Macmillan, 1971.

Leal, Juan Felipe. *México: Estado, burocracia, y sindicatos.* Mexico City: Ediciones El Caballito, 1976.

Leff, Nathaniel. "Monopoly Capitalism and Public Policy in Developing Countries." *Kyklos* 32 (1979):718-738.

Little, Ian, Tibor Scitovsky, and Maurice Scott. *Industry and Trade in Some Developing Countries: A Comparative Study.* London: Oxford University Press, 1970.

Looney, Robert E. *Mexico's Economy: A Policy Analysis with Forecasts to 1990.* Boulder, Col.: Westview, 1978.

Lukes, Steven. *Power: A Radical View.* London: Macmillan, 1974.

Marcos, Ernesto. "Origen y objectivos de la nueva política automotriz." In Cámara Nacional de Industrias de Transformación, *Memoria I: Primer simposium de actualización operacional de la industria automotriz en México.* Mexico City: CANACINTRA, 1978, pp. 60-63.

Marx, Karl. "The Eighteenth Brumaire of Louis Bonaparte." In Robert C. Tucker, ed., *The Marx-Engels Reader*, pp. 436-525. New York: W. W. Norton, 1972.

Menge, John A. "Style Change Costs As a Market Weapon." *Quarterly Journal of Economics* 76 (1962):632-647.

Meyer, Lorenzo. "Historical Roots of the Authoritarian State in Mexico." In José Luis Reyna and Richard S. Weinert, eds., *Authoritarianism in Mexico*, pp. 3-22. Philadelphia: ISHI Press, 1977.

———. *Mexico and the United States in the Oil Controversy, 1917-1942.* Austin: University of Texas Press, 1977.

Middlebrook, Kevin J. "International Implications of Labor Change: The Mexican Automobile Industry." In Jorge I. Domínguez, ed., *Mexico's Political Economy: Challenges at Home and Abroad*, pp. 133-170. Beverly Hills, Calif.: Sage, 1982.

———. "Political Change and Political Reform in an Authoritarian Regime: The Case of Mexico." *Working Papers*, no. 91, Latin America Program, Woodrow Wilson International Center for Scholars. Washington, 1980.

Mikesell, Raymond F. "Conflict in Foreign Investor–Host Country Relations: A Preliminary Analysis." In Raymond F. Mikesell, ed., *Foreign Investment in the Petroleum and Mineral Industries: Case Studies of Investor–Host Country Relations*, pp. 29-55. Baltimore: The Johns Hopkins University Press, 1971.

Miliband, Ralph. *The State in Capitalist Society.* New York: Basic Books, 1969.

Moran, Theodore. "Multinational Corporations and Dependency: A Dialogue for Dependentistas and Non-Dependentistas." *International Organization* 32 (1978):79-100.

———. *Multinational Corporations and the Politics of Dependence: Copper in Chile.* Princeton: Princeton University Press, 1974.

Munk, B. "The Welfare Costs of Content Protection: The Automotive Industry in Latin America." *Journal of Political Economy* 77 (1969):85-98.

Navarrete, Ifigenia M. de. "La distribución del ingreso y el desarrollo económico de México." Mexico City: Instituto de Investigaciones Económicas, Escuela Nacional de Economía, 1960.

Navarrete López, Jorge Eduardo. "Hacia una política de integración industrial en México." *Comercio exterior*, Aug. 1962, pp. 512-514.

———. "La marcha de la integración de la industria automovilística." *Comercio exterior*, Mar. 1963, pp. 156-158.

Newfarmer, Richard. "International Industrial Organization and Development: A Survey." In Richard Newfarmer, ed., *Profits, Progress and Poverty: Case Studies of International Industries in Latin America.* Notre Dame: University of Notre Dame Press, 1984.

Newfarmer, Richard, and William Mueller. *Multinational Corporations in Brazil and Mexico: Structural Sources of Economic and Non-Economic Power.* Report prepared for the Subcommittee on Multinational Corporations of the Senate Committee on Foreign Relations. 94th Cong., 1st sess., 1975.

Offe, Claus. "Structural Problems of the Capitalist State." In Klaus von Beyme, ed., *German Political Studies*, pp. 31-57. Beverly Hills, Calif.: Sage, 1976.

Offe, Claus, and Volker Ronge. "Theses on the Theory of the State." *New German Critique* 6 (1975):139-147.

Packenham, Robert A. *Liberal America in the Third World.* Princeton: Princeton University Press, 1973.

Padgett, Vincent. *The Mexican Political System*, 2nd ed. Boston: Houghton Mifflin, 1976.

Parenti, Michael. "Power and Pluralism: A View from the Bottom." *Journal of Politics* 32 (1970):501-530.

Parkinson, Jack H. "The Automotive Industry Decree: Tooling Up for More Exports." In *Business/Mexico*, pp. 245-248. Mexico City: American Chamber of Commerce of Mexico, 1979.

Parsons, Talcott. "On the Concept of Political Power." *Proceedings of the American Philosophical Society* 107 (1963):232-262.

Petras, James T. *Latin America: From Dependence to Revolution.* New York: John Wiley, 1973.

Poniatowska, Elena. *La noche de Tlatelolco.* Mexico City: Biblioteca Era, 1971.

Poulantzas, Nicos. "The Problem of the Capitalist State." In Robin Blackburn, ed., *Ideology in Social Science*, pp. 239-258. New York: Vintage, 1973.

Purcell, Susan Kaufman, and John F. H. Purcell. "State and Society in Mexico: Must a Stable Policy Be Institutionalized?" *World Politics* 32 (1980):194-227.

Reyna, José Luis. "Redefining the Authoritarian Regime." In José Luis Reyna and Richard Weinert, eds., *Authoritarianism in Mexico*, pp. 155-171. Philadelphia: ISHI Press, 1977.

Reynolds, Clark. *The Mexican Economy: Twentieth-Century Structure and Growth.* New Haven: Yale University Press, 1970.

Rhys, D. G. *The Motor Industry: An Economic Survey.* London: Butterworth, 1972.

Riding, Alan. "Taming the Mexican Passion for More." *New York Times*, Sept. 12, 1982, p. 3.

Rippy, Merrill. *Oil and the Mexican Revolution.* Luden, Netherlands: E. J. Brill, 1972.

Robbins, Sidney M., and Robert B. Stobaugh. *Money in the Multinational Corporation.* New York: Basic Books, 1973.

Ronfeldt, David. *Atencingo: The Politics of Agrarian Struggle in a Mexican Ejido.* Stanford: Stanford University Press, 1973.

Rostow, Walt W. *The Stages of Economic Growth: A Non-Communist Manifesto.* Cambridge: Cambridge University Press, 1960.

Roxborough, Ian. "Labor in the Mexican Automobile Industry." In Richard Kronish and Kenneth S. Mericle, eds., *The Political Economy of the Latin American Motor Vehicle Industry*, pp. 161-194. Cambridge: MIT Press, 1982.

Sacristán Roy, Emiliano. "Apoyos del programa de fomento." In Cámara Nacional de Industrias de Transformación, *Memoria II: Segundo simposium de la industria automotriz mexicana*, pp. 35-39. Mexico City: CANACINTRA, 1980.

Salas Vargas, Guillermo. "Política industrial e industria automotriz en México, 1947-79." Master's thesis, El Colegio de México, 1980.

Salinas Lozano, Raúl. *Memoria de labores, 1963.* Mexico City: Secretaria de Industria y Comercio, 1963.

Sánchez Marco, C. "Introduction to the Mexican Automobile Industry." Paris: OECD Development Center, Industrialization and Trade Project, 1968.

Sanders, Thomas G. *Devaluing the Peso: Background and Implications.* North American Series, no. 5. Hanover, N.H.: American Universities Field Staff, 1982.

Schattschneider, E. E. *The Semi-Sovereign People.* New York: Holt, Rinehart and Winston, 1960.

Scherer, F. M. *Industrial Market Structure and Economic Performance.* Chicago: Rand McNally, 1980.

Schydlowsky, Daniel M. "Latin American Trade Policies in the 1970s: A Prospective Appraisal." *Quarterly Journal of Economics* 86 (1972):263-289.

Scott, Robert E. *Mexican Government in Transition.* Urbana: University of Illinois Press, 1964.

Sepúlveda Amor, Bernardo, Olga Pellicer de Brody, and Lorenzo Meyer. *Las empresas transnacionales en México.* Mexico City: El Colegio de México, 1974.

Sevier, John D. "Review and Prospects for the Automotive Industry." In *Business/Mexico*, pp. 237-244. Mexico City: American Chamber of Commerce of Mexico, 1979.

Simpson, Eyler N. *The Ejido: Mexico's Way Out.* Chapel Hill: University of North Carolina Press, 1937.

Skocpol, Theda. "Bringing the State Back In: False Leads and Promising Starts in Current Theories and Research." Working paper prepared for the Conference on States and Social Structures, Seven Springs Conference Center, Mount Kisco, New York, Feb. 25-27, 1982.

Slocum, William G. "The Automotive Industry—Key to Growth." *Mex-Am Review*, Mar. 1975.

Smith, Peter. *Labyrinths of Power: Political Recruitment in Twentieth-Century Mexico.* Princeton: Princeton University Press, 1979.

Smith, Robert F. *The United States and Revolutionary Nationalism in Mexico, 1916-1932.* Chicago: University of Chicago Press, 1972.

Snell, Bradford. *American Ground Transport: A Proposal for Restructuring the Automobile, Truck, Bus, and Rail Industries.* Washington: Government Printing Office, 1973.

Spaulding, Rose. "State Power and Its Limits: Corporatism in Mexico." *Comparative Political Studies* 14 (1981):139-161.

Stein, Barbara, and Stanley J. Stein. *The Colonial Heritage of Latin America.* New York: Oxford University Press, 1970.

Stepan, Alfred. *The State and Society: Peru in Comparative Perspective.* Princeton: Princeton University Press, 1978.

Stevens, Evelyn P. *Protest and Response in Mexico.* Cambridge: MIT Press, 1974.

Stopford, John, and Louis T. Wells. *Managing the Multinational Enterprise.* New York: Basic Books, 1972.

Sunkel, Osvaldo, "Big Business and 'Dependencia.'" *Foreign Affairs* 50 (1972):517-531.

———. "National Development Policy and External Dependence in Latin America." *Journal of Development Studies* 6 (1970):23-48.

Toder, Eric J., Nicholas Scott Cardell, and Ellen Burton. *Trade Policy and the U.S. Automobile Industry.* New York: Praeger, 1978.

Torre, José de la. "Foreign Investment and Export Dependency." *Economic Development and Cultural Change* 23 (1974-1975):133-150.

Tucker, William. "The Wreck of the Auto Industry." *Harper's*, Nov. 1980, pp. 45-60.

Tugwell, Franklin. *The Politics of Oil in Venezuela.* Stanford: Stanford University Press, 1975.

Vaitsos, Constantine. *Intercountry Income Distribution and Transnational Enterprises.* Oxford: Clarendon Press, 1974.

———. "Power, Knowledge, and Development Policy: Relations between Transnational Enterprises and Developing Countries." Paper presented at the 1974 Dag Hammarskjöld Seminar on the Third World and International Economic Change, Uppsala, Sweden, Aug. 1974.

Vatter, H. G. "The Closure of Entry in the American Automobile Industry." *Oxford Economic Papers* 4 (1952):213-234.

Vázquez Tercero, Héctor. *Una década de política sobre la industria automotriz: Bases para una nueva política.* Mexico City: Editorial Tecnos, 1975.

Vernon, Raymond. *The Dilemma of Mexico's Development.* Cambridge: Harvard University Press, 1963.

———. *Sovereignty at Bay: The Multinational Spread of U.S. Enterprises.* New York: Basic Books, 1971.

———. *Storm over the Multinationals: The Real Issues.* Cambridge: Harvard University Press, 1977.

Vidali, Carlos. "La industria de automotores en México." *Visión,* July 1, 1970.

Villarreal, René. "The Policy of Import-Substituting Industrialization, 1929-1975." In José Luis Reyna and Richard S. Weinert, eds., *Authoritarianism in Mexico,* pp. 67-107. Philadelphia: ISHI Press, 1977.

Villaseñor, Victor Manuel. *Memorias de un hombre de izquierda.* Vol. 2. Mexico City: Editorial Grijalbo, 1976.

Warman, Natan. "Política de estímulos a la inversión." In Cámara Nacional de Industrias de Tranformación, *Memoria I: Primer simposium de actualización operacional de la industria automotriz en México,* pp. 11-14. Mexico City: CANACINTRA, 1978.

Wells, Louis T., Jr. "Automobiles." In Raymond Vernon, ed., *Big Business and the State,* pp. 229-254. Cambridge: Harvard University Press, 1978.

West, Peter. "The World Tire Industry." In Richard Newfarmer, ed., *Profits, Progress and and Poverty: Case Studies of International Industries in Latin America.* Notre Dame: University of Notre Dame Press, 1984.

Whetten, Nathan L. *Rural Mexico.* Chicago: University of Chicago Press, 1948.

White, Lawrence J. *The American Automobile Industry since 1945.* Cambridge: Harvard University Press, 1971.

Whitehead, Laurence. "Mexico from Boom to Bust: A Political Evaluation of the 1976-79 Stabilization Programme." *World Development* 8 (1980):843-864.

Wilkins, Mira. *The Emergence of Multinational Enterprise.* Cambridge: Harvard University Press, 1970.

———. *The Maturing of Multinational Enterprise: American Business Abroad from 1914 to 1970.* Cambridge: Harvard University Press, 1974.

Wionczek, Miguel. *El nacionalismo mexicano y la inversión extranjera.* Mexico City: Siglo XXI, 1967.

Wionczek, Miguel, Gerardo Bueno, and Jorge Eduardo Navarrete. "La transferencia de tecnología a la industria de automotores." Chap. 3 in *La transferencia internacional de tecnología: El caso de México.* Mexico City: Fondo de Cultura Económica, 1974.

Wolf, Eric. *Peasant Wars of the Twentieth Century.* New York: Harper and Row, 1973.

Womack, John, Jr. *Zapata and the Mexican Revolution.* New York: Vintage, 1969.

Wonnacott, Paul. "Canadian Automotive Protection: Content Provisions, the Bladen Plan, and Recent Tariff Changes." *Canadian Journal of Economics and Politics* 31 (1965):98-115.

Wright, Harry K. *Foreign Enterprise in Mexico: Laws and Policies.* Chapel Hill: University of North Carolina Press, 1971.

BIBLIOGRAPHY

B. Decrees, Regulations, and Unpublished Materials

Acuerdo que establece las reglas de aplicación del decreto para el fomento de la industria automotriz." *Diario oficial,* Oct. 18. 1977.

Cámara Nacional de Industrias de Transformación, Sección de Autopartes. "Incremento de la industria automotriz: Memoria de cálculos." Apr. 1976.

"Decreto para el fomento de la industria automotriz." *Diario oficial,* June 20, 1977.

"Decreto que establece los estímulos fiscales para el fomento del empleo y la inversión en las actividades industriales." *Diario oficial,* Mar. 6, 1979.

"Decreto que fija las bases para el desarrollo de la industria automotriz." *Diario oficial,* Oct. 24, 1972.

"Decreto suplementario del 21 de octubre de 1969." *Diario oficial,* Oct. 21, 1969.

"Directrices de una política que norme el desarrollo de la industria automotriz." Report prepared for Carlos Tello, Minister-designate of the Ministry of Program and Budget, 1976.

Ford, Charles A. "Past Development and Future Trends in Mexican Automotive Policy: Implications for United States–Mexican Trade Relations." Motor Vehicle Manufacturers Association, April 1980.

Ford Motor Company. "Estudio sobre contenido nacional y generación de divisas por exportaciones." May 1976.

———. "Programa de fabricación de automóviles y camiones." Sept. 1962.

———. "Proposal for Automotive Manufacturing in Mexico." Apr. 1960.

———. "A Study of Automotive Manufacturing in Mexico." Apr. 1960.

Metzenbaum, Senator Howard M. Press release, Feb. 21, 1980.

Motor Vehicle Manufacturers Association. "Views of the Motor Vehicle Manufacturers Association of the U.S. on the President's Report to the Congress on North American Trade Agreements." Feb. 6, 1981.

Nacional Financiera. "Elementos para una política de desarrollo de la fabricación de vehículos automotrices en México." NAFIN, 1960.

———, Gerencia de Programación Industrial. "La industria automotriz terminal mexicana." NAFIN, 1970.

"Programa de fomento para la industria nacional fabricante de autopartes." *Diario oficial,* Jan. 21, 1980.

"Resolución sobre anticipos y contrabilización de divisas de las empresas de la industria automotriz terminal." *Diario oficial,* Aug. 27, 1980.

"Resolución sobre planeación concertada de la industria automotriz." *Diario oficial,* Oct. 3, 1980.

Secretaria de Hacienda, Dirección General de Promoción Fiscal. "Informe de resultados de visitas de control efectuadas a las empresas de la industria automotriz terminal para la verificación del año modelo 1979." Jan. 1981.

Secretaria de Industria y Comercio, Comisión Intersecretarial de la Industria Automotriz. "Programa para una nueva estructura de la industria automotriz mexicana (industria terminal y de autopartes)." 1976.

————. "Resolución sobre la producción de motores de la industria terminal." Aug. 27, 1980.

Secretaria de Patrimonio y Fomento Industrial. *Plan nacional de desarrollo industrial, 1979-82*. SEPAFIN, 1979.

United Nations. Economic Commission for Latin America. *Perspectivas y modalidades de integración regional de la industria automotriz en América Latina.* New York: ECLA, 1973.

INDEX

A. O. Smith Company, 135
Abed family, 120, 121
Adams, Walter, 66n
Aguinaga, Sebastian, 235n
Almond, Gabriel A., 5n
Althusser, Louis, 40n
Altos Hornos, 143
American and Foreign Power, 131
American Chamber of Commerce of Mexico, 216
American Motors, 125, 197, 199, 213, 222, 274
Anderson, Charles, 25n, 26n
Asociación Mexicana de la Industria Automotriz (AMIA), 155, 167, 202, 215
Asociación Mexicana de Productores de Partes Automotrices (AMPPA), 202, 235
Asociación Nacional de Fabricantes de Productos Automotrices (ANFPA), 202, 235
Auto Union-DKW, 120-122
automobile industry: in Europe, 57-58; in Japan, 59-60; in Mexico, 3, 51-55, 65, 99-100; in the United States, 56-57; world automobile industry, 55-56, 61-63, 106-107, 191-192, 194-199; world industry in LDCs, 63, 107, 192-194
automobile industry decrees: 1962 decree, 105, 114-116, 117, 151, 155-156, 269; 1969 acuerdo, 155, 165, 173, 175, 176, 206, 269; 1972 decree, 176; 1976 draft decree, 201, 203; 1977 decree, 204-205, 209-211, 227, 232, 233, 238; 1983 decree, 273-275
Automotriz O'Farrill, 124
Automoviles Ingleses, 124
Avila Camacho, Manuel, 26-27
Azcárraga, Gaston, 98, 126-128, 158-160, 173

Bachrach, Peter, 82n
Bailey, John J., 229n
Bain, Joseph, 61, 62n, 66n
Balassa, Bela, 157n
Baldrige, Malcolm, 245
Baldwin, David, 85n

Banco Nacional de Mexico, 131
Bank of Mexico, 20, 22, 43, 160
banking system, 22-23, 33; nationalization, 231
Baranson, Jack, 64n, 147n, 150n
Baratz, Morton, 82n
bargaining: agenda setting in, 81-84; between Mexican state and transnational automobile corporations, 259-263; between state and transnational corporations (TNCs), 4, 9, 80-94, 251; decision-making in, 84-92; implementation of agreements, 92
Barnet, Richard, 76n
barriers to entry, 73
Becker, Guillermo, 176, 201
Behrman, Jack, 147n
Bendix, Reinhard, 5n
Bennett, Douglas, 20n, 28n, 36n, 41n, 46n, 64n, 139n, 182n, 212n
Bergsten, D. Fred, 217, 217n
Bernstein, Marvin, 24n
Bierstecker, Thomas, 75n
Blachman, Morris, 36n, 46n
Black, Cyril E., 5n
Block, Fred, 45n
Bloomfield, Gerald, 65n
Boatler, Robert, 181n
Bodenheimer, Suzanne, 6n
Bonilla, Frank, 6n
Borgward, 122-124
Brandenburg, Frank, 20n, 39n
Bravo Aguilera, Luis, 155, 162, 171
Brock, William, 245, 246
Brooke, Michael Z., 138n
Brothers, Dwight, 34n
Bueno, Gerardo, 189n
Burton, Ellen, 192n
Bustamante, Eduardo, 96

Cafiero, Eugene, 161
Calles, Plutarco Elías, 19, 20, 25
Campos Salas, Octaviano, 148-149, 155, 159, 162-163, 171
Cardell, Nicholas Scott, 192n
Cárdenas, Lazaro, 19, 23, 25-26

Mann, U.S. Ambassador Thomas, 109
Manufacturas Metálicas de Monterrey, 135
manufacturing industries, compared with extractive industries, 8, 88-89, 262
Marcos, Ernesto, 207, 208n
market, structure of, 70, 255-256. *See also* fragmentation of the market
Martínez Tárrago, Trinidad, 36n, 178n, 181n
Marx, Karl, 3n
Meislin, Richard J., 274n
Menge, John A., 57n
Mercedes-Benz, 120-121
Metzenbaum, Senator Howard M., 245, 245n
Mexicanization, 101, 105; consequences of, 136-140
Meyer, Lorenzo, 24n, 36n, 49n
Middlebrook, Kevin, 31n, 98n, 213n
Mikesell, Raymond F., 80n, 89n
Miliband, Ralph, 39n
Moctezuma Cid, Julio Rodolfo, 203, 207
modernization approach, 5-7
Molina, Edgar, 97, 109, 113, 131, 135
Montes de Oca, Luis, 141
Moran, Theodore H., 16n, 75n, 76, 76n, 78n, 80n, 87n, 89n, 90, 90n, 262n
Motores y Refacciones (MORESA), 133-134
Mueller, Willard, 36n
Muller, Ronald, 76n
Munk, B., 147n

Nacional Financiera (NAFIN), 20, 22, 43, 50, 94, 94n, 144-145
NAFIN report (1960), 94-95, 97, 102-103, 108-109, 263
national champions, 59, 267
National Properties, Ministry of (*Patrimonio*), 145
National Properties and Industrial Development, Ministry of (SEPAFIN), 145, 207, 208, 233, 236
Navarrete, Ifigenia, 29n
neoclassical economics, 70, 75, 147, 156, 182
Newfarmer, Richard, 36n, 75n, 77n, 78n
Nissan, 59, 60, 170, 192, 199, 203, 213, 222, 261

Offe, Claus, 45n
oil, in Mexico, 226, 227-229, 273
oligopolistic reaction, 69. *See also* defensive investment
Organization of Petroleum Exporting Countries (OPEC), 195
Ortiz Mena, Antonio, 96, 97, 159-160, 162-163, 171, 172
Oteyza, Jose Andres de, 203, 207, 215
ownership (as component of industry structure), 70-72, 257-258; public vs. private, 71, 73, 100-101; transnational vs. national, 71-72. *See also* denationalization, Mexicanization, state ownership

Packenham, Robert A., 5n
Padgett, Vincent, 31n
Pagliai, Bruno, 141
Parenti, Michael, 80n
Parsons, Talcott, 85n
Partido Revolucionario Institucional (PRI), 20, 25, 31
parts supply firms: as participants in bargaining, 166-167, 202; growing predominance of those with foreign equity, 177-178; interests of, 206-207; separation from terminal automobile manufacturers, 103, 116; tensions with terminal firms, 150-151, 234-237, 266-267
Pellicer de Brody, Olga, 36n
Perfect Circle, 132
performance requirements, 217-218, 243-247
Petras, James T., 6n
Planta, Reo, 110, 111, 119
Poulantzas, Nicos, 40n
power, 84-92; as affected by internal characteristics of actors, 85-87; as shaped by structures, 87-92
Prebish, Raúl, 157n
price controls, 149, 210
product life-cycle, 73
production quotas, 117, 151-152, 163-164, 179-180, 210
Promexa, 108, 124-125. *See also* Volkswagen
Purcell, John F.H., 39n
Purcell, Susan Kaufman, 39n

LIBRARY OF CONGRESS CATALOGING IN PUBLICATION DATA

Bennett, Douglas C., 1946-
Transnational corporations versus the state.

Bibliography: p.
Includes index.
1. Automobile industry and trade—Government policy—
Mexico. 2. International business enterprises—Mexico.
3. International business enterprises—Developing
countries. I. Sharpe, Kenneth Evan. II. Title.
HD9710.M42B46 1985   338.8′87   85-42674

ISBN 0-691-07689-8 (alk. paper)
ISBN 0-691-02237-2 (pbk. : alk. paper)